Also by Frank-Jürgen Richter

THE DYNAMICS OF JAPANESE ORGANIZATIONS (*edited*)

BUSINESS NETWORKS IN ASIA: Promises, Doubts, and Perspectives (*edited*)

THE DRAGON MILLENNIUM: Chinese Business in the Coming World Economy (*edited*)

STRATEGIC NETWORKS: The Art of Japanese Interfirm Cooperation

THE ASIAN ECONOMIC CATHARSIS: How Asian Firms Bounce Back from Crisis (*edited*)

The East Asian Development Model

Economic Growth, Institutional Failure and the Aftermath of the Crisis

Edited by

Frank-Jürgen Richter

First published in Great Britain 2000 by
MACMILLAN PRESS LTD
Houndmills, Basingstoke, Hampshire RG21 6XS and London
Companies and representatives throughout the world

A catalogue record for this book is available from the British Library.

ISBN 0–333–92063–5

First published in the United States of America 2000 by
ST. MARTIN'S PRESS, LLC.,
Scholarly and Reference Division,
175 Fifth Avenue, New York, N.Y. 10010

ISBN 0–312–23305–1 (cloth)

Library of Congress Cataloging-in-Publication Data

The East Asian development model: economic growth, institutional failure and the
aftermath of the crisis / edited by Frank-Jürgen Richter.
p. cm.
Includes bibliographical references and index.
ISBN 0–312–23305–1 (cloth)
1. Financial crises – East Asia. 2. East Asia – Economic conditions. 3. East
Asia – Economic policy. I. Title: Economic growth, institutional failure and the
aftermath of the crisis. II. Richter, Frank-Jürgen.

HB3816.5 .E17 2000
338.95 – dc21
99-045254

This book is printed on paper suitable for recycling and
made from fully managed and sustained forest sources.

10   9   8   7   6   5   4   3   2   1
09   08   07   06   05   04   03   02   01   00

Printed in Great Britain by Antony Rowe Ltd, Chippenham, Wiltshire

Contents

List of Figures and Tables

Figures

Tables

Notes on the Contributors

Caroline Benton holds an MBA from Tsukuba University and a PhD in Management Engineering from the Tokyo Institute of Technology. She was formerly a director of a Japanese subsidiary of a European manufacturer, and has been chief consultant at a marketing consulting firm for foreign-affiliated companies in Japan over the last five years.

Hock-Beng Cheah is a Senior Lecturer at the School of Economics and Management, University College, University of New South Wales. His teaching and research interests include Human Resource Management, Organisational Development and Entrepreneurship. In 1989 he was a visiting Research Fellow at the Snider Entrepreneurial Center, Wharton School, University of Pennsylvania, where he examined the Schumpeterian and Austrian conceptions of entrepreneurship and proposed a new perspective on the entrepreneurial process. Since then he has extensively explored the ramifications of this perspective for organisations, management and economic development.

Yi Feng received a PhD in Political Science from the University of Rochester in 1992 and is currently an Associate Professor at Claremont Graduate University, Claremont, California. His areas of specialisation include International Political Economy and Methodology. He has published extensively and his papers have appeared in such journals as the *British Journal of Political Science,* the *European Journal of Political Economy,* the *Journal of Peace Research,* the *Journal of Conflict Resolution* and *International Interactions.*

Usha C. V. Haley is an Associate Professor at the School of Management, New Jersey Institute of Technology, New Jersey. She is also a Research Associate for the 'Managing Business in Asia Program' at the Research School of Pacific and Asian Studies, Australian National University, Canberra. She received her PhD in Business Administration, specialising in International Business and Management, from the Stern School of Business, New York University. Her current research interests include the management of business–government relations and the successful conducting of business in the Asia-Pacific region and Mexico. Her award winning book, *New Asian Emperors: The Overseas Chinese, Their*

Strategies and Competitive Advantages (with Chin-Tiong Tan and George Haley), was published in 1998.

Ha Huong is a lecturer at Technology Management Center, Singapore. She received a Masters Degree in Public Policy from the National University of Singapore in 1997. Her publications and conference papers concentrate on topics such as IT policy, urban planning policy, creative teaching and the policy making process, environmental policy.

Harold R. Kerbo is a Professor of Sociology at California Polytechnic State University, San Luis Obispo. He has been a Fulbright Professor at Hiroshima University, Japan, a Fulbright-Hays grant recipient to study in Thailand, a visiting professor at two universities in Thailand, a visiting professor at Duisburg University, Germany, and most recently at the University of Zurich, Switzerland. He is the author of several books and articles on subjects such as social stratification, elites and corporate structure, and modern Japan, including *Social Stratification and Inequality* and *Who Rules Japan? The Inner Circles of Economic and Political Power* (coauthored by John McKinstry). He has conducted extensive research on Japanese corporations in Germany and, together with Professor Robert Slagter, American and Japanese corporations in Thailand.

Wolfgang Klenner is Professor of East Asian Economics at the Ruhr-Universität Bochum, Germany. He has been a visiting professor at the University of Tokyo, the University of Nagoya, the University of International Business and Economics, Beijing, and various American universities. His research projects include China's economic policy and reforms, Japan's industrial structure and organisation, economic relations between Western and East Asian companies, and cooperation and competition in East and Southeast Asia.

Jacek Kugler is the Elisabeth Helm Rosecrans Professor of International Relations at the Claremont Graduate University, Claremont, California. He received his PhD from the University of Michigan in 1973. His research interests include political and economic development, and political demography. He is the author of *The War Ledger* and *Power Transitions*, and he co-edited *Political Capacity and Economic Behavior*.

Christopher Lingle is an independent corporate consultant and adjunct scholar of the Centre for Independent Studies in Sydney. He has been a university teacher since earning his PhD in Economics from the University of Georgia in 1977. Most of his academic career has been spent in universities in Africa, Asia and Europe. He is the author of *The Rise and Decline of the Asian Century.*

Phillip Hookon Park is an Assistant Professor at the School of International and Public Affairs, Columbia University, and a visiting fellow at Columbia University's East Asian Institute and APEC Study Center. He is the author of *The Cause of the Acute Food Crisis in the Democratic People's Republic of Korea,* and teaches a course entitled 'Globalization, Human Development, and Economic Reforms in East and Southeast Asian countries'.

Subramaniam S. Pillay is an Associate Professor at the Finance Division of the School of Management, University of Science Malaysia (USM). He teaches international finance and economics and has been at the USM since 1980. He obtained his BSc in Physics and Chemistry from USM, his MBA from the University of California, Berkeley, and his PhD from the University of British Columbia. He has previously worked at Hewlett-Packard (Malaysia). His current research interests are the political economy of the financial and economic crises in Malaysia and the economic integration of East Asia.

Frank-Jürgen Richter holds a management position with a European multinational corporation and is currently working in Beijing, China. Having studied business administration and mechanical engineering in Germany, France and Mexico, he conducted his PhD research at the University of Tsukuba, Tokyo.

Fred Robins holds a BA and MA in economics and a MSc and PhD in marketing. He teaches and researches at the Graduate School of Management, University of Adelaide. He is also a member of the University of South Australia's Marketing Science Centre. Prior to his academic career he had public sector experience in Europe and Asia, and later worked in the private sector in the fields of public relations and marketing. More recently he has researched the activities of Australian businesses in ASEAN markets and has published articles on Asian business in international academic journals. He has also written on the contrast between Asian and Australian trade and industry policies.

Hilton L. Root is a senior fellow at the Milken Institute, where his research focuses on the global economy. With expertise in Asia and Southeast Asia in particular, Root has extensively studied developing countries and the relationship between their economies and political systems. A frequent contributor to the *Asian Wall Street Journal* and the *International Herald Tribune*, he is the author of six books and numerous articles. One of his books, coauthored with J. Edgardo Campos, *The Key to the East Asian Miracle: Making Shared Growth Credible*, recently won the International Political Science Association's Charles H. Levine Award for best book of the year. He has also won the best book prize awarded by the Economic History Section of the Social Sciences History Association for *The Fountain of Privilege: Political Foundations of Markets in Old Regime France and England*. Root received his PhD in economics and history from the University of Michigan in 1983.

Dongyoub Shin is Assistant Professor of Management at Yonsei University in Seoul, South Korea. He was a winner of the 1991 Thompson Outstanding Paper Award from the Organizations and Occupations Division of the American Sociological Association. He was a Mellon Foundation and a John D. Rockefeller III Fellow. His research interests include interorganisational networks, strategic alliances, interfirm innovation networks, the dynamics between competition and cooperation, and institutional organisation theory.

Robert Slagter is Associate Professor of Political Science at Birmingham-Southern College in Birmingham, Alabama. For the last ten years he has pursued his interest in political and economic development in Asia and the role of culture in the success or failure of transplanted institutions, especially corporations. Along with Harold Kerbo he has recently published a sociology text, *Modern Thailand*.

Yoshiya Teramoto is Professor of Social System Design at the Graduate School of Knowledge Science, Japan Advanced Institute of Science and Technology. He is also a visiting Professor of Organization Theory at the Graduate School of Asia-Pacific Studies, Waseda University, and a visiting researcher at the National Institute for Science and Technology Policy, Science and Technology Agency, Japan. He has written and lectured widely on organisational learning and knowledge management.

Paul J. Zak received his PhD from the University of Pennsylvania in 1994 and is currently Assistant Professor of Economics at the Claremont Graduate University in Claremont, California. His research interests are centred around economic growth and governance. He recently edited *Currency Crises, Monetary Union, and the Conduct of Monetary Policy* and is the author of numerous journal articles.

1 Economic Development and Crisis in East Asia

Frank-Jürgen Richter

THE AFTERMATH OF THE CRISIS

The Asian crisis is now history. The region's emerging economies and markets are in the process of recovery, and the restoration of financial health is making progress. While much remains to be done, a lot has been learned from the crisis, and business practices are being altered. Perhaps most significantly, the crisis triggered important changes that will have lasting effects on economic development.

Nonetheless, unfinished skyscrapers in cities across Asia stand as silent monuments to an era gone wrong, and the reputations of many of the architects of Asia's boom lie in the dust. After a decade of 10 per cent annual growth, East Asian economies contracted and stockmarket values went into free fall. In 1997 the crisis spread from Thailand to Indonesia and South Korea, then to Hong Kong and Malaysia, and finally to Japan.

As one of the world's most successful developing region, East Asia was able to attract several hundred billion dollars of international bank loans in the first half of the 1990s. A huge proportion of these loans were short term, that is, with a maturity of under one year. However most Asian financial institutions and capitalists were not entirely capable of channelling the increased inflows into profitable investments. Even traditional, hard-working business people were snared by the lure of easy money. One could easily borrow US dollars at rates lower than local currency deposits. So traditional value builders ended up arbitraging – with disastrous results when the local currencies collapsed.

Politically connected individuals and institutions were widely perceived to be backed by implicit government guarantees, but they were not subject to effective supervision. This was an invitation to risk-taking, and became especially dangerous after 1990 as foreign capital began to be freely available. The result was a huge stock of mistakes: heavy lending to speculative real estate ventures, overambitious corporate expansions and so on. By the

1

mid 1990s, the Asian financial markets were inflated by a major bubble that had to burst sooner or later.

The impact of the Asian economic crisis was substantial. Currencies plunged, enterprises failed, financial institutions closed their doors, and rapid growth turned into recession. A number of Asian countries are still having to deal with the severe consequences of this crisis. Unemployment, bankruptcy, hunger and increased ethnic conflict are very prominent, leading in Indonesia's case to President Suharto having to step down in 1998. But he has not been the only victim: many of the power elite have dropped off their pedestals – South Korean President Kim Young Sam, Thai Premier Chavalit Yongchaiyudh and Japanese Premier Ryutaro Hashimoto being the most prominent ones.

A better understanding of the roots of the Asian economic crisis is essential if the broken pieces of the Asian economies are to be put together again. The crisis essentially resulted from a financial-sector malfunction within the affected economies and from faults in the international financial architecture. Bad investments left governments and businesses incapable of fulfilling their financial obligations. Short-term capital left the country, putting fixed exchange rates under pressure and ultimately leading to the devaluation of Asian currencies. Asian governments and politicians such as Malaysia's Mahathir Mohamad (1999) even pronounced that the Asian crisis was a sinister plot by Western politicians, managers and investment bankers.

The International Monetary Fund (IMF), functioned as a buffer by bailing out outstanding loans. Certain conditions, such the restriction of government expenditure, reform of the banking sector and cancellation of subsidies, have been applied to the East Asian economies. Also, the persistence of conglomerates such as the Korean *chaebol*, the Japanese *keiretsu* and the Overseas Chinese network groups in Southeast Asia has been sharply criticised. When events turn out as badly as they have in Asia, one naturally wonders whether the supposed rescue team actually did its job correctly. There has been a lot of criticism of the IMF, particularly within the ranks of the affected Asian governments. One could accuse – as Western observers have pointed out (Garnaut, 1998; Godement, 1999; Henderson 1998) – the IMF of failing to understand the panic element in the Asian crisis, and of concentrating on disciplining countries when it should have concentrated on reassuring markets.

The Asian economic crisis is causing a sea change in international perceptions of the region's major players. After a dazzling century in which Japan emerged first as a feared military power and then as formidable economic one, its influence may be on the wane. Thus Japan, which had previously been seen as the engine of the region's economic growth, is increasingly viewed as part of the problem rather than part of the solution. China, on the other hand, is emerging as the new economic power of Asia. Beijing's leaders are being praised for their handling of the crisis, principally their declaration that they will not devalue the renminbi. However, the impact on China from other Asian economies which have gone wrong will be substantial. Despite Beijing's protestations that China is immune from the Asian crisis, it is not. No one should be shocked if the thunderclaps of bad loans, collapsing banks, and plummeting equity prices that have already rolled through Japan, South Korea and Southeast Asia hit China forcefully.

The Asian economic crisis took place against a background of a debate that will continue well into the next millennium: a debate about the so-called 'East Asian development model' versus the 'Western' or more precisely – 'Anglo-Saxon model'.[1] It is amazing what an economic crisis can do to international perception. In the late 1980s, it was normal to criticise the Anglo-Saxon tendency to ignore longer-term corporate prospects while focusing on quarterly profit reports. The Anglo-Saxon fascination for the ability of well-functioning markets to allocate resources efficiently, was increasingly questioned throughout the 1980s and the first years of the 1990s (Fallows, 1996; Thurow, 1992; Zysman, 1983). Now, again, the talk is about the virtues of the market, the importance of competition and transparency, and the horrors of nepotism.

With this book we do not want to add fuel to chauvinist sentiments. What the contributors of this book are talking about is not a battle between states but a comparison of systems of economic organisation which *per se* are neither good nor bad. General – or even universal – theories meant to explain similar economic processes across cultures are almost certain to mislead. Differing historical traditions will almost always intervene to make economic development unique in each nation.

THE EAST ASIAN DEVELOPMENT MODEL

Asian countries have often seen themselves as the victims of exploitation by other countries – and their colonial history gives them some reason for that view. Many of Asia's emerging nations moved towards a considerable degree of government control of the economy and planning to catch up with the former colonisers. However there was no homogeneous approach to economic development in East Asia as each nation developed its own policies. Therefore there is no established and agreed definition of the East Asian development model, as noted by most commentators (for example Adams and James, 1999; Akyuz, 1999; Berger, 1988). There are enough commonalties, however, for a general East Asian model of economic development to be described, primarily in contrast to the Anglo-Saxon model. The key distinguishing feature of the East Asian development model compared with its Western counterpart may be that governments played a proactive part in the industrialisation process. In the USA and the UK, on the other hand, individuals, rather than government, make the majority of decisions on economic activities and transactions. Other features of the East Asian development model include high insider shares and weak roles for outsiders in corporate governance, close bank–firm relations and weak reliance on stock markets in investment financing, static labour markets and a monopolistic domestic market with little foreign firm presence.

After being liberated from decades or even centuries of economic depression and varying periods of stagnation, Asian governments and their citizens appeared to be captivated by the creation of wealth and economic growth at any cost. As a group, the East Asian high-growth economies recorded an average of 5.5 per cent per capita income growth during the period 1960–90.[2] This was about double the rate of growth of the mature, high-income, industrialised economies of the West.

The governments of East Asian economies initially adopted what is commonly referred to as an inward-oriented strategy of economic development, which promotes industrialisation by fostering industries to replace imports and stimulate production for the home market. Tariffs and import restrictions were used to shelter domestic producers from foreign competition, and some producers were given subsidies in the form of tax and credit preferences. A burst of industrial growth ensued as many new industries were created, largely to produce simple consumer products and – after a further period of growth – technologically sophisticated products. At a later stage, Asian governments adopted an outward-oriented strategy and pushed their domestic industries to export their products. This growth process, however, was diluted in the 1990s when these governments pursued economic growth at any cost and Asian firms targeted increasing turnover instead of increasing profits.

Economic organisation and economic behaviour in Japan – notably employment relations, trading relations between firms and the financing of firms – were rather different from the prevailing patterns in Europe and the USA. Japan's rapid industrialisation after the Second World War was made possible by the state guiding and directing the economy. Behind the state was what is often referred to as the 'iron triangle' of elites – ministry officials, politicians and managers of the big conglomerates (*keiretsu*). There was a high level of unity between them – directed at the vision of rapid and substantial economic growth. The spirit of this 'Japanese development model' comes across in the widely used epithet 'Japan Inc.' As this label suggests, the concept really reflects a perception that Japan had somehow managed to develop a collective cohesion through which the country succeeded in making economic progress. This differed sharply from the Anglo-Saxon experience. Moreover it was closely linked in the Western mind with notions of 'strong' or 'authoritarian' government.

Subsequently relabelled the 'East Asian development model' (Fallows, 1996) the Japanese model was applied elsewhere in the region. The most prominent proponents of the Japanese/East Asian development model included Malaysian Prime Minister Mahathir Mohamad and the Japanese Diet member Shintaro Ishihara (Mahathir and Ishihara, 1996), Eisuke Sakakibara, the former Japanese vice minister of finance (Sakakibara, 1993), and Lee Kuan Yew, the former prime minister of Singapore (Lee, 1998). They emphasised a shift in economic superiority from West to East and promoted the East Asian development model as being distinctively non-Western. Malaysia, for instance, adopted a 'Look East Policy', drawing on the Japanese approach of economic development. As Mahathir (1999, pp. 81–90) puts it:

> Japan's magnificent economic success was to rightfully become a role model for many East Asian countries striving to launch their own economic miracles. ... I instigated a 'Look East Policy' in the early 1980s to systematically learn from the successful elements of Japanese management and business practices, instead of always looking to the West to show the way. ... Visitors to Malaysia today will often hear businesspeople ... talk about 'Malaysia Incorporated'. That this term originates in Japan is a fact which all may not be aware of, but the concept has become an integral part of our business culture.

One element of the formula of looking East was the renaissance of a set of Asian or Confucian values. The resurgence of a public Confucianism, competing with the civic philosophy of the European tradition, built up the theme of Asian values as separate from mainstream thinking. Confucian tenets portrayed Asian cultures as being able to retain their distinctive identity, and to exercise some control over their destiny in the face of industrial progress and modernisation. Confucianism expects a strict social order wherein individuals have no existence of their own outside their local community. Confucius taught that everyone has their correct place in society, denoted by their title, and must act according to the rules associated with that position. Mahathir (Mahathir, 1999, p. 69), advocates that 'whereas Western values clearly emphasize individual rights, we in Asia tend to stress the community's rights, and if an individual tramples on the rights of the community, that person is really stealing from the rights of the majority and selfishly pursuing his own rights'.

And, defending Asian values, he further argues (ibid., p. 77), that

> the basic Asian values I have mentioned above clearly had very little to do with the origins of the Asian economic crises, and thus it is of utter nonsense to now argue that our economic hardships should have proved Asian value systems to be wrong. If any value system has been proved to be wrong, it is the purely profit-oriented, excessively materialistic values embedded in the global financial system in the West.

Indeed, within the framework of the Western financial system mentioned here, contracts determine the transactions that are undertaken. In arm's length transactions the level of mutual dependency of the business partners is much lower than in relationship-based systems. As a result institutional links matter less and the market becomes a more important medium for governing the terms of transactions. Relationship-based systems, on the other hand, ensure a return to the capitalist by granting him some form of power over the organisation being financed. An important distinction between these two systems is their different degree of reliance on legal enforcement. Relationship-based systems in general and Asian values in particular can survive in environments where laws are poorly drafted and contracts not enforced. Central to relationship-based systems such as the East Asian development model is the phenomenon of *market failure*: characterised by Williamson (1975) as the predictable inability of market mechanisms to achieve maximum efficiency and to encourage growth when confronting economies of scale. Transaction cost theory states that when market failure occurs the normal economic pressure on economic actors to perform effectively breaks down and has to be replaced by hierarchical controls.

The original version of the model was provided by Japan's Ministry of International Trade and Industry (MITI). The MITI has played a major role in promoting wide discussion of, and creating a national consensus on the strategic directions in which the economy should be restructured. And it has provided the organisational frameworks for the promotion of a wide range of industrial research and development.

Japan and South Korea relied on a similar system of industrial planning, huge interlinked conglomerates, lifetime jobs in big companies, export assistance and protected domestic industries. In the Korean variant of the model, subjective judgements as to who and what would receive preference – were exercised by the government, the industrial conglomerates (*chaebol*) and the government associated banks (see Chapter 8 of this volume). There is broad evidence that Malaysia, Singapore, Thailand and Indonesia borrowed from the development model as well. In Indonesia and Malaysia, for instance, economic development has been very much under the control of former President Suharto and Prime Minister Mahathir.

States played an important role in each country's economic development. Economic growth was a foremost priority of state action. East Asian governments have exercised a high degree of autonomy and capacity in implementing development policies. As the consequence the East Asian development model produced accomplishments. Despite these favourable outcomes such as effective mechanisms for technology transfer, and high savings, investment accumulation, there are downsides to the East Asian development model which will be further discussed in this book.

Although the problems of the Asian economies are quite severe, the main argument of this book is anything but gloating. We do not want to reinforce a Eurocentric view of Asia, attacking Asia with almost pure Occidentalism, as probably done by Patten (1998), Backman (1999) and Mallet (1999). Nor do we intend to venerate the 'Asian miracle', as done by Fallows (1996) and Naisbitt (1997). Our position lies in the middle of the two. The potential for fairly high growth is still there – the current crisis does not mean that Asia has lost its economic potential.

One way or another the period of crisis and readjustment will pass. Asia will eventually return to the fundamental course of growth that was characteristic of the last two decades of the twentieth century. The old school of economic thinking, which prescribes economic growth at all costs, however, has to be abandoned. Asia has to recover its talent for entrepreneurship, which laid the basis for sustainable development in Japan after the Second World War, in South Korea after the Korean War and in Southeast Asia during the period of economic awaking (1970–95). The collapse of the East Asian development model is not a defeat for Asia. On the contrary, it may give the region a new dynamism.

THE LOGIC OF THE BOOK

The aim of this book is to advance the search for a new paradigm of economic development in Asia. In this connection, questions of interest are as follows. What are the main features of the East Asian development model? Is the model itself in crisis or is there alternative explanation for the general crisis in East Asian countries? Why were Asian conglomerates such effective corporate engines for the rapid economic growth of East Asia? What went wrong with the Asian institutions and organisations, which used to look highly effective? Why did the East Asian system of economic development, which has been credited with fuelling the miraculous growth in the region, suddenly implode? What economic policies are consistent with and complementary to the model? In particular, what lesson can be drawn from countries' experiences with reforms? How might Asia's crisis and its post-crisis development policies affect the world economy?

This book should be seen against the background of these emerging questions. It will mainly attempt to draw lessons from the recent economic experience of East Asia in order to reevaluate the East Asian development model and its alternatives. The chapters represent a range of perspectives on the topic.[3]

The first section includes four overviews of the Asian economic crisis – the event which triggered the questioning of the mode of economic development in Asia. At the outbreak of the crisis, Asian capitalism was characterised by huge investment, extensive borrowing and a lack of market discipline in general. The individual chapters look at the crisis from different angles. Fred Robins (Chapter 2) offers a summary overview of the economic crisis and the still-unfolding consequences. Christopher Lingle (Chapter 3), on the other hand, reflects on the institutional basis of the crisis. He draws a link between the underlying political culture and the set of institutional arrangements it engenders. Yi Feng (Chapter 4) sums up the experiences of the various economies during the crisis and argues that while political stability and economic freedom have facilitated economic development in East Asia over the past three decades, political liberalisation and broad-based economic reform are needed to cope with the causes and consequences of the crisis. Hock-Beng Cheah (Chapter 5) puts the crisis into a broader context: he calls for a more economically, socially and ecologically sustainable development process in the world to avoid future crises. This could be achieved by departing from the debate between the purists of free enterprise on the one hand and those championing state planning on the other.

Part Two highlights the different variants of the East Asian development model. In particular the economies of Thailand and Japan (Harold Kerbo and Robert Slagter, Chapter 6), Taiwan (Phillip Hookan Park, Chapter 7), South Korea (Chapter 7 and Dongyoub Shin, Chapter 8), Malaysia (Subramaniam Pillay, Chapter 9), Indonesia (Hilton Root, Chapter 10), and Singapore (Ha Huong, Chapter 11) are analysed and compared. For instance there has been much less government involvement and economic growth policy in Thailand with compared with other Asian nations. Of the rapidly developing Asian nations, Thailand is the only one without strong Confucian traditions or an Islamic influence to create a public expectation and desire for a strong but benevolent central authority to establish security and provide guidance. Singapore and Malaysia can be seen as lying at the other end of the spectrum, promoting public guidance and state control of economic development.

China and its economic development are the focus of two chapters (Wolfgang Klenner, Chapter 12; Yi Feng, Jacek Kugler and Paul Zak, Chapter 13). To the surprise of many observers, China achieved an enormous economic bubble by applying similar economic thinking as its Asian neighbours – and has survived until now. One might argue, however, that China needs a crisis in order to overcome inefficiencies and achieve economic catharsis. Klenner believes that China's financial stability is due to a specific 'China mix', consisting of restricted foreign access to China's financial assets, the government's successful balancing of short-term credits with long-term credits, and the personal ties between business and administration. Feng, Kugler and Zak point out another phenomenon that may further promote China's economic health: demographic stability, which is regarded as a source of economic development. Statistically, the effect of fertility on growth is negative, so China's population stability policy has had a positive effect on economic development.

The authors agree that the respective economies need to build new competencies. They are worried, however, about how these economies will compete in the future without the advantages of a developmental government. Different models to cope with and develop the variants of the Asian development model are presented and discussed. The proposed recommendations can be summarised as follows:

- Authoritarian leadership should be reduced.
- Minority shareholders should be better protected.
- Social welfare systems should be established.
- Market mediation should become an imperative.

The economic crisis and capital shortage has provided a rare opportunity for institutional reform. Rather than reconstituting the old monopolies, East Asian economies may be well advised to take advantage of the crisis to reinvent themselves.

Part Three draws on various levels of analysis to explore the strategic responses of Asian firms to the ongoing changes within the framework of their respective economies. Throughout Asia, firms have been worrying about the modes of economic development as external factors in the economic crisis, and they are right to be concerned about these. However the foundations of economic policy are more or less beyond their control. Internal factors, on the other hand, such as their general ways of doing business, are well within their power to change. In Part Three a number of organisational and structural changes are proposed.

Usha C. V. Haley (Chapter 14) argues that the structural and regulatory changes made in the wake of the crisis have created a new set of opportunities for multinational corporations and local companies. She examines some of the strategies followed by companies that appear to be winning in the new economic environment. Yoshiya Teramoto and Caroline Benton (Chapter 15) propose a new business model for a 'post-matured' Japanese industrial sector. Japan's economic growth cannot be significantly enhanced by following the Western mould of capitalism. Rather, in order to meet the challenges of the global, knowledge-centred environment, Japan must take advantage of the country's long history of economic development. The fusion of Western and Japanese wisdom may trigger a new era of economic growth in Japan. Frank-Jürgen Richter and Usha C. V. Haley (Chapter 16) draw a similar conclusion: it is no accident that the region that has generated the world's most explosive economic growth is also the region where an economic organisation peculiar to East Asia – networks of firms such as the Japanese *keiretsu*, the Korean *chaebol* and the overseas Chinese networks – is pervasive. Changes in internal and global economic conditions, however, do require organisational transformations. Yet many of the benefits of the Asian way of economic organisation may remain. New types of business networks have to lead the region through yet another of its transformations.

East Asia probably does not need too much in the way of theory – a new, specifically Asian model of economic development masterminded by economists of both Asian and Western origin. Rather it needs to be entrepreneurial. There is a broad consensus that entrepreneurial risk taking has been at the heart of the global success of Asian firms (Cheah, 1999; Haley *et al.*, 1998; So and Chiu, 1995; Richter and Teramoto, 1995; Zahra *et al.*, 1999). The new economies of Asia have been created by thousands of entrepreneurs from the bottom up. Governments should now move aside and allow the economic power and vigour of Asian entrepreneurs to be unleashed. Throughout Asia ideology has to give way to economic reality and the outstanding capacities of its entrepreneurs.

In the past, the best approach to economic development in Asia was the fast and successful catch-up. It is quite possible in the twenty-first century to take a dramatically different approach, focusing on the innovative and creative skills of Asian entrepreneurs. It likely, that open and democratic governments will foster the 'new model' and create the necessary conditions for it to succeed, which may not be the case with purely authoritarian governments. For the present at least, the Asian economic crisis is driving governments and businesses alike towards a more market-oriented version of capitalism. However this does not mean that the Asian countries will mindlessly adopt the Anglo-Saxon model.

Taiwan could serve as a model for the other Asian economies (see Chapter 7 of this volume). Despite the crisis, Taiwanese companies are continuing to push back the technological boundaries and fight for greater dominance in the high-tech markets they have already captured. The island's government has been successful in nurturing home-grown companies to succeed on the world stage. The Taiwanese model of economic development is less government-controlled than that of its neighbours and is exemplified by the cult of the entrepreneur. Taiwanese firms are free to compete for funding in the country's capital markets. As policymakers throughout Asia start to rebuild their economies, they may look at Taiwan for direction.

Asian entrepreneurs should use the crisis as a catalyst for openness, flexibility and economic change. Asians are very pragmatic – they will find solutions to the current crisis and the failure of the old development model.

Notes

1. It should be understood that the 'Anglo-Saxon model' is not the only approach to economic development adopted by Western industrialised nations. Despite global economic integration and considerable harmonisation of the financial markets, the distinctive characteristics and economic functions of national economic systems have not necessarily been undermined. In continental Europe, particularly in Germany and France, government intervention is widely accepted. Sometimes called the 'social market economy' because it relies largely on markets but also on the government to direct the economy, this system has been predominant in Europe. In Germany, for instance, the unique aspects of the welfare system financed by contributions and backed by the state, which provides security for the individual, have persisted despite powerful pressure for change.
2. East Asia, as it is defined as unit of analysis throughout this book, comprises Japan, South Korea, China, Taiwan, Singapore, Malaysia, Thailand, Indonesia and the Philippines.
3. Some of the world's leading scholars on the Asian economies have been invited to contribute to this volume.

References

Adams, F. G. and W. E. James (eds) (1999) *Public Policies in East Asian Development: Facing New Challenges* (Westport, CT: Praeger).

Akyuz, Y. (ed.) (1999) *East Asian Development: New Perspectives* (London: Frank Cass).

Backman, M. (1999) *Asian Eclipse. Exposing the Dark Side of Business in Asia* (Singapore: Wiley).

Berger, P. L. (ed.) (1988) *In Search of an East Asian Development Model* (New York: Transaction Publications).

Cheah, H. B. (1999) 'Raising the Dragon: Adaptive Entrepreneurship and Chinese Economic Development', in F. J. Richter (ed.), *The Dragon Millennium. Chinese Business in the Coming World Economy* (Westport, CT: Quorum, forthcoming).

Delhaise, P. F. (1999) *Asia in Crisis. The Implosion of the Banking and Finance Systems* (Singapore: Wiley).

Fallows, J. (1996) *Looking at the Sun: The Rise of the New East Asian Economic and Political System* (New York: Vintage Books).

Garnaut, R. (1998) 'Economic Lessons', in R. H. McLeod and R. Garnaut (eds), *East Asia in Crisis. From being a Miracle to Needing One?* (London: Routledge), pp. 352–66.

Geogh, L. (1998) *Asia Meltdown. The End of the Miracle?* (Oxford: Capstone).

Godement, F. (1999) *The Downsizing of Asia* (London: Routledge).

Haley, G. T., C. T. Tan and U. C. V. Haley (1998) *New Asian Emperors. The Overseas Chinese, their Strategies and Competitive Advantage* (Oxford: Butterworth-Heinemann).

Henderson, C. (1998) *Asia Falling? Making Sense of the Asian Currency Crisis and its Aftermath* (Singapore: McGraw-Hill).

Johnson, C. (1995) *Japan: Who Governs?: The Rise of the Developmental State* (New York: Norton).

Krugman, P. (1994) 'The Myth of Asia's Miracle', *Foreign Affairs*, vol. 73, no. 6, pp. 62–78.

Lee Kuan Yew (1998) *The Singapore Story* (Englewood Cliffs, NJ: Prentice Hall).

Mahathir, M. (1999) *A New Deal for Asia* (Subang Jaya: Pelanduk Publications).

Mahathir, M. and S. Ishihara (1996): *The Voice of Asia: Two Leaders Discuss the Coming Century* (Tokyo: Kodansha International).

Mallet, V. (1999) *The Trouble with Tigers: The Rise and Fall of Southeast Asia* (London: HarperCollins).

Naisbitt, J. (1997) *Megatrends Asia. The Eight Asian Megatrends that are Changing the World* (London: Nicholas Brealey).

Patten, C. (1998) *East and West: China, Power, and the Future of Asia* (New York: Times Books).

Richter, F. J. and Y. Teramoto (1995) 'Interpreneurship: A New Management Concept from Japan', *Management International Review*, vol. 35 (special issue), pp. 91–104.

Sakakibara, E. (1993) *Beyond Capitalism: The Japanese Model of Market Economics* (Lanham: University Press of America and Economic Strategy Institute).

So, Y. A. and S. W. K. Chiu (1995) *East Asia and the World Economy* (London: Sage).

Thurow, L. (1992) *Head to Head* (New York: Morrow).

Williamson, O. E. (1975) *Markets and Hierarchies: Analysis and Antitrust Implications* (New York: The Free Press).

World Bank (1993) *The East Asian Miracle: Economic Growth and Public Policy* (New York: Oxford University Press).

Zahra, S. A., G. George and D. M. Garvis (1999) 'Networks and Entrepreneurship in Southeast Asia: The Role of Social Capital and Membership Commitment', in F. J. Richter (ed.), *Business Networks in Asia. Promises, Doubts, and Perspectives* (Westport, CT: Quorum), pp. 39–60.

Zysman, J. (1983) *Governments, Markets and Change* (Oxford: Robertson).

Part One
The Asian Economic Crisis

2 Asia's 1997 Crash: its Character, Causes and Consequences

Fred Robins

INTRODUCTION

Most of East Asia's high-growth economies shuddered to a dramatic, unforecast halt after 2 July 1997. I remember that day very well. I was in Dublin to address MBA graduates from across Europe on market opportunities in the 'booming, high performance, economies of the Far East'. On the way I had glanced at my newspaper. A headline announced that the Bank of Thailand had floated the baht. By the time my session was over, during which I had spoken much of Asian commercial dynamism and big annual increases in expenditures, the baht had lost 15 per cent of its value, other regional currencies were coming under pressure, and a decade-old mindset of regional stability had begun to be superseded by one of regional fragility. Although few then clearly realised what was happening, there was early recognition, at least among the business community, that it was something important.

This chapter offers a summary overview of these events and of their still-unfolding consequences; not just for East Asia but for the global economy as a whole.

THE BEGINNING: THAILAND – EPICENTRE OF A CRASH

It probably was no accident that the crisis broke in Thailand. In October 1996 *Asia Week* had already labelled Thailand the region's worst performer – despite over 6 per cent GDP growth in that year. But the health of Thailand's financial sector had been a cause of concern for some time. The Bangkok Bank of Commerce had sunk in a sea of scandal even before 1997. A real estate company, Somprasong Land, had defaulted on a Eurobond loan in February 1997 and the country's largest finance company, Finance One, had been effectively closed down on account of bad debts by the Ministry of Finance (Lauridsen, 1998, p. 147).

At the same time, Thailand was experiencing a worrying balance of payments deficit. During 1996, economic and export growth had fallen to their lowest rates in a decade and domestic interest rates were already relatively high to protect the baht, which was pegged to a dollar-dominant basket of major currencies. As the current account deficit exceeded 8 per cent of GDP, a number which had become symbolic in financial circles as a result of the Mexican crisis of 1994, markets became uneasy and there were several speculative moves against the Thai currency. One came in December 1996, another in March 1997, then on 16 May the Bank of Thailand spent nearly $10 billion defending the baht's peg (Jumbala, 1998, p. 279). Nevertheless it is worth noting that Thailand had experienced a balance of payments deficit in excess of 8 per cent in 1990 without precipitating a crisis.

What occurred has been fully documented. A detailed chronology of events, compiled by New York academic Roubini, is freely available to all (www.stern.nyu.edu/-nroubini/asia); a remarkable public service. Much of the financial detail is to be found in a book published by a bank analyst based in Hong Kong (Delhaise, 1998, pp. 84–95). Essentially, appreciation of the baht against the yen and weaknesses in the Thai financial system made it difficult to maintain the established parity of the baht. Nonetheless the Bank of Thailand, for whatever reasons, steadily squandered the country's reserves trying to maintain it. Worse, it hid its actions from public view by failing fully to disclose swap transactions. By June 1997 these off-balance-sheet trades were almost equal to Thailand's national reserves. Consequently the time had arrived when another speculative challenge would force the Thai authorities to face reality. This occurred and on 2 July 1997 the Bank of Thailand announced a managed float of the baht. They also sought assistance from the International Monetary Fund (IMF). The baht fell 15–20 per cent and triggered the East Asian crisis.

With the benefit of hindsight it is very easy indeed to recognise both financial and economic weaknesses in the Thailand of 1997. Indeed if we were to look more closely at the detail of the country's political, economic and financial affairs at that time, we might even question why some kind of crisis had not occurred earlier. This is in fact a revealing perspective, for any attempt to explain the timing of Thailand's crisis offers the first clue to any reasonable understanding of these events. This is because the onset of the crisis in July 1997 cannot be explained by examining Thailand alone. Any full explanation must also to take Thailand's creditors fully into account, and other foreign financial interests also. The latter include overseas currency traders, fund managers, financial institutions such as hedge funds and, most importantly, foreign banks.

Some nine months afterwards, at a media briefing in Washington on 16 April 1998, representatives of the IMF spoke publicly about these events. The following is what Barry Eichengreen, a senior policy adviser at the IMF, is reported to have said (Hughes, 1998):

> 'Hedge funds triggered Thailand's financial crisis, building up large positions against the Thai baht and contributing to a devaluation that sparked Asia's devastating financial turmoil. However there is no concrete evidence that the hedge funds had built up large positions against other Southeast Asian currencies.'

In examining the Asian crisis, what we are really seeking to understand is more than an isolated event in a single country. Rather it is a regional event embracing many countries that turned out to have major global repercussions. What occurred in Thailand was just the start. The crisis quickly spread to embrace almost all of Southeast Asia and South Korea as well. Within just a few months Thailand's 'currency crisis' had become Asia's 'financial crisis', and later Asia's 'economic meltdown'. The rapid spread of crisis across the region is a most noteworthy and worrying feature of these events; it was essentially a phenomenon of fast and effective global financial markets. Financial markets provided the conducting mechanism by which the crisis in Thailand spread with such speed to other countries. The efficiency of this market mechanism reflected both modern communications technology and the characteristics of modern fund management.

The 'Asian crisis' was financial panic on a grand scale. The leap from country to country became known as 'the contagion effect'. Very soon there was a region-wide crisis of confidence, which, given lack of understanding and institutional rigidities, quickly spread from financial markets to the 'real' economies of the region with disastrous economic and social effects. The latter were and still are momentous and are bound to be of lasting impact; but they are not the focus of this chapter.

THE CRISIS SPREADS: 'CONTAGION'

Floating the baht precipitated 'capital flight' from the entire region. There was a rush by Thai banks and businesses with dollar-denominated debt, of which there were very many, to buy dollars and otherwise hedge their currency exposures. There was an even greater rush by outside interests to liquidate their baht exposures as speedily as possible. However these responses were not limited to Thailand or the baht; they quickly spread to nearly every nearby country, other than those which still blocked the free movement of capital. Within a few weeks the Philippine peso, Malaysian ringgit and Indonesian rupiah were all well down in value. Then on 24 October, speculators even attacked the Hong Kong dollar. Hong Kong, unlike the others, possessed huge foreign currency reserves and could fight back successfully. Yet all across the region previously respected currencies lost 20–40 per cent of their dollar value and at the same time regional stock market capitalisations were halved. After Hong Kong, the contagion spread to South Korea. Within the Association of Southeast Asian Nations (ASEAN), only Brunei and Singapore escaped major losses. By the end of 1997 Thailand, Indonesia, the Philippines and South Korea had been forced to seek, or renew in the case of the Philippines, IMF loans and support to remain solvent. Malaysia did not go to the IMF but was similarly afflicted. What had begun as a currency crisis in one country had within six months become a regional economic crisis of very considerable proportions. Currencies had tumbled, foreign reserves fallen alarmingly, economic growth suddenly halted, and the powerful foreign capital inflows of the earlier 1990s, including the first half of 1997, moved into rapid reverse.

In fact, in the days following Thailand's devaluation, investors sold off Brazilian real and Polish zloty as well as regional currencies (Hale, 1997). Inevitably, in such turmoil there were political repercussions too (Crone, 1998, p. 13). Indeed by the time Japan's famed Yamaichi Securities stockbroking firm collapsed on 23 November, some voices claimed that the Asian crisis had become a global crisis. However such voices did not yet include US President Clinton's, who at the APEC summit in Vancouver described the Asian financial turmoil as just 'a few glitches on the road'. Nonetheless there was already little doubt that the crisis was the most serious economic event in East Asia since the end of the Second World War (Noordin, 1998).

This was confirmed by information subsequently released by the Bank for International Settlements (Brenchley, 1998), which stated that in the second half of 1997, global markets had already been stretched to breaking point by the unfolding crisis in Asia and that the crisis had already sparked such a sharp international credit squeeze that the world financial system was on the brink of collapse. Japan's 'Mr Yen', vice-minister at the Ministry of Finance, Eisuke Sakakibara, reached a somewhat similar conclusion. In an interview with *The South China Morning Post* (Fulford, 1998) he said: 'I do not think it is an Asian crisis so much as a crisis of global capitalism. It was caused by large volumes of capital pouring into Asia.' Later, in September 1998, when calling for joint action on the crisis by the 'Group of Seven' (G7) industrialised countries, President Clinton asked the richer countries of the world to address 'the biggest financial challenge facing the world in half a century' (Gray, 1998a).

So what exactly was happening? The sequence of events in the second half of 1997 was as follows. After the floating of the Thai baht on 2 July, the Malaysian ringgit required central bank support on 8 July and on 24 July there was what seemed like a currency meltdown with the baht, rupiah, ringgit and peso all slumping. In August the IMF offered Thailand a $17.2 billion rescue loan package; and the Malaysian ringgit plunged again. In September, Indonesia sought to keep control of events by going to the IMF for support before being forced to do so; the rupiah plunged thereafter. In October, world currency and stockmarkets were in chaos, the Hong Kong dollar was attacked by speculators and Indonesia was offered a $23 billion rescue package – the first of three. In November, 16 Indonesian banks were closed on IMF advice, some Japanese financial institutions failed, the won plunged and Seoul sought an IMF bailout. The extreme urgency of the Korean situation, coupled with the size of Korea's economy, the world's eleventh largest, was sufficiently alarming to US monetary authorities for the USA to start giving the Asian crisis priority attention. As a result, by the time of the APEC summit in Vancouver the USA, Japan and the IMF were all prepared to give South Korea the generous financial support that was required. With active US Treasury involvement, the IMF approved a $21 billion loan to South Korea on 4 December; with record speed. The year-on-year effect on regional currencies and stock market indices, both of which very clearly demonstrate the severity of the crisis, are shown in Tables 2.1 and 2.2.

By the end of 1997 many Western 'experts' were quietly optimistic, believing the worst to be over and the crisis contained. In reality, as Table 2.2 shows, dramatic currency depreciation continued into 1998. However, neither Russia nor Brazil was yet causing widespread concern and the sick economies of Asia had been prescribed what the IMF thought the right medicine. It then became increasingly apparent that some patients, notably Indonesia, did not want to take their medicine – worse, some thought it the wrong medicine anyway. From almost the outset, respected voices were

Table 2.1   Currency depreciation in the worst affected countries

	$ value 31 Dec. 96	$ value 19 Dec. 97	% change
Thailand	25.63 baht	44.85 baht	− 42.9
Malaysia	2.5264 ringgit	3.815 ringgit	− 33.8
Indonesia	2362.25 rupiah	5100.00 rupiah	− 53.7
Philippines	26.30 peso	39.65 peso	− 33.7
South Korea	844.5 won	1557.0 won	− 45.8

Source: (1997) *Business Times,* Singapore, 20 December, p. 3.

Table 2.2   Asian currency and stock index
changes, 1 July 1997 to 16 January 1998
(per cent)

	Currency	*Stock*
Thailand	−52	−33
Malaysia	−41	−50
Indonesia	−71	−46
South Korea	−45	−36
Hong Kong	−2	−41
China	−1	−45
Japan	−12	−20

Source: (1998) *Nihon Keizai Shimbun*, Tokyo,
17 January, p. 5.

heard to oppose both the IMF diagnosis of the problem and its recommended cure. In particular, critics argued that the IMF was wrongly
imposing credit squeeze policies on Asian countries. These were similar to
those which had been successfully adopted by Mexico in 1995, but in Asia's
different circumstances they were arguably inappropriate; instead, many
thought the priority should have been the maintenance of commercial confidence. Most strikingly, there was public disagreement about the whole
nature of the crisis between Stanley Fischer, first deputy managing director of the IMF (Fischer, 1998) and Joseph Stiglitz, senior vice president
and chief economist of the World Bank (Stiglitz, 1998). The tenor of this
public spat can be gauged by the following paragraph from the financial
press (Gray, 1998b): 'The World Bank has publicly parted company with
its sister agency, the International Monetary Fund, and the US Treasury,
arguing that hard-line rescue strategies for crisis-hit countries have failed
because of the disastrous social consequences.'

In fact an increasingly vigorous intellectual debate took off among those
trying to understand the crisis, and naturally enough, those who came to
different conclusions about causation prescribed different remedies. It was
noticeable that on all sides of this debate American commentators and
economists, despite the tardiness of their government's official response,
took the lead. There were important voices in several other parts of the world
as well, but this observer noted with regret that Europe conspicuously failed
to pull its intellectual weight in the debate.

In the course of 1998 the fallout from the crisis continued. Within
Southeast Asia, economic conditions deteriorated through the first quarter
of the year. However, except in Indonesia, where political uncertainties

dominated attention, and Hong Kong, where the currency remained pegged to the dollar, the region as a whole appeared to have 'bottomed-out' by mid-year (Kranenberg, 1998). However, it was also in 1998 that the impact of Asia's crisis was strongly felt outside the region; notably in the other 'emerging markets' of Eastern Europe and Latin America and also, very importantly, on Wall Street. Since these more distant repercussions powerfully influenced 'expert' thinking about the nature of the crisis, they cannot be overlooked.

The most important consequences outside Asia were as follows. In early June, came renewed turmoil on currency markets. Stabilisation followed after 17 June as a result of combined US Treasury – Bank of Japan intervention in the market to lift the value of the Yen but then there was major loan default by the Russian government on $40 billion of rouble bonds. This occurred just over one year after the crisis began in Asia, in August 1998. The default came despite Russia receiving IMF support and during a period of near panic among foreign investors. It is estimated that American banks and hedge funds lost at least $8 billion as a result (Deans, 1998). This default, in turn, led to the technical bankruptcy of one of the world's most prominent hedge funds, Long Term Capital Management (LTCM). This event marked a new phase of the crisis. The strength of its impact can be gauged from the words of a leading article in the *Financial Times* of 3 October 1998: ' ... the folly of bankers, who punted such huge sums on an over-borrowed hedge fund, that the whole US financial system was put in danger.' Even the quasi-official salvaging of LTCM rattled Wall Street and American banks began to tighten lending requirements to other investment funds (Morgenson, 1998).

It seemed there could no longer be any doubt that the Asian crisis had gone global. Through the last part of the year and into 1999, there followed a long-anticipated debt management and currency crisis in Brazil. Both Russian and Brazilian crises were partly due to 'contagion' from Asia. Western investment institutions, which had become frightened of exposure to Asia, quickly became nervous of exposure to other emerging markets and promptly withdrew their funds, weakening stockmarkets and putting downward pressure on exchange rates as a result. In the case of Brazil, the US government feared currency collapse might quickly snowball to other Latin American countries. For this reason the US itself offered $5 billion and mobilised support from 20 nations for Brazil, in addition to an $18 billion IMF loan. This was in November 1998 but it proved insufficient to prevent a currency devaluation of some 38 per cent on 13 January 1999. At the time of writing (June 1999) this Latin American currency crisis had not spread beyond Brazil; but it may be too soon to be confident that it will not. A leading article in the *Financial Times* of 10 October 1998 put it this way: 'Since the Russian debacle (August) and the derailment of the LTCM hedge fund (September)...contagion has spread the Asian disease to the developed world. *The difficulty is that the global economy is increasingly hostage to the world of finance*' (emphasis added).

Taken together, these 'global' events critically influenced the climate of intellectual opinion about Asia's crisis. First, Russian default, more than Asian rescheduling, really hurt foreign investors, who collectively lost at least \$33 billion (Coggan *et al.*, 1998) and the event caused many to look again at the quality of their risk assessment. It also underlined more than ever the increased global interdependence of the world's money markets. Second, the effective collapse of LTCM starkly highlighted the systemic risk to the global financial system resulting from the extremely high levels of leverage enjoyed by hedge funds and others; further, LTCM's rescue, which was orchestrated by the Federal Reserve and involved many of the world's most prominent financial institutions, alerted everybody to the wide and legitimate public interest in the internal affairs of highly leveraged institutions. The near-collapse of LTCM proved a decisive event in terms of moulding informed opinion. In particular it alerted the US authorities to the fact that the threat posed by highly leveraged institutions was dangerous not just to individual economies but also to the stability of the global financial system as a whole (Sikri, 1998). Third, crisis in Brazil, by far the largest economy of South America, focused concern about contagion in Washington and boosted support for developing mechanisms to limit it. On 2 October 1998, unlike at the APEC meeting in November 1997, President Clinton announced a US proposal to provide countries threatened by economic crisis with new emergency lines of credit (Blustein, 1998).

Meanwhile, within the region speculative activity remained a factor in currency markets. As a consequence there were a number of important restrictive moves. The Central Bank of China in Taipei banned dealing in three types of derivative used in foreign exchange transactions from 25 May 1998 (Hsu, 1998). Renewed speculation against the Hong Kong dollar gave rise to an unprecedented \$3 billion purchase of local shares by the Hong Kong Monetary Authority on 14 August 1998 (Oldfield, 1998). The government said this had been necessary to prevent speculators from profiting by 'shorting' these equities. Revealingly, this effective initiative was criticised by the international investment community (Jacob, 1999). More interestingly, one fund manager offered a more informed and balanced view in the *Far Eastern Economic Review* (Bhala, 1998). Anyway, the outcome was that attacks on the currency dwindled, interest rates fell and share prices rose (Granitsas, 1998). As in the previous year, competent officials backed by huge foreign currency reserves saw off the speculative attack.

Bigger non-financial problems remained, but calm returned to Hong Kong's financial markets. Then on 1 September Malaysia became the first country in the region to reintroduce comprehensive capital controls and a fixed exchange rate. When announcing these measures Dr Mahatir said that 'People can no longer stay with the free-market system.' Arguably, however, by the time these moves were made the crisis had peaked and to date it seems as though little difference was made. Either way, no other country in the region chose to follow Malaysia's example.

A credible, global perspective of the time is nicely encapsulated in the following: 'The contagion of the Asian crisis, within Asia, spreading through Russia and Latin America, and now threatening a global recession next year, has laid bare the substantial weaknesses of our international and regional institutions to handle the crisis' (*The Australian Financial Review*, 25 September 1998).

At the end of 1998, with the future of the Brazilian currency still hanging in the balance, informed voices were more cautious than twelve months before. Yet within a few months it would be seen that the Brazilian float did not destabilise other Latin American currencies, most of the afflicted Asian economies seemed to bottom out and begin to recover, and the international financial atmosphere was more relaxed. So much so that US Treasury Secretary Rubin could announce his departure without causing jitters. By the middle of 1999, whatever official or institutional energy had earlier existed to tackle the inadequacies of the 'international financial architecture' appeared to be fast ebbing away.

Yet by this time it had become quite clear that the mechanism of contagion was the international financial market; in particular those elements dealing in derivatives purchased on margin. During 1998 this had been publicly recognised by both the IMF and the World Bank. John Williamson of the World Bank said so explicitly during a panel discussion organised by the American Economic Association of New York in January 1999. Jack Boorman, director of the IMF's Policy Department, put it this way 'These countries opened themselves to great vulnerability by accepting short-term capital flows in a way that ultimately proved destabilising' (IMF, 1999).

CAUSES

Perspective

In examining causes, it should be stressed at the outset that opinions on the balance of causation of Asia's crisis do differ; it is still difficult to speak with confidence of a majority view. So while what follows refers to the judgements of some well-known and well-placed individuals, it is just a practical attempt to make sense out of the disagreement among economists and the inherent complexity of events. It is only personal opinion.

A good number of factors have been put forward to explain the crisis. In the months after July 1997 most commentators sought explanation within the afflicted economies themselves. Some pointed to specific economic factors, such as balance of payments deficits; some to institutional factors, such as inadequate prudential supervision of banks; and yet others to more cultural factors, such as cronyism and a predilection for sweetheart deals. Some blamed all of these and suggested that until the Asian economies cleaned up their act and adopted business practices more like those of the West, market forces would continue to exact a high price.

If the author believed that any of these factors did cause the Asian crisis he would investigate them in detail. However common sense suggests an obvious flaw in these arguments; namely that most or all of these factors had characterised the East Asian economies for years and they had not suddenly appeared in the run-up to 1997. Indeed many of these factors had been characteristic of East Asian economies for the preceding 30 years, during which they had achieved the fastest, most dramatic rise in economic activity and living standards the world had ever witnessed (World Bank, 1993, p. 4). So while these factors might indeed be negatives for the East Asian economies, they could not have caused the crisis of 1997.

Macroeconomic

A more convincing explanation might be found in the policy of fixed exchange rates that was followed by the countries of the region prior to the crisis. This policy operated in a way that effectively tied regional currencies to the American dollar. This provided exchange rate stability with the currency in which most international trade is denominated and might therefore be seen as an advantage. More significant, however, was the direct impact of this quasi-dollar peg on competitiveness. Typically, the countries of the region relied on buying intermediate goods from Japan in yen and exporting to the USA and EU in dollar prices. As it happened, between 1989 and 1995 the yen appreciated strongly against the dollar and Japanese manufacturers moved into the other Asian countries to establish local, lower-cost production. The recipient economies benefited from this inward direct investment and at the same time were able to continue to develop their dollar-priced exports. Then from 1995 the currency trends reversed. The dollar began to appreciate strongly against the yen and the output of most

East Asian economies became less internationally competitive as a result. So the Asian economies began to suffer slower export growth. Naturally other factors were affecting regional export growth as well, notably the 1996 slump in demand for consumer electronics in the USA. Yet the dollar peg must have eroded their ability to compete, especially against rival Chinese products.

At first sight, an appealing reason for rejecting exchange rate relativities as a cause of the crisis is that adverse balance of payments figures are country specific, whereas what has to be explained is a region-wide phenomenon. However there were important similarities among many of the economies of the region, not least the 1996 export slowdown and their dollar-pegged currencies. So it makes sense to examine the argument further by looking at some of the figures (Tables 2.3 and 2.4). These summary figures suggest a deteriorating situation in at least two of these countries, with Thailand clearly the hardest hit by the export slowdown. Such evidence is at least consistent with the view that adverse currency movements caused the crisis. But is such evidence sufficient and convincing? Some are largely convinced (for example Warr, 1998, p. 55) but certainly not everybody (for example Hale, 1998, p. 269). In particular, it can be shown that Thailand's balance of payments in 1997 was no worse than

Table 2.3   Annual export growth
(percentage of US$ values)

	1994	1995	1996
Thailand	23	25	−1
Malaysia	25	26	6
Indonesia	9	13	10

Source: World Trade Organisation.

Table 2.4   Current account balance as
percentage of GDP

	1994	1995	1996
Thailand	−5.9	−8.0	−8.0
Malaysia	−5.9	−8.5	−5.3
Indonesia	−1.6	−3.4	−3.4

Source: Asian Development Bank.

it had been in 1990. Furthermore, countries in other parts of the world had worse balance of payments at the time, and anyway it does not make a lot of sense to look at balance of payments figures in isolation.

There are, however, theoretical reasons for considering the argument that a major change in currency relativities caused the Asian crisis. Paul Krugman (1979), in what IMF staff have called a seminal paper (Kaminsky *et al.*, 1997), attempted to identify the causes of financial crises. He concluded that under fixed exchange rates, appreciating currencies and worsening trade balances generally precede the speculative attacks that trigger financial crises. In other words, his theoretically derived statement seems consistent with the situation of Thailand in 1997. Indeed it may be that without the underlying conditions that Krugman's early work on financial crises focused upon, the Asian crisis could not or would not have occurred.

The potential of changing currency relativities comes across with particular clarity in the following statement from a London financial adviser:

In 1995, when the yen soared to nearly 80 to the greenback, dollar-linked Asia enjoyed its highest rate of export growth in a decade. After Tokyo authorities cut rates and took other measures to weaken the yen in late 1995, export growth in Malaysia, Singapore, South Korea and Thailand went into free fall (Michael Howell of *Cross-border Capital*, quoted in *Business Week*, 22 September 1997, p. 23).

The primacy of this factor was also accepted by the editors of *The Nikkei Weekly*, which in a leading article on 15 June 1998 simply stated that 'The Asian crisis was triggered by the yen's depreciation due to the lengthy slump in Japan.' There remains nonetheless the awkward question of whether currency changes by themselves offer an adequate and sufficient explanation of events. The answer is almost certainly no.

The basic weakness of the currency and balance of payments argument, as a suggested cause of the crisis, is that it cannot explain the timing of the crisis. Payments data show that worrying current account deficits emerged in Southeast Asia at least a couple of years before the crisis broke; as is crystal clear in the case of Malaysia from Table 2.4 above. Moreover this is acknowledged by Stanley Fischer of the IMF (Jomo, 1998, p. 10). What the argument fails to consider and what Krugman failed to consider until many years later (1998), a very prominent feature of the Asian crisis of 1997 was the very large-scale movement of international capital. It is the role of these global capital flows that we now need to consider.

Financial markets

First, even if seldom remembered it is worth noting that in 1996 the IMF
formally warned Asia of the risks it faced in this regard (*World Economic
Outlook*, September 1996). Interestingly, this warning referred both to the
crisis-warning signals identified by Krugman and to the potential effects
of heavy foreign capital inflow. This warning was given front page status,
under the headline 'IMF's warning to Asia – financial crisis looms as
economies overheat', in *The Australian Financial Review* of 26 September
1996, which spoke in the following terms:

> the IMF highlights one of the key economic dilemmas confronting the
> developing countries of Asia ... how to prevent *large-scale foreign cap-
> ital inflows* overheating their economies, fuelling speculative inflation,
> blowing out their balance of payments and producing a repeat of
> Mexico's financial market crunch.
>   It particularly names Malaysia, which last year ran a current account
> deficit equal to more than 8 per cent of its gross domestic product...
>   The Mexican financial crisis provided a strong reminder of the poten-
> tial for sudden changes in financial markets' assessments of a country's
> economic policies and prospects (emphasis added).

The notable thing is that to accept that global capital flows could have
played an important part in the Asian crisis, is to accept that we have to
look *outside* the afflicted countries to explain events. In the post-crisis
months of 1997, few in the West were willing to do this. Since that time,
in contrast, especially since the LTCM affair, this has become the preferred approach. Indeed by May 1999 the Japanese press were publicly
warning Asian markets against accepting 'hot money' for a second time
(TNW, 1999). So let us now examine the size and nature of these external
capital flows. While the data are neither exact nor complete, in the context
of the crisis two factors are of particular interest:

- The *magnitude* of the external capital flows relative to GDP.
- The institutional *mechanism* driving and changing these flows.

According to figures issued by the Institute of International Finance (IIF,
1998), in the five Asian countries most affected by the crisis – Thailand,
Malaysia, Indonesia, Philippines and South Korea – the net capital flow
changed from an *in*flow of $93 billion in 1996 to an *out*flow of $12 billion
in 1997. There was a dramatic turnaround of $105 billion within six months.
This is the equivalent of more than 10 per cent of these countries' combined

GDP. Quite obviously, such a turnaround could have been destabilising. On top of this, according to the Bank for International Settlements, international bank lending to Asia fell by $51.7 billion, or 14 per cent, in the first half of 1998. This was the biggest recorded decline in a decade.

In the case of both Thailand and Malaysia, the average annual net private capital inflow over the period 1992–96 was about 10 per cent of GDP; in the case of the former this was predominantly loans and portfolio investment rather than direct investment. It is obvious that sudden reversals in volumes of this magnitude could well destabilise a country's domestic credit availability, currency value and/or foreign currency reserves. In the case of Thailand the foreign liabilities of banks and financial institutions rose from 5 per cent of GDP in 1990 to 28 per cent of GDP in 1995 (Radelet and Sachs, 1999). It is undeniable that more foreign funds were made available than were actually needed or could safely be swallowed (Delhaise, 1998, p. 85). Not only did international banks rush to invest in East Asia but so too did pension funds, investment houses and others. The implications of these free, unregulated, cross-border capital flows are several and not necessarily obvious. For clarity, it is worth making some general observations.

First, where cross-border capital movement is scarcely regulated, as in Southeast Asia in 1997, financial transfers can be made at will. They can also be made cheaply and instantaneously, even automatically, by computer. With such speed comes an inescapable risk of volatility. Second, investors need not invest in a particular economy in order to earn a return from the 'real' economy. Rather they have the option of making a purely speculative play on financial markets. Offering scope for speculation attracts funds into an economy that might otherwise stay away, further increasing the risk of volatility. Third, the financial instruments available to contemporary speculators are increasingly sophisticated and include many that can be purchased with just a small deposit. Speculators who act in this way can leverage their investments; often highly, as indicated below. This institutional facility to leverage speculative plays adds further to the potential volatility of open capital markets. It comes about because those who buy on margin are generally obliged to sell very quickly indeed when prices move against them, if they wish to avoid crippling losses.

At this point it is worth noting a couple of facts. These were established beyond any doubt by the 28 April 1999 report by President Clinton's working group on financial markets, led by Treasury Secretary Rubin and Federal Reserve Chairman Greenspan; their report is as authoritative as any document on this subject can be. It describes the increasing tendency of financial companies to leverage their bets on financial markets with borrowed money: 'leading securities firms use even more borrowed money relative to capital than LTCM did the ratios of borrowed money to capital at the top five investment banks average 27 to 1'.

Boyd (1999), writing at about the same time, stated that 'LTCM had a leverage of 50 because banks were falling over each other to lend to it'. Anyway, partly as a consequence of the working party report, the US government is considering direct regulation of both hedge funds and derivatives dealers, which are now largely free of supervision (Kahn, 1999). Derivatives are known to have been an important mechanism of contagion in the crisis. In this context it is interesting to note remarks made by Jan Kregel of the Jerome Levy Economics Institute in New York, as quoted in *The New York Times* of 17 February 1999: 'Western banks made incomparably more money selling derivatives than making loans and that in any case much of the lending was linked to derivatives as well. Most major American banks – Bankers Trust, Chase and JP Morgan – were actively selling derivatives in Asia'. In addition, Kregel is quoted as stating that 'South Korea in particular invested in high risk securities tied to Thailand, Russia, Indonesia and Latin America, including 40% of one Russian bond issue and almost 100% of a Colombian bond issue.'

So against this background let us now return to the basic issue of the magnitude of the capital flows into and out of the East Asian economies in 1997. There can be no doubt that following the steady capital market liberalisations of the 1990s, those Asian economies which received major flows of funds from overseas exposed themselves to risk of a sudden destabilising, withdrawal of funds (Delhaise, 1998, p. 30). Of course there may well have been benefits too, but that is not the issue here. In a 1998 paper, a senior World Bank official (Severino, 1998) recommended that governments should 'think carefully about the regime that integrates their domestic financial sectors with foreign capital flows'. In other words, short-term capital inflows can be a very mixed blessing. Another World Bank official (Stiglitz, 1998, p. 8) has gone further: 'A consensus is beginning to form that governments, *and possibly the international system*, need to do more to restrain the movement of capital, especially of short-term hot money' (emphasis added).

It is also worth noting, as Federal Reserve Chairman Alan Greenspan often does, that modern communications and computerised trading have greatly reduced the cost of global financial dealing. These facts, together with the wide availability of leveraged instruments such as derivatives, have enabled the trading departments of banks and specialised intermediaries such as hedge funds to develop a profitable business in moving large concentrations of funds quickly between markets in order to exploit perceived arbitrage opportunities (Hale, 1998, p. 271). Indeed the chairman of the Federal Reserve Board said earlier this year (Greenspan, 1999a) that

> By far the most significant event in finance during the past decade has been the extraordinary development and expansion of financial derivatives. ... At year-end, US commercial banks, the leading players in global derivatives markets, reported outstanding derivatives contracts with a notional value of $33 trillion, a measure that has been growing at a compound annual rate of around 20 percent since 1990.

In addition, looking at currency markets, it is estimated that by 1995 foreign exchange spot transactions amounted to 67 times the value of international trade in goods, or some 40 times the total value of trade in goods and services (Jomo, 1998, p. 10). Obviously there is a sense in which the market for foreign exchange is largely divorced from the real economy. In a typical day it is said that $1.5 trillion changes hands on the world's foreign exchange markets – an eightfold increase since 1986 and equivalent to total world trade for four months (Kristoff and Wyatt, 1999).

So it is easy to see that when the huge investment capacities of the world's major financial institutions are focused on an emerging economy, a relatively small shift in fund allocation by a major investment house might overwhelm the capital market of a relatively small economy. As Delhaise (1998, p. 88) put it in the context of Thailand in 1997: 'A seemingly innocuous decision to reallocate funds, taken in a NY boardroom, could move markets in Asia.' The same point is put more generally, more forcefully and with total clarity by a highly respected columnist of the *Financial Times* (Wolf, *Financial Times*, 20 January 1999, p. 5):

> Yet without the banks there would have been no crisis: for the five most affected Asian economies, three-quarters of the net swing in private external finance, between 1996 and 1998, was accounted for by the commercial banks alone. The banks, in particular, and debt-creating inflows, in general, have therefore been behind all the volatility.

Such moves need not relate to the economic fundamentals of the country at all. If it is assumed that institutions that are big enough to move emerging markets are aware of their power, and this is a completely realistic assumption, it follows that they may well choose to move markets for their own private gain. In such cases, when international market plays give rise to destabilising local consequences, these consequences are caused by outside interests and, in a proximate sense at least, not by forces within the country itself. So despite the sometimes gross imperfections of economic management in the afflicted Asian economies, we need to recognise that the Asian crisis may not be Asia's fault. Put rather differently, Malaysian Prime Minister Mahatir, warts and all, probably has much better reason to feel aggrieved than has been publicly recognised.

One commentator (Weinstein, 1998) wrote as follows: 'Fickle investors, controlling trillions of dollars, can drive currency values up and down in huge swings for seemingly no valid economic reason. Sudden currency swings play havoc with people's lives.'

The detail of the Asian crisis gives fully adequate reason for believing that short-term foreign currency debt can be a major liability in a world of unregulated capital flows. This does not necessarily mean that short-term capital movements were the sole cause; but it does mean they were the most important cause. This observer does judge that money market moves directly triggered the collapse of the Thai baht and by this means set off the Asian crisis. The judgement rests on the following evidence. First and most obviously, hedge funds accounted for the timing of the floating of the baht, as later acknowledged by the IMF and already noted above. It had very probably been desirable to devalue the baht for some time but it was hedge-fund currency speculation that forced the issue. Second, the speed and magnitude of the well documented reversal of foreign capital into and out of the afflicted countries, before and after the baht was floated, could reasonably explain the speed and magnitude of the currency and stockmarket falls the region experienced. These are shown in Table 2.2 above. In contrast the economic fundamentals of the countries concerned cannot explain changes of this speed and magnitude. In addition, the financial market responses were disproportionately violent in relation to the relatively minor economic imbalances in the Southeast Asian economies in 1997. Third, given the record of contagion, it is hard to identify any mechanism in the real economy that could respond with such speed across different economies; apparently ignoring some diverse economic fundamentals. Last but not least, it can be observed that the market forces that created the Asian crisis did not bring about market corrections, but gave rise to such severe 'overshooting' that they left the afflicted economies enfeebled rather than invigorated.

CONSEQUENCES

Perspective

The Asian crisis has had powerful national, regional and global consequences. Moreover these are still unfolding. Many are likely to have long-term significance. Even cursory familiarity with these events, as offered above, makes clear that the full impact embraces financial, economic, political, social and institutional consequences. The latter, which will eventually include improvements to the 'global financial architecture', which the crisis has shown to be necessary, still lie in the future.

One short chapter cannot deal with such matters comprehensively. As indicated earlier, most of the intellectual energy invested in understanding these events has been American and, not surprisingly, most of this has focused on the global consequences of the crisis. The purpose here is different. It is to focus on just one particular set of consequences: the likely impact of the crisis on Asian business. For simplicity, this set of consequences may be categorised as follows:

- Impact on the financial sector of East Asian economies.
- Impact on the corporate sector of these economies.
- Impact on business–government relations in these economies.
- Impact on industry policy in the East Asian economies.

Following this, it is interesting to speculate on the impact of the crisis on the so-called Asian model of development.

All these consequences are already being felt throughout the afflicted region. Yet what we see, so far, is probably just the start of a fairly long adjustment process. Even if the worst of the crisis is already over, as many believe, the full adjustment may still come to embrace more fundamental political and social change than is yet evident, in which case the impact will prove profound and will be felt for many years to come. Moreover, as was said of the Great Depression of the 1930s, the most profound consequence of all is its impact on the mind of a generation.

The Financial Sector

Given that the crisis originated as a currency and stockmarket crash, it is appropriate to begin with financial sector changes. Far and away the most obvious and most important has been the unpegging and floating of regional currencies.

Prior to 1997, as noted at the outset, pegged exchange rates were the region's norm. The peg provided apparent stability but allowed regional currencies to rise to unsustainable levels against the dollar. This proved not to be in the interest of regional economies. In addition the pegged rates encouraged local borrowers to raise dollar-denominated loans and risk leaving these unhedged. This was not in their interest either; in fact it proved an unmitigated disaster. Today, with the exception of the regulated ringgit and still-pegged Hong Kong dollar, the freely convertible currencies of the region all float. Nearly everyone looks upon this change positively.

The crisis also highlighted the risk of holding too much short-term debt. So it may safely be assumed that regional administrations are now giving renewed thought, some under IMF tutelage, to the associated issues of financial system regulation and disclosure. In 1997 most regional governments and central banks had little idea of the volume of short-term, foreign currency debts held by their banks or their corporate sectors. The need to improve on this state of affairs is now recognised everywhere. Regulatory changes and new disclosure requirements will probably make such ignorance a thing of the past. The crisis has also shown that central banks do need to be able to exercise effective authority in difficult times. Events have shown that prudence requires domestic financial systems to be liberalised, internationalised and made competitive before they are fully opened up to global capital. If not, small, emerging money markets will be at the mercy of more powerful foreign interests. A related lesson of the crisis is that financial liberalisation requires strict, impartial regulation and close prudential supervision at the national level if it is to work well. Emerging markets now know that if they are to inspire confidence and work satisfactorily they must achieve this. At the same time it is noteworthy that all the Southeast Asian countries possessed elaborate prudential controls before the crisis. It was implementation and enforcement that was lacking.

The conventional tools of prudential regulation had mostly been phased in during the early 1990s. These related to capital adequacy, lending to associated borrowers, percentage limits on individual foreign currency and interest exposures, and so on. However there tended to be very lax rules governing provisioning for non-performing loans. (Fane, 1998, pp. 293–5). This was a major weakness and after the crisis all the countries of the region announced plans for much stricter provisioning requirements. Both Thailand and Malaysia are now adopting US-style conventions for classifying loans and providing for losses. Malaysia has gone further and in 1998 began quarterly public disclosure of prudential information on individual banks. In addition the central bank now demands that banks under its supervision include a monthly 'stress test' to supplement their internal controls. In Indonesia, prudential supervision of the 240 banks that existed prior to the crisis showed itself to be totally ineffective due to complete lack of enforcement. In this particular case, however, state-owned banks were in practice often required to grant loans to members of the president's family (*Time*, 1999, p. 45) and these were not necessarily serviced or repaid. Nevertheless, since the crisis even Indonesia has raised minimum capital requirements and necessarily moved towards fewer, stronger banks.

So it can safely be said that a further consequence of the 1997 crash is region-wide recognition of the need for much higher quality prudential regulation of the financial sector with a much clearer focus on essentials than in the past. This means higher capital adequacy ratios – Hong Kong had an average ratio of 17.7 per cent in 1996, twice the Basle minimum of 8 per cent – plus tight rules on the classification of loans, continuously, impartially and rigorously implemented. Unlike before, circumvention needs to be actively countered. Looking back at the precrisis situation, Delhaise (1998, p. 299) described the situation in the following terms: 'It turned out that there had been a chasm between the controls that existed on paper and those that were actually implemented, as the widespread flouting of the prudential regulations had demonstrated even before the crisis occurred.'

In Korea, the banking system has been well characterised as a 'disaster' and merchant banks as 'an interesting case of uncontrollable madness' (Delhaise, 1998, pp. 105–15). Although Korean banks have the advantage of being less exposed to speculative real estate investment than banks elsewhere in Asia, their Japanese-style practices render their accounting procedures largely worthless for prudential purposes. Delhaise suggests that, in aggregate, Korean banks were already bankrupt in 1996, even before the major bankruptcies of Hanbo Steel and the Kia group, and that Thomson Bank Watch had shown that Korean banks lacked positive net worth several years before the Asian crisis broke. In fact, as Alan Greenspan (1999b) later said: 'South Korea's short-term debts, including those owed by South Korean banks, were more than three times the level of the country's foreign exchange reserves in December 1996, the year before the Asian currency crisis struck that nation.' Indeed, when Kia collapsed in 1997 three merchant banks were found to have lent the equivalent of over 120 per cent of their own capitalisation to the group. Given the major equity investments of Korean banks, they were in a very much worse situation after the crisis.

In any case, as in the other afflicted economies of the region, the classification rules governing non-performing loans in Korea have long been extremely loose. Nonetheless, loans so classified rose from 4.1 per cent at the end of 1996 to 6.8 per cent in September 1997 on the eve of the crisis in Korea (Chang, 1998, p. 223). Furthermore the merchant banks were highly exposed to foreign currency loans in the absence of any prudential regulations governing them in this regard (Smith, 1998, p. 74). Moreover the central bank had an established practice of compensating banks for some of their losses. On the credit side, the government is now opening up its banking sector to foreign competition. Bankrupt Seoul Bank and Korea First Bank were both (Veale, 1999, p. 26) sold to foreign interests, and on 17 April 1999 Goldman Sachs bought a 17 per cent stake in Kookmin Bank. Yet Korea, more than any of the other afflicted economies, faces cultural and institutional problems as well as technical problems in bringing its financial system up to an internationally acceptable standard. Even with the best will in the world, this will take time.

In the region as a whole, financial institutions require fundamental upgrading to reach internationally acceptable standards. Whilst this remains a major challenge there is at least an understanding of why it is important. Before the crisis there was complacency. Since the crisis, spurred by events, we have begun to see an improvement.

The Corporate Sector

All five of the most afflicted economies experienced a severe credit crunch after the currency collapses of 1997. Consequently business firms, especially those which had borrowed in foreign currency, faced steep increases in debt servicing costs. As a result many businesses collapsed. In Asia, unlike the West, that did not necessarily mean they stopped trading. Some did, many others did not. Typically, firms defaulted on their loans, stopped providing or supporting normal trade credit and cut back sharply on operations, but remained in business at a more modest level. Although technically bankrupt, the absence of modern bankruptcy laws or lack of established procedures for dealing with insolvency on a large scale, as in Thailand and Indonesia, enabled enterprises to remain in existence and continue trading.

Businesses in all five meltdown economies, on a devastating scale, faced the same core problem of unmanageable indebtedness. Despite differences between countries, this core problem was everywhere the same. This section offers a summary of what has been happening as a result. In each of the countries we can find instances of nationalisation, especially of banks, enforced mergers of both public and private enterprises, asset sales, the raising of new equity finance and the introduction of new business partners, often foreign partners for the first time. We may fairly say that the crisis is changing the face of Asian business.

An example or two, taken from the respected monthly *Asian Business* (April 1999, pp. 22–9), indicate the character of this broad picture. In Thailand, the introduction of Western style bankruptcy legislation proved one of the most delicate and time-consuming institutional adjustments made. As a result, corporate restructuring proceeded very slowly indeed. Thai Petrochemical Industry, for example, one of Thailand's biggest defaulters with $4.2 billion of overdue debts, has been haggling with creditors without conclusion for more than two years. On the other hand Siam Cement, which has managed to avoid default, is voluntarily restructuring to reduce debt and better cope with the crisis conditions. The company president calls it 'business restructuring' rather than 'debt restructuring' (Mertens, 1999, p. 24). In Indonesia, the worst hit economy, where unresolved political problems compound the crisis, an estimated 70 per cent of businesses are insolvent. Nevertheless few companies have been declared bankrupt because the new IMF-backed bankruptcy law lacks teeth. Some giant conglomerate groups, for example Salim and Gadjah Tunggal, are nonetheless having changes forced upon them by the official Indonesian Bank Reconstruction Agency. Unlike Chinese conglomerates, the ethnic Indonesian or *pribumi* Bakrie group has apparently successfully split itself into a good half and a bad half and offered its many hundreds of creditors a debt–equity swap option that has drawn an encouraging response. The company is being advised by Chase Manhattan Bank and Salomon Smith Barney. At the same time, however, *Asian Business* (April 1999, p. 29) tells us Aburizal Bakrie, head of the Indonesian Chamber of Commerce, is lobbying for corporate debt relief from government. South Korea is a somewhat different case. As a rule, Korean businesses are more globally exposed, their sophistication is greater and their debts are bigger too. Yet in common with companies in Southeast Asian countries, Korean businesses are accustomed to close government involvement and support. The difference is that in Korea, half of the top thirty conglomerates, or *chaebol*, are formally bankrupt or have been placed under court receivership. The giant 'top five', in contrast, have considered themselves too big to be leaned on by government and have up to the last possible moment resisted change. The government's policy for these biggest conglomerates is twofold. First, they are to reduce their extraordinarily high gearing levels of around 500 per cent to 200 per cent by the end of 1999. Second, they must rationalise their business activities so that they are not all participating in the same industries; and are subsequently able to focus on their remaining core businesses. From end of 1997 to mid 1999, however, this restructuring process was half hearted at best. Some limited swapping of subsidiaries has occurred, but not without a deal of bickering among the contestants. In addition some new equity has been gained, but not necessarily as the government wished; they have raised money through rights issues and so avoided dilution of ownership. The underlying problem is that most of the *chaebol* are still family controlled and their owners do not want to share power. While they would now welcome an injection of foreign funds, they would not welcome foreigners on their boards. The surviving smaller *chaebol*, with their debts pressing, have responded more actively. The star performer is possibly Hanwha, the eighth largest. It escaped collapse only through half a billion dollars worth of 'cooperative loans' from its creditor banks in a government-directed rescue. It then sold off whole or partial stakes in nine affiliates and lowered its debt ratio from 1200 per cent in 1997 to 255 per cent by mid 1999 (Lee, 1999, p. 42). The remaining businesses are now being grouped into three areas of activity in which future investment will be determined by cash flow and value creation rather than growth potential as in the past. The company claims it now 'operates on an entirely different paradigm'.

Whilst Singapore is definitely not one of the meltdown economies, it is notable that Singapore, too, is in a phase of active corporate restructuring. Driven by competitive ambition rather than necessity, Singapore is forcing mergers and higher standards on both its corporate sector and its financial institutions. The objective is to enhance national competitive strength and to help local players survive and prosper when the local market is fully open to global competition.

A process of massive corporate restructuring on a region-wide scale is well underway. It is forcing centralisation and attention to profit on Asia's sprawling conglomerates. It is forcing asset sales in the drive towards debt reduction. It is making short-term profitability the priority, at least for now, for large and small businesses alike. At the same time it is putting greater pressure than ever on management and a premium on strategic business thinking.

Business–Government Relations

In a magazine article written shortly after the crisis began, Paul Krugman (1997, p. 13) stated that 'The biggest lesson from Asia's troubles isn't about economics, it's about governments.' Krugman went on to suggest, as he had before the crisis began (1994), that the contribution of Asian governments to economic development had not been truly significant. The accuracy or inaccuracy of this assertion is the big question that lies behind most assessments of day-to-day Asian government involvement in business. The underlying economic and ideological question of whether it is primarily governments or markets that have 'managed' the Asian economic development success until 1997 will not be explored here; the question is too hotly debated and too far from resolution. The following comments relate more narrowly, and perhaps more superficially, to the *character* of day-to-day Asian government involvement in business and to the question of how the crisis may be changing this involvement.

When discussing post-crisis changes in government–business relations it is important to recognise that these changes are as likely to relate to non-controversial issues as to controversial ones. For example, improvement in the handling of bankruptcy and insolvency, which is widely desirable across Asia, requires legislation by governments and implementation by the courts, free of favour. The same holds for improvements in corporate auditing, accounting and reporting procedures. It follows that the very process of reform, the need for which has been highlighted and made urgent by the crisis, itself requires the active involvement of political leaders, legislatures and bureaucracies. Only in the much narrower sense of a government's direct, developmental role in 'industry policy' as a so-called 'developmental state', may it be useful to separate governmental responses from corporate responses to the crisis. Otherwise the responsibilities and needs of each are closely interrelated and to a degree symbiotic.

Perhaps the most urgent post-crisis task facing the region has been the resuscitation of sick banks and the nationalisation or sale of those beyond repair. While what has been done varies somewhat between countries, whatever has been done has required public money and directly involved government. In Thailand, for example, the government has given capital support to some banks in the form of ten-year bonds in return for preference shares. In return the banks are required to boost their core capital. Similarly the Malaysian government has established an asset management company, Danaharta, to take over non-performing loans and a second institution, Danamodal, to recapitalise ailing banks (Yeoh, 1998). Both agencies are funded through the issue of government bonds. In addition the governments of the region are facilitating bank mergers and even sales to foreigners. For example GE Capital has taken control of Korea First Bank in Seoul and Standard Chartered has taken over Nakornthon Bank in Bangkok. In both countries, foreign control of domestic banks is new; it would not have been acceptable to either government before the crisis.

Government influence on the conventional non-financial corporate sector represents a more delicate side of government–business relations. In all of the afflicted economies, government and business have long been closely intertwined. In Indonesia this came about through the commercial dominance of former President Suharto's family and friends. In Korea it came about through the government's control of credit and provision of 'policy loans'. The Asian crisis mercilessly exposed such intimate but not necessarily competitive government–business relations. The consequence so far is that these particular kinds of government influence over business have been permanently weakened, and are perhaps in the process of ending altogether.

On the other side of the balance sheet, in Indonesia as in China, the military arm of government has long engaged in business. The Indonesian military's business operations range from plantations and mining to real estate and protection. Among the many office buildings owned by the military is the Jakarta Stock Exchange (Thoenes, 1998). In Indonesia, unlike China, there is as yet no sign that this particular involvement will cease.

In all the afflicted countries, one response to the crisis has been to open up hitherto protected sectors of the economy to foreign investment and competition. Indonesia claims to have opened 26 sectors and lifted its ban on investment by large firms, domestic or foreign, in sectors that were previously the sole preserve of small enterprises. The latter include, notably, distribution and retail. Similarly Thailand is revising its restrictive Alien Business Law and will remove a 49 per cent limit on foreign ownership in the hotel, tourism and advertising sectors. All such moves represent a further step in the integration of local economies with the emerging global marketplace. At the time of writing it looks as though all the crisis-affected economies – even Malaysia, which has reintroduced capital and exchange controls – will emerge from the experience with a more liberal foreign direct investment regime, greater privatisation of monopolies and increased integration of local business with the outside world through ownership and trade. Of course the dramatic currency devaluations that triggered the crisis have increased the international competitiveness of these local businesses.

Much government influence on business in the afflicted economies, as in Japan, has been non-transparent. This influence has been substantially weakened but not removed by the crisis. Where the crisis has either coincided with or accelerated political change, as in all three countries under IMF tutelage, old 'crony' relationships have been devalued. However this is not to say that new ones cannot arise. In the case of Indonesia, many of the indebted conglomerates whose leaders are closely associated with former President Suharto have recently found that the government is less willing than in the past to give them support. At the same time, long-term relationships do not disappear overnight. For example Soegianto, head of Indonesia's giant, state-owned oil company, Pertamina, was replaced without public explanation in December 1998 after less than one year in the job. With all probability this was due to the continuing influence of ex-President Suharto's family, whose business interests were being adversely affected by Soegianto's decisions (Praginanto, 1998). It is known that Pertamina wanted to terminate contracts awarded earlier to Suharto family firms, without competitive bidding, because Soegianto judged them 'unfair' to Pertamina. The sacked man had earlier claimed to have identified 159 such contracts and had already terminated some of them. Such events as his removal suggest that while political direction and crony connections are quite likely to diminish as business influences, old habits do tend to linger on.

Industry Policy

The most interesting dimension of East Asian government–business relations is the role of the government as midwife to industrialisation, or
'industry policy'. With the partial exception of the Philippines, the governments of all the crisis economies, like Japan before them, possess active
industry policies to accelerate and direct their industrialisation and development. Indeed it was the conspicuous developmental success of these
economies that largely accounted for the close interest of so many of the
world's governments, global financial institutions and development economists in industry policy and associated business–government relations.
The question here is what consequences, if any, the 1997 crash has had on
such policies.

South Korea is the classic 'tiger' economy. There, more than elsewhere,
we can point with confidence to a government that has played a decisive
role as initiator, promoter and master of the industrialisation process
(Amsden, 1989). The crisis-afflicted Southeast Asian countries are different; they are both behind Korea on the development ladder and have
employed far less comprehensive and less prescriptive industry policy
practices. Unlike Korea, they have courted foreign direct investment and
to a greater or lesser extent welcomed other foreign involvement in their
economies. Nevertheless the governments of these countries have played
a central role in the establishment of new industries from scratch.
The Malaysian national car, Proton, is but one example. Less obviously,
Thailand's single most important regional industrial development project,
the Eastern Seaboard Project, would not have been possible without government initiative (Jomo *et al.*, 1997, p. 76). Where government itself
directly negotiates the establishment of new enterprises, it is reasonable to
suppose that close business–government relations are established.

Our focus here is whether the crisis is changing the role of East Asian
governments in economic development. After all, it could be that the practices and mechanisms of past industry policy are now no longer appropriate.

The first step in answering this question is to note that industry policy,
as practiced in Asia over the past 40 years, was under challenge before
the crisis began. First, it was under challenge from theoretical economists
in the West who viewed close government involvement in business as
unwarranted and efficiency-reducing interference, or 'intervention', in
otherwise welfare-maximising markets. We agree with Takahashi (1997,
p. 293) that 'industrial policy has been a dirty word among neoclassical
theorists for many years'. Second, to the extent that industry policy was
seen to embrace special advantages or favours to local producers, it was
also under political and diplomatic threat from Western, especially

American, trade negotiators and regulators. Third, and closely related to the previous point, industry policy mechanisms that were seen as nationally discriminatory were under potential threat from action under the World Trade Organisation's rules on competition. So industry policy was already a controversial policy issue before the 1997 crisis struck. Many classic industry policy mechanisms – those which involved government fiat, centralised or preferential allocation of resources, or identifiable subsidies and preferences – were believed most unlikely to be WTO-compatible and were therefore doomed.

So against this background, what difference has the crisis made? Although many believe that the worst of the crisis is already over, it is too soon to be sure. The most certain feature is that the dominant commercial trends of the decade – liberalisation, deregulation, privatisation and globalisation – show every sign of continuing unabated. These four words, taken together, capture what is both an intellectual and a practical current of our time. The crisis has not changed that. Indeed the crisis itself is probably best regarded as a manifestation of these trends. Moreover, with just one notable exception, the impact of the crisis has been to strengthen these developments. The single exception is short-term capital movement; the 1997 crash has put global financial markets under very critical scrutiny and, as noted earlier, the volatility of short-term capital markets and their potential to destabilise economic activity suggests much closer prudential regulation in the future. Otherwise liberalisation, deregulation, privatisation and globalisation look set to progress further in the future.

There are those who would argue the crisis has accelerated these trends. Support for this view can be found by scrutinising government responses to the crisis. As already noted, Thailand, Korea and Indonesia, the three countries under IMF tutelage, have since 1997 opened up their economies to greater foreign investment, including foreign control of businesses in hitherto protected sectors. This particular move embraces both liberalisation and closer integration into the global economy. Importantly, these consequences will be felt in both financial and traded goods sectors and will enhance their international competitiveness across the board. Even in Malaysia, the one crisis-affected economy that has chosen to reverse the liberalisation trend, it is notable that the reintroduced capital controls exempt foreign direct investment and international trade. Furthermore, companies associated with the government's Multimedia Super Corridor project are also exempted (Mahbob, 1998); the latter, please note, is itself an example of government-inspired industry policy.

It is in the context of major global trends that the impact of the crisis on industry policy is best examined. This author is aware of no evidence that the crisis has caused any regional government to reduce its commitment to economic development. So, to the extent that industry policy is still seen to offer a path to development, it is likely to be retained and employed by regional governments. Despite growing and critical scrutiny of 'crony' relationships in some countries, and despite growing and critical scrutiny of corruption in most of them, and even despite criticism of some particular mechanisms of industry policy, notably in Korea, there is no clear evidence that industry policy, in principle, is under criticism. This is quite unlike the West. Rather the evidence of government actions across the region suggests that regional politicians and bureaucrats approach development issues with very great pragmatism. The priority of the day is recovery. To this end, bank bailouts, forcing big *chaebol* to rationalise, encouraging conglomerates to divest non-core assets, liberalising foreign investment regulations, and anything else that works, is all fine. Circumstances have changed and the objective is the reestablishment of fast growth. So where industry policy is still seen to offer advantage it will still be employed. The new problem in this context is not a consequence of the crisis; rather it is today's need to make any industry policy acceptable to trading partners and the world at large. The problem is the practical difficulty of ensuring that the mechanisms of industry policy are commercially effective at the domestic level and yet permissible at the global level. This may not be so easy. It is likely to require both sophistication and ingenuity. Still, if judged useful, it is likely to be done.

The Asian Model

Discussion of industry policy leads easily into the slightly broader topic of the so-called 'Asian model' of development; sometimes termed 'Asian capitalism'. The Asian model cries out for definition, but sadly there is no established and agreed definition available. The World Bank is not alone in acknowledging this (Jomo *et al.*, 1997, p. 157). Yet the label usefully encapsulates core aspects of the political economy of Japan and that small group of East Asian 'tiger' economies that have successfully achieved unprecedented and sustained economic growth over recent decades. This political economy amounts to more than just a close business–government relationship of the kind described above; after all, corporatist state–business partnerships have been evident in other societies. The key distinguishing feature of Asian capitalism, irrespective of private ownership of industrial property, is that the government has been firmly in the driving seat and has itself played a major and proactive part in the industrialisation process (Henderson and Applebaum, 1992, p. 2). The spirit of the Asian model of development, as perceived in the West, comes across in the widely used epithets 'Japan Inc', 'Malaysia Inc' and so on. As such labels suggest, the concept really reflects a perception that the East Asian states have somehow managed to develop a collective national cohesion through which they have succeeded in making startling economic progress. This differs sharply from the Anglo-American experience. Moreover it is closely linked in the Western mind with notions of strong or authoritarian government. Perhaps not surprisingly, therefore, majority Western opinion finds it rather unappealing. This negative attitude may reflect political perceptions and preferences as much as simplistic, neoclassical economic ideology.

There is a further complication. Once we focus on the political dimension of the Asian model it is easy to drift into the much broader debate over so-called 'Asian values'. Proponents of the latter seek to account for Asia's economic success in terms of authoritarian political structures, which in turn are viewed as a reflection of widely shared, usually Confucian, Asian values. This chapter avoids such contentious issues, even though the line between a proactive government stance on industrialisation and the institutional character of policy implementation in general is not always a clear one.

There is a solid body of research findings that corroborate the effectiveness of East Asian approaches to development. Yet others have explained the Asian miracle, from the same evidence, in terms of the benefits gained from allowing market forces to hold sway. This debate is summarised elsewhere (Wade, 1992). The issue here is the narrower one of whether the events of 1997 are likely to have a lasting impact on what are commonly accepted as peculiarly Asian approaches to development. In mid 1999, the time of writing, any answer to this question must be speculative.

In the West, the 1997 crisis has been widely seen as much more than 'the end of the Asian miracle'. It has, also been enthusiastically welcomed as a signal that the Japan-inspired development model, the Asian model, has now failed. Indeed some Western press comments along these lines have been labelled 'triumphalist'. So it is interesting to assess whether the crisis has really changed the mindset of the Asian elite. Prior to the crisis, as noted, the main debate centred on how the Asian model succeeded in achieving development, on whether this was primarily through government guidance or primarily by leaving market forces free to do their work. Since the crisis, attention has shifted to whether or not the Asian model will survive. This is quite a change; but it is largely a change in Western focus.

Given that the model originated in Japan and largely owes its regional appeal to Japan's global commercial success, it is sensible to look first at Japanese attitudes. Unlike those economies most affected in 1997, Japan's economy has been stagnating since 1991. The vice-minister at the Ministry of Finance, Dr Sakakibara, once a firm supporter of 'the Japanese way', now wants to change the model. He recently said that Japan's core problem was 'the rigidity of our organisations' and 'Japanese institutions need to have major restructuring to keep up with globalisation and techno-logy'(Hartcher and Cornell, 1999). So although Japan is not one of the crisis economies, it is instructive to note such a dramatic change of view from one of the most prominent supporters of the model (Sakakibara, 1993) and someone who has been so directly involved in the crisis itself. Yet on the other side of the argument we might note the Japanese gov-ernment remains intimately involved in public sector–private sector col-laboration, for example in the development of a 300-seat, supersonic commercial aircraft (TNW, 1997).

Similarly Steve Parker, an economist with the Asian Development Bank Institute in Tokyo, has been reported as saying that 'Asian governments are entering new and uncharted territory. This time around, there's a new dynamism at work, You can't just invest and save your way out of this cri-sis' (Zielenziger, 1999). This comment goes to the heart of the high-saving, high-investment Asian model. Parker is emphasising that Asian economies cannot rely on export-led growth to the same extent as before; they must now save less and consume more. Such an adjustment would mean slower GDP growth and take a central piece out of both the input side and the output side of the Asian model. It implies a post-crisis future in which Asian growth is less rapid and in which the performance of the residual Asian model will be less distinctive. Yet this implies only macroeconomic and performance changes. It does not necessarily imply changes to policy priorities, the mindset of the administrative elite or political structures.

A more dispassionate view is offered by Garran (1998:4). He argues:

> The Asian model was only ever useful for countries behind the frontier of technology and industrialisation. Once Japan, Korea, Singapore, Hong Kong and Taiwan caught up with the rich world's level of tech-nology the model had little to offer. And even if the 1997 crash shows that economic conditions have changed in fundamental ways, ... Asia's leaders, and their boosters in the West, ... applauded the strengths of the Asian model – and their success shows its virtues were considerable – without recognising its weaknesses.

Despite the measured tone of this evaluation, the present writer is less than convinced. For the time being the evidence on the ground still seems very mixed. For brevity, I shall comment on Korea alone, the country which looks like emerging first from the crisis. On one side of the argument,

President Kim Dae-jung has praised the role and policies of the IMF in putting his country on the road to economic recovery (Lee, 1999). So he apparently applauds the conventional 'Western', IMF, 'hands-off', perspective on business–government relations. It is certainly the case that he personally owes nothing to Korea's established politician–bureaucrat–bank–business networks. Yet the Korean economy cannot instantly escape its own past. This can be recognised from its own government's actions. On the other side of the argument, Kim's Minister of Commerce, Industry and Energy, Park Tae-young, recently announced government plans (Sohn, 1999) for Korea to enhance its position in the global footwear industry. The '*government*', he said 'will finalise plans to establish shoe manufacturing centers and other support facilities … ' In addition, to promote research and development in footwear manufacturing: 'the *Ministry*, would reinvigorate research centers by sharply enhancing administrative support' (emphasis added).

He even said: 'the *Ministry* plans to improve the quality of Korean made footwear … while devising differentiated export strategies' (emphasis added). Speaking more generally, rather than just about the footwear industry, he went on to refer to the government's target trade surplus. To achieve it, he said, 'the government will develop 200 export items for niche markets overseas'.

Even leaving on one side the fact that the government has a target trade surplus, itself a characteristic of the Asian developmental state, this all sounds like very intimate government involvement in industry. Actually, it sounds like pre-crisis Korea. Evidence like this suggests it may well be premature to assume that the crisis has really changed attitudes significantly. This is particularly the case if, as June 1999 suggests, the stricken economies are already on the mend and with the passage of time the crisis will come to appear short-lived.

Overall, it does not appear to this writer that the relationships which were the underpinning of the Asian model are dying quickly. The crisis has certainly jolted the Asian economies into greater openness and closer integration with the rest of the world. However this may still leave them a very long way from University of Chicago capitalism. Contemporary adjustments may be judged to represent some modest measure of convergence on the part of Asian economies towards Western norms but this is unlikely to be sufficient to leave the Asian model indistinguishable from the American model. As Jusuf Wanandi, chairman of the policy research centre in Jakarta has put it (Kristof, 1998):

Everybody has been liberating markets to take advantage of globalization and the world economy. So we are all moving more to the American model. But this does not mean that Asian countries will adopt the American model outright. Many Asians are still not on friendly terms with the market forces that over the last few months have demolished their currencies and stock markets.

A former Japanese trade official, Naohiro Amaya, regarded as a theorist of the Japanese model (Kristof, 1999), has been quoted as speaking similarly: 'When you go hunting you have to shoot at a target. But your neoclassical school of economics says you can fire in all directions at once and the "market" will insure you hit the target. Well, we don't accept that line of reasoning ...'

For the present, the jury judging the contemporary value of the Asian model is still out. Arguments for and against it, in whole and in part, can be heard within all the afflicted Asian economies. It is this debate within the region rather than Western comment, or even IMF pressure, that is likely to be decisive in the end. Judgement now is premature. The Asian crisis has most certainly given these economies a battering but, as spelt out earlier in this chapter, this crisis was not uniquely their fault. It follows that it was not necessarily the fault of their Asian model of development either. Yet the future value of the model is most certainly being reassessed. The outcome may be either its retention or its rejection, or, most likely, modification and a bit of both.

CONCLUSION

This chapter has addressed three broad questions and offered partial answers to each of them. In briefest possible summary, the answers in the opinion of this author are as follows. The *character* of the 1997 Asian crash was that of a sudden, deep and region-wide economic depression; the worst experienced by some countries of the region since their modern industrialisation began. The principal *cause* was the herd-like behaviour of fund managers[1] in an inherently unstable global financial system; one in which some highly leveraged participants have the ability to 'move' markets. The *consequences* have been profound and extend beyond the region to the world at large. The regional consequences are social and political as well as financial and economic. Among the consequences still working themselves out are massive corporate restructuring, changes in the regulatory frameworks governing business and finance, reassessment of business–government relations in general, and critical scrutiny of the so-called Asian model of economic development. This model and the business–government relations that lie at its heart are likely to be weakened, but will not disappear.

Note

1. Whom Paul Krugman (1997) has aptly characterised as 'an extremely dangerous flock of financial sheep'.

References

Amsden, Alice (1989) *Asia's Next Giant: South Korea and Late Industrialisation* (Oxford: Oxford University Press).

Bhala, Kara Tan (1998) 'In Praise of Intervention', *Far Eastern Economic Review* (Hong Kong), 3 September, p. 29.

Blustein, Paul (1998) 'U.S. Offers Plan to Aid Global Economy', *Washington Post*, 3 October, p. A1.

Boyd, Tony (1999) 'Banks lurking in the hedge', *The Australian Financial Review*, (Sydney), 31 March, p. 14.

Brenchley, Fred (1998) 'BIS speaks out on global danger', *The Australian Financial Review*, (Sydney), 9 March, p. 1.

Chang, Ha-joon (1998) 'South Korea: The Misunderstood Crisis', in K. S. Jomo (ed.), *Tigers in Trouble:Financial Governance, Liberalisation and Crises in East Asia* (London: Zed Books).

Coggan, Philip, Tracy Corrigan, Clay Harris, William Lewis, Edward Luce and John Thornhill (1998) 'Investors face $33bn losses from Russian bond default', *Financial Times* (London), 27 August.

Crone, David (1998) 'Southeast Asia: A Year When High Ambition Was Challenged', in Derek de Cunha and John Funston (eds), *Southeast Asian Affairs 1998* (Singapore: Institute of Southeast Asian Studies), pp. 3–17.

Deans, Alan (1998) 'Turning tide of economic opinion', *The Australian Financial Review* (Sydney), 5–6 September.

Delhaise, Philippe (1998) *Asia in Crisis: the implosion of the banking and finance systems* (Singapore: Wiley).

Fane, George (1998) 'The role of prudential regulation', in Ross McLeod and Ross Garnaut (eds), *East Asia in Crisis: from being a miracle to needing one?* (London: Routledge), pp. 287–303.

Fischer, Stanley (1998) 'Economic Crises and the Financial Sector', speech prepared for the Federal Deposit Insurance Corporation Conference on Deposit Insurance, Mayflower Hotel, Washington DC, 10 September; downloaded from IMF website.

Fulford, Benjamin (1998) 'Markets must heed the call of capital', *South China Morning Post*, Internet Edition (Hong Kong), 27 June.

Garran, Robert (1998) *Tigers Tamed: the end of the Asian Miracle* (St. Leonards, Australia: Allen & Unwin).

Granitsas, Alkman (1998) 'What's the Plan? *Far Eastern Economic Review* (Hong Kong), 17 September, p. 53.

Gray, Joanne (1998a) 'Clinton, G7 to co-ordinate policy response', *The Australian Financial Review* (Sydney), 16 September, p. 1.

Gray, Joanne (1998b) 'World Bank, IMF split on strategy', *The Australian Financial Review* (Sydney), 8 October, p. 14.

Greenspan, Alan (1999a) Remarks by Chairman Alan Greenspan before the Futures Industry Association, at Boca Raton, Florida, 19 March; downloaded from the Federal Reserve Board website on 11 May 1999.

Greenspan, Alan (1999b) quoted by Associated Press in 'Greenspan Says Euro Will Grow', *New York Times on the web* (New York), 29 April.

Hale, David (1997) quoted by Peter Hartcher in 'Why Soros may be Mahatir's red herring', *The Australian Financial Review* (Sydney), 26 August, p. 11.

Hale, David (1998) 'Will Mexico's recovery from crisis be a model for East Asia?', in Ross McCleod and Ross Garnaut (eds), *East Asia in Crisis: from being a miracle to needing one*? (London: Routledge), pp. 266–86.

Hale, David (1999) 'Reform will fortify emerging economies', *The Australian Financial Review* (Sydney), 16 February, p. 17.

Hartcher, Peter and Andrew Cornell (1999) 'Defender of the Japanese way calls for modernisation', *The Australian Financial Review* (Sydney), 25 May.

Henderson, Jeffrey and Richard Appelbaum, (1992) 'Situating the State in the East Asian Development Process', in Richard Appelbaum and Jeffrey Henderson (eds), *States and Development in the Asian Pacific Rim* (Newbury Park, CA: Sage Publications), pp. 1–26.

Hsu, Michelle (1998) 'Central Bank Restricts NDF Trading to Curb Speculation', *China Economic News Service* (Taipei), 24 May.

Hughes, Duncan (1998) 'Baht lone currency shorted in crisis', *South China Morning Post*, Internet Edition (Hong Kong), 18 April.

IIF (1998) Figures released by the IIF in Zurich, reported by Fred Brenchley in 'Emerging markets wounded as Asian crisis slashes capital flows', *The Australian Financial Review* (Sydney), 30 January, p. 28.

IMF (1999) 'IMF Finds Design of Policy Recommendations "Basically Appropriate" in Asian Crisis Review', *IMF Survey*, vol. 28, no. 2, pp. 20–23.

Jacob, Rahul (1999) 'Hong Kong: Intervention pays off', *Financial Times*, 27 March.

Jomo, K. S. *et al.* (1997) *Southeast Asia's Misunderstood Miracle* (Boulder, Co: Westview Press).

Jomo, K. S. (1998) 'Introduction: Financial Governance, Liberalisation and Crises in East Asia', in K. S. Jomo (ed.), *Tigers in Trouble: Financial Governance, Liberalisation and Crises in East Asia* (London: Zed Books), pp. 1–32.

Jumbala, Prudhisan (1998) 'Thailand: Constitutional Reform Amidst Economic Crisis', *Southeast Asian Affairs 1998* (Singapore: Institute of Southeast Asian Studies), pp. 265–91.

Kahn, Joseph (1999) 'More Scrutiny is Sought for Firms that Run or Lend to Hedge Funds', *The New York Times on the web* (New York), 29 April.

Kaminsky, Graciela, Saul Lizondo and Carmen Reinhart (1997) IMF Working Paper 97/79: 'Leading Indicators of Currency Crises', available from the IMF website: http://www.imf.org

Kranenberg, Hendrick (1998) Executive vice-president of Standard & Poor's, quoted by Larry Wee in 'Most Asia sovereign ratings have hit bottom', *Business Times Online* (Singapore), 25 April.

Kristof, Nicholas (1998) 'Crisis Pushing Asian Capitalism Closer to US-Style Free Market', *The New York Times on the web* (New York), 17 January.

Kristof, Nicholas and Edward Wyatt (1999) 'Who Sank, or Swam, in Choppy Currents of a World Cash Ocean', *The New York Times on the web*, 15 February.

Krugman, Paul (1979) *A Model of Balance of Payments Crises* (New York: Basic Books).

Krugman, Paul (1994) 'The Myth of Asia's Miracle', *Foreign Affairs*, vol. 73, no. 6 (November–December), pp. 62–78.

Krugman, Paul (1997) 'Whatever happened to the Asian Miracle?', *Fortune*, 18 August, pp. 12–14.

Krugman, Paul (1998) 'What Happened to Asia?', unpublished MIT paper, January. See also 'Asia: What Went Wrong', *Fortune*, 2 March.

Lauridsen, Laurids (1998) 'Thailand: Causes, Conduct, Consequences', in K. S. Jomo (ed.), *Tigers in Trouble: Financial Governance, Liberalisation and Crises in East Asia* (London: Zed Books), pp. 137–61.

Lee, Chang-sup (1999) 'Pres. Kim Lauds IMF for Korea's Recovery', *Internet Hankookilbo Korea Times* (Seoul), 10 May.

Mahbob, Sulaiman (1998) 'Investors Still Welcome', *Far Eastern Economic Review* (Hong Kong), 24 September, p. 36.

Mertens, Brian (1999) 'Putting back the pieces: Asia's restructuring gathers pace', *Asian Business* (Hong Kong), vol. 35, no. 4, (April), pp. 22–9.

Morgenson, Gretchen (1998) 'Seeing a Fund as Too Big to Fail, New York Fed Assists its Bailout', *The New York Times on the web* (New York), 24 September.

Noordin, Sopiee (1998) Speaking as chairman and CEO of the Malaysian Institute of Strategic and International Studies, quoted in *The Nikkei Weekly* (Tokyo), 7 September, p. 11.

Oldfield, Stewart (1998) 'Global bid to defend intervention', *South China Morning Post*, Internet edition (Hong Kong), 17 August.

Praginanto, L. (1998) 'Firing of Indonesian oil chief suggests Suharto still powerful', *The Nikkei Weekly* (Tokyo), 20 December.

Radelet, Steven and Jeffrey Sachs (1999) 'What Have We Learned, So Far, From the Asian Financial Crisis?', unpublished paper dated 4 January; partially sponsored by the Office of Emerging Markets, US Agency for International Development (USAID).

Roubini, Nicholas (1998) *Chronology of the Asian Currency Crisis and its Global Contagion*; website address: http://www.stern.nyu.edu/-nroubini. asia /AsiaChronology

Sakakibara, Eisuke (1993) *Beyond Capitalism: The Japanese Model of Market Economics* (University Press of America and Economic Strategy Institute, USA).

Severino, Jean-Michel (1998) *East Asia: The Road to Recovery;* quoted by Joanne Gray in 'World Bank seeks $17bn growth spur', *The Australian Financial Review* (Sydney), 30 September, p. 8.

Sikri, Apu (1998) 'Fear of wider damage fueled long-term bailout', *Business Times Online* (Singapore), 26 September.

Smith, Heather (1998) 'Korea', in Ross McLeod and Ross Garnaut (eds), *East Asia in Crisis: from being a miracle to needing one?* (London: Routledge), pp. 66–84.

Sohn, Tae-soo (1999) 'Pusan to be developed into global mecca of footwear industry', *Korea Herald Online* (Seoul), 24 February.

Stiglitz, Joseph (1998) 'The Role of International Financial Institutions in the Current Global Economy', address to the Chicago Council of Foreign Relations, 27 February; downloaded from the World Bank website on 5 May 1999.

Takahashi, Takuma (1997) 'The Industrial Policies of Developed and Developing Economies from the Perspective of the East Asian Experience', in Seiichi Masuyama, Donna Vandenbrink and Chia Siow Yue (eds), *Industrial Policies in East Asia* (Singapore and Tokyo: ISEAS and Nomura Research Institute), pp. 293–325.

Thoenes, Sander (1998) 'Indonesia: Army has an eye to profit', *Financial Times* (London), 3 December.

Time (1999) 'Suharto's Billions', *Time*, 24 May, pp. 36–48.

TNW (1997) 'MITI piloting commercial aircraft project', *The Nikkei Weekly* (Tokyo), 1 September, p. 7.

TNW (1999) 'Asian markets on rebound should guard against hot money', editorial in *The Nikkei Weekly*, 24 May.

Veale, Jennifer (1999) 'Asia: How Real Is Its Recovery?', *Business Week*, Asian edition, 3 May, pp. 24–7.

Wade, Robert (1992) 'East Asia's Economic Success', *World Politics*, vol. 44 (January), pp. 270–320.

Warr, Peter (1998) 'Thailand', in Ross McCleod and Ross Garnaut (eds), *East Asia in Crisis: from being a miracle to needing one?* (London: Routledge), pp. 49–65.

Weinstein, Michael (1998) 'When Lending Money Just Isn't Enough: Critics Seek a New Role for the IMF', *The New York Times on the web* (New York), 30 September.

World Bank (1993) *The East Asian Miracle: economic growth and public policy* (New York: Oxford University Press).

Yeoh, Oon (1998) 'Malaysia's slide suggests economy not yet out of woods', *The Nikkei Weekly* (Tokyo), 7 December.

Zielenziger, Michael (1999) 'Old formulas insufficient for Asia economies', *San Jose Mercury News, Asia Report Online*, 24 April.

3 The Institutional Basis of Asia's Economic Crisis

Christopher Lingle

The analysis of the Asian crisis offered in this chapter departs from an understanding of the nature of the interaction of economic and political institutions with market processes. A link is drawn between the underlying political culture and a set of institutional arrangements that it engenders. In turn, this institutional infrastructure defines a set of incentives within which economic decisions are made. Faulty institutions will send misguided signals such that decisions that appear to be rational when judged by internal criteria are proved to be irrational and inefficient when compared with external standards. A number of propositions or observations will be outlined and then explored.

First, the economic crisis afflicting East Asia after July 1997 can be considered as being self-inflicted in that it reflected a general failure of governance. In effect, the turmoil resulted from systematic politicisation of domestic financial markets. Policies of directed development were followed in most of the countries in the region. As such, investments for development were directed through banks while domestic capital markets were suppressed.

Second, it follows, then, that global capital flows were not the cause of the crisis. These footloose flows merely transmitted the message that the institutional framework of the East Asian economies would no longer be considered compatible with the demands of the international marketplace. Overall conditions of competition changed the rules of the game. Political and economic institutions that were once thought to help promote growth in the region began to serve as a drag. Judging from the resignation of former Indonesian President Suharto, global capital can now be seen as a liberating force that displaces dictators and inept rulers.

Third, East Asia's problems are deepseated and arise from elements of political culture and similar development policies that are evident throughout the region. As such, resolution of the crisis requires radical changes that must include the introduction of greater political accountability and increased financial transparency. Participation in the global marketplace will induce reluctant leaders to embrace modernisation of their political and economic institutions.

Fourth, before these economies can recover, they must first stabilise. Stabilisation can only begin after they reach bottom. Japan's state of arrested collapse that began at the end of the 1980s inspires little confidence that its neighbours can act more quickly or more resolutely. There are no good estimates of how much longer Indonesia will experience economic decline. Even though there are some encouraging signs of progress in South Korea and Thailand, the crisis is in the early stages in Malaysia and Singapore.

Fifth, recovery from the crisis involves a long-term structural adjustment. These problems are not merely a brief cyclical downturn. Restoration of confidence in Asia's economic future, and with it the return of foreign capital, will depend on a willingness to abandon culturally imbedded institutions. This may require decades or even generations.

Sixth, there is widespread misunderstanding of the modernising process brought about by the global economy. An oft-repeated confusion is that modernisation is linked to Westernisation or even Americanisation. Such suggestions are misplaced and smack of an inappropriate sense of cultural triumphalism (Lingle, 1998). Modernisation is a universal process and is best interpreted as the implementation and evolution of individualist-based institutions.

WHY (FREE) INSTITUTIONS MATTER

Institutions are systems of rules, conventions, laws or customs that serve as enabling mechanisms discovered through the process of human interaction. Such arrangements emerge and endure inasmuch as they reinforce stability within a community or facilitate change by reducing uncertainty. The rule structure of institutions provides an aspect of predictability in the course of social interplay. This predictability arises from the incentive structures embodied in the institutions that guide individual choices and shape the social impacts of these decisions.

Since institutions define incentives and impact on choice, the overall institutional arrangements have considerable economic import. In particular, markets both depend on and set the stage for the emergence of a contract culture and commercial morality. In turn institutional frameworks will evolve to reinforce and reward or punish actions in reference to the agreements and the legal institutions that support them.

Virtually every country in the world has voluntarily undertaken to participate in the international market economy. Therefore success, as measured by sustainable growth, will require an environment that is compatible with markets.

Countries with institutions that provide strong protection of property rights, along with relatively low costs for innovations, can be expected to have economies that perform better. An effective system of property rights vests the ownership and control of productive properties and means of distribution in private hands. These rights require a firm legal underpinning that includes constitutional guarantees, effective laws and an independent judicial system with the will and ability to ensure enforcement. The qualities of innovation and receptivity to change are not limited to the economic realm and should include politics. In this latter regard, valuable lessons might be learned about political and corporate accountability associated with the rise and decline of the East Asian economies.

Cultural change and economic growth reflect the speed of learning expressed through the learning process. Entrepreneurial action is the search and application of new knowledge that occurs when there are adequate pay-offs from the expense of their quests. As such, institutional arrangements that are based on openness and encourage competition will offer greater opportunities for entrepreneurial innovation. In contrast the presence and enforcement of monopoly, imposed by government mandate, will retard learning and put a brake on economic growth. Consequently a strong case can be made for the linkage between economic liberty, as seen in institutional arrangements that promote free markets and high growth.

THROUGH THE PAST, BRIGHTLY

While the pace of material advance in East Asia since the early 1970s has been admirable, the idea of an ascendant 'Asian century' has proven to be fraught with difficulty. One crucial flaw was that it was based on an understanding that expanding international trade is a zero-sum game, with Asia portrayed as a 'winner' at the expense of 'losers'. Second, continued success with high economic growth has proved to be more difficult than predicted by those who assumed that it would arise from a simple extrapolation of past performance.

A fruitful approach to understanding the past and anticipating the future for East Asia lies in an examination of the institutional arrangements and development strategies common to much of East Asia. This requires a long view combined with an understanding of the requirements for market-driven growth to be sustainable. Following this line of reasoning, there is good reason to doubt a rapid return to stability and a recovery in the high growth rates once enjoyed by the economies in the region.

The inherent conservatism and inflexibility of East Asia's economic and political institutions was once widely seen as the basis of high growth in the region. However it has become clear that the institutional arrangements were incompatible with the demands of an increasingly efficient global market. In particular the boom period for many East Asian economies was coincidental with a form of corporatism as a guiding paradigm for economic development. This framework involved a close cooperative relationship between politicians, technocratic bureaucrats and an established business elite, often with the collusion of trade unions. The German and French economies have operated along these lines, where 'insiders' oversee policies to protect their special interests, which often serves to disadvantage 'outsiders'. In general, outsiders are consumers who pay higher prices and have less choice, workers not covered by the arrangements or small or medium sized firms that are or will be new market entrants.

Asian traditions act upon economic and political structures to create a regional variant, identified here as 'Confucian corporatism', that reflects corporate practices familiar elsewhere. For example key elements of Confucianism such as 'filial piety', 'saving face' and 'society above self' serve to reinforce the hegemony and hierarchical political structures of Asian corporatist arrangements. In Japan this arrangement became known as an 'iron triangle' (Richter, 1999), wherein bureaucrats, businesses and politicians work together in close consultation.

Corporatist arrangements are credited with increasing harmony and cooperation in the workplace, but they might simply have been coincidental with initial high rates of economic growth. Corporatism was also associated with the 'miracle' economy of postwar Germany. However it is likely that the current economic malaise in both countries has arisen from rigidities associated with their institutional arrangements.

Historical experience suggests that corporatist institutions suffer from internal contradictions in that they spawn rigidities in economic relations that retard economic growth rates. Ironically the institutional arrangements previously said to be part of the winning formula for many East Asian regimes are undermining stabilisation and inhibiting recovery of their economies.

For example the growth strategy of most East Asian countries included substantial government involvement. This included government-directed investment, funded through taxes and forced savings. In addition governments often guided bank lending to promote export-oriented industries and offered subsidies and tax incentives to multinationals. This was combined with capital-friendly policies to encourage foreign direct investment and technology transfers.

But most of these policies can only be part of a short-term strategy. In the face of economic fundamentals, subsidies are unnecessary. Indeed they are economically irrational since they have no positive net impact on jobs. Such attempts to protect employment in one sector generate price distortions and the misallocation of resources in other sectors to offset job losses.

In sum, most governments in the region overlooked the necessary development of their infrastructure for their modernisation. While prudent actions were often undertaken to provide physical infrastructure (roads and railways, communications, seaport and airport facilities), there was a neglect of intangible infrastructure expenditure and human capital investment. In general, this meant that the institutional arrangements were not in place that would make their economies compatible with the changing demands of the global capital market.

The presumed successes of the Asian model provided a cover for the dysfunctional democracy of one-party or one-family regimes. In most East Asian regimes, political longevity was seldom due to the true and unshakeable approval of their citizens. More often than not, electoral success reflected a grip on power based on either the carrot of cronyism or the stick of fear. More benign methods involved coopting key elements of the civil society through trade unions, guided by supporters of the regime, filling key university posts with sycophants or concocting laws to tame the media.

An underlying element of the crisis emerged from the politicisation of the domestic financial markets throughout the region. Their policy of directed development involved a purposeful weakening of capital markets so that commercial and industrial investments were directed through the banking system. Bank managers were much easier to control than the millions of individual investors participating in open markets for equities and bonds. Government-directed investments and subsidised interest rates resulted in massive conglomerates such as the Japanese *keiretsu* and Korean *chaebol* diverting vast funds into non-economic activities.

On the one hand, stunting the growth of long-term debt markets supported the policy objectives of the government but encouraged domestic capital to be used inefficiently. On the other hand, in absence of an active domestic bond market, foreign portfolio funds went into the stock market. But the heavy reliance of corporate enterprises upon bank financing meant that equities were thinly traded and proved to be vulnerable to fickle foreign capital flows.

ECONOMIC GROWTH: INSPIRATION, PERSPIRATION, LUCK ...?

A key element of the catch-up process in much of East Asia was the shift of labour and other resources from agrarian production towards industrial output, especially in Japan, Korea and Taiwan. As these economies modernised, labour resources were released from farming and were combined with increasing numbers of women seeking employment. This massive mobilisation of the overall labour force allowed a substantial boost in production when combined with new capital investment.

The consequence of this input-driven approach to growth became the object of an interesting and lively debate, stimulated by Paul Krugman in an article in *Foreign Affairs* (Krugman, 1994). Krugman pointed out similarities between the East Asian experience and the early stages of development in the USSR. Although many of the East Asian economies have made large expenditures on physical and human capital, these actions are non-repeatable.

In this context, economic growth in much of East Asia has arisen from massive increases in inputs that will inevitably boost output, at least initially. Growth may continue, but it will increase at a decreasing rate. Without gains in productivity, the rates of growth will eventually decline. An economy with high rates of investment will eventually attain a higher level of income than one with lower rates of investment, but income gains will experience diminishing returns. Furthermore, since investment involves the sacrifice of current consumption, excessive levels of saving and investment will reduce economic welfare.

Maintaining increases in productivity became more difficult as operating costs rose rapidly in most of the high-growth regions of East Asia. With rising costs exceeding productivity gains, production facilities began to migrate to areas with lower costs and greater profit opportunities. This problem may become more acute in China. In early 1996 the Beijing regime rescinded the tax breaks that were previously offered as a lure for new foreign investment. Meanwhile the costs of housing for expatriates in controlled property markets have soared, and there is continued interference and financial impositions by corrupt officials. There is also a scarcity of skilled labour and management talent, and delivery costs are rising due to regulations in the transport industry. There will have to be substantial increases in productivity gains or growth will begin to slow dramatically.

While the economic logic in the Krugman logic is intact, the crisis afflicting East Asia did not stem from this process. In this sense, Krugman was right about the fact that growth would slow in East Asia, but for the wrong reason. Problems with returns to scale would probably not have arisen until well into the next millennium.

Indeed the 'miracle' growth of the East and Southeast Asian economies may be no different from the high-growth record exhibited by other countries during the early stages of development (Witley, 1992). Most East Asian economies relied heavily on off-the-shelf technology and access to markets in the mature economies to fuel their growth. If they fail to develop their own domestic entrepreneurial talent and promote self-generated technological advance, the East Asian economies will be followers instead of world-class leaders. Like Germany and America prior to the First World War, the East Asian economies have benefited as much from expanding product and resource markets as they have from their own development strategies.

The sustainability of economic growth has also been undermined in those countries which depend heavily on the exploitation of non-renewable resources. The limit of this was reached in the Philippines during the 1970s and it is now becoming apparent in Indonesia and Thailand. The obsessive drive for adding to material wealth in the short run may lead to a serious deterioration of the environment in many of the Asian countries. In many cases, such problems have arisen out of the type of government action that leads to overzealous exploitation as politicians and bureaucrats scramble to cut themselves in on sweetheart deals.

AUTHORITARIANISM, COLLECTIVISM AND ECONOMIC GROWTH?

The East Asian crisis has caused a number of casualties in respect of views on the role of governments in economic development. The first is the myth that authoritarianism is good for growth. A corollary to this view stressed the importance of political connections as a necessary and sufficient condition for business success in the region. Another mistaken view was that collective decision making would provide superior results than reliance on individualist-based institutions.

Many Asian cultures rely on methodical deliberation to reach a voluntary or enforced consensus. This reflects a belief that the imposition of order provides better results than the messiness associated with the open discourse of competitive processes. However a good case can be made for encouraging the involvement of a large number of free thinkers when issues become increasingly complex. My own experience as a professor has revealed that uninitiated students ask the most interesting questions and answers because they do not know better!

Much of the now dormant debate revolved around claims that the Asian version of democracy combined the 'positive' features of authoritarianism with popular rule. Authoritarian regimes invoked the notion of 'Asian democracy' to provide a legitimising veil while they restrained all modernisation and change that threatened to disrupt the political *status quo*.

One serious side effect of the institutionalised collectivism that is common in parts of East Asia will be an accelerated 'entrepreneurial brain drain'. The discouragement of institutions that promote individualism frustrates native entrepreneurs, who are likely to seek a more hospitable environment outside the region. An entrepreneur does more than buy low and sell high. It is unlikely that ersatz entrepreneurs will have the innovative spark of those true entrepreneurs who improve market efficiency by exploiting market share opportunities or instigating changes to the rigidified policy framework. The subsequent shortage of domestic entrepreneurial talent will eviscerate one of the most important internal sources of innovation-based development. Consequently these countries are likely to remain dependent on foreigners for access to markets and creative invention.

Despite its potentially disruptive impact on one-party politics, the high-growth Asian economies must allow increased flexibility and efficiency in information flows as a precondition for future production. Just as continued world economic growth depends on a regime of expanding free trade in goods and services, the modern global economy requires access to and production of knowledge-based commodities. Social progress also depends on open competition among political and cultural institutions, regardless of their geographic origin. Unfortunately many Asian authoritarian regimes have imposed a form of 'cultural protectionism' that is designed to inoculate their citizens against modernising influences that might encourage the liberalisation of individual rights and freedoms. However impediments to cultural and intellectual exchanges are likely to be as self-defeating as politically inspired trade protectionism.

The daunting challenges of the ongoing crisis are especially problematic for the authoritarian regimes in the region. This is because successful resolution will involve choices that are antithetical to one-party regimes. On the one hand, an inability or refusal to adapt to the constantly changing realities of the globalised economy will postpone the process of stabilisation and push recovery further into the future. This undoes the claim of delivering prosperity in return for popular support. On the other hand, relaxation of government economic controls will, *per se*, undermine the basis of political dominance. Furthermore the increasingly complicated political relationships that inevitably accompany economic modernisation will undermine the management and control capacity of authoritarian leaderships. In the long run, East Asian authoritarian regimes must either adapt or die, a choice faced by all economies.

GOVERNMENT FAILURES AND CURRENCY CRISES IN EAST ASIA: OVERINVESTMENT OR MALINVESTMENT?

If Krugman was wrong about what went wrong, what is the explanation of the business failures in East Asia? The surprise and confusion over the currency and financial crises sweeping through the region in late 1997 and early 1998 reflected the belief that the fundamentals were intact to promote economic growth. A report by the World Bank in 1994 praised the East Asia leadership for getting the 'basics rights' (World Bank, 1994). This notion must have been in part wishful thinking, since there would be no discussion of a long-term crisis if the fundamentals had been in place.

Following conventional wisdom, observers have interpreted the turmoil sweeping through the Asian economies as evidence that markets are irrational and unstable. A common notion is that the East Asian economies were victims because they went too far and too fast in liberalising their markets. It seems as if the discussion of the East Asian development has been locked into ideological confrontations between left and right in the West – with an ensuing loss of clarity and logic.

Most East Asian governments pursued a policy that provided government guarantees of subsidised loans to specific producers for an expansion of their operations that exceeded market rationality. But it is not easy to see how these guarantees could lead to *most* companies overinvesting even when they had access to foreign savings. Government subsidy costs would simply be very high. Massive and unpopular conversions of domestic savings into taxes to pay the subsidies would then follow.

The problems confronting East Asia have arisen from a concentrated mass of distorted investments because government guarantees distorted incentives that encouraged investment based on technocratic or political considerations instead of commercial viability and profitability. In the absence of properly functioning domestic capital markets, funds were squandered on ill-conceived projects that exposed their economies to the non-compromising market logic of global capital.

Such malinvestment occurred directly through public spending or the promotion of government-favoured businesses, such as South Korea's *chaebol*. However, such misdirected investments were principally inspired by monetary or credit policies. In turn, illusory signals arose so that consumers and the business community misinterpret increased money and credit flows as real, permanent changes in the economy instead of mere monetary changes.

Unfortunately, government-guaranteed investments divert funds that might be placed elsewhere in more economically rational applications.

As rates of interest are forced down through credit expansion, there is an illusion that certain activities will be more profitable, especially in higher stages of production. In effect production is misdirected by artificial changes in relative prices. The extent of malinvestments depends on the vigour of the induced expansion. The vigorously manipulated expansion in East Asia simply ran into a financial wall, which was the cause of the abrupt decline in production in the region. As investors began to understand that the boom was unsustainable, speculative pressures were brought to bear. Although condemned by governments in the region, the motivations behind the speculative actions were homegrown. Speculators were acting as countervailing forces to the counterfeit expansion and provided a force that burst speculative bubbles throughout the region.

Every speculative bubble eventually bursts when consumers and producers realise that changes in activity are based on an inflationary surge. Governments must then choose whether to curb the inflationary consequences of their loose credit policies, or succumb to self-correcting forces triggered by inflation. Inflation will expose and restore the actual relations in the economy – prices will rise, relative prices will change and exchange rates will fall until a balance between the different parts of the economy has been reached.

Asia's problems have been heavily compounded by industry policies that have created their own malinvestments and added to those created by inflation. Even in the absence of inflation such policy-created malinvestments have the effect of slowing down productivity growth. The logic of market economics suggests that when politicians and bureaucrats rather than the market allocate resources, there will be a decline in the rates of return on capital and productivity. Only markets allocate to generate conditions of the highest efficiency.

Much attention has been given to the degree of corruption in Asia and its role in the recent financial events. While corruption added to the turmoil, it did not create it. Even in the total absence of corruption the meltdown would still have happened. Interventionist policies that politicised financial markets made it inevitable. The blame for East Asia's crisis lies with a failure of governance, not speculators or irrational investors or market imperfections.

TRUTH HURTS: WHY THE EAST ASIAN CRISES SURPRISED SO MANY

It is interesting to consider why the economic turmoil in the region was not better anticipated. There was no conspiracy of silence; however there was a pattern of slinking away from the truth. Many Asia watchers who were unable to anticipate what lay ahead apparently chose not to see. While some were bereft of an understanding of the economic fundamentals behind the operations of markets, others suffered from conflicts of interests that kept them from offering an honest appraisal. Rating agencies were of little help. As in the case of the Mexican peso crisis, their warnings lagged behind newspaper reports that were themselves both tardy and too often uncritical.

In fairness, few journalists have the training to sniff out theoretical or practical inconsistencies in economic policies. And custom or legal restraints thwart even those with the ability or inclination to ask the sort of tough questions that might reveal such disharmonies. Many Asian countries require questions to be submitted in advance. In many other countries press restrictions or the rough handling of 'uncooperative' journalists runs the gamut from assassination to blatant censorship to limiting the circulation of periodicals to expulsion. Local media often face similar or even heavier constraints, plus a lower level of investigative initiative based partially on social conventions. For example it was nosy foreign journalists who uncovered most of Japan's big political scandals and local coverage followed the presentation in the international press.

Foreign diplomats assigned to the region or visiting politicians are congenitally loath to criticise or challenge conventional wisdom. Indeed many people assigned to the region bought into the idea that the Asian model represented a third way between free market capitalism and socialism (Arogyaswamy, 1999). Consequently they were incapable of seeing the rot beneath the surface, arising from fatal contradictions with the demands of the global economy.

International bureaucrats at the IMF and the World Bank were no better than foreign service personnel, even though they had or could have had access that would have alerted them to impending problems, for example the IMF and the governments of the affected countries were aware of the imbalances in the financial sectors of the crisis economies. In particular the excessive accumulation of short-term debt was public knowledge, but no steps were taken to rectify this problem.

Then there were investment houses and brokers who were mostly mute or irredeemably bullish on East Asia, especially those trying to sell the junk paper offered by many of the regimes. There was also the characteristic lack of independent analysis among the region's academics that was combined with weak political opposition. The tendency for persistent dominance by a particular political party, often leading to a single-party state, meant that parliamentary challenges were unheard of and inquiries into potential economic disorder were few and uncritical.

Behind much of the unwillingness to see was an abiding belief that political connections were sufficient to ensure profitability. At the same time there was a presumption that authoritarian regimes were inherently stable and would contribute to economic growth. Based on these myths, political risks were underestimated and financial risk was simply set aside, because with political support losses could be passed on to local taxpayers.

East Asia's economies exhibited a series of flaws that led to an avoidable doom. Unfortunately there were few rewards for telling the truth and punishment was often excessive for those who were willing to be critical.

GLOBAL CAPITAL AS LIBERATOR OF THE MASSES

Global capital flow has become the vanguard of a new revolution. It has undermined despotism, revealed the unsustainable nature of corruption and motivated change in policies that curtail domestic competition or impose the high costs of protectionism. A key to understanding this process is that capital can no longer be thought of as having a specific national base. A world without national capital is one where attempts by governments to control or restrain capital will cause it to migrate. No hegemonic forces or small groups of financiers control the capital markets. The migration of capital reflects the will of the many small individual savers in all countries who require their funds to be placed prudently so that risk is balanced against return.

Although there will be substantial adjustment costs, in the future there will be rounds of vigorous institutional competition that will lead to the discovery of arrangements that best attract capital. This 'race to the top' will mean that those countries with the most attractive arrangements for capital will be rewarded with the highest rates of economic growth and job creation.

Successful economic development in the future will depend on a number of conditions that shape and define the so-called global economy. Perhaps the most important momentum behind the internationalisation of economic activities arises from the high degree of capital mobility. The capacity of capital to migrate and reside elsewhere more or less at will ensures that the search for the gains from trade arising from comparative advantage is temporary, elusive and increasingly contested. It will be increasingly important for countries to develop greater flexibility and responsiveness in their economic and political institutions. Otherwise the automatic adjustment mechanisms that contribute to stability and aid growth will be obstructed.

Countries wishing to be players in the global marketplace will have to face up to the implications of this simple observation. It will be important to countries in the early stages of development that might pursue development through the promotion of export-oriented production, and the more advanced economies that need to tease higher rates of growth to keep living standards high and unemployment low in order to maintain social harmony.

Aspirants in the global marketplace that wish to remain competitive and enjoy economic success will be guided towards policy mixes and institutional arrangements that are flexible and responsive. Otherwise industrial and commercial aspirants will lose market share to competitors while national economies will experience an exodus of capital. In the event of a truly global economy, the institutions of every country will be affected by external shocks generated by repetitive waves of competition. Those countries with inadequate institutional flexibility will simply break down in face of these challenges. Indeed this is what happened when the East Asian economies stumbled at the first hurdle in July 1997.

On the micro side, small and medium-sized enterprises will be well placed with nimble responses to exploit niche opportunities. This will work best in situations where there is extensive domestic competition among firms, including allowing foreign producers in to contest local markets. On the macro side, capital-friendly policies combined with a liberal trade regime will increase and enhance linkages with international markets that facilitate trade and capital flows.

There are risks and challenges associated with such arrangements, not least of which is the risk that upsetting traditional relationships will lead to some political instability. However the political stability associated with the cosy relationships between many Asian governments and commercial interests has proved to be a recipe for disaster.

Unfortunately there is impatience with certain aspects of progress in developing countries, whether with emerging economies or not. In essence there is a presumption that the institutional infrastructure required for long-term success in the global market can be implemented overnight. Optimists who wish good things for the region as well as apologists for 'Asian values' tend to overlook several deficiencies in the institutional environment of the region. Many governments have embraced the voting rules associated with democracy (majority rule elections). However the mere superimposition of such trappings on a collectivist culture creates a number of internal, perhaps fatal contradictions. In the conservative political culture of much of East Asia, vigorously contested, multiparty elections are far from the norm. One-party and one-family states dominate the civic landscape.

Most countries in the region pursued similar policies for growth, whereby export-led, 'directed' development involved the politicisation and underdevelopment of domestic capital markets. Not only did this provide opportunities for corruption and nepotism, it also led to substantial malinvestment, whereby funds were directed towards projects with little or no economic merit or commercial viability. Indeed the hundreds of billions of dollars in bad debt burdening the region arose principally from these homegrown circumstances.

As a matter of policy, industrial and commercial investments were funded principally through the banking system. This approach allowed for greater political control over investment flows since bank managers could be influenced to direct funds toward activities or sectors favoured by technocrats or politicians. While some investments were based on technocratic inspiration, political considerations and cronyism drove many others. In all these cases, proper risk analysis was not seen as necessary since government support meant that profits would be privatised and losses would be nationalised and paid by taxpayers.

In contrast, controlling capital markets is similar to herding a room full of cats. Participants are independent and disconnected, with disparate plans. What links them is a desire for some sufficiently high rates of return relative to associated risk by demanding that asset managers exercise due diligence in seeking adequate information.

The inefficiency of the underdeveloped domestic financial markets meant that most of the economies in the region were dependent on international capital. In contrast to comments by Malaysian Prime Minister Mahathir, the exposure of East Asian economies to the whims of global capital reflects policy decisions by governments in the region. It reflects the outcome of their failure of governance and is not a neocolonial conspiracy.

East Asian leaders did not seem to realise that by engaging in the world trading system they were riding a tiger. As in Indonesia, this tiger is global capital markets that dethrone autocratic or inept governments. It will come as a shock to Marxists that the greatest force for democratic change and freedom is global capital.

MODERNISATION AND INSTITUTIONAL REFORM

Much of the high growth experienced by the East Asian economies reflected the extension of the radical changes that Margaret Thatcher introduced to the world. The familiar core of her reform package included the privatisation of state-run enterprises and extensive deregulation to increase competition, and the opening up of the country to international investment. Many countries wishing to introduce Thatcherite reforms of their capital markets failed to understand that the most crucial requirement was supportive institutional arrangements. This oversight was not accidental since it would require a dramatic change in their respective political cultures. In sum, the full benefits of interacting in a market-based global economy require an ascendancy of individualist-based institutions. As such there must be a shift from collective decision making and control towards arrangements where individuals play a decisive role in shaping political and economic outcomes.

In a macro context this implies increased democratic involvement by citizens and greater accountability by politicians. At the same time, arbitrary rule by rulers or ruling parties has to be replaced by non-arbitrary outcomes governed by the rule of law. In a micro context, expanded individual and private property rights allow for greater self-ownership by each and every market participant. This allows for entrepreneurial-driven growth and provides greater corporate accountability.

There are few countries where Thatcher's wisdom has been completely implemented. However it is in East Asia where the contradictions wrought by incomplete implementation have been so fully and fatally exposed. Throughout most of East Asia, governments intervene extensively in the workings of the market. Political considerations too often reflect inept and inappropriate interference with the logic of the market and are motivated by a collectivist mentality. The resulting economic and political institutions tend to limit individualism. Political slogans such as 'society above self' and 'the exposed nail is hammered down' express the collective instincts that are reflected in many of East Asia's institutions.

For many it is counterintuitive that individualist-based institutions can provide social harmony. The political philosophy in favour of 'Asian values' gains its deepest inspiration from the idea that individuals should transfer power and initiative to collective institutions. The rapid economic change in East Asia has – after almost twenty years of phenomenal growth – reached the point of social development where it is clear that individualist-based institutions are the logical and necessary outcome of the process of modernisation.

Civil society reflects the spontaneous emergence of voluntary associations of individuals in order to limit abuses of power by governments, groups or other individuals. These associations may support special interests (such as trade unions or producer groups) or seek to promote general interests (such as freedom of speech as advanced by a free, open media).

These groups serve to offset the type of authoritarianism advocated in the 'Asian values' concept and liberate individuals in a way that is implicitly criticised by the same philosophy. The market can act as a civilising force on individuals because economic exchange becomes more impersonal. Economic arrangements in emerging economies tend to be based on personal relationships that limit the scope of exchange. Under these conditions there is little mutual trust outside narrow groups defined by personal, ethnic, racial, regional or other characteristics. Those who do not possess these specific attributes are generally the objects of discrimination. The ethos of the group may even endorse the cheating of others.

In more advanced markets there is tendency to break down discrimination. Individuals expand their scope of trust and respect for others in order to expand their market reach to increase their wealth. Market processes also expose people to the need for compromise and provide greater confidence in surviving what may initially appear to be chaotic change.

The economies of East Asia have been characterised by communal, personalised institutions wherein individual attributes are not valued so are sometimes discouraged. Herein lies an important development problem in the Asian model. Since entrepreneurs are the true engines of change and economic growth, their actions are the key to sustained economic growth. Entrepreneurs are essentially individualists who aim to break up the economic or political *status quo*.

Activities initiated by individual entrepreneurs are often described as part of the 'creative destruction' process. Economic innovations destroy older structures because of their higher productivity (Schumpeter, 1976). An open economy introduces creative destruction through trade and capital flows even if domestic innovation is low. This process works against the cosy relationships and the ideal of social stability that have historically existed between most East Asian governments and conglomerates such as the *keiretsu* in Japan and the *chaebol* in Korea.

Similarly the high value of consensus evident in East Asian political culture is counterproductive to the modern market economy. The search for political harmony has often resulted in limits on free speech and the secretive protection of information flows in order to control or shape public opinion. These actions further restrain the entrepreneur by restricting access to information that would inspire them to create new products or services.

The East Asian crisis can be interpreted as part of the ongoing struggle in the competition between modern, individualist-based institutions and conservative, collectivist institutions. Resolution of the economic crisis in

East Asia will occur only when there is deeper commitment to the lessons of Thatcher's grand experiment.

INTO THE FUTURE, DARKLY

The simple explanation for the decline of East Asia's 'miracle' economies lies in the incompatibility of their political and commercial institutions with an increasingly efficient global capital market. While these arrangements worked under other conditions, they did not allow for a ready response to the external competitive shocks that visited their shores.

Ultimately, those countries with the most flexible and efficient institutions that can support responsive economic arrangements will attract foreign capital. These conditions underlie innovation-driven growth, which differs from the sort of catch-up growth experienced by most East Asian economies. Innovation-driven growth is long-lived, because creative problem solving and invention constantly rejuvenate it.

In contrast, although catch-up growth may appear to be meteoric, it is short-lived because it only represents the belated incorporation of technology or ideas developed elsewhere. Thus governments characterised by strict and inflexible hierarchical rule will inadvertently hinder high rates of economic growth by stunting innovation. In the context of global megacompetition, such a politically self-serving approach is fatally flawed. Unless these governments can create an intellectual environment that is conducive to technological innovation, the 'miracle' of Asia's stunning economic successes will be short-circuited. Unfortunately the East Asian economies faced the same sort of catastrophic contradictions faced by the communist economies. In the end, the prospect of an 'Asian century' was no more likely than a 'Soviet century'.

According to the 1999 Global Competitiveness Report of the World Economic Forum, prepared in collaboration with the Harvard Institute of International Development, China (World Economic Forum, 1999), Indonesia, Japan, South Korea, Taiwan, Malaysia, Thailand and the Philippines rank quite low in technological capability and in the quality of their governmental institutions. To a considerable degree their lack of technological capacity reflects a dearth of research collaboration between universities and industry, and there is a serious shortage of qualified scientists and engineers.

The next century might best be characterised as the beginning of a 'Global millennium', where competition among institutions and cultures is as vigorous as any competition in goods and services. This new order of expanding international trade relations has been facilitated by the confluence of increased capital mobility and easier access to information and technology. Economic success in this coming era will require further separation between the economic and political spheres, greater tolerance of institutional innovation, and increased transparency and accountability on the part of the existing economic and political structures.

These conditions are as important for the mature Western economies as they are for developing economies, in Asia or elsewhere. Regimes that attempt to frustrate this marketplace of ideas will undermine their long-term survival. Just as economic protectionism leads to avoidable economic costs, cultural isolationism involves self-inflicted social and political costs. Neither wishful thinking nor strong-armed authoritarian rule will be able to revive hopes for an 'Asian century', and neither can they hold back the positive forces of a 'Global millennium'.

While the restoration of stability in the East Asian economies will be difficult, the slow pace of institutional changes will make the process of recovery an even longer one. Indeed it may take a generation for some East Asian economies to replicate the necessary institutional infrastructure for sustainable economic growth that will be required by the increasingly efficient global capital market.

References

Arogyaswamy, B. (1999) *The Asian Miracle, Myth, and Mirage* (Westport, CT: Quorum).

Krugman, P. (1994) 'The Myth of Asia's Miracle', *Foreign Affairs*, vol. 73, no. 6, pp. 62–78.

Lingle, C. (1998) *The Rise and Decline of the Asian Century* (Hong Kong: Asia 2000).

Richter, F. J. (1999) *Strategic Networks: The Art of Japanese Interfirm Cooperation* (Binghamton, NY: International Business Press).

Schumpeter, J. A. (1976) *Capitalism, Socialism and Democracy*, 5th edn (London: Allen and Unwin).

Witley, R. D. (1992) *Business Systems in East Asia; Firms, Markets and Societies* (London: Sage).

World Bank (1994) *Sustaining Rapid Development in East Asia and the Pacific* (Washington, DC: World Bank).

World Economic Forum (1999) *Global Competitiveness Report* (Washington, DC: World Economic Forum).

4 Political Foundations of Economic Management: an Interpretation of Economic Development and Economic Crisis in East Asia

Yi Feng

INTRODUCTION

East Asia has witnessed a profound political and economic change in the past few decades. Not only has the region experienced spectacular economic growth until recently, it also has undergone fundamental political change, leading to democracy in South Korea, Taiwan and the Philippines.[1] This chapter discusses a politico-economic model of growth and development. It uncovers some political mechanisms for economic transformation in this region. The general conclusion of this study is that political stability, political consensus and political as well as economic freedom all promote economic growth and development. From a theoretical perspective, this model explains the economic success in East Asia from the 1960s to the 1990s. It also sheds light on political institutions accountable for a series of recent Asian political and economic crises that occurred first in Thailand in July 1997. We argue that while political stability and economic freedom have facilitated economic development in East Asia over the past three decades, political liberalisation and broad-based economic reform are needed to cope with the causes and consequences of the recent financial crisis.

The second section compares economic development in East Asia with that in other regions of the world, exploring the difference in their growth trajectories. The third section posits a theoretical model that explains the anomalies exposed in the preceding section. The fourth section empirically investigates the theoretical implications in the context of East Asian countries. The fifth section uses Indonesia as a template to derive policy implications for the recent financial crisis in Asia. The sixth section concludes the chapter.

A COMPARATIVE FRAMEWORK OF ECONOMIC DEVELOPMENT

In recent years, Feng (1999a), Feng and Zak (1999), Feng and Hsiang (1998) and Feng and Wu (1998) have compared economic development in East Asian developing nations with that in other parts of the world. They find that the former have attained significantly faster growth rates than the latter. Three East Asian newly industrialising countries (NICs) – South Korea, Singapore and Taiwan – and four Eastern Asian newly exporting countries (NECs) – Indonesia, Malaysia, the Philippines and Thailand – have made impressive strides in their economic expansion.

Figure 4.1 is based on real GDP per capita data from Summers and Heston (1995), who have adjusted national income levels according to the purchasing power parity standard, thus overcoming the complications caused by using foreign currency exchange rates. All the East Asian developing countries in Figure 4.1 had lower per capita incomes than Latin American countries in the early 1960s. By 1990 all four East Asian NICs had surpassed their Latin American counterparts (Argentina, Brazil, Chile, Mexico, Colombia, Jamaica, Peru and Venezuela) by a large margin. Among the East Asian NECs, Malaysia had surpassed all Latin American countries except Mexico and Venezuela. Thailand has accelerated its rate of growth since 1986 and led Colombia, Jamaica and Peru in per capita income.

Compared with the growth trends for East Asian countries, most Latin American countries have experienced low or even negative growth. During

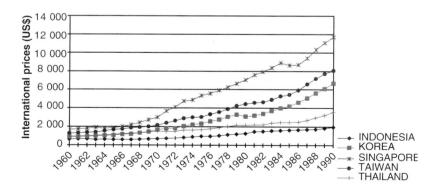

Figure 4.1   Real GDP per capita in East Asian developing nations
Source: Summers and Heston (1995).

the 1980s several high-income Latin American countries (Venezuela, Mexico and Argentina) suffered from substantial negative growth, while Chile and Peru went through massive fluctuations. During the period 1975–90 the average growth rate of real GDP per capita at the international price level was about 5 per cent for the seven East Asian countries, but only 0.04 per cent for the eight Latin American countries mentioned above.

Similarly in 1960 the ten largest Sub-Saharan African economies – Algeria, Congo, Gabon, Ivory Coast, Madagascar, Mauritius, Mozambique, Seychelles, South Africa and Swaziland – on average had higher income levels than East Asia, ranging from US$1 120 for Ivory Coast to US$2 862 for Mauritius in terms of international prices. However the growth rate of real GDP per capita in the ten African countries has been neither high nor stable. Many of these countries experienced periods of negative growth throughout these years, including high-performing Mauritius (with a per capita income of about US$6 000 in 1990). The income levels in Mozambique and Madagascar were even lower in 1990 than in 1960. The average growth rate for the ten countries over the period 1975–90 was only 0.3 per cent.

Though the economies in East Asia grew rapidly until recently, the development experiences of the seven nations discussed here have differed. The NICs (Taiwan, South Korea and Singapore) have performed better than the NECs (Indonesia, Malaysia, the Philippines and Thailand). Figures 4.2 and 4.3 show the growth rates of real GDP per capita for these countries from 1960–99.

From 1961 to 1997 Taiwan, South Korea and Singapore enjoyed higher growth rates than Malaysia, Thailand, Indonesia and the Philippines. Although the former nations did experience negative growth in a number of years, the degree of economic shrinkage was significantly lower in the former than the latter. The average growth rates were 6.7 per cent for Taiwan, 6.6 per cent for South Korea and 6.1 per cent for Singapore. By comparison, South Korea was hit hard by the Asian economic crisis. In January 1997 Hanbo Steel collapsed under $6 billion worth of debts; this was the first bankruptcy of a leading conglomerate in a decade. In March 1997 Sammi Steel failed, triggering further concern about the looming debt crisis. In July 1997 Kia, Korea's third largest automobile maker, suffered from a credit crunch and asked for emergency loans; Kia was subsequently nationalised in October 1997 as the result of its failure to acquire loans from banks. Since then the world's eleventh largest economy has suffered a series of setbacks in terms of capital flight, credit downgrading and currency depreciation. Despite all this, South Korea has been able to adjust itself to economic shocks by reforming its banking system, improving its financial

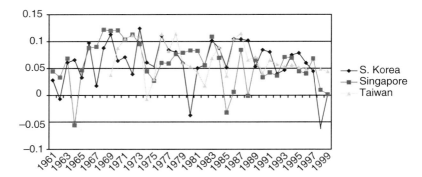

Figure 4.2   Growth rates of GDP per capita (1990 prices) for three Asian
NICs, 1961–99 US$

sector and modifying its labour laws and social security programme. As a
result the prospect of its recovering from the crisis seems bright.

The other two NICs – Taiwan and Singapore – suffered far less damage
from the financial crisis, though their growth rates have slowed down. In
contrast to South Korea, both of these countries have had current account
surpluses in recent years. In 1997 the current account surpluses as a ratio
of GDP were 14 per cent in Singapore and 3 per cent in Taiwan, the only
two of the seven East Asian countries to have a positive current account
since 1990. The two countries have also had the lowest inflation rates in
recent years. In 1997 the inflation rates were about 1 per cent in Taiwan
and 2 per cent in Singapore. The macroeconomic fundamentals in these two
economies have been relatively solid, which makes them less vulnerable
to the financial crisis than others.

The growth rates for the four Asian NECs were lower than for the three
NICs. From the 1960s to the 1990s, prior to the Asian economic crisis,
the fastest growing economy in this group was Thailand, with an average
growth rate of 5.1 per cent, followed by Malaysia (4.5 per cent), Indonesia
(3.8 per cent) and the Philippines (1.4 per cent). The economy that has suffered most from the Asian economic crisis has been Indonesia. In contrast
to South Korea, the prognosis for its economic and financial problems is
nothing but grim. The projected growth rates of GDP for Indonesia are
−16.5 per cent for 1998 and −2.8 per cent for 1999. Thailand suffered
extensively from the crisis, but seemed to recover steadily. The Philippines
and Malaysia were relatively less damaged by the financial turbulence than
Indonesia and Thailand, as the levels of economic openness in the former
were lower than in the latter.

Since 1998 the consequences of the financial crisis in these nations have been mitigated to different degrees. For instance in Korea and Thailand interest rates declined markedly as currency pressures eased, leading to a drop in interest rates to their precrisis levels. The two nations have also made significant progress in macroeconomic stabilisation and have begun to implement structural reforms. In Indonesia, the modified policy programme introduced in late June 1998 has been implemented broadly as planned, though the recovery is far slower than expected. The causes of the financial crisis have been multifaceted, ranging from 'irrational exuberance' on the part of the global financial market to domestic market imperfections. The purpose of this chapter is not to explore these factors, but to study the constraints of domestic political institutions on economic development and their effect on the recent financial crisis in Asia.

A POLITICO-ECONOMIC THEORY OF GROWTH

The puzzle of uneven growth introduced in the preceding section can be illustrated by what happened in one country in East Asia. In the 1950s the Philippines was considered the best performer in East Asia and the most promising in the long run. Optimism grew following an economic report by the World Bank in November 1957.

The Philippines has achieved a rapid rate of economic growth in the post-war period (since 1949). Production has continued to grow at an annual rate of 7 percent, despite the disrupting effects of the HUK movement, which hampered economic activity until 1952.... By comparison with most underdeveloped countries, the basic economic position of the Philippines is favorable. It has a generous endowment of arable land, forest resources, minerals, and normal potential. Through a comparatively high level of expenditure on education, transport, communications, and industrial plant over the past 50 years, the Philippines has achieved a position in the Far East second only to Japan, both in respect to its level of literacy, and to per capita production capacity.... The prospects of the Philippines economy for sustained long-term growth are good. [Apart from a] generous endowment of material resources and high level of literacy, other favorable factors are the growth of the labor force, the availability of managerial skills, the high level of savings and investment, rather good prospects for most of the Philippine exports, and considerable possibilities for import substitution.[2]

The Philippines, however, has not lived up to the World Bank's evaluation and forecast. The average growth rate of real GDP per capita in the Philippines from 1960–97 was only 1.4 per cent, the lowest among the three NICs and four NECs in East Asia. By 1990 South Korea, which had compared unfavourably with the Philippines in the report, surpassed it by almost 400 per cent. Taiwan, which had about the same level of GDP per capita as the Philippines in 1960, more than quadrupled the GDP of the latter.[3] How could the Philippines have failed to achieve the high expectations reported with such enthusiasm and optimism by the economists at the World Bank? An understanding of the political institutions in the Philippines provides a key to unravelling the reasons for this.

The data in Figure 4.3 indicate that prior to 1998 the Philippines experienced two periods of negative growth: 1983–86 and 1991–92. The worst period was 1983–86 with the economy shrinking about 10 per cent in 1984. Ironically the most pronounced negative growth occurred after the period of martial law, which lasted from 1972–81. The years between 1983 and 1986 mark one of the most turbulent historical periods in the Philippines, beginning with the assassination of opposition leader Benigno Aquino and ending with the vindication of the 'people power' revolution when Aquino's widow Corazon took office as Marcos fled to Hawaii.

Likewise the other negative growth period preceded a change in political power. Though Aquino won a May 1987 vote of confidence in the legislature, military unrest and slow economic growth continually plagued her government. In December 1989 a military coup was suppressed only with the help of the US Air Force. During Aquino's last two years in office the economy shrank (4 per cent in 1991 and further 1 per cent in 1992).

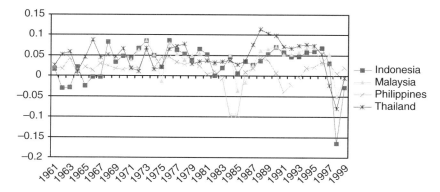

Figure 4.3   Growth rates of GDP per capita (1990 prices) for
four Asian NECs, 1991–99
Sources: 1961–97 data from IMF (1999); 1998–99 data from Straszheim (1998).

In 1992 Aquino declined to stand for reelection, instead endorsing the eventual winner, former Defence Secretary Fidel Valdez Ramos. After Ramos assumed office the economy started to stabilise. By 1996 the Philippines had joined the ranks of free nations, with a significant decline in rebel insurgence and a reduction in the political and economic influence of the nation's traditional ruling families.[4]

Political features such as these would be important to the growth trajectory of any country. To understand their effects on growth, we need to construct a theoretical framework of conceptual relations and references in the abstract. Chen and Feng (1996) and Feng and Chen (1996) have developed a mathematical model to study the relationship between politics and growth. Their model isolates three aspects of political institutions as the basic components of the political environment for economic growth and socio-economic development. Political instability, political polarisation and government repression all condition and constrain an individual's economic decision to invest in reproducible capital in the marketplace.[5] Economic growth, a function of the accumulation of reproducible capital, will increase or decrease as a function of these factors. A theoretical discussion of this model is provided below.

An assessment of the political environment is embedded in an investor's reasoning with regard to investment and consumption. When individual economic agents decide how much money they should invest and how many goods they should consume, they examine the current and future political parameters. In particular they are concerned about the likelihood of the current regime being replaced in the future, the degree of polarisation between the opposing political parties and how much political and economic freedom is permitted in the society. Both the likelihood of regime change and the large degree of political polarisation will add to the uncertainty of the economy, thus reducing the agents' incentive to invest. Furthermore, government repression implies that some gains from investment will be expropriated by or lost to the government, decreasing the agents' incentive to invest, thus reducing economic growth.

The probability of political regime change, no matter how minor, always exists. According to the model, an individual born in the current period is assumed to be uncertain of a future government's policy and its implications. Associated with the probability of a new government replacing the current one is the notion that the policy of the future government has not been tested in or experienced by the marketplace. Given that investors are risk averse, they prefer to wait rather than risk their investment today, particularly if there is a strong probability that the current government will be superseded by a new one. Reducing capital inflow and economic growth, radical political change involving different regimes particularly adds to the uncertainty of investment decision making[6] though it is dramatic to say that one can make money in any policy environment as long as it remains unchanged, investors do appreciate consistent public policy, which comes more easily if the government does not change. By contrast some countries have experienced military coups without concurrent changes in the economic system and policies installed by the previous government. Economic growth should not be seriously affected as a result.

The theoretical model and subsequent empirical discussion in this chapter focus on regime change rather than constitutional government change. While the former occurs outside the constitutional framework, thus creating political uncertainty, the latter represents policy adjustment, usually as the consequence of a political election. In a simultaneous equation model of political stability, democracy and growth, Feng (1997a) distinguishes between unconstitutional government change major constitutional government change and minor constitutional government change. It can be concluded that it is extra-constitutional change (such as a military coup) that has a pronounced negative consequence on economic growth, rather than regular government change (which represents policy adjustments rather than fundamental change to the political system).

Investors will discount the effect of political regime change on growth if political polarisation is low, that is, if the difference between the current and future regimes is negligible. In this chapter, policy polarisation is defined as a disagreement over public policy between the government and its opponents.[7] It stands for a change in the current social policy, or a deviation from the current level of government repression, by a new government in the future. It captures the difference between the new and old regimes in their basic political orientation of running an economy or organising a government.[8] Investors will normally place a high premium on liquidating or consuming assets today, rather than making a commitment to long-term investment, if they perceive that the future government will be very different from the current government in its policy. What is implied in this reasoning is a high level of uncertainty about a potentially large policy shift from the current government. While the future policy could be more or less repressive than the current one, political uncertainty ensues from the concern that the market has not tested the policy of the drastically different government that might be installed in the future.

The effects of five kinds of political actions on growth are compared in Feng and Chen (1996); these are coups *d'état*, revolutions, riots, strikes and assassinations. It should be noted that as indicators for political polarisation, these events reflect the scale and intensity of disagreement about the political management of a country; they are more likely to be the consequence of political polarisation than its cause. The levels of significance of the polarisation variables show a pattern: the most violent or the most extensive political actions (that is, coups and revolutions) tend to be significant, while less violent or less extensive political actions (riots, strikes and assassinations) tend to be less significant. The results from using the standardised coefficient estimates are consistent with the above analysis.[9] As the most organised and most violent political actions, coups and revolutions have the largest negative effect on growth. Riots have a greater negative effect on the economy than assassinations and strikes, and assassinations lead strikes in the degree of adverse impact on economic growth. This pattern is consistent with the theoretical argument that a higher degree of political polarisation is associated with a lower level of economic growth.

Government repression is a third political structural factor that affects economic growth; it implies that the government will forfeit some gains from investment. Compared with political uncertainty and polarisation, where the relevancy lies in the future, government repression is a current choice. Originating in the current government's political and economic orientation, it stands for policies that depress private investment.[10] The government may adopt a policy from a set of options (ranging from the highest to the lowest political, economic and social freedoms), which have an impact on economic agents' investment decisions. Among the examples of government repression affecting investment and growth are infringements of property rights, lack of patent protection, the abuse or misuse of resources to satisfy interest groups, government corruption and violations of human and civil rights.

The government may also initiate and provide public goods such as national defence, infrastructure, education, a framework for property rights and other institutions necessary for growth. For example it may adopt a social policy that reduces income inequality with a view to facilitating continued and sustained growth. The public goods provided by a government can be regarded as negative social costs. In accordance with the level of government repression and the amount of public goods provided by the state, investors formulates their strategy to maximise their utility between consuming today and investing for tomorrow.

Government repression in the model implies both political freedom and economic freedom, which can be different from each other, if not totally orthogonal. In this section government repression is treated broadly and philosophically; it represents any government policy that imposes a social cost on economic growth. Generally speaking, long-run economic growth requires both political and economic freedom.

The following theoretical conclusions are made. First, *ceteris paribus*, the lower the probability of the survival of the current regime, the lower the growth rate. Second, the more polarised the policy positions of opposing parties, the lower the growth rate. Third, the more repressive the government, the lower the growth rate.

Figure 4.4 presents an illustration of the three variables, using three countries. Political freedom and economic freedom are combined into a single dimension, defined as social freedom, which is obtained by totalling and averaging the political rights score from Freedom House data and the economic freedom score from Gwartney *et al.* (1996), assigning them equal weights.[11] The value on regime stability is derived from subtracting from one the probability of regime change in Feng (1997a). Finally, policy consensus is indexed by one minus the average year of revolutions, the data on which are from Banks (1996).[12] The period in question is 1970–80, for which the average values of the variables are taken to obtain an aggregate environment for economic growth and development. All values range from zero to one, with one indicating the highest value for the most desirable condition for economic performance according to the theoretical model.

Of the three countries in Figure 4.4, the USA and Singapore have the highest levels of regime stability, social freedom and political consensus; they also enjoy the best economic performance in this group of countries. Regarding social freedom, Singapore has the highest level of economic freedom (second only to New Zealand and Hong Kong) but only a modicum of political freedom, reducing its overall social freedom level. By comparison the regimes of the Philippines and Zaire were fairly stable during this period, probably owing to the high-handed authoritarian control of national politics; their levels of political consensus are, however, marred by domestic

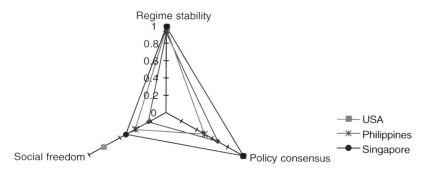

Figure 4.4   Example of the model

revolutions and insurgencies. In addition their social freedom levels are noticeably lower than those of the USA and Singapore. Finally, Bolivia and Peru have unstable regimes, and the probability of irregular government change is higher than in the other countries. Compared with the USA and Singapore, their social freedom is low. Bolivia also has the highest frequency of revolutions.

COMPARATIVE EMPIRICAL ANALYSIS: EAST ASIAN AND OTHER COUNTRIES

This section presents a preliminary empirical look at some political determinants of economic growth. As it stands, the approach used here does not constitute a multivariate test of the model described in the preceding section.[13] We shall focus on the broad implications of the approach exemplified in the model. The framework introduced in the previous section has three implications in terms of how to look at the data and what one should expect to find.

First, the theoretical model introduced in the previous section emphasises the uncertainty associated with a substantial change in government; empirically, we should look at drastic government transfers that are likely to produce high levels of uncertainty. The particular focus is the effect on growth of regime change, which usually causes great uncertainty in the marketplace, rather than government change, which may or may not cause political uncertainty. Regime change is defined as a transfer of the national executive from one leader or group to another, accomplished outside the conventional legal procedures in place at the time.[14]

Additionally, the theoretical approach in the previous section is *ex ante* rather than *ex post*. Though the completion of regime change may bring about certainty about who is currently in power, the likelihood of such a change has already discouraged investors from investing because of the entry and exit costs associated with investment.[15] Even after regime change occurs, investors may still remain uncertain for some time about the new government, whose policies need to be tested in the marketplace. This delay in investment by actors implies a reduction in economic growth.

Second, the model suggests that differences in the views of political groups reduce economic growth. Empirically, we would expect that certain intense political actions would decrease economic growth as they stem from divergence in political views. Third, the model suggests that government repression has a deleterious effect on growth. Empirically, we would expect to find that policies that seriously repress market conditions and activities have a negative effect on economic growth.

Several groups of countries are further analysed: the OECD group, the G7 group, Latin American countries, Sub-Saharan African countries, the eight Latin American and ten African countries discussed above, and seven East Asian countries (PA7). Both the G7 and PA7 countries have had a very low probability of irregular government change, with the average probability of such change in a given year being 2 per cent for the latter and 0.5 per cent for the former. Latin American countries have had the highest likelihood of regime change for all groups, with the probability of 6.7 per cent, followed by African countries with 5.7 per cent.

The G7 and PA7 countries also have the highest degree of economic freedom, with an average score of 5.6 for the former group and 5.7 for the latter. Economic freedom is essential for economic activities. 'Economic miracles' depend on the protection and promotion of economic incentives, at the centre of which are secure property rights and the ability freely and voluntarily to exchange such rights. Despite its importance in growth and development, economic freedom alone cannot solve the difficulties embedded in the course of development. For instance, in a society of high inequality, economic freedom in favour of the rich that results in greater inequality in the ownership of wealth will not help economic growth. Where it efficiently enriches one section of the society while pauperising others, economic freedom hampers economic growth, as it has been found that inequality is systemically associated with slow growth.[16] Therefore the effect of economic freedom on growth should be controlled by political freedom and income distribution.

Both the OECD and PA7 countries have low-income inequality, as measured by their Gini coefficients, which may serve as another indicator of policy polarisation. The relatively even distribution of wealth in these countries is conducive to growth, especially when – in combination with economic freedom – it enhances wealth acquisition for all or most social groups. Two variables show that PA7 countries differ from OECD countries. First, the incidents of revolution were much higher in the former than in the latter group. Second, political freedom was much lower in the former than in the latter. Domestic revolutionary movements engendered the relatively high frequency in the Asian Pacific Rim countries. For instance two separate forces – the Communist New People's Army and the Moro National Liberation Front – were waging guerrilla wars on the government of the Philippines during the 1970s. In every year from 1975 to 1990, with the exception of 1980, the Philippines was recorded as having at least one revolution.

In Indonesia, a crisis arose in December 1975 with that nation's invasion of the former Portuguese colony of East Timor. United Nations human-rights organisations claim that during the subsequent Indonesian annexation of East Timor the Indonesian army may have killed more than 100 000 people. Ongoing political tensions in the region eventually led to the death of pro-independence demonstrators at the hands of Indonesian soldiers in November 1991. Revolutions aimed either at independence or the overthrow of the government also occurred in Thailand, Korea and Malaysia. Figure 4.5 shows the frequency of revolutions in the seven East Asian countries.

Clearly, the relatively high average frequency of revolutions in East Asia was caused by one country, the Philippines, which recorded 24 revolutions during the period. By comparison Thailand had five revolutions, South Korea four and Indonesia three. There were none in Singapore and Taiwan.[17] Without the Philippines, the average number of revolutions per year in the region would have been 0.14 (compared with 0.33 when the Philippines is included). This would compare East Asia favourably to Latin America (0.30) and Sub-Saharan Africa (0.29). It does not seem coincidental that the two countries with the best economic performance, Singapore and Taiwan, had no revolutions during this period while the Philippines and Indonesia, the two East Asian countries where revolutionary movements were, for a while, most threatening, have had the lowest growth in the region.

The other political variable that separates the East Asian countries from the OECD countries is the degree of political rights. It should be understood that even though the average level of political freedom in East Asia is not as high as it is in OECD countries, or even in Latin American countries, it is not extremely low. The average political freedom level during 1975–90 was 0.454 for East Asia compared with 0.215 for Sub Saharan Africa, 0.50

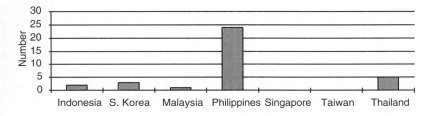

Figure 4.5 Revolutions in East Asia, 1975–90
Source: Adapted from Banks (1996).

for Latin America and 0.946 for the OECD countries. The role of democracy in economic growth should be understood in a broad and complex context. Democracy affects economic growth mostly through the indirect channels of reducing irregular government change, promoting private investment, improving human capital formation, alleviating income inequality and safeguarding economic freedom (Feng, 1999b). Democracy is likely to promote economic growth by relaxing these political and economic constraints where the accumulation of physical and human capital is slow, the probability of a military coup is high, income distribution is markedly unequal and economic freedom is lacking.[18] The role democracy can play in promoting growth is limited where economic freedom is emerging (for example Singapore), the chance of irregular government change is infinitesimal (for example Taiwan), savings and investment are abundant (for example Malaysia) and human resources have been vastly improved (for example South Korea). In the long run, however, these facilitating conditions for growth tend to erode if there is no transition to political freedom. The indirect effects of political freedom on economic development imply that the conditions favourable for marketplace and social environment will improve with political decentralisation and franchise, which will lay the political foundation for social and economic development. Political stability, economic freedom and policy cohesiveness have been contributory factors in the economic growth of some East Asian countries in the past three decades, which makes a difference between these countries and others, accounting for the varying growth trajectories uncovered in the second section of this chapter.

It should be understood that on their own none of the three conditions – political stability, policy consensus and freedom – are sufficient or necessary conditions for economic growth. If the government is very strong and the probability of its demise is extremely low, then political polarisation will not matter a great deal in terms of constraining the behaviour of people when reaching their political and economic decisions. Similarly, if there is no substantial difference between the government and its opposition, then the party in power may not be a crucial factor in economic decision making. Only when all three conditions are violated will the economy surely head towards a crisis.

The recent financial crisis provides an opportunity to examine the difference in policies and, more importantly, their outcomes given the shocks on the financial market. The next section provides a case study of Indonesia in the light of the theoretical discussion in this chapter.

THE ASIAN CRISIS AND THE INDONESIAN EXPERIENCE

East Asia's rapid growth came to an end in the early hours of 2 July, 1997.

> Bangkok's top bankers were awakened before dawn and summoned to a 6:30 a.m. meeting in a low-rise building facing Bankhumpron Palace, as the ornate Bank of Thailand headquarters is known. The nervous group was told the government was abandoning the baht's peg to the US dollar. When the market opened a few hours later, the baht plunged 15% against the greenback, creating a vortex that quickly sucked in the rest of East Asia.
>
> (Chanda, 1998, p. 8)

In the following months, currencies collapsed in Indonesia, the Philippines and Malaysia, causing massive business failures. Currency depreciation in these countries also created pressures in Hong Kong, China, Taiwan and Singapore, threatening the expansion of their economies.

The proximate cause of the Asian crisis can be found in the foreign capital flows into these economies from the USA, Europe and Japan in the early 1990s. According to the International Monetary Fund, by the end of 1996, East Asian countries had borrowed $318 billion from European banks, $260 billion from Japanese banks and $46 billion from US banks. Much of this was in the form of short-term loans. Next to Hong Kong and Singapore, the two main financial centres, the highest international borrowing was by South Korea ($100 billion), followed by Thailand ($70.2 billion), Indonesia ($55.5 billion), Taiwan ($22.4 billion) and Malaysia ($22.2 billion).[19]

The losses in the banking and composite sectors as a result of the financial crisis were substantial. The financial markets in all these nations suffered a massive setback. Speculative forces in globalisation and the lack of financial market rules and regulations in these countries caused the problems associated with the current crisis. The factors discussed in the preceding sections helped the rapid growth in East Asia, which attracted an undue amount of capital from the rest of the world. Meanwhile the domestic financial markets in these countries were still backward, partly due to imperfect political conditions and particularly due to the deficiency of political rights and civil liberties. The lack of a franchised political system or in experience in democratic rule meant that these countries were unfamiliar with or unprepared for a modern market system associated with political decentralisation and sound macroeconomic regulation independent of political motivation.

For the previous three decades the Indonesian economy had grown at an average annual rate of 7 per cent. In this broad-based growth period, the percentage of the population living below the poverty line dropped from over 60 per cent in the early 1970s to around 11 per cent in 1996 (Radelet, 1999). The Asian financial crisis of 1997 caught the world by surprise. In a period of months it wrecked the economies of the fastest growing region in the world. Among the Asian nations, Indonesia suffered the most damaging blow and its subsequent recovery has been the slowest. From July 1997 to October 1998 the equity market in Indonesia declined sharply, with a 90 per cent loss in its banking sector and 56 per cent damage to its composite index. In comparison Taiwan, Hong Kong and Japan sustained relatively light damage.

The Indonesian currency, the rupiah, lost nearly 80 per cent of its value. Many banks and corporations went bankrupt. Unemployment rose rapidly. For a time inflation ran at an annual rate of 50–60 per cent and several million people lost their jobs. The economy was severely disrupted. Some areas experienced serious food shortages. The value of real estate in the metropolitan areas dropped by 50 per cent. Riots erupted across the country, most of which were directed at ethnic Chinese, who made up 3 per cent of the population but controlled approximately 75 per cent of the nation's wealth. The world's fourth most populous nation with over 200 million people, experienced a major crisis. In 1997 it became the recipient of US$10.1 billion, the third largest bailout ever by the International Monetary Fund.[20]

The fundamental cause of the economic problems in Indonesia was a political one. The deeply divided society belied the appearance of political stability imposed by the government. In addition, economic liberalisation had provided only precarious and temporary relief to the ordinary people in Indonesia while tremendously enriching the families of the political elite. As discussed below, the narrowly based economic freedom in Indonesia hampered long-term and sustainable development, a process that was accentuated by the lack of political freedom and a polarised society.

Economic freedom in Indonesia was greater before the financial crisis than in the early years of its economic development. The measure of economic freedom had been on the rise and then stalled before the outbreak of the financial crisis in 1997. Even though the level of economic freedom in Indonesia ranks low in terms of the selected countries in the region, it is higher than in Denmark, France, Italy, Spain, Sweden, Greece, India, Bangladesh and Nepal, and about the same as in Belgium, Germany, Peru, Uruguay and Oman.

From the 1980s Indonesia made significant progress towards economic liberalisation. The government intended to activate its economy through a series of economic reforms. In the mid 1980 it introduced a series of trade and industrial deregulations to encourage producers to export labour-intensive manufactured products to the world market. Such products included textiles, garments, footwear, toys, furniture and electronics, 'creating millions of jobs in the late 1980s and early 1990s and lifting many Indonesians out of poverty' (Radelet, 1999).

Over the years, taxes were cut, barriers to trade were lowered and the economy was opened to foreign investment. Protectionism in Indonesia was considered low, with an average tariff rate of 6 per cent, though strict licensing was applied to a number of products such as rice. The dramatic rise in Indonesia's export industries had been an engine for economic growth in the past.

Indonesia reformed its foreign investment code to allow 100 per cent foreign ownership and to open many sectors that were formerly closed to foreign investment, such as electricity, telecommunications, shipping, airlines, railways, roads and water supplies. From 1969 no foreign banks were granted a license, but this restriction was relaxed in the late 1980s. Though foreign banks are still regulated in Indonesia, they are allowed to participate in the market through a joint venture with Indonesian domestic banks, which tend to gain independence from the government (Johnson and Sheehy, 1996).

Along with the relatively open and free structure of the Indonesian economy, 'Indonesia's regulatory environment is characterized by bribery, kickbacks and corruption. Many regulations are applied arbitrarily, and bribes may be necessary to receive an 'exemption' from a government regulation' (ibid., p. 169). Although the market is supposed to determine prices, government regulation has remained high. The government regulates the price of certain 'strategic' items (for example rice), setting price ceilings or floors. The government also uses subsidies to promote the agricultural sector. Government enterprises are often protected from market competition.

Moreover Indonesia does not have a modern commercial code system that is compatible with economic activities. 'The legal structure provides public officials with too much arbitrary authority. When the discretion of government officials replaces the rule of law, the security of property rights is undermined and corruption (for example, bribes, selective enforcement of regulations and favoritism) becomes a way of life' (Gwartney and Lawson, 1997, p. 117). Court rulings leave much room for inconsistency and arbitrariness. Finally, Indonesia has a very large black market (Johnson and Sheehy, 1996).

Indonesia opened its domestic capital market without first establishing a set of competitive and efficient mechanisms. Capital liberalisation before the establishment of sound domestic financial markets leads to inefficient resource allocation. Capital inflows can cause serious consequences for the recipient country because of the market failures in the movement of factors and goods, as well as policy failures in achieving a consistent and credible domestic macroeconomic policy.

There has been a healthy debate on the sequence of opening capital and current accounts (see Feng, 1999c). Some countries (for example Chile and Taiwan) liberalised the current account first, followed by the opening or gradual opening of the capital account, while others (for example Uruguay and Argentina) prioritised the liberalisation of the capital account over that of the current account. In Indonesia the liberalisation of the two accounts seemed to be simultaneous. As certain sectors benefit from state protection or regulation, the inflow of foreign capital tends to be allocated to these protected yet inefficient sectors, causing distortion of the economy.

In Indonesia the inflow of foreign capital created financial instability, underlined by the lack of sound market mechanisms, despite the appearance of an open economy. The liberalisation of the capital market was premature and out of pace with the country's development. The capital market was opened too fast and too early, particularly in light of the absence of sound regulatory and supervisory institutions and the rampant corruption associated with the Suharto family.

From the 1980s domestic credit began to rise and a series of financial reforms aimed at liberalisation were launched in the late 1980s. The number of banks more than doubled from 108 to 232 between 1988 and 1993 (Radelet, 1999). The ill-regulated and ill-supervised expansion of the financial sector resulted in a tremendous increase in non-performing loans. Until the financial crisis, the increase in lending was dramatic. Taking into consideration the lack of sound market mechanisms, as discussed above, such huge amounts of lending implies that the degree of inefficiency and distortion in the market worsened in the 1990s. The seeds of financial disaster were sown.

When the financial crisis started in 1997, countries that had relatively open economies but lacked sound economic policies were hit hardest. Creditors quickly withdrew their lending and borrowers with huge foreign debts tried to cover their positions. The value of the US dollar against the rupiah increased from 2 450 rupiah per dollar in the second quarter of 1997 to 3 275 in the third quarter. By the second quarter of 1998 it had reached 14 000. The Indonesian currency had fallen faster than the dollar had in the Great Depression (Lamb, 1998).

Prior to the crisis the families of the political elite had benefited from the liberalisation reforms. The Suharto family and their close circle of friends had controlled a large proportion of the country's economic activities.

The cronyism and favouritism associated with the first family had expanded as the ruler's children came of age in the late 1980s and early 1990s, when economic reforms had increased lucrative opportunities and imposed few constraints on their greedy enterprises.

> Foreign financiers, fully aware of the growing weakness of the financial sector and the corruption associated with the Suharto family businesses, were more than happy to finance these activities. After all, they earned high profits on these loans, and presumed (along with everyone else) that these protected enterprises could not fail and would be able to make all their debt payments.
>
> (Radelet, 1999)

With the end of Suharto's 32-year rule, most Indonesians feel robbed – they are suffering from the economic catastrophe but Suharto and his family are believed to have enriched themselves tremendously. The Indonesia Business Data Centre, a consulting firm in Jakarta, estimates that the family assets amount to 200 trillion rupiah – about $17.5 billion at the June 1998 exchange rate, or $80 billion at the 1997 rate (*The Economist*, 6 June 1998). The richest families in Indonesia benefited from an economic 'liberalisation' that was fraught with corruption. 'Corruption allowed elite business interests to trample on the rights of rural society and thereby exploit the forest

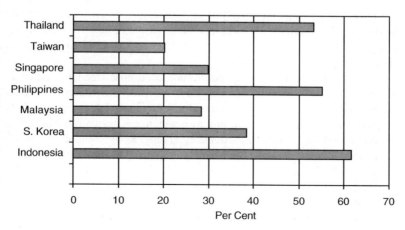

Figure 4.6 Percentage of total market capitalisation
controlled by the 15 richest families
Source: Adapted from Claessens *et al.* (1998).

and mineral wealth without having to succumb to the niceties of the law or due process' (Root, 1999, p. 45).

Under such circumstances, economic liberalisation does not necessarily contribute to economic growth because there is no broad base of support for the national policy of economic development. Income inequality also implies that in the presence of economic difficulties the poor will suffer more than the rich, thus breeding political instability and violence, as demonstrated by the series of riots in Indonesia in the late 1990s. Figure 4.6 shows the percentage of total market capitalisation controlled by the 15 richest families. Indonesia ranked number one in this category, with the 15 wealthiest families possessing 61.7 per cent of total market capitalisation, followed by the Philippines (55.1 per cent) and Thailand (53.3 per cent).

It should be noted that after the financial crisis hit Thailand in July 1997, Indonesia seemed to adopt a classic liberalisation policy. It floated the rupiah, eased foreign investment regulations and refrained from spending its foreign reserves. None of this prevented the onset of the same crisis in Indonesia. What many fail to understand is that investors who had taken advantage of the weak economic system and strong political clout now started to exit the market because they anticipated that the worst was about to emerge.

A fundamental answer to the deterioration of Indonesia's economy lies in the contradiction between the country's economic liberalisation policy and its fossilised political system. Indonesia had been enmeshed in an incongruity of rapid economic liberalisation and slow political democratisation. Economic liberalisation had favoured the *nouveau riche* and the families of the political elite. Helped by speculative investors at home and abroad, they had been able to take advantage of the absence of a democratic legal system in order to get rich fast, thus contributing to the bubble economy that finally burst in 1997.

As Figure 4.7 demonstrates, Indonesia's economic freedom stalled in the mid 1990s, following its ascendance in the preceding decade. As time passed, political repression increased and Indonesia was left as the only fully autocratic country among the nations with which it is normally associated – the four newly industrialising countries (Hong Kong, Singapore, South Korea and Taiwan) and the four newly exporting countries (Indonesia, Malaysia, the Philippines and Thailand). The rest of this section explains the rise of political autocracy in Indonesia and its implications for economic development. It is argued that distorted economic liberalisation and rising political repression were responsible for Indonesia's crisis today.

The monopoly of politics by the political party Golkar in Indonesia severely retarded political freedom and civil liberty in the country; it also facilitated the influence of the political elite in business and economic affairs.

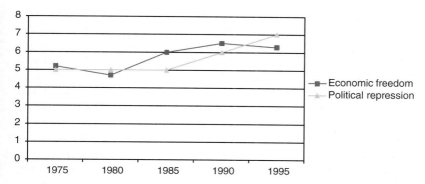

Figure 4.7 Political repression and economic freedom in Indonesia
Sources: Freedom House, 'Tables of Independent States: Comparative
Measures of Freedom' (various years); Gwartney and Lawson (1997).

During Suharto's 32-year rule repressive measure were applied intensively
in order to silence and neutralise the opposition. Interethnic, interreligious
or interclass issues were prohibited from public discussion. Political parties with religious motivations were suppressed. The goal was to force
cohesion among Indonesia's ethnic and religious groups. Despite this
effort, polarisation in Indonesia underscored the political and economic
crises in the country for years to come.

Emphasising authority, the political system reinforced Suharto's personal
power, making him comparable to a traditional Javanese king (Demaine
with Cribb, 1998). Suharto also enjoyed the support of the military, which
occupied half of the provincial governorships (Mydans, 1998). Concurrent
with the ascendance of statism, political influence in the economic sphere
intensified, which thwarted the deepening of economic liberalisation.

> When the forces of reform hit up against the immovable object of polit-
> ical interests, reform makes a detour ... the reason for the foot-dragging
> is that reform has reached the point where the only interests left unchal-
> lenged are those close to the hearts of some very powerful people ... the
> business activities of the Suharto family blanket everything from cars,
> telecoms, petrochemicals, and toll roads to power plants, airlines, taxi
> cabs – and even birds' nests.
>
> (McBeth, 1998, pp. 128–9)

Political monopoly prevented true economic liberalisation designed to
benefit the whole country, rather than a handful of the most powerful people
and their families.

The contradiction between political freedom and economic liberalisation in Indonesia has been a source of economic crisis. We argue that one fundamental source of Indonesia's current economic crisis is the incompatibility of liberalisation programmes and the repressive political system. The double goals of political stability and economic growth were short-lived and crisis-ridden in Indonesia because of the incongruity and incompatibility of the two kinds of freedom discussed in this chapter. Without political liberalisation, economic liberalisation can lead to premature development and economic stillbirth. Indonesia's real challenge and opportunity lie in the institutionalisation of a liberal-democratic government that will deprive the ruling class of their political and economic prerogatives and restore the basic human value of equality and justice for all. Such a political system will foster the economic freedom that once existed but was stunted by a repressive government, and it will promote social and economic development in the long run.

CONCLUDING REMARKS

Political stability, policy consensus and social freedom (the latter including political rights and economic liberties) are the core of the political foundation for economic management. Their effects on economic growth have been deduced in a mathematical model and statistically tested on cross-country data (Feng, 1997; Chen and Feng, 1996). The case studies of the development experience in East Asia, and in particular the financial crisis of late 1997, have further supported our argument.

Those East Asian countries that have been able to maintain high growth trajectories in the past several decades have had stable political regimes and pursued economic policies that enjoyed broad-based support. In tandem with economic prosperity, some of these nations have made the political transition to liberal democracy while others are still struggling with their political identity and destiny.

Economic and financial globalisation has embraced these nations as a consequence of their export-oriented development strategies. Despite all the benefits associated with integration into the world economy, globalisation presents risks for developing economies, particularly in the case of those which lack a sound political foundation for the modern marketplace. Indonesia is one example of this point. Despite its high growth rates, the nation collapsed during the financial crisis. It can be argued that other nations in the region, including democracies (for example South Korea), also suffered from the recent crisis. However their political foundation (that is, political stability, consensus and freedom) and economic conditions (for example the extent to which the country was integrated in to the world economy) determined the degree of damage they suffered in the crisis and the likelihood of a speedy recovery.

Democracy provides a stable political environment that reduces unconstitutional government change at the macro level; yet along with regime stability, democracy also offers flexibility and the opportunity for substantial change to the political system. This juxtaposition of macropolitical certainty and micropolitical adjustability should be regarded as the ultimate basis for sustainable economic growth and expansion. Such an argument forecasts a faster recovery in South Korea than in Indonesia and may serve as a theoretical insight into economic activities in East Asia and the rest of the world.

Acknowledgement

The author would like to thank the Fletcher-Jones Foundation for the faculty research grant that facilitated this research.

Notes

1. Singapore became the first East Asian developing country to be classified as a developed country by the World Bank (January 1996), and Taiwan was classified as a free country for the first time by the Freedom House survey following its first direct presidential election in April 1996.
2. Quoted in World Bank (1993), p. 14. Note that this section uses GDP data from Summers and Heston (1995), which may differ somewhat from World Bank data.
3. Summers and Heston (1995).
4. Karatnycky (1997).
5. The theory of reproducible capital focuses on the fact that the way in which individuals allocate their time between various activities in the current period affects their productivity in future periods (Romer, 1986; Lucas, 1988).
6. Even if the policy remains the same, investment is still negatively affected by changes in the government's ability to carry out the policy. See Feng and Chen (1997).
7. See Cukierman *et al.* (1992).
8. Roemer (1995) uses a deductive model to show that potential government change in a democratic political system creates uncertainty because of the difference in policy between political parties. The difference in policy between opposition parties regarding unconstitutional government change should be even larger, thus creating a higher level of uncertainty.
9. The standardised coefficient estimates the predictive importance of the independent variables. Feng and Chen (1996) take into account the variation of the independent variable in the sample by multiplying the parameter esti-

mate by the ratio of the standard deviation of the independent variable over the standard deviation of the dependent variable.
10. See Ozler and Rodrik of (1992).
11. The sources are Gastil (1989) and Gwartney *et al.* (1996).
12. Revolutions are defined as any illegal or forced change in the top government elite, any attempts to bring about such a change, and any successful or unsuccessful armed rebellion whose aim is independence from the central government.
13. See Chen and Feng (1996) and Feng and Chen (1996) for the multivariate statistical results.
14. For similar definitions, see Easton (1965) and Sanders (1981).
15. See Feng and Chen (1996); Chen and Feng (1996).
16. See Persson and Tabellini (1994); Alesina and Perotti (1996).
17. The following are the years in which revolutions occurred in these countries. Indonesia: 1979 and 1990; South Korea: 1977 and 1979; Malaysia: 1977; The Philippines: 1975–79 and 1981–90; Singapore: none; Taiwan: none; Thailand: 1976, 1977, 1981, 1984 and 1985. Note that multiple revolutions occurred in some of the years. Source of data: Banks (1996).
18. Feng (1995, 1997b) has found that democracy promotes growth in Latin America and Sub-Saharan Africa where the structural constraints on growth leave a lot of room for improvement in respect of the relaxation of political freedom. See Feng (1995, 1997b).
19. See Chanda (1998), p. 10.
20. South Korea received an IMF bailout package of US$21 billion in 1997 and Mexico was rescued by an IMF package of US$17.6 billion in 1996.

References

Alesina, A. and R. Perotti (1996) 'Income Distribution, Political Instability, and Investment', *European Economic Review,* vol. 40, pp. 1203–28.
Banks, A. S. (1996) *Cross-National Time-Series Data* (Binghamton, NY: SUNY Binghamton).
Chanda, N. (1998) 'Rebuilding Asia', in Dan Biers (ed.), *Crash of '97: How the Financial Crisis is Reshaping Asia* (Hong Kong: Review Publishing Company), pp. 8–17.
Chen, B. and Y. Feng (1996) 'Some Political Determinants of Economic Growth', *European Journal of Political Economy,* vol. 12, pp. 609–27.
Claessens, S., S. Djankov and L. H. P. Lang (1998) 'Who Controls East Asian Corporations?', World Bank working paper (Washington, DC: World Bank).
Cukierman, A., S. Edwards and G. Tabellini (1992) 'Seigniorage and Political Instability', *The American Economic Review,* vol. 82, pp. 537–55.
Deininger, K. and L. Squire (1996) 'Measuring Income Inequality: A New Data Base', World Bank working paper (Washington, DC: World Bank).
Demaine, H. with R. Cribb (1998) 'Indonesia: Physical and Social Geography', *The Far East and Australasia Yearbook* (London: Europa Publications) pp. 389–415.
Easton, D. (1965) *A Systems Analysis of Political Life* (New York: Wiley).

Feng, Y. (1995) 'Regime, Polity, and Economic Performance: The Latin American Experience', *Growth and Change*, vol. 25, pp. 77–104.

Feng, Y. (1997a) 'Democracy, Political Stability and Economic Growth', *British Journal of Political Science*, vol. 27, pp. 391–418.

Feng, Y. (1997b) 'Democracy and Growth: The Sub-Saharan African Case, 1960–1992', *Review of Black Political Economy*, vol. 25, pp. 93–124.

Feng, Y. (1999a) 'Political Institutions, Economic Growth, and Democratic Evolution: The Pacific Asian Scenario', in Bruce Bueno de Mesquita and Hilton Root (eds), *Governing for Prosperity* (New Haven, CT: Yale University Press).

Feng, Y. (1999b) 'Democracy, Governance, and Economic Performance: Theory, Data Analysis, and Case Studies', completed manuscript under review.

Feng, Y. (1999c) 'Capital Account Liberalization: Sequencing and Implications', in B. Chen (eds), *Financial Market Reform in China: Progress, Problems and Prospect* (Boulder, CO: Westview).

Feng, Y. and B. Chen (1996) 'Political Environment and Economic Growth', *Social and Economic Studies*, vol. 45, pp. 77–105.

Feng, Y. and B. Chen (1997) 'Government Capacity and Private Investment: A Study of Developing Countries', in Marina Arbetman and Jacek Kugler (eds.), *Political Capacity and Economic Behavior* (Boulder, CO: Westview Press), pp. 97–108.

Feng, Y. and A. Hsiang (1998) 'Economic Development in Latin America: A Comparative Analysis', in Kuotsai Tom Liou (ed.), *Handbook of Economic Development*, New York: (Marcel Dekker), pp. 523–49.

Feng,Y. and Q. Wu (1998) 'China at the Crossroads: Tradition, Evolution and Transformation' *National Security Studies Quarterly*, vol. 4, pp. 121–35.

Feng, Y. and J. P. Zak (1999) 'Determinants of Democratic Transitions', *Journal of Conflict Resolution,* vol. 46 (forthcoming).

Freedom House (1990) 'Tables of Independent States: Comparative Measures of Freedom', *Freedom at Issue*, vol. 112, pp. 18–19.

Freedom House (1995) 'Tables of Independent States: Comparative Measures of Freedom', *Freedom Review*, vol. 26, pp. 15–16.

Gastil, R. D. (1985) 'Table of Independent Nations: Comparative Measures of Freedom', *Freedom at Issue*, vol. 8, pp. 8–9.

Gastil, R. D. (1989) *Freedom in the World* (Westport, CT: Greenwood Press).

Gwartney, J. and R. Lawson (1997) *Economic Freedom of the World 1997: Annual Report* (Vancouver, BC: Fraser Institute).

Gwartney, J. D., R. Lawson and W. Block (1996) *Economic Freedom of the World: 1975–1995* (Vancouver, BC: The Fraser Institute).

International Monetary Fund (IMF) (1999) *International Financial Statistics CD-ROM* (March).

Johnson, B. T. and T. P. Sheehy (1996) *1996 Index of Economic Freedom* (Washington, DC: The Heritage Foundation).

Karatnycky, A. (1997) 'Freedom on the March' *Freedom Review,* vol. 28, pp. 1–7.

Kormendi, R. C. and P. G. Meguire (1985) 'Macroeconomic Determinants of Growth: Cross-country Evidence', *Journal of Monetary Economics,* vol. 16, pp. 141–63.

Lamb, D. (1998) 'Clouds Haven't Lifted in Post-Suharto Indonesia', *Los Angeles Times*, 1 October, p. A4.

Lucas, R. E. (1988) 'On the Mechanics of Economic Development', *Journal of Monetary Economics,* vol. 22, p. 3–42.

McBeth, J. (1998) 'Dept. of Connections', in Dan Biers (ed.), *Crash of '97: How the Financial Crisis is Reshaping Asia* (Hong Kong: Review Publishing Company), pp. 128–34.

Mydans, S. (1998) 'Role of Military: A Potential Unifier Split by Conflicting Goals', *New York Times,* 15 May, p. A6.

Ozler, S. and D. Rodrik (1992) 'External Shocks, Politics and Private Investment', *Journal of Development Economics,* vol. 39, pp. 141–62.

Pastor Jr, M. and E. Hilt (1993) 'Private Investment and Democracy in Latin America', *World Development,* vol. 21, pp. 489–507.

Persson, T. and G. Tabellini (1994) 'Is Inequality Harmful for Growth? Theory and Evidence', *The American Economic Review,* vol. 84, pp. 600–21.

Radelet, S. (1999) 'Indonesia's Implosion', *Harvard Asian Pacific Review,* forthcoming.

Roemer, J. (1995) 'On the Relationship between Economic Development and Political Democracy', in Amiya Kumar Bagchi (ed), *Democracy and development* (New York: St Martin's Press), pp. 28–55.

Romer, P. M. (1986) 'Increasing Returns and Long-run Growth', *Journal of Political Economy,* vol. 94, pp. 1002–37.

Root, H. (1999) 'Suharto's Tax on Indonesia's Future', working paper (Santa Monica, CA: The Milken Institute).

Sanders, D. (1981) *Patterns of Political Instability* (New York: St Martin's Press).

Summers, R. and A. Heston (1995) *The Penn World Table (Mark 5.6)* (Cambridge, MA: National Bureau of Economic Research).

Straszheim, D. (1998) 'The Realities of Global Competition', International Studies Association West Meeting, Claremont, October.

World Bank (1993) *Sustaining Rapid Development in East Asia and the Pacific* (Washington, DC: World Bank).

5 The Asian Economic Crisis: Three Perspectives on the Unfolding of the Crisis in the Global Economy

Hock-Beng Cheah

There is a single set of events that dominates the world economic scene today as it has for more than a year: the global economic crisis that began in Thailand on July 2, 1997, spread from there to Indonesia and Korea, then to Russia, then to Latin America. Few countries have not been touched by the global forces that this crisis – by some accounts the worst since the 1980s debt crisis – has unleashed. Some countries have gone, in the space of a few short months, from robust growth to deep recession. The social consequences of this economic downturn are already manifest, with interrupted education, increased poverty, poorer health.

(World Bank, 1999, p. ix)

INTRODUCTION

This chapter examines three perspectives on the so-called Asian crisis: (a) the perspective of international financial and development organisations, which emphasise deficiencies in the practices of firms and of financial and governmental institutions in Asia; (b) the perspective of Soros (1998) and Strange (1986), who perceive it as part of a broader crisis of the global financial system; and (c) an even broader perspective of the process and consequences of catching up and slowing down in the global system.

The International Monetary Fund (IMF) and others have promoted the term 'the Asian crisis' (IMF Staff, 1998) and initially treated the issue as predominantly an Asian problem, focusing narrowly on economic (and, more specifically, financial) difficulties. More recently the Asian crisis has become known as the Asian 'contagion', which has infected other parts of the globe such as Russia and Brazil (Walker, 1998). However it can be argued that the crisis is not only an Asian crisis but also a fundamentally global one. From this perspective, the principal reason why other locations and regions in the world are vulnerable to infection is that the preconditions already exist globally for its diffusion, regardless of the origin of the outbreak. Furthermore, while the crisis has significant financial and economic aspects, it is much more pervasive and systemic. It is a production as well as a financial crisis. It is a crisis of the export-oriented industrialisation (EOI) development model. It is a crisis of free-market (unregulated) capitalism. It particular it is a crisis of orthodox (fundamentalist) free-market economics.

However, all these constitute only one set of a 'triple whammy' of crises to hit the world as it approached the millennium. The other two global crises are the technology crisis (in the form of the Y2K computer design flaw) and the leadership crisis; both of which will be extremely serious singly but, in combination with the first, will have profound and unpredictable compounding effects that could fundamentally cripple the global economy and society.

CAUSES AND CONSEQUENCES OF THE ASIAN CRISIS: THE PERSPECTIVE OF INTERNATIONAL FINANCIAL AND DEVELOPMENT ORGANISATIONS (IMF AND WORLD BANK)

IMF staff (1998) have identified the following causes of the Asian crisis:[1]

- Overheated economies stemming from large external deficits and inflated property and stock market values.
- Prolonged maintenance of pegged exchange rates to the US dollar at unsustainable levels, coupled with wide swings in the dollar–yen exchange rate that undermined international competitiveness (see also Rana, 1998a; Brooks et al., 1998).
- Excessive external (especially short-term) borrowing, leading to excessive exposure to foreign exchange risk in both the financial and corporate sectors (see also Rana, 1998b).
- Lack of enforcement of prudential rules and inadequate supervision of financial systems, coupled with government-directed lending practices that led to a sharp deterioration in the quality of banks' loan portfolios.
- The limited availability of data and a lack of transparency hindered market participants from taking a realistic view of economic fundamentals.
- International investors underestimated the risks as they searched for higher hields at a time when investment opportunities appeared less profitable in Europe and Japan, owing to their sluggish economic growth and low interest rates.

- Governance problems and political uncertainties worsened the crisis of confidence, fuelled the reluctance of foreign creditors to roll over short-term loans, and created downward pressure on currencies and stock markets.
- Excessive government intervention in the economy, widespread political patronage, nepotism and lax accounting practices.

In addition the World Bank (1998, pp. 23–8) has pointed to narrow specialisation in the electronics industry, competition from China and other low-cost exporters, and the domino effect transmitted through intra-Asian trade as contributory causes of the crisis.

The financial and economic crisis has had significant adverse social effects in the affected countries. According to the World Bank (ibid., p. 2),

> Unemployment is rising. Real wages of low-income urban workers have plummeted, and the region's major cities are filled with idle workers looking for ways to make a living. Inflation has risen, with the possible effects of worsening income distribution and further reducing the real wages of low-income groups ... The effects of falling incomes are felt most severely by poor women and children. Also, in some countries economic pressures have ignited latent social prejudices against minorities and immigrants.[2]

IMF staff (1998) propose the following solutions for the Asian crisis:[3]

- Firm monetary policy to restore investor and market confidence.
- Restructure and recapitalise weak but viable financial institutions, and close insolvent ones or merge them with stronger institutions.
- Improve public sector and corporate sector governance and strengthen transparency and accountability.
- Adopt fiscal policies that reduce reliance on external savings and promote the restructuring and recapitalisation of domestic banks.
- Reallocate resources from unproductive public expenditures, minimise the social cost of the crisis and strengthen social safety nets.

The last point was emphasised earlier and more strongly by the World Bank (1998, pp. 122, 124), which stressed that low-income groups should be protected during the crisis and share in the eventual recovery.

DISINTEGRATION OF THE GLOBAL FINANCIAL SYSTEM: THE PERSPECTIVE OF STRANGE AND SOROS

Strange (1986) and Soros (1998) go much further than the IMF, the World Bank and the ADB in linking the crisis to a more fundamental systemic disorder in the global financial system. More than a decade ago Strange (1986, p. 119) noted that:

> It would seem that uncertainty ... has substantially increased in the past decade or so, as the number of volatile variables in the monetary and financial structure of the international political economy has multiplied. This has often been the result ... of certain specific political decisions or non-decisions taken by the leading financial authorities, especially in the United States. The uncertainty has started a vicious cycle of risk-averse responses, which in turn have added to the volatility of the variables and consequently to the general sense of confusion and the faltering confidence in the long-term viability of the global financial system. This erosion of social trust and confidence has been exacerbated as human and other resources have been diverted either to gambling and speculation, or to self-defence against. Thus, far from stabilising the system by damping its ups and downs, the devices such as futures markets – developed to deal with uncertainty – have actually served to exaggerate and perpetuate it.

More recently the renowned international fund manager George Soros admitted that 'I was fully cognizant of the Asian crisis – indeed my fund management company anticipated it six months before it happened – but I had no idea how far-reaching it would turn out to be. I was explaining why the global capitalist system was unsound and unsustainable, but until the Russian meltdown in August 1998, I did not realise it was in fact disintegrating' (Soros, 1998, p. xi).[4]

According to Soros (ibid., p. 123) the Asian crisis of 1997 was precipitated by a rise in the US dollar, but Soros also placed responsibility on the IMF for the crisis, claiming that there was an asymmetry between its treatment of lenders and borrowers. It imposed conditions for assisting borrowers to manage financial crises, but not on the lenders that contributed to the crisis. In this way, 'IMF programs have served to bail out the lenders and thereby encouraged them to act irresponsibly; this is a major source of instability in the international financial system' (ibid., p. 180).

Echoing similar earlier observations by Strange, Soros (ibid., p. xx) argues that at present 'Global financial markets are largely beyond the control of national or international authorities ... the current state of affairs is unsound and unsustainable. Financial markets are inherently unstable and there are social needs that cannot be met by giving market forces free rein.' This leads Soros to see the problems as a manifestation of the crisis of free-market (unregulated) capitalism. He claims that 'the capitalist system by itself

shows no tendency toward equilibrium. The owners of capital seek to maximise their profits. Left to their own devices, they would continue to accu-
mulate capital until the situation became unbalanced' (ibid., p. xxvii).[5] In
the process, investors and speculators would drive the system from 'near
equilibrium' to 'far-from-equilibrium' situations. In this regard, Strange
had drawn attention to Keynes' belief that the situation would progress so
far from equilibrium as to be unmanageable:

> Keynes argued that the capitalist system did not function evenly nor effi-
> ciently; that is to say, it was liable to slumps and depressions and it did not
> always keep up enough real investment in production to maintain eco-
> nomic growth. Nor could it be saved from its own inherent weaknesses by
> the use of merely monetary policies. Although governments had the power
> to control the rate of interest and could make it act as a brake by raising it,
> and as an accelerator by lowering it, that would not work because the
> changes that would be politically practicable in either direction could
> never be big enough to offset in one case the enthusiasm of optimistic
> investors nor, in the other case, the reluctance of pessimistic ones.
>
> (Strange, 1986, p. 134)

Sharing this Keynesian insight, Soros links the origins of the crisis to a fundamental mistake in conventional belief in how financial markets operate:

> The global capitalist system is based on the belief that financial mar-
> kets, left to their own devices, tend to equilibrium. They are supposed to
> move like a pendulum: they may be dislocated by external forces, so-
> called exogenous shocks, but they will seek to return to the equilibrium
> point. This belief is false. Financial markets are given to excesses and if
> a boom/bust sequence progresses beyond a certain point it will never
> revert to where it came from. Instead of acting like a pendulum financial
> markets have recently acted more like a wrecking ball, knocking over
> one economy after another.
>
> (Soros, 1998, p. xvi)

From this perspective the crisis in the global financial system also represents a crisis of orthodox (fundamentalist) free-market economics. Soros
argues that:

> The global capitalist system is supported by an ideology rooted in the
> theory of perfect competition. According to this theory, markets tend
> toward equilibrium and the equilibrium position represents the most

efficient allocation of resources. Any constraints on free competition interfere with the efficiency of the market mechanism; therefore they should be resisted.

(ibid., pp. 126–27)

Market fundamentalism endangers the open society inadvertently by misinterpreting how markets work and giving them an unduly large role to play.

(ibid., pp. xxii–xxiii)

It is market fundamentalism that has rendered the global capitalist system unsound and unsustainable ....It is market fundamentalism that has put financial capital into the driver's seat.

(ibid., p. xx)

In this situation, the developing countries are more vulnerable that the more developed economies because 'In times of uncertainty, capital tends to return to its place of origin. That is one reason why disturbances in the global capitalist system tend to have a disproportionally larger effect at the periphery than at the center' (ibid., p. 124). This effect on the periphery is a negative one, but the effects on the centre (at least initially) are positive, as the return of capital boosts economic activity in the centre. However in the longer term the problems in the periphery will spread to the centre.

THE CRISIS FROM A GLOBAL EVOLUTIONARY PERSPECTIVE: CATCHING UP AND SLOWING DOWN IN THE DEVELOPMENT PROCESS

The two perspectives presented above may be incorporated into a third, broader global evolutionary perspective. This locates the Asian crisis and the current global financial instability within a global evolutionary development process that involves 'catching up' and 'slowing down' (see Cheah, 1995, 1998a).

Empirical evidence of changes in revealed comparative advantage point to the occurrence in Asia of a catching up process in the 'flying geese' pattern (see Watanabe, 1983, 1992, pp. 148–60; Yamazawa *et al.*, 1991; Akamatsu, 1961; Cheah, 1995; Radelet and Sachs, 1997). Several other industry and firm-level studies in the car, electronics and other industries also provide supporting evidence of changes in competitiveness between firms in different countries (see Dertouzos *et al.*, 1989; Womack *et al.*, 1990).

The causes of the significant shifts in competitive advantage can be attributed to the power of adaptive entrepreneurship,[6] the diffusion of technology from more advanced countries and the supportive (and protective) efforts of governments, which enabled Asian countries to catch up rapidly with the more advanced industrial countries (see White, 1988; Wade, 1990; MacIntyre, 1994; Li, 1988; Pang, 1992). These developments were facilitated earlier by the favourable postwar international economic environment and US goodwill (see Hersh, 1993). Specifically, in the immediate decades after 1945 several Asian countries benefited from the creation of the Bretton Woods system of fixed exchange rates and the increasing liberalisation of world trade. These were influenced by liberal and supportive US policies, which were influenced by Cold War politics. These developments were very significant for the development of various Asian countries and for Europe too (see Hersh, 1993; Schwartz, 1994, p. 205 ff). In this environment, governments in the Asian region actively promoted national production capabilities and competitiveness.

The rapid postwar growth of Japan and other Asian countries may also be attributed, among other things, to the smaller economic base upon which production resumed after the war, the lower wage levels, the importation of newer technology and the building up of new capital stock. The need to pay for increased imports encouraged these countries to promote the exportation of their manufactures. The success of these and other economic efforts made it possible, by the late 1960s, for Japanese enterprises to begin to compete directly with US firms in the larger international market.

Similarly Asian NICs benefited from their pursuit of an export-oriented industrialisation strategy, and from the influx of direct foreign investment. First, the strategy capitalised on the growth in the international economy and contributed significantly to domestic growth and development. Second, the inflow of foreign investments into these countries increased international interest in their well-being. Third, rising employment and wage levels contributed to improvements in living standards. Fourth, the proliferation and growth of local private and state enterprises strengthened indigenous productive capacity and expanded the bases for local capital accumulation. Fifth, industrial and economic diversification in these countries added to the strength of their economies and increased their domestic capacity to cope with adversity. Finally, these countries were able to secure a lead over other developing countries and to derive various advantages from that.

One result of the process of catching up by Japan and other Asian countries has been the corresponding rise in their general standard of living. Empirical data indicates that Japan in particular, together with Hong Kong,

Singapore and South Korea, have narrowed the gap with (and in some instances surpassed) the developed Western countries, represented by the USA, Canada and Australia, based on comparisons of per capita gross national product, the human development index and indicators of welfare levels. This represented a significant shift in the centres of growth, wealth and power in the world.

The narrowing of the technology gap, the diminution of US competitive advantages and its large budget and trade deficits eventually reduced the USA's capacity to sustain growth in its economy, as well as to serve as the 'engine of growth' for the international economy. The result has been a general tendency towards recession and friction in the international economy (see Cheah, 1987, pp. 79–112; Hersh, 1993, p. 75 ff; Schwartz, 1994, p. 302 ff).

One result of these developments has been a significant rise in the intensity of competition, resulting from surplus production capacity, and stagnant or declining demand. This has led to a tendency towards deflation in the economy. Deflationary tendencies arise from price cutting among a host of products and industries. These have ranged from agricultural commodities to petroleum products, integrated circuits and computers, which have all experienced a substantial fall in price.

The intensification of competition has also encouraged Japanese and other Asian firms to place increased emphasis on product and process innovation and to undertake their own foreign direct investment. However, many competitors have directed their efforts at promoting the same activities, products or industries. The contrast between the high degree of complementarity in the economies of the USA, Europe and Japan in the 1950s, and the increased competition resulting from the convergence of economic capabilities in the 1990s, was highlighted by Thurow (1993, pp. 29–30). This intensified the tendency for zero-sum situations to arise.

At the same time the achievements of the Asian countries (especially Japan, Hong Kong, Singapore, Taiwan, South Korea, Malaysia and others) also helped to undermine their previous competitive advantages. This occurred through rising wage rates as a consequence of higher levels of employment and growing labour shortages, appreciation of the exchange value of their currencies, as well as increasing capital outflows in the form of direct foreign investment into both developed and developing economies.

These developments can be appreciated better from a Schumpeterian perspective than from the orthodox, neoclassical economics perspective. Unlike the conventional approach, the Schumpeterian approach expects development to be an uneven and discontinuous process, a process that tends to be characterised by changing phases. Schumpeter conceived of the development process as passing through the phases of recovery, boom, recession and depression. For him, each recovery is powered by a new group of products, industries and technology. These constitute the new starting points of the development process, and it is the diffusion and maturation of the earlier products, industries and technologies that bring each cycle of development to its end. In Schumpeter's conception, these dynamic processes and their associated changes do not lead to a situation of history merely repeating itself in recurring cycles; rather they lead to fundamental changes in the economic system, that is, to its transformation.

Moreover, for Schumpeter, the new generally does not arise from the old, nor does it operate largely to complement the latter; instead the new competes with the old for resources and markets, as well as in shaping the very forms and directions of development. Thus the different growth experiences (the slowing down of the mature economies and catching up by the emerging economies) leads to a relative convergence of economic structures and productive capacities. The tendency for a relative convergence of economic structures and production capacities, over time (observed, among others, by Knies, 1853, p. 117; Hoffmann, 1958, p. 147; League of Nations, 1945), is likely to create major structural problems for at least three reasons.

First, the expansion of existing capacity is generally less difficult than the initial efforts to establish production capability where none yet exists. Second, the establishment and expansion of productive capacity are both easier than the dissolution of this capacity, once it has come into existence (see Salter, 1966, p. 22). Consequently the problems of surplus capacity can easily become endemic (see Downie, 1958, pp. 117–20; Strange, 1979; Strange and Tooze, 1981). Third, the existence of substantial surplus capacity and the accompanying recession is likely to slow down the rate of implementation of technical innovations (Downie, 1958, p. 119). This helps to prolong the problem of surplus capacity and, with it, the intense competitive pressures in industry.[7]

Finally, a resort to increasingly round-about methods of production, the extension of 'machines to make machines', is not, as was once believed, ultimately any solution at all to the problem of markets for final consumption goods, nor to the slowing down of the rate of economic growth. Indeed this extension or lengthening of the production process, in time, reproduces the problem of excess capacity over wider and wider areas of the production process. This then leads to pressures for the exportation not only of final consumption goods, but also of capital goods.

Given the differences in the stages of development reached by different countries, initially there is relatively little difficulty for an advanced industrial country (AIC) to export final manufactures to a less advanced or newly industrialising country (NIC). However, as the latter acquires greater domestic technological and production capacity, the composition of the former's exports to the latter shifts increasingly towards capital goods. In time the NIC acquires sufficient domestic capacity in the production of both consumption and capital goods, and the problem of domestic surplus capacity, which the AIC earlier resolved through exports, reappears (if it ever vanished at all) over a wider area. Indeed if the same process also causes the NIC to experience a surfeit of capacity in various activities, the problem will become a general one.

Thus excess capacity in the production of final consumer goods leads, in time, to the extension of the problem to capital goods; and the resolution of this domestic problem in one country through exports, eventually reproduces the problem at the international level. This, and in particular the rapidity of the late developers' forward surge at particular phases in the international development process, creates Schumpeter's 'swarm effect' on a world scale. The general consequences associated with this are a marked rise in the level and intensity of competition, severe profit squeeze, the ending of the boom, a slide into recession, a 'shake-out' of competitors within the system and the 'end' of development.[8]

The economic recession (crisis) is a generalised one; its causes are fundamentally structural (or systemic) in nature; and from a Schumpeterian perspective its resolution is likely to require dynamic discontinuities in the development process – that is, development takes new forms and directions. This could produce substantial modifications in the international division of labour and, consequently, significant shifts in the centres of growth, wealth and power.

Contrary to the belief of conventional, neoclassical economics, development does not occur in a continuously harmonious process of evolutionary change. Schumpeter was conscious of the realities of the development process when he warned that 'industrial change is never harmonious advance with all elements of the system moving or tending to move in step. At any given time, some industries move on and others stay behind; and the discrepancies arising from this are *an essential element* in the situations that developed' (Schumpeter, 1939, pp. 101–2, emphasis added). Over time the economic lead is transferred from mature economies to emerging ones. This conception of the shifting starting points and directions of development, of changes in its agents and locations, is fundamentally incompatible with the conventional neoclassical conception of development as a process of evolutionary and harmonious progression.

The shifts in the growth centres result partly from the problems of economic maturity among the leading economies, which contribute to their relative slowing down in the development process. In contrast various factors assist a process of catching up by later developers. Together these lead to a situation of relative convergence in the world economy, which creates a 'swarming effect' on a world scale. These result in the intensification of competition, recession, crisis in the world economy and stresses on international economic relations.[10] The difficulties can only be reduced through significant institutional and structural changes, accompanied by technological, organisational and other innovations. These changes provide the foundation for the emergence of new leaders in the world economy, whose rapid growth generates a relative divergence of economic structures and the reestablishment of complementarity between countries, and lays the foundation for a(nother) period of harmonious international economic relations[11] (Cheah, 1987, pp. 18–43). Over a broad historical time scale such fluctuations may be tentatively depicted as in Figure 5.1 (see also Bienefeld, 1982; Beenstock, 1983; Adachi, 1985; Arrighi, 1994; Kennedy, 1993; Weber, 1997).

This perspective provides a useful general framework for viewing developments in the world economy, and among Asia-Pacific economies in particular. It helps us to identify the (changing) bases for complementarity and conflict in the region, and to consider how the processes of economic transformation can be better managed.

From this perspective the recent economic difficulties experienced by several Asian countries have a more fundamental systemic cause. While many

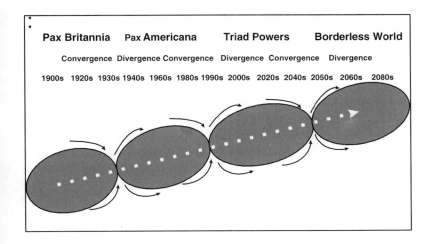

Figure 5.1 Catching up and slowing down: a stylised long-wave perspective of the evolution of the global economy

observers, including the IMF, have placed the blame one 'crony capital-ism', poor banking practices, property speculation, currency speculation, authoritarian governments and corruption, these were at best precipitating factors in the crisis. Indeed these factors were present much earlier, even during the catching up phase.[12] It was only when the global effects of catching up led to substantial excess productive capacity in a host of indus-tries and countries, as well as severe competitive pressures in the global economy, that the basis emerged for a general crisis to be precipitated.

IMPLICATIONS FOR FUTURE DEVELOPMENT

In this context the difficulties for all countries seeking to make a success-ful transition to a higher level of development have increased markedly, including those Asian countries that had previously experienced rapid eco-nomic growth. The most important need is for the regeneration of global complementarity by promoting a redivergence of national and regional economic structures. Innovations in economic, social and political institu-tions at the enterprise, national and international levels can assist signifi-cantly in this regard. Adaptive entrepreneurship and innovation will continue to be particularly important in transitional and less developed countries, while the need for creative entrepreneurship and innovation will be greater in the more advanced countries.

At the enterprise level, firms will face continued pressure for further cost reductions and improved performance. Efforts to lower the costs of undertak-ing an economic activity by exploiting the possibility of sourcing cheaper inputs from lower-cost producers abroad and transferring part or all of pro-duction operations to those locations will help to diffuse modern technology and management more widely (see Kaplinsky, 1994; Elger and Smith, 1994).

Moreover, when competition is for the global market and rivals are world-class competitors, it is no longer possible to trade off one or two advantages (such as lower labour costs and more compliant employees) against the few special advantages held by other competitors (such as bet-ter technology and management). All global operators will be seeking to combine multiple advantages from the best technology and management, the cheapest source of funds, the most productive labour force and so on into an overall competitive edge over other global competitors. These will require a substantial degree of both adaptive and creative entrepreneurship. The recent emergence of the 'lean production system' and its displacement of the older 'mass production system' can be perceived in this light.

Consequently, at the national level, policies to promote and support entrepreneurship are just as important as policies to support economic adjustment and restructuring; to resolve problems associated with technical obsolescence, poor management, inefficient and uncompetitive enterprises and industries. The latter will require new investment, relocation, retraining and retooling. However these involve substantial current costs (often unaffordable by firms, employees, communities or countries that do not have sufficient savings or are already in substantial debt), while the benefits (if they are realised) will only materialise in the future. Part of the solution is to facilitate the diffusion of production capabilities to regions that have not yet benefited significantly (or sufficiently) from the development process. This will help to expand global purchasing power, and consequently expand the global market for many more goods and services, and thus help to reduce the existing problems of surplus capacity.

At the national level, too, effective policies can be introduced to lower the cost of living and the cost of undertaking economic activity systematically by exploiting the increasingly pervasive deflationary tendency in the economy.

Finally, at the international level there is an urgent need for better, more effective global institutions for the management, coordination and regulation of an increasingly integrated but unevenly developing global economy (see Shonfield, 1984; Reinicke, 1997; Ayres and Braithwaite, 1992). This also involves finding ways to tap the vast potential (unmet) demand of the population in the underdeveloped countries. The problem of a 'crisis of production' is associated with underconsumption in that there is a substantial surplus capacity in many industries, which cannot find markets with an effective demand.

This does not mean that the world's need for goods and services in these industries has been fully satisfied. The problem is that those who have the purchasing power want less or no more (the problem of diminishing demand or saturation of demand), while those who still want (more of) these goods and services are constrained by limited, declining or zero purchasing power. The solution lies partly with international support for the coordination of adjustment programmes on a bilateral as well as a multilateral basis. However, for the most disadvantaged communities, regions and countries, a new form of 'Marshall Plan' is necessary, one that will substantially further than current bilateral and multilateral development aid programmes.

The Technology Crisis

At the time of writing (1999) there is a looming global crisis in the form of the year 2000 (Y2K) computer malfunction. This problem, associated with a date specification flaw in computer hardware and software, will cause severe disruptions in many organisations and countries (see Subcommittee on Government Management, Information and Technology, 1998; Public

Management Service, 1998; International Trade Administration, 1999). Among other consequences, it threatens serious domestic and international disruptions to trade and financial flows. The remedy for this problem is expensive and time-consuming. Consequently it is likely that most organisations and economies will fail to resolve the difficulties effectively and in time. Indeed serious difficulties in domestic and international transactions are likely to occur even prior to the beginning of the year 2000. Unfortunately many countries in Asia and elsewhere have not responded proactively to the situation and thus are poorly prepared for its severe impact.

The Leadership Crisis

Soros (1998, p. xxx) argues that, 'With the right sense of leadership and with clarity of purpose, the United States and its allies could begin to create a global open society that could help to stabilise the global economic system and to extend and uphold universal human values. The opportunity is waiting to be grasped.' In this regard Soros looks to coordinated international efforts to provide the solutions, including the creation of an International Credit Insurance Corporation and a more balanced treatment of debtors and creditors on the part of the IMF.

However, Strange argues that it is naive to expect international leadership to provide solutions to the problems. She contends that the solutions have to originate from national efforts, in particular from American initiatives: 'The problem of managing and stabilising a financial system that is fundamentally out of order and control is a global one. But the solution is a national one. It is absolutely no use looking to international organisations ... the reform must start with a change of mind in Washington' (Strange, 1986, p. 170).

Strange, however, is far from optimistic on this point. She notes that, 'in making certain key decisions affecting the international financial system, successive US governments have been far more swayed by short-term domestic considerations than by any awareness of the long-term national interest in building a healthy, well-ordered and stable financial system capable of sustaining a healthy, stable and prosperous world economy' (ibid., p. 23). It is arguable that this situation still persists.

CONCLUSION

When a single car has an accident on a bend in the highway, one might infer something about the driver or his car. But when, at the same bend, there are accidents day in and day out, the presumption changes – there is probably something wrong with the road. The fact that such a large number of countries have been affected by this crisis and required large official bailouts suggests some fundamental systemic weaknesses.

(Joseph Stiglitz in World Bank, 1999, p. xii)

In previous decades, several Asian countries experienced significant growth and development. For some observers the ultimate goal seemed to be unambiguous: higher living standards for all, based on a transition towards open market economies and liberal democratic societies (see Fukuyama, 1992). However the process has been protracted, and for some countries the goal still seems distant. In this regard, do the recent development experiences in Asia offer any lessons on what is (not) attainable and the means (the kinds of strategies, policies and efforts) to do so? The answer must be a qualified one: the past and recent development experiences of various Asian countries point to significant possibilities as well as serious constraints and pitfalls.

There will undoubtedly continue to be significant opportunities for development for all developing economies, not least through a myriad adaptive entrepreneurial activities, which will continue to offer possibilities for catching up with the more developed industrialised economies. However there have been significant changes in the international economy (between the 1960s and the 1990s) which have altered the conditions and development prospects for all states. In particular the problem of convergence of economic structures needs to be resolved by finding means to regenerate complementarity by promoting the divergence of economic structures and activities. Solutions need to be found through entrepreneurial ingenuity at the enterprise level, through national programmes and through international collaboration and coordination. Consequently the development outcomes for the Asian economies, as well as for others, will be determined only partly by their own efforts.

The times immediately ahead are likely to be more difficult for most countries. In the near future we are likely to see, in a more forceful fashion, the collapse of many established companies and the (further) disintegration of some previously viable economies. In the months ahead, when the global economic crisis is compounded by the year 2000 computer malfunction and by failures of national and global leadership, the world would be confronted by a 'triple whammy'. It will once again become a jungle out there.

In these circumstances it will be necessary to look ahead at least a decade or more, after the combined crises have demolished the present tottering financial and industrial structures, within countries as well as in the world at large. Then it will be necessary to rebuild from the debris of the collapse new industries and institutions that are more effective and more appropriate for the twenty-first century. It is principally on that context, not just the present one, that attention must be focused in our search for a better basis for global development. In this regard, creative efforts must focus on the need for a more economically, socially and ecologically sustainable development process in the world. This will have to include a revolutionary transformation of production and consumption processes (see Cheah, 1998b), as well as new combinations of market and non-market mechanisms (see Godfrey, 1997; Cheah, 1997), because the existing market mechanisms can be as unreliable and as problematic as the non-market mechanisms upon which the former socialist countries have relied so far (see Strange, 1986; Levinson, 1988; Gray, 1998b, *Business Week*, 1998). This can only be achieved by departing from the sterile debate between the purists of free enterprise on the one hand, and those championing state planning on the other. It is necessary to be able to recognise the flaws and limitations inherent in both, discover new and innovative ways to promote their respective strengths and to integrate the merits of both market and non-market mechanisms, within nations and in the world at large (see World Bank, 1998, pp. 111–29; Shonfield, 1984).[13] By these means the achievement of sustainable abundance for all of the world's population might be conceivable.

Notes

1. See also Alba *et al.* (1998), Pomerleano (1998), Shin and Hahm (1998), World Bank (1998, pp. 1–61).
2. See also Pernia and Knowles (1998), World Bank (1999, pp. 101–10).
3. See also World Bank (1998, pp. 111–29).
4. For a participant's account of the events, causes and consequences of the crisis see Soros (1998, pp. 135–74).
5. One example of the degree of the extreme imbalance may be observed from the case of the experiences of one hedge fund: 'Long-Term Capital Management carried a balance sheet of over $100 billion on an equity base of less than $5 billion. In addition, it had off-balance sheet liabilities in excess of $1 trillion. The dislocations caused by the Russion melt-down eroded the equity base until it was down to $600 million at the time of the rescue. If Long-Term Capital Management had been allowed to fail, the counterparties would have sustained losses running into billions' (Soros, 1998, pp. 190–1). This example also suggests that lack of transparency, poor institutional governance, and cronyism are not unique to the countries that experienced the Asian crisis.

6. Adaptive (or Austrian) entrepreneurship refers to the many different forms of incremental innovation, such as product imitation in the early stages of economic development. It is contrasted with creative (or Schumpeterian) entrepreneurship which results in radical innovations (see Cheah, 1993, Cheah and Yu, 1995).

7. For a sceptical view on this issue see Krugman (1997).

8. During this phase the tendency for a shift from productive investment into highly speculative investment ('casino capitalism'), highlighted earlier by Strange (1986) and more recently by Soros (1998), becomes increasingly pronounced. The development in recent decades of new financial instruments, and the implementation of electronic technology to promote easier financial transactions, are both complementary responses to as well as facilitators of this tendency, enabling it to be raised to previously unprecedented levels.

9. From a Schumpeterian perspective, evolutionary change is periodically disrupted by revolutionary changes in the economy. Schumpeter's perspective of the development process emphasises the reality of change through competition, displacement or elimination, and through a general transformation of the economy. Moreover, owing to the dynamic and competitive nature of the development process, development, in Schumpeter's conception, does not occur continuously and evenly over time and place. Instead the phenomenon is primarily an episodic, transient and discontinuous one. For Schumpeter, generalised economic fluctuations (economic cycles) are an integral aspect of the competitive development process (see Schumpeter, 1934, 1939, 1976).

10. During such periods, mercantilist practices and ideology become more prominent; and so too does the tendency for conflict to occur, under a variety of guises (see Huntington, 1993; Gray, 1998a).

11. During such periods, *laissez faire* policies and ideology are in vogue again.

12. The Asian 'miracle' was always less miraculous and more flawed than it was made out to be by its admirers; and it always had its critics, the most recent being Lingle (1997) and Backman (1999). Despite the protestations of the critics, in the past institutions such as the IMF, the World Bank and the Asian Development Bank largely overlooked, deliberately ignored or treated as inconsequential the deficiencies that they have recently attributed as the principal causes of the Asian crisis.

13. One specific implication is that the reform of authoritarian, inefficient and corrupt institutions in the former socialist countries should not mean a rush into unfettered private enterprise, for there is an important need for strong social institutions to maintain capital, help the poor and moderate inequity in the development process.

References

Adachi, F. (1985) 'Trade, growth and international economic conflicts', International Economic Conflict Discussion Paper no. 21 (Nagoya: Economics Research Center, Nagoya University).

Akamatsu, K. (1961) 'A theory of unbalanced growth in the world economy', *Weltwirtschaftliches Archiv*, vol. 86, no. 2, pp. 196–217.

Alba, P. *et al.* (1998) 'Volatility and contagion in a financially integrated world: lessons from East Asia's recent experience', World Bank Policy Research Working Paper no. 2008 (Washington, DC: World Bank).

Arrighi, G. (1994) *The Long Twentieth Century* (London: Verso).

Ayres, I. and J. Braithwaite (1992) *Responsive Regulation: transcending the deregulation debate* (Oxford: Oxford University Press).

Backman, Michael (1999) *Asian Eclipse: Exposing the dark side of business in Asia* (New York: Wiley).

Beenstock, M. (1983) *The World Economy in Transition* (London: Allen and Unwin).

Bienefeld, M. (1982) 'The international context for national development strategies: Constraints and opportunities in a changing world', in M. Bienefeld and M. Godfrey (eds), *The Struggle for Development* (London: Wiley).

Brooks, D. *et al.* (1998) 'The Yen depreciation and its implications for East and Southeast Asia', EDRC Briefing Notes no. 1 (Manila: Asian Development Bank).

Business Week (1998) 'The perils of red capitalism', 26 October, pp. 22–6.

Cheah, H. B. (1987) *International Competition in the Pacific* (Singapore: Institute of Southeast Asian Studies).

Cheah, H. B. (1993) 'Dual modes of entrepreneurship: revolution and evolution in the entrepreneurial process', *Creativity and Innovation Management*, vol. 2, no. 4, pp. 243–51.

Cheah, H. B. (1995) 'Changes in competitive advantage in East Asia and the Pacific: Causes and consequences', International Economic Conflict Discussion Paper no. 87 (Economics Research Center, School of Economics, Nagoya University, Japan).

Cheah, H. B. (1997) 'Can governments engineer the transition from cheap labour to skill-based competitiveness? The case of Singapore', in Martin Godfrey (ed.), *Skill Development for International Competitiveness* (London: Edward Elgar).

Cheah, H. B. (1998a) 'Catching up': adaptive entrepreneurship and economic development in Asia', in Y. Takahashi, M. Murata and K. M. Rahman (eds), *Management Strategies of Multinational Corporations in Asian Markets* (Tokyo: Chuo University Press), pp. 243–63.

Cheah H. B. (1998b) 'Beyond the crisis: entrepreneurship challenges towards the millennium', paper presented at the University of Illinois at Chicago and American Marketing Association Research Symposium on Marketing and Entrepreneurship, 12–13 June, Hong Kong.

Cheah, H. B. and T. Yu (1996) 'Adaptive response: entrepreneurship and competitiveness in the economic development of Hong Kong', *Journal of Enterprising Culture*, vol. 4, no. (3), pp. 241–66.

Dertouzos, M. *et al.* (1989) *Made in America: Regaining the productive edge* (Cambridge, Mass.: MIT Press).

Downie, J. (1958) *The Competitive Process* (London: Duckworth).

Elger, T. and C. Smith (1994) *Global Japanization : the transnational transformation of the labour process* (New York : Routledge).

Fukuyama, F. (1992) *The End of History and the Last Man* (New York: The Free Press).

Godfrey, M. (1997) 'Introduction', in M. Godfrey (ed.), *Skills Development for International Competitiveness* (Cheltenham: Edward Elgar), pp. xv–xxix.

Gray, J. (1998a) 'Global utopias and clashing civilizations: misunderstanding the present', *International Affairs*, vol. 74, no. 1, pp. 149–64.

Gray, J. (1998b) 'World Bank attacks management of crisis', *Australian Financial Review*, 4 December.

Hersh, J. (1993) *The USA and the Rise of East Asia since 1945* (New York: St Martin's Press).

Hoffmann, W. G. (1958) *The Growth of Industrial Economies* (Manchester: Manchester University Press).

Huntington, S. (1993) 'Clash of civilizations', *Foreign Affairs,* vol. 72, no. 3, pp. 22–49.

IMF Staff (1998) 'The Asian crisis: causes and cures', *Finance and Development*, vol. 35, no. 2.

International Trade Administration (1999) *The Year 2000 Problem and the Global Trading System* (Washington, DC: US Department of Commerce).

Kaplinsky, R. (1994) *Easternisation: The spread of Japanese management techniques to developing countries* (London: Frank Cass).

Kennedy, P. (1993) *Preparing for the Twenty-first Century* (New York: Vintage).

Knies, K. (1853) *Die Politische Okonomie vom Standpunkte der Geschichtlichen Methode* (Braunschweig).

Krugman, P. (1997) 'Is Capitalism too productive?', *Foreign Affairs*, vol. 76, no. 5, pp. 79–94.

League of Nations (1945) *Economic Instability in the Post-war World: The conditions of prosperity after the transition from war to peace* (Princeton, NJ: Princeton University Press).

Levinson, M. (1988) *Beyond Free Markets* (Lexington: Lexington Books).

Li, K. T. (1988) *The Evolution of Policy behind Taiwan's Development Success* (New Haven, CT: Yale University Press).

Lingle, C. (1997) *The Rise and Decline of the Asian Century: false starts on the path to the global millennium* (Hong Kong: Asia 2000).

MacIntyre, A. (1994) *Business and Government in Industrialising Asia* (Ithaca, NY: Cornell University Press).

Pang, C. K. (1992) *The State and Economic Transformation: The Taiwan case* (New York: Garland).

Pernia, E. and J. Knowles (1998) 'Assessing the social impact of the financial crisis in Asia', EDRC Briefing Notes no. 6 (Manila: Asian Development Bank).

Pomerleano, M. (1998) 'The East Asia crisis and corporate finances: the untold micro story', World Bank Policy Research Working Paper no. 1990 (Washington, DC: World Bank).

Public Management Service (1998) *The Year 2000 Problem: Impacts and actions* (Paris: OECD), http://www.oecd.org/puma/

Radelet, S. and J. Sachs (1997) 'Asia's reemergence', *Foreign Affairs*, vol. 76, no. 6, pp. 44–59.

Rana, P. (1998a) 'The East Asian financial crisis: implications for exchange rate management', EDRC Briefing Notes no. 5, (Manila: Asian Development Bank).

Rana, P. (1998b) 'Controls on short-term capital inflows: the Latin American experience and lessons for DMCs', EDRC Briefing Notes no. 2, (Manila: Asian Development Bank).

Reinicke, W. (1997) 'Global public policy', *Foreign Affairs,* vol. 76, no. 6, pp. 127–38.

Salter, W. E. G. (1966) *Productivity and Technical Change*, 2nd edn (Cambridge, Mass.: Cambridge University Press).

Schumpeter, J. A. (1934) *The Theory of Economic Development* (Cambridge, Mass.: Harvard University Press).

Schumpeter, J. A. (1939) *Business Cycles*, 2 vol (New York: McGraw-Hill).

Schumpeter, J. A. (1976) *Capitalism, Socialism and Democracy*, 5th edn (London: Allen and Unwin).

Schwartz, H. (1994) *States versus Markets* (New York: St Martin's).

Shin, I. S and J. H. Hahm (1998) 'The Korean Crisis: causes and resolution', paper prepared for the East-West Center/KDI Conference on the Korean Crisis, Honolulu, 8 August.

Shonfield, A. (1984) *In Defence of the Mixed Economy* (Oxford: Oxford University Press).

Soros, G. (1998) *The Crisis of Global Capitalism* (New York: Public Affairs).

Stigler, G. J. (1968) 'The division of labour is limited by the extent of the market' in W. Breit and H. M. Hochman (eds), *Readings in Microeconomics* (London: Holt, Rinehart and Winston), pp. 151–9.

Strange, S. (1979) 'The management of surplus productive capacity', in N. M. Kamrany and R. H. Day (eds), *Economic Issues of the Eighties* (Baltimore, MD: John Hopkins University Press), pp. 226–46.

Strange, S. (1986) *Casino Capitalism* (Oxford: Blackwell).

Strange, S. and R. Tooze (1981) *The International Politics of Surplus Capacity* (London: Allen and Unwin).

Subcommittee on Government Management, Information and Technology (1998) *The Year 2000 Problem*, a report by the Committee on Government Reform and Oversight to the U.S. House of Representatives, Washington, DC, 8 October. http://www.house.gov/reform/gmit/y2k/y2k/report/

Thurow, L. (1993) *Head to Head* (New York: Warner).

Wade, R. (1990) *Governing the Market: Economic theory and the role of government in East Asian industrialisation* (Princeton, NJ: Princeton University Press).

Walker, W. C. (1998) 'Contagion: how the Asian crisis spread', EDRC Briefing Notes no. 3 (Manila: Asian Development Bank).

Watanabe, T. (1983) 'Asia's high-growth region', *Japan Echo*, vol. 10, no. 3, pp. 42–51.

Watanabe, T. (1992) *Asia: Its growth and agony* (Honolulu: East–West Center).

Weber, S. (1997) 'The end of the business cycle?', *Foreign Affairs*, vol. 76, no. 4, pp. 65–82.

White, G. (ed.) (1988) *Developmental States in East Asia* (London: Macmillan).

Womack, J., D. Jones and D. Roos (1990) *The Machine that Changed the World* (New York: Harper).

World Bank (1998) *East Asia: The Road to Recovery* (Washington, DC: World Bank).

World Bank (1999) *Global Economic Prospects and the Developing Countries 1998/99: beyond financial crisis* (Washington, DC: World Bank).

Yamazawa, I., A. Hirata and K. Yokota (1991) 'Evolving patterns of comparative advantage in the Pacific economies', in M. Ariff (ed.), *The Pacific Economy: Growth and external stability* (Sydney: Allen and Unwin).

Part Two
Variants of the East Asian Development Model

6 Thailand, Japan and the East Asian Development Model: the Asian Economic Crisis in World System Perspective

Harold R. Kerbo and Robert Slagter

INTRODUCTION

The development of sociology as an academic discipline can be traced to classic theorists such as Marx, Weber, Durkheim, Tonnies and the many others who focused much of their work on the dynamics of 'modernisation' and economic development that were underway at the time and the implications for European societies of these processes. Indeed much the same can be said of the discipline of political science, and of course Western economic theory. More recently, the literature on economic development has expanded much further with a focus on less developed nations leading to detailed economic analysis of such things as investment strategies, import substitution versus export strategies, and education policies, as well as other topics. Despite this very substantial literature, however, there are considerable gaps in the analysis and understanding of the causes and processes of economic development resulting from neglect as well as outright misunderstanding that sociological research can usefully address.

In the present chapter we begin with a discussion of some of the inadequacies of standard liberal theories of economic development resulting from a too narrow focus on purely economic aspects of development while neglecting cultural, historical and institutional factors. We then turn to modern world systems/dependency theory and the biases in its application to Asian industrialising states that result from ignoring recent research on the effects of investment by advanced industrial nations in some of the less developed countries (see Rapley, 1996, for a full discussion of development theories). We then consider what has been called the East Asian development model, the roots of this model in the modern Japan, and the question of what may be termed 'flaws' in the model that have become evident, especially in Japan during the 1990s but in other countries as well since the Asian economic crisis started in July 1997. Finally, we consider the extent to which Thailand has followed the standard version of the East Asian development model, the nature of the flaws in this model with the Asian economic crisis of the late 1990s, the continued viability of the model, and the prospect of Thailand and other Asian nations overcoming the problems with their economic development process.

THE WESTERN BIAS IN MODERN THEORIES OF ECONOMIC DEVELOPMENT

Modern sociology developed in the age of great societal transformations in Europe, and of course during the age of colonialism. The only world well known by theorists such as Marx, Weber, Durkheim and others was the world of nineteenth century Europe. And in fact it is clear that much of the material sociologists such as Weber had to rely on for their limited writings on Asian subjects in the 1800s was simply wrong on many facts about Asian societies (Golzio, 1985; Minear, 1980; Mouer and Sugimoto, 1985; Frank, 1998). Thus we can perhaps be justified in forgiving Marx, Weber, Durkheim and the others of their time for some of their Western biases – but not modern social scientists who continue many of these biases more than a century after they were first applied.

Recent criticisms of Western theories of economic development have focused on the individualistic value assumptions and Western views of a *laissez-faire* state (Fallows, 1994; Johnson, 1982; Dore, 1987; Frank, 1998; Pye, 1985). It is not our intention to provide a detailed analysis of these criticisms in this chapter. We need only note that these and other criticisms indicate that according to standard Western economic theory, the East Asian development model, along with the rise of modern Japan and the other 'Asian Tigers', should have been impossible! Throughout departments of economics in the United States and Britain, one could see smirks on academic faces as Japan began to falter in the early 1990s, and then almost hear a collective sigh of relief as in quick order the economies of many Asian nations fell into crisis from July 1997. As we shall attempt to show towards the end of this chapter, however, the East Asian development model is not necessarily fatally flawed, but only in need of a more realistic understanding of the nature of ruling elites in the process of political and economic development. Thus if our analysis is correct, the collective smiles on the faces of most Western academic economists could very well be short lived.

Another body of research and theory that must be considered with regard to the East Asian development model and the current Asian economic crisis is that which refutes what might be called the superpower bias in standard theories of economic development. The theories and analysis of Wallerstein (1974, 1980, 1989), Frank (1967, 1975, 1978), Chirot (1977, 1986) and others utilising the 'modern world system' paradigm argue that the standard economic development theories, especially the assumptions of 'stages of economic development' made famous by Rostow (1962, 1975), are inaccurate when trying to understand the situation of countries trying to develop in the second half of the twentieth century. The argument is that what the 'stages of economic growth' model most neglects are the realities experienced by the poorer nations that are currently trying to develop in the face of outside intervention by dominant (core) nations in the world economy. When European nations went through the first stages of economic growth in the nineteenth and early twentieth centuries there were no already developed nations in existence to intervene in their development processes, to create structural distortions in their economies, and simply take out resources and profits that were needed for future economic development. In the world systems perspective the industrialising nations of Asia are assigned to a semiperiphery status and the analysis of their development falls under dependency theory. From this perspective semiperiphery industrial development necessarily has the following characteristics: (1) development is an artificial enclave industrialisation with few linkages to the broader international economy, (2) it is exceptionally vulnerable to swings in world economic conditions, and (3) capital and markets are heavily influenced by multinational firms. The result is likely to be the domination of national markets by these multinationals, the absence of indigenous entrepreneurship, and economically weakened states. In the long run, dependency-linked structural problems result in economic stagnation and heightened inequality across regions, economic sectors and income groups (Barrett and Chin, 1987).

Current world system theory also purports to explain how the interests of political and economic elites in developing countries today tend to become more closely tied to the interests of elites from rich core nations than with their own people, which in turn leads to the adoption of economic policies beneficial to the core nations and harmful to the long-term interests of the masses in the poorer countries. Considerable empirical research comparing developing nations around the world has supported the world system theoretical conclusion that political and economic intervention from rich nations tends to harm the long-term development chances of less developed countries (for example see Bornschier *et al.*, 1978; Bornschier and Chase-Dunn, 1985; Bornschier and Ballmer-Cao, 1979; Chase-Dunn, 1975, 1989; Rubinson, 1976).

When we look more closely at Asian developing nations, however, we find research that reaches conclusions contrary to the proposal that the intervention of multinational corporations from the core nations in developing economies tends to reduce the prospect of long-term economic growth (Barrett and Whyte, 1982; Hill, 1994; Kerbo, 1996, pp. 422–4). However for most Western dependency theorists the development successes of East Asian states are merely interesting counterexamples or deviant cases to the causal relationships predicted by world systems/ dependency theory (Barrett and Chin, 1987). Again, it seems clear that another kind of Western bias exists in much of the world systems/dependency approach even though it is critical of standard liberal economic development theories (Frank, 1998). In this case there is an underestimation and misunderstanding of how the East Asian development model can operate to overcome some of the negative effects of the outside economic intervention that have been found more commonly in Africa and Latin America.

Finally, there is another, more widespread problem in the theory building and research of most economists and sociologists in the subject area that leads to misunderstandings of the process of economic development in all nations – rich and poor, Western and non-Western. There is a strong tendency in modern social science to build *general* models of economic development, models backed by mathematical equations that seem highly scientific, and above all, models claimed to be valid across all nations and time periods (see van Wolferen, 1999). But despite other problems he may have created for current social scientists trying to understand the process of economic development in Asia, Max Weber cautioned us that general theories that are meant to explain similar social and economic processes across time and national boundaries are almost certain to mislead. Differing historical traditions, values and geography, to list only a few factors, will almost always intervene to make the details of something such as economic development at least somewhat unique in each nation. One may start with what Weber called an 'ideal type' of some economic or political process, but such an ideal type must be considered as only a general model to be used to understand the political, economic and/or social reality in a particular situation or nation (Pye, 1985, p. 10). Thus in what follows we shall also briefly consider, with the case of Thailand, how proponents of the East Asian development model have overplayed their theoretical hands when claiming that there is one model of economic development common to all or most of the Asian nations that showed remarkable economic growth in the second half of the twentieth century. There certainly may be some common characteristics among Asian nations experiencing rapid economic development, but an East Asian development model is best considered as an ideal type, with considerable variance in how the model has been, and perhaps must be, used in each nation.

THE EAST ASIAN DEVELOPMENT MODEL

It is important to specify, at least briefly, what is generally meant by the East Asian development model, for as we have implied above, in many ways it remains a somewhat murky and vague concept. And it is worth noting again that there are, no doubt, a dozen or more East Asian development models, varying models in Japan depending on the time frame selected (Raphael and Rohlen, 1998) and differing models depending on the country of reference (see Rowen, 1998). There are enough commonalities, however, for a general East Asian development model to be described, primarily in contrast to its Western counterpart.

Two separate aspects of the model must be distinguished – the purpose of economic development and the means of economic development – though to a large degree the purpose shapes the choice of means. Fallows (1994, p. 208) provides a simple description of the contrasting development models. In the Anglo-American model, the basic reason to have an economy is to raise the individual consumer's standard of living. In the Asian model, it is to increase the collective national strength. Fallows goes on to suggest that the focus on national strength is a reaction to the long repression of Asians by European colonialism, though we disagree on this point. A broader look at history suggests that the same Asian goals for an economic and political system existed long before colonial repression (Frank, 1998). Rather, we can refer to a fundamentally different orientation or value system in Asian societies when compared with the West. There is now substantial evidence that Asian societies are collectivist or group oriented, in contrast to the more individualistic value orientation generally ascribed to Western societies. From this perspective the purpose of development is, at least in large part, historically and culturally determined. Therefore in the Western model 'economic development means "more".' 'If people have more choice, more leisure, more wealth, more opportunity to pursue happiness, society as a whole will be a success' (Fallows, 1994, p. 209). This definition of the purpose of development reflects an individualist value orientation in which individuals are largely responsible for themselves and individual goals are emphasised. In contrast the more collectivist value orientation of Asian societies emphasises group goals to a greater extent. In Asia people are relatively more concerned about how well the group is doing – the family, the work group, the company, the nation – than with purely individual success.

Despite the common charge of oversimplification, there is rather strong empirical support for these differing value orientations. Hofstede's (1991) data from over 50 countries puts the USA highest on his 'individualism vs. collectivism scale', with Britain, Canada, New Zealand and Australia close behind, while most Asian nations line up towards the other end of the scale. Hampden-Turner and Trompenaars (1993) found much the same thing with their questionnaires to business people around the world, as did Verba (1987) in his study of national elite attitudes towards inequality and the goals of government between the USA and Japan. And while other national opinion polls seldom include data from Asian nations other than Japan, most questions involving the purpose of government and government regulation of the economy generally reveal that North Americans are mostly opposed (with the British usually closer to the American view) and the Japanese are mostly in favour (Ladd and Bowman, 1998).

With respect to the means of economic development, it logically follows that in a more collectivist nation some agent representing the group or nation should have some authority over the economy. At the national level this agent is always the polity in one form or another (king, emperor, president, parliament, bureaucracy, the military and so on). In an excellent work that shows the differences between as well as the similarities among Asian nations, Pye (1985) convincingly shows that power and authority in Asian nations have been viewed differently when compared with Western nations. Pye notes that Asian nations are in the process of change, but still there is 'the common denominator of idealizing benevolent, paternalistic leadership ... . Thus, although Europe did succeed in imposing on Asia its legalistic concept of the nation-state, the Asian response has been a new, and powerful, form of nationalism based on paternalistic authority' (Pye 1985, p. vii).

Following Pye, we can understand why the East Asian development model readily contains the assumption of what Myrdal (1968, 1970) calls a 'hard state'. Others writing about the nature of the state in the East Asian development model generally agree (see Vogel, 1991; Kim, 1997; Fallows, 1994; Pye, 1985, ch. 1), with Johnson (1982) preferring the term 'capitalist development state'. In essence a 'hard state' is both capable of and willing to use its influence to press for national development goals even in the face of opposition from various internal interest groups, including powerful interest groups from the upper and upper-middle classes who stand to lose in the short term because of the policies followed by the development state. The 'hard' or 'developmental' states stand in contrast to the Western model of the 'regulatory' state, which intervenes in the economy to enforce rules such as preventing monopolies or protecting consumers and wherein many competing groups force the adoption of policies that may be detrimental to economic growth (Chan, 1993). Of course hard or capitalist development states must also have the power to resist demands from outside powers wanting policies that are harmful to the long-term interests of the nation.

With respect to the elites in charge of the hard state, they must, in order successfully to promote development, be motivated to serve national interests rather than selfish narrow interests. In those Asian nations that developed rather dramatically in the second half of the twentieth century, there is wide agreement that elites do generally share this characteristic relative to elites in many other developing nations (Pye, 1985, p. 4; Johnson, 1982; Vogel, 1991; Kerbo and McKinstry, 1995; Fallows, 1994; Koh, 1989; Kim, 1997). This is not to say that Asian political elites or ministry officials are completely altruistic and totally opposed to helping powerful cronies, but such collusion on behalf of the rich and powerful is more often tempered by restraint for national and popular interests. It is not possible here to consider in detail the sources of such restraint among Asian elites, but it has been argued that they are found in Asian collective value orientations, collectivist religions and other traditions of civilisations in Asia, and that these sources endured during the period of economic and political confrontation with the West in the nineteenth and twentieth centuries. Similar traditions, to the degree they existed, did not survive the impact of colonisation in Africa and Latin America.

It is interesting to note that in contrast to American and British social scientists, Asian social scientists seem to be more aware that the theoretical underpinning of the East Asian development model can be traced to the early nineteenth-century German economist Friedrich List (1983), who viewed collective rather than individual interests as more important for national economies (Fallows, 1994, pp. 179–96). However, most of the practical details of the East Asian development model, as Johnson (1982) shows, were worked out through trial and error by the Japanese bureaucratic elite from the 1920s, through the Second World War and well after the war to create the 'Japanese economic miracle'. Johnson demonstrates how the Japanese ministry elite learned to use the authority of the state with techniques such as planning and administrative guidance to build up the Japanese economy to its second-place position behind the USA early in the second half of the twentieth century.

THAILAND AND THE EAST ASIAN DEVELOPMENT MODEL

While Thailand varied more than other Southeast and East Asian nations from the ideal type of East Asian development model, there is agreement that Thailand did follow many of the basic practices of the model (Muscat, 1994; Pasuk and Baker, 1997, 1998; Girling, 1981; Kulick and Wilson, 1996). During the second half of the nineteenth century there were even a few interesting parallels between Japan's and Thailand's attempts to confront Western colonialism with rapid development. Somewhat like Japan during the Meiji Restoration in the second half of the nineteenth century, in the same time period Thailand began to develop a state bureaucracy intent on 'modernisation' and economic development under King Chulalongkorn (Girling, 1981; Keyes, 1989; Wyatt, 1984). A military coup in 1932 removed absolute rule by the king and began the tradition of alliance between state bureaucrats and the military, and those who organised the coup had economic development as an objective. But the more significant Thai push for economic development, in which some elements of the model demonstrated successfully in Japan were adopted, did not begin until well after the Second World War. It was primarily under Prime Minister Sarit from 1958 that the Thai ministry elite had sufficient training and education, along with the strong support of a powerful prime minister (and military) and substantial aid from the USA, for economic development policies really to take off in Thailand. The development programme devised was strongly influenced by the liberal market-oriented focus of the USA and the World Bank, as well as the Japanese model, and represents an amalgamation of the two models.

As described well by Muscat (1994) and others, from the early 1960s policies were focused on agricultural development and import substitution. But by the 1980s the focus was on the development of export industries, especially agriculture, cars and electronics. During the period prior to the export-oriented phase there were substantial controls on foreign capital going into Thailand, especially the '51 per cent rule', which in most cases required foreign corporations to form a joint venture with a Thai company or companies, with the latter owning at least 51 per cent of the joint venture. Tariffs as high as 50 per cent were placed on foreign imports competing with Thai products. There were domestic content rules on production, along with minimum wage laws.

As noted above, however, the East Asian development model must be seen as only an ideal type, with Asian nations varying in the details of how the model is viewed and implemented. Compared with other East and Southeast Asian nations, several relatively unique characteristics of Thailand can be noted. As commonly stressed, along with Japan, Thailand is the only nation in the region that has not been colonised, though there has certainly been considerable Western influence, particularly from Britain, since the mid 1800s. Traditional institutions and authority relations were somewhat less disrupted in Thailand, and many people claim that development was less conflict-ridden as a result (Keyes, 1989). Also, in contrast to the other Southeast Asian nations, there has been much more acceptance of ethnic Chinese (who tend to dominate the economies of the region), with a long history of cooperation between rich Chinese capitalist families and the Thai bureaucratic/military elite as a crucial component of Thai economic development (Girling, 1981, p. 80; Kulick and Wilson, 1996; Keyes, 1989; Wyatt, 1984). Because of this, especially compared with Malaysia and Indonesia, there has been a much less conflict-ridden process of development in Thailand.

In the case of Thailand, however, it can probably be said that the development model varied most from the norm because the 'hard state' was less hard in Thailand. The basic paradigm for the state's involvement was established under the Sarit government in the late 1950s. Under this regime an implicit agreement was reached between the major competing factions – the technocrats and the politicians (the military and some senior bureaucrats) – in the undemocratic system. The technocrats would be given control of macroeconomic policy while sectoral and microeconomic management would be given to the politicians (Christensen and Siamwalla, 1993). The result was an enduring pattern of stable macroeconomic policy and a non-interventionist policy style at the industry level. The most unique feature of the Thai model in comparison with the Japanese is the level of government intervention in the economy. As one analyst has noted, 'There can be little argument that state economic policies, through establishing an open, market oriented economy based on trade and private enterprise, have produced a climate in which industrialization has taken root and flourished' (Falkus, 1995, p. 23).

The primary explanation of why there has been less government involvement in the Thai economy compared with other Asian nations focuses on social structure and values (Muscat, 1994, pp. 4–5). Of the rapidly developing Asian nations, Thailand is the only one that lacks strong Confucian traditions or an Islamic influence to create the expectation and desire for a strong but benevolent central authority to establish security and provide guidance (Pye, 1985). This less authoritarian orientation of Thai society in the Asian context may result from the particular mix of Buddhism and Hinduism in Thai culture (Osborne, 1995) and material factors such as agricultural abundance and plentiful land (Pasuk and Baker, 1997), resulting in less inclination for a hard state. Our perspective is that another major contributory factor to the relative absence of a hard state in recent Thai history is the existence of individualism and the value placed on personal independence in Thai culture.

As early as the 1950s Western anthropologists were noting the relative independence of Thais, with Thai society being loosely structured in comparison with other Asian societies (Embree, 1950). This was later confirmed by the field research of other social scientists (for example, Phillips, 1993). These early descriptions of Thais as individualistic are now viewed as overly simplistic and Thai society is now seen as more complex (Mulder, 1992, pp. 43–4). In some regards Thais are rather like most other Asians as they have been found to be quite group oriented when it comes to important, closely knit groups, especially the family and sometimes the work group or a less formal social circle, but they are more independent and 'unstructured' in wider public relations (Slagter and Kerbo, 2000). For example in Hofstede's (1991) study Thais are put far on the collectivism side of the individualism–collectivism scale as well as high on the power–distance scale used to measure levels of hierarchy in societies. Other research measuring Thai value orientations, however, describes Thai society as 'first and foremost hierarchically structured ... where individualism and social relations are of the utmost importance' (Komin, 1991), an 'individualist and hierarchical society' in contrast to the United States, which is 'individualistic egalitarian' (Rokeach, 1979). As a Thai saying goes, 'to be able to do what one wants is to be a real Thai' (see Akin, 1996, p. xx).

It follows, then, that given the Thai social structure and value orientations the East Asian development model would be implemented at least somewhat differently in Thailand from elsewhere in Asia. While there has certainly been a relatively hard state, with ministry direction of the economy, most agree that there has been less of this than in most other Asian developing nations (Muscat, 1994). Thus compared with these other Asian nations, the style of Thai economic development has been different, with less government regulation and more entrepreneurial spirit. The development policies of Thailand can help explain why Thailand was the first to fall in the Asian economic crisis from 1997, but also one of the first to implement the reforms needed to overcome the crisis.

A key point needs to be emphasised here: a hard state of some type is a common feature of the East Asian development model, and a hard state means *powerful government elites dominating the economy*. As has been quoted many times, 'power corrupts and absolute power corrupts absolutely'. This means that it is necessary to examine the nature of elites and changes in elite composition over time in order to understand elites' roles in the development process. Before we take up the issue, however, we should briefly consider a few details of the Asian economic crises of the 1990s.

THE ASIAN ECONOMIC CRISES

Let us be clear why we have referred in the plural to Asian economic *crises*. Primarily we suggest that the economic crisis that began in Japan soon after the 1990s began to be separated from the more widespread Asian economic crisis sparked by the Thai government's decision to allow the baht to float from 2 July 1997, although they are related in that Japan's long recession had created problems for the Southeast Asian economies. This second Asian crisis was the one that led Thailand, Malaysia, Indonesia and South Korea to fall into economic crisis in quick succession, with other countries such as Taiwan and Singapore also affected, although to a lesser degree. These two crises, we shall argue, had similar roots even if they differed considerably in the details.

The Japanese economic crisis was set off by the chief of the Bank of Japan, Mr Mieno, when he began to manipulate interest rates in order to stop the boom in the Japanese real estate sector and the stock market. From Mieno's perspective the boom signified that the economy was overheating and would harm the interests of ordinary Japanese (Kerbo and McKinstry, 1995). Related to this, many Japanese were becoming angry and resentful about the rapid rise of inequality as they observed the new super rich apparently wasting money in conspicuous consumption. There are now hard data showing that the Japanese public did indeed develop strong attitudes about the rapid rise in inequality (Kerbo, 2000, ch. 2; Smeeding *et al.*, 1990; Mishel *et al.*, 1999). In response to concern about the future of the Japanese economy and popular discontent, Mieno burst the 'bubble economy', but the result was a much harder landing than anyone had imagined. Unsound financial practices and rampant corruption (Schlesinger, 1998) during the bubble economy years of the 1980s had created the preconditions for an economic crisis once Mieno's stimulus set it off.

In the other Asian economic crisis, beginning in July 1997, there was also a stimulus from financial markets; in this case it was the Thai government's decision to let the baht float after months of denying it was necessary or that it would even do so. Again a bubble economy was burst, setting off a chain reaction with other economies in the region. There were similarities to the earlier situation in Japan, especially the inflated real estate sector and an overvalued stock market, although the stock market had peaked in 1994. There was an investment pattern characterised as 'golf course capitalism', which produced speculative projects in high-rise office buildings, luxury condominiums and, of course, golf courses. These investments neither earned the export income upon which Thailand depended nor created the kind of long-term growth industries that could both service the domestic economy and provide long-term employment. The crisis broke in the context of other problems, as many reports by the IMF, the World Bank and other international agencies pointed out. There was, for example, excess industrial capacity throughout Asia, which few people took seriously before July 1997. And there was, in Thailand at least, a significant increase in income inequality that went along with the bubble economy, creating considerable popular discontent and, as some have noted, likely problems for future consumer demand (Pasuk and Baker, 1998; Kerbo, 2000, ch. 13).

A component of the July 1997 crisis that did not exist in the bursting of the earlier Japanese bubble was the role of international finance. As part of a long-term liberalisation agenda the US government had pushed for the opening of financial markets throughout Asia. In Thailand, as in most countries in the region, the financial markets were heavily protected from foreign penetration, competition and ownership. During the Clinton presidency this liberalisation agenda was strongly pushed and some success was achieved. Many US government officials have now admitted that the US government, urged on by the US financial sector and Treasury Secretary Rubin, contributed to the Asian economic crisis by insisting that the financial markets be opened rapidly (see *International Herald Tribune*, 16, 17 and 19 February 1999). Many US government officials now agree that financial institutions and government agencies in developing Asian nations were not ready for liberalisation and exposure to the powerful forces of international finance. Banks did not operate to international standards, government regulation – to the degree that it existed – was ineffective and substantial corruption was built into the system. The crises have elicited considerable scepticism about the future of the East Asian development model. Is it still viable? Is it worth emulating? Are there lessons for developed and less developed nations in the causes and remedies of these crises?

THE EAST ASIAN DEVELOPMENT MODEL:
ITS (NON-FATAL?) FLAWS

Before examining the failures in the East Asian development model that contributed to the crises it is useful briefly to examine the successes achieved with the model. First, in the case of Japan, and later throughout East and Southeast Asia, the general East Asian development model produced something unique among the less developed nations: rapid and sustained economic growth. Between 1945 and the 1970s the war-devastated economy of Japan was transformed into the second largest economy in the world and provided an extremely high standard of living for virtually all of its citizens. Thailand, which in the 1950s seemed one of the nations least likely to develop, experienced more than three decades of economic growth. And while inequality varied considerably during this period, including a sharp increase in the bubble years, poverty was very substantially reduced by anyone's measure. Between 1970 and 1993 life expectancy increased from 58 years to 69 years and infant mortality declined from 73 per thousand live births to 36 (Ahuja *et al.,* 1997, p. 14), while in 1993 per capita GDP was more than 3.6 times what it had been in 1970 (Dixon, 1999, p. 16). During the same time period inequality increased greatly, but the percentage of the population living in poverty (defined by the World Bank's 1985 dollar per capita per day standard) decreased substantially from 8.1 per cent to less than 1 per cent in the 1975–95 period (Ahuja *et al.,* 1997, p. 10). The data indicate that economic growth was great enough substantially to overcome the negative effects of increasing income inequality on the incidence of poverty (ibid., pp. 46–7).

Despite all this economic success in Asia, the late 1990s have brought denunciations of the East Asian development model and the charge that it is no longer viable. The criticisms emanate from both the liberal orthodox and the world system/dependency schools of thought discussed earlier. From the liberal orthodox perspective the crises demonstrate, in the case of Japan, the fatal flaw of excessive government interference in the economic sphere and, in the case of Thailand, the failure of its regulatory functions. For both countries the problems are seen as primarily to do with politics and government and the inadequate brands of capitalism it has spawned. In the case of Japan, it is argued that powerful vested interests continue to thwart any attempt at meaningful economic reform in the interests of true international competition (Schlesinger, 1998; Smith, 1997) and that the bureaucracy is no longer competent and honest. With regard to Thailand the crisis is seen as a natural outcome of an *ersatz* capitalism that is complacent and unwilling to commit resources to increasing savings or upgrading technology. It is a capitalism characterised by undue emphasis on speculation and quick profits, and entrepreneurs whose major efforts are directed towards seeking benefits from the government, and most especially it is corrupt (Yoshihara, 1999). In other words these economies are not sufficiently *laissez-faire* or market driven, and in the case of Thailand regulation is either lacking or is characterised by partiality.

The crises in Southeast Asia also provide fodder for criticising the development process in these countries from a world systems/dependency perspective. Despite the impressive economic achievements of the Southeast Asian nations the crisis was seen as demonstrating a fundamental flaw in the entire development process. The crises have exposed these nations' extreme vulnerability to international markets and the perils of exposure to the financial power of the developed nations and the international financial system. In one assessment from this perspective, several key flaws of the Thai development model are identified: excessive dependence on foreign capital and exports, increasing inequality in income distribution, and the overwhelming priority given to market forces and the private sector in development, with the government abandoning its planning monitoring and guiding role (Bello *et al.*, 1998). The policy response argued for is withdrawal from the global system and an emphasis on national self-sufficiency in the economic sphere.

Most of these responses are too extreme. Rather than total rejection of the East Asian development model we suggest that a more realistic approach is to consider its specific flaws or problems, and whether or not these flaws are 'fatal' or temporary problems in need of adjustment. With respect to Japan, Kerbo and McKinstry (1995) suggest that the basic flaw is related to the nature of the elites formed under the hard state of the East Asian development model, as practised in Japan. Few will question that politicians in Japan have been generally corrupt, self-serving and short-sighted for most of the post-Second World War period. But until recently, the Japanese ministry elites, the true powers behind economic development, have been highly dedicated, nationally motivated and almost beyond corruption, according to detailed studies (Koh, 1989; Johnson, 1982; Kerbo and McKinstry, 1995, ch. 5). The first generation of postwar Japanese ministry elites saw themselves as the only saviours of their nation, were highly idealistic and self-sacrificing, and in most cases the top graduates from elite universities in Japan, primarily Tokyo University. The second generation of ministry elites, beginning in the 1980s, are seen as much less dedicated, more often leaving the government at an early age for more highly paid corporate jobs (in the industries they previously regulated), and as many recent scandals have shown, they are increasingly corrupt. It is particularly in the Ministry of Finance where inaction, corruption and self-serving policies have been singled out in the late 1990s. Even powerful business groups such as Keidanren, which in the past have benefited considerably from the structure of government ministry power in Japan, are calling for massive reform of the ministry.

Much like Japan, Thai ministry bureaucrats have been highly dedicated, honest and among the most talented people in the nation (Muscat, 1994,

p. 79), especially those in the Finance Ministry and the Bank of Thailand, which provided the stable macroeconomic policy that was so crucial for economic growth. And while this may be less the case today, in contrast to Japan the problem in Thailand is the increasing power of politicians seeking very particularistic benefits for their constituencies, politicians who are now more likely than those in the past to be able to manipulate government ministries for their short-sighted and selfish ends (Pasuk and Baker, 1997, 1998). From the 1970s the political power of the Thai military steadily declined, as did the power of their allies in the state bureaucracy, so that by the 1990s these old elite centres of political power had been clearly supplanted by the political side of government (Kulick and Wilson, 1996; Muscat, 1994). A cycle that can be found in most democratic polities has a particular variant in the Thai case. It takes money to win elections, lots of it, including money for direct payments to voters, or vote buying. In some cases legitimate businessmen spend their own money, in other cases local *chao pho* (godfathers) with both legitimate and illegal business interests enter the political arena (for Thai electoral politics and provincial politicians see Somrudee, 1993; Anek, 1996; Ockey, 1996; Robertson, 1996). To a large degree, then, Thai electoral politics is a direct business venture rather than a public service, with those who have invested their money, whether politicians or donors, hoping to reap quick profits on their investments. As a consequence the long established division of responsibility wherein technocrats controlled macroeconomic policy has been disrupted. Beginning in the late 1980s the Finance Ministry and the Bank of Thailand – the central macroeconomic agencies – became politicised (Muscat, 1994, p. 278). The culmination of this politicisation came with the onset of the crisis as the government had four finance ministers in a six-month period from June 1997 to the end of the year (Doner and Ramsay, 1999). Therefore it became possible for politicians and their business supporters both to stimulate and to participate in the financial and real estate speculation that marked the boom (bubble?) of the early 1990s (Pasuk and Baker, 1998, pp. 83, 180).

Thus in both Japan and Thailand we find that changes in the elites in the developmental state that had been so important in fostering development set the stage for economic crisis. In Japan it was increasing corruption and policies protecting privilege and power that were behind the economic crisis and blocked attempts to take significant action to remedy the situation. In Thailand it was not so much change among the ministry bureaucrats as a power shift towards corrupt politicians, who were then able to influence economic policy. These institutional changes alone do not account for the onset of the crises – in both Japan and Thailand the blame can also be put on a 'hard state' that for different reasons could not or would not continue the previous sound policies that had made the economic 'miracle' possible in both countries. The hard state continued to have power, but now that power could be used in both Japan and Thailand for different interests. In Thailand especially, increasing pressure on the ministry dealing with financial affairs by politicians from the 1980s made the economy ripe for crisis when the US government pushed for openings for US corporate investment (that is, it pushed for less control over financial institutions).

COMPETITION IN THE MODERN WORLD SYSTEM, GLOBAL MARKETS AND THE ASIAN ECONOMIC CRISIS

As noted at the beginning of this chapter, research shows that most of Asia has escaped many of the common negative effects of nations trying to develop while economic superpowers disrupt the process for their own economic interests. In contrast to most of Africa and Latin America, these studies show that outside investments from the rich nations have not retarded economic development as much in Asia during recent decades. To a large degree, we have argued, the implementation of the East Asian development model, with the inclusion of the necessary 'hard state', has been responsible for the difference between the Asian situation and that of developing nations in Africa and Latin America.

Once they achieve a higher level of economic development, however, nations enter another type of competition in the modern world system, one that has been going on for several centuries, wherein dominant nations are in strict competition with other dominant nations to increase their economic position relative to others, or to prevent their position from declining. The great revolutions of recent centuries – including the French Revolution of 1789, the Chinese Revolution through many decades of the twentieth century and the Russian Revolution of 1917, as well as the collapse of the Soviet Union more recently – all came about because the old governments could not ensure their countries' competitive position in this world competition (Skocpol, 1979).

Herein, it seems, lies the dilemma with regard to the East Asian development model: this model and the hard state included in it are necessary to escape exploitation by the dominant superpowers in the modern world system. However once a higher level of economic development has been achieved and the goal is to remain competitive, the hard state becomes a hindrance. Increasingly corrupt and inflexible elites – put in place by the capitalist development state (the hard state) – will attempt to maintain their power and prestige, blocking the changes needed to become more competitive at the new level of development. Competitive nations in today's modern world system, for example, need financial institutions that make decisions based on sound financial principles, thus the more inflexible coordination of the economy for long-term development (as done by MITI in Japan) must give way to policies that give firms the necessary independence to compete, and fail if they are inefficient. These types of reform are what almost all observers call for in Japan, but they are still blocked by the old ministry elite (Kerbo and McKinstry, 1995). In the case of Thailand, we have argued, the problem has been the hard state, which performed rather well in the first stages of Thai economic development but was then captured by self-serving politicians, who have increased their power since the later years of the 1980s.

CONCLUSION

Moving from dominance by the elites of the capitalist development state (the hard state), which was once necessary for development but now a hindrance, is of course, no simple task. It is perhaps comforting to suggest that such a task seems less difficult than removing the dominance of an old Stalinist state, but still the task seems daunting, as the Japanese have discovered in recent years. And following our Weberian qualitative analysis, requiring us to understand how unique combinations of historical forces and traditions have shaped each nation, we must suggest that there is no simple method of changing from an old capitalist development state that has outlived its usefulness. Each nation must struggle to find its own solutions while keeping in mind that many elements of the capitalist development state have outlived their usefulness.

One set of forces stimulating change towards less corrupt and more transparent governmental institutions in Asian nations today, ironically, consists of the IMF, the World Bank and the global capital markets, said by many to have brought about the Asian economic crisis in the first place. This is ironic because the IMF and the World Bank have been blamed for (and now admit that) many of the policies in developing nations have done more harm than good. As we noted earlier in this chapter, it was the US government's push for financial institutions to be opened to US investment in developing nations in Asia that stimulated the economic crisis. However, in order to receive IMF loans and entice global capital markets to return to Asia, these nations are being pressured to reform both their financial institutions and any government regulations that are seen as blocking their competitiveness. These are the same financial institutions that are protected by the old elites of the capitalist development state that have often outlived their usefulness. Because of the damage caused by these international capitalist institutions in the past, one can understand the reluctance of Asian nations to trust their policies at present. A realistic understanding of the nature of the East Asian development model, along with its merits and flaws, however, seems to suggest that these international financial institutions can now lead the pressure for reform that will move Asian nations to a dominant economic position in the twenty-first century.

References

Ahuja, Vinod, Benu Bidani, Francisco Ferreira and Michael Walton (1997) *Everyone's miracle?: Assessing Poverty and Inequality in Southeast Asia* (Washington, DC: World Bank).

Akin Rabibhadana (1993) *Social Inequality: A Source of Conflict in the Future?* (Bangkok: Development Research Institute).

Akin Rabibhadana (1996) *The Organization of Thai Society in the early Bangkok Period, 1782–1873* (Bangkok: Amarin Printing).

Anek Laothamatas (1996) 'A Tale of Two Democracies: Conflicting Perceptions of Elections and Democracy in Thailand', in R. H. Taylor (ed.), *The Politics of Elections in Southeast Asia* (Washington, DC: Woodrow Wilson Center Press and Cambridge University Press), pp. 201–23.

Barrett, Richard E. and Soomi Chin (1987) 'Export-oriented industrializing states in the capitalist world system: similarities and differences', in Frederic C. Deyo (ed.), *The Political Economy of East Asian Industrialization* (Ithaca, NY: Cornell University Press), pp. 23–43.

Barrett, Richard and Martin King Whyte (1982) 'Dependency Theory and Taiwan: Analysis of a Deviant Case', *American Journal of Sociology*, vol. 87, pp. 1064–89.

Bello, Walden, Shea Cunningham and Li Kheng Poh (1998) *A Siamese Tragedy: Development and Disintegration in Modern Thailand* (London: Zed Books).

Bornschier, Volker and Christopher Chase-Dunn (1985) *Transnational Corporations and Underdevelopment* (New York: Praeger).

Bornschier, Volker and Thank-Huyen Ballmer-Cao (1979) 'Income Inequality: A Cross-National Study of the Relationships Between MNC-Penetration, Dimensions of the Power Structure and Income Distribution', *American Sociological Review*, vol. 44, pp. 487–506.

Bornschier, Volker, Christopher Chase-Dunn and Richard Rubinson (1978) 'Cross-National Evidence of the Effects of Foreign Investment and Aid on Economic Growth and Inequality: A Survey of Findings and a Reanalysis', *American Journal of Sociology*, vol. 84, pp. 651–83.

Chan, Steve (1993) *East Asian Dynamism: Growth, Order, and Security in the Pacific Region* (Boulder, CO: Westview Press).

Chase-Dunn, Christopher (1975) 'The Effects of International Economic Dependence on Development and Inequality: A Cross-National Study', *American Sociological Review*, vol. 40, pp. 720–38.

Chase-Dunn, Christopher (1989) *Global Formation: Structures of the World-Economy* (Oxford: Oxford University Press).

Chirot, Daniel (1977) *Social Change in the Twentieth Century* (New York: Harcourt Brace Jovanovich).

Chirot, Daniel (1986) *Social Change in the Modern Era* (New York: Harcourt Brace Jovanovich).

Christensen, Scott and Ammar Siamwalla (1993) *Beyond Patronage: Tasks for the Thai State* (Bangkok: Thailand Development Research Institute).

Deyo, Frederic C. (1987) 'Coalitions, institutions and linkage sequencing – toward a strategic capacity model of East Asian development', in Frederic C. Deyo (ed.), *The Political Economy of East Asian Industrialization* (Ithaca, NY: Cornell University Press), pp. 227–47.

Dixon, Chris (1999) *The Thai Economy: Uneven Development and Internationalization* (London: Routledge).

Doner, Richard F. and Ansil Ramsay (1999) 'Thailand: From Economic Miracle to Economic Crisis', in Karl D. Jackson (ed.), *Asian Contagion: The Causes and Consequences of a Financial Crisis* (Boulder, CO: Westview), pp. 171–207.

Dore, Ronald (1987) *Taking Japan Seriously* (Palo Alto, CA: Stanford University Press).

Embree, J. F. (1950) 'Thailand: A "Loosely Structured" Social System', *American Anthropologist*, vol. 52, pp. 181–93.

Falkus, Malcolm (1995) 'Thai Industrialization: an Overview', in Mehdi Krongkaew (ed.), *Thailand's Industrialization and its Consequences* (New York: St. Martin's Press), pp. 13–32.

Fallows, James (1994) *Looking at the Sun: The Rise of the New East Asian Economic and Political System* (New York: Pantheon).

Frank, Andre Gunder (1967) *Capitalism and Underdevelopment in Latin America* (New York: Monthly Review Press).

Frank, Andre Gunder (1975) *On Capitalist Underdevelopment* (Bombay: Oxford University Press).

Frank, Andre Gunder (1978) *Dependent Accumulation and Underdevelopment* (New York: Monthly Review Press).

Frank, Andre Gunder (1998) *ReOrient: Global Economy in the Asian Age* (Berkeley, CA: University of California Press).

Girling, John L. S. (1981) *Thailand: Society and Politics* (Ithaca, NY: Cornell University Press).

Girling, John L. (1996) *Interpreting Development: Capitalism, Democracy, and the Middle Class in Thailand* (Ithaca, NY: Cornell Southeast Asia Program Publications).

Golzio, Karl Heinz (1985) 'Max Weber on Japan: The Role of the Government and the Buddhist Sects', in Andreas E. Buss (ed.), *Max Weber in Asian Studies* (Leiden, Netherlands: E. J. Brill), pp. 90–101.

Hampden-Turner, Charles and Alfons Trompenaars (1993) *The Seven Cultures of Capitalism* (New York: Doubleday).

Hewison, Kevin (1997) 'Thailand: Capitalist Development and the State', in Garry Rodan, Kevin Hewison and Richard Robison (eds), *The Political Economy of Southeast Asia: an Introduction* (Australia: Oxford University Press), pp. 93–120.

Hill, Hal (1994) 'ASEAN Economic Development: An Analytical Survey – The State of the Field', *Journal of Asian Studies,* vol. 53, pp. 832–66.

Hofstede, Geert (1991) *Cultures and Organization: Software of the Mind* (New York: McGraw-Hill).

Johnson, Chalmers (1982) MITI and the Japanese Miracle (Stanford, CA: Stanford University Press).

Kerbo, Harold R. (1996) *Social Stratification and Inequality: Class Conflict in Historical and Comparative Perspective*, 3rd edn (New York: McGraw-Hill).

Kerbo, Harold R. (2000) *Social Stratification and Inequality: Class Conflict in Historical, Global, and Comparative Perspective*, 4th edn (New York: McGraw-Hill).

Kerbo, Harold R. and John McKinstry (1995) *Who Rules Japan?: The Inner Circles of Economic and Political Power* (Westport, CT: Greenwood/Praeger).

Kerbo, Harold R. and Robert Slagter (1996) 'Japanese and American Corporations in Thailand: Work Organization, Employee Relations, and Cultural Contrast', unpublished manuscript.

Keyes, Charles F. (1989) *Thailand: Buddhist Kingdom as Modern Nation-State* (Boulder, CO: Westview Press).

Kim, Eun Nee (1997) *Big Business, Strong State: Collusion and Conflict in South Korean Development, 1960–1990* (Albany, NY: State University of New York Press).

Kim, Young C. (ed.) (1995) *The Southeast Asian Miracle* (New Brunswick, Transaction Publishers).

Koh, B. C. (1989) *Japan's Administrative Elite* (Berkeley, CA: University of California Press).

Komin, Suntaree (1989) *Social Dimensions of Industrialization in Thailand* (Bangkok: National Institute of Development Administration).

Komin, Suntaree (1991) *Psychology of the Thai People: Values and Behavior Patterns* (Bangkok: National Institute of Development Administration).

Komin, Suntaree (1995) 'Changes in Social Values in the Thai Society and Economy: a Post-Industrialization Scenario', in Mehdi Krongkaew (ed.), *Thailand's Industrialization and its Consequences* (New York: St. Martin's Press), pp. 251–66.

Kulick, Elliot and Dick Wilson (1996) *Time for Thailand: Profile of a New Success* (Bangkok: White Lotus).

Ladd, Everett and Karlyn H. Bowman (1998) *Attitudes Toward Economic Inequality* (Washington, DC: American Enterprise Institute).

List, Friedrich (1983) *The Natural System of Political Economy* (London: Frank Cass).

MacIntyre, Andrew (1998) 'Political Institutions and the Economic Crisis in Thailand and Indonesia', *ASEAN Economic Bulletin*, vol. 15, pp. 362–72.

Minear, Richard (1980) 'Orientalism and the Study of Japan', *Journal of Asian Studies*, vol. 30, pp. 507–17.

Mishel, Lawrence, Jared Bernstein and John Schmitt (1999) *The State of Working America, 1998–99* (Ithaca, NY: Cornell University Press).

Mouer, Ross and Yoshio Sugimoto (1985) *Images of the Japanese* (New York: Routledge & Kegan Paul).

Mulder, Neils (1992) *Inside Thai Society: An Interpretation of Everyday Life*, 4th edn (Bangkok: Editions Duang Kamol).

Mulder, Neils (1997) *Thai Images: The Culture of the Public World* (Chiang Mai, Thailand: Silkworm Press).

Muscat, Robert J. (1994) *The Fifth Tiger: A Study of Thai Development* (Armonk, NY: M. E. Sharpe).

Myrdal, Gunnar (1968) *Asian Drama: An Inquiry into The Poverty of Nations* (New York: Pantheon).

Myrdal, Gunnar (1970) *The Challenge of World Poverty* (New York: Pantheon).

Ockey, James (1996) 'Thai Society and Patterns of Political Leadership', *Asian Survey*, vol. 36, pp. 345–60.

Osborne, Milton (1995) *Southeast Asia: An Introductory History*, 6th edn (Australia: Allen and Unwin).

Pasuk Phongpaichit and Chris Baker (1997) *Thailand: Economy and Politics* (Kuala Lumpur: Oxford University Press).

Pasuk Phongpaichit and Chris Baker (1998) *Thailand's Boom and Bust* (Chiang Mai, Thailand: Silkworm Books).

Phillips, H. P. (1993) *The Integrative Art of Modern Thailand* (Washington: University of Washington Press).

Preston, Peter W. (1998) 'Reading the Asian Crisis: History, Culture and Institutional Truths', *Contemporary Southeast Asia*, vol. 20, pp. 241–60.

Pye, Lucien W. (1985) *Asian Power and Politics: The Cultural Dimensions of Authority* (Cambridge, Mass.: Harvard University Press).

Raphael, James H. and Thomas P. Rohlen (1998) 'How Many Models of Japanese Growth Do We Want or Need', in Henry S. Rowen (ed.), *Behind East Asian Growth: the Political and Social Foundations of Prosperity* (London: Routledge), pp. 265–96.

Rapley, John (1996) *Understanding Development: Theory and Practice in the Developing World* (Boulder, CO: Lynn Rienner).

Robertson, Philip S. Jr (1996) 'The Rise of the Rural Network Politician: Will Thailand's New Elite Endure?', *Asian Survey*, vol. 36, no. 9, pp. 924–41.

Rokeach, M. (1979) 'Change and Stability on American Value Systems, 1968–71', in M. Rokeach (ed.), *Understanding Human Values: Individual and Societal* (New York, The Free Press).

Rostow, Walter W. (1962) *The Stages of Economic Growth: A Non-Communist Manifesto* (Cambridge: Cambridge University Press).

Rostow, Walter W. (1975) *How It All Began: Origins of the Modern Economy* (New York: McGraw-Hill).

Rowen, Henry S. (1998) 'What Are the Lessons', in Henry S. Rowen (ed.), *Behind East Asian Growth: the Political and Social Foundations of Prosperity* (London: Routledge), pp. 241–8.

Rubinson, Richard (1976) 'The World Economy and the Distribution of Income Within States: A Cross-National Study', *American Sociological Review*, vol. 41, pp. 638–59.

Schlesinger, Jacob M. (1998) 'Shadow Shoguns: The Origins and Crisis of Japan, Inc.', *The Washington Quarterly*, vol. 21, pp. 135–48.

Skocpol, Theda (1979) *States and Social Revolutions: A Comparative Analysis of France, Russia and China* (New York: Cambridge University Press).

Slagter, Robert and Harold Kerbo (2000) *Modern Thailand: A Volume in the Comparative Societies Series* (New York: McGraw-Hill).

Smeeding, Timothy M., Michael O'Higgins and Lee Rainwater (1990) *Poverty, Inequality, and Income Distribution in Comparative Perspective: the Luxembourg Income Study* (Washington, DC: Urban Institute Press).

Smith, Patrick (1997) *Japan: A Reinterpretation* (New York: Pantheon).

Somrudee Nicro (1993) 'Thailand's NIC Democracy: Studying From General Elections', *Pacific Affairs*, vol. 66, pp. 167–82.

van Wolferen, Karl (1999) 'The Global Conceptual Crisis', *New Perspectives Quarterly*, vol. 16, pp. 17–26.

Verba, Sidney (1987) *Elites and the Idea of Equality* (Cambridge, Mass.: Harvard University Press).

Vogel, Ezra (1991) *The Four Little Dragons: The Spread of Industrialization in East Asia* (Cambridge, Mass.: Harvard University Press).

Wallerstein, Immanual (1974) *The Modern World System: Capitalist Agriculture and the Origins of the European World-Economy in the 16th Century* (New York: Academic Press).

Wallerstein, Immanual (1980) *The Modern World System II: Mercantilism and the Consolidation of the European World-Economy, 1600–1750.* (New York: Academic Press).

Wallerstein, Immanual (1989) *The Modern World System III: The Second Era of Great Expansion of the Capitalist World-Economy, 1730–1840s* (New York: Academic Press).

Weber, Max (1946) *From Max Weber: Essays in Sociology*, ed. H. H. Gerth and C. Wright Mills (New York: Oxford University Press).

Wyatt, David K. (1984) *Thailand: A Short History* (New Heaven, CT: Yale University Press).

Yoshihara, Kunio (1999) *Building a Prosperous Southeast Asia: from Ersatz to Echt Capitalism* (Richmond, Surrey: Curzon Press).

7 A Reflection on the East Asian Development Model: Comparison of the South Korean and Taiwanese Experiences

Phillip Hookon Park

INTRODUCTION

Since the 1970s the economic development of East Asia has increasingly attracted the attention of development economists and those interested in development studies. East Asia's newly industrialised economies (NIEs) – Singapore, Hong Kong, Taiwan and South Korea – grew at annual rate of 9 per cent during the 1971–80 period and 8.3 per cent from 1981–90, while the world economy grew at the average rate of 2.9 per cent from 1981–90. As well as geographical proximity, the East Asian NIEs share some common characteristics in terms of economic development, such as export-oriented industrialisation, state guidance and involvement in economic development and high investment in human capital formation. Because Singapore and Hong Kong are city states, their economic development can hardly serve as a model for other developing countries. Many developing countries, including those in Southeast Asia (the so called ASEAN-4: Indonesia, Malaysia, Thailand and the Philippines), tried to emulate Taiwan and South Korea, and experienced tremendous success until 1996. The development success of the East and Southeast Asian countries seemed to confirm the validity of the East Asian model.

However in the last quarter of 1997 financial crisis spread through Asia and undermined the economic performance and sometimes the political stability of some of the East and Southeast Asian countries. One of the hardest hit was South Korea. As a result it experiencied negative growth for the first time in 20 years; moreover in a just six months the unemployment rate doubled from 3 per cent to 7 per cent while per capita GNP shrank by more than 40 per cent. Observing this crisis, some scholars and significant figures such as the chairman of US Federal Reserve Board, Alan Greenspan, commented that the East Asian model could no longer be considered valid and declared the US-style free market system triumphant. On the other hand the contagion did not spread to Taiwan, another adherent of the East Asian model. Although Taiwanese economic growth fell from 8 per cent in 1997 to 5.6 per cent in 1998, its economy continues to show robustness and flexibility in the eyes of most observers.

The aim of this chapter is to analyse and compare the economic development of the East Asian model economies of South Korea and Taiwan from the 1960s to 1997. Until 1997, both countries were heralded as exemplars of the East Asian model. Today South Korea is in deep economic crisis, but to date Taiwan has not only avoided the East Asian financial contagion, but has also continued to grow at a respectable rate. This chapter will attempt to identify and explain this difference. In particular the following questions will be addressed:

- How did the economic policies of and management in South Korea and Taiwan differ?
- How can a star performer such as South Korea end up in a crisis of such magnitude and severity as the one that occurred in 1997?
- How has Taiwan escaped the financial contagion in East Asia and managed to grow at a respectable rate?
- What role did reforms of the financial sector and greater capital market integration play in bringing about the crisis in South Korea?

This chapter will also attempt to draw lessons from the recent economic experience of South Korea and Taiwan to reevaluate the highly acclaimed East Asian model. In this respect the questions of interest are as follows. What are the main features of the East Asian model? Is the model itself in crisis or is there an alternative explanation for the general crisis in East and Southeast Asian countries? What economic policies are consistent with and complementary to the model? In particular, what lesson can be drawn from these countries' experiences with reforms (for example financial reforms), especially in the highly globalised trade and investment regimes?

THE EAST ASIAN DEVELOPMENT MODEL

When we consider South Korea's and Taiwan's development experiences, three important characteristics of the East Asian development model stand out.

First of all the state plays an important and sometimes decisive role in each country's economic development. In Johnson's words, they are developmental states characterised by three features of the developmental state (Johnson, 1987). First, economic development is the foremost priority of state action. The state emphasises economic development as the principal goal and does not hesitate to intervene in an otherwise market-dominated economy in pursuit of this goal. Second, since the developmental state is a capitalist state it is firmly committed to private property and the market. The market, however, is closely governed by state managers who formulate strategic industrial policy to promote development. Third, within the state bureaucracy pilot agencies (such as the Ministry of International Trade and Industry, MITI, in Japan) play a key role in strategic policy formulation and implementation. Such agencies are given sufficient scope to take initiatives and operate effectively, and are staffed by the best available managerial talent in the state bureaucracy (So and Chu, 1995). Fourth, as a recent World Bank study indicates, these countries have sound 'policy fundamentals', which allow rapid capital accumulation, aggressive investment in human capital and improvement in factor productivity. All of these contribute to rapid growth within a framework of sound macroeconomic management (World Bank, 1993). Fifth, East Asian governments are relatively autonomous and strong *vis-à-vis* local interest groups. The state allows a high degree of bureaucratic autonomy in the implementation of development policies (Onis, 1991).

These are the salient features of the 'East Asian model' and form the core of the experiences of South Korea and Taiwan. However these common features do not mean that the two countries have implemented identical policies. For instance economic policy in South Korea has emphasised growth while macroeconomic stability is given higher priority in Taiwan. Big business conglomerates, known as *chaebol*, dominate the South Korean economy whereas small- and medium-sized firms play a central role in the Taiwanese economy. These differences are important in explaining the different outcomes in the late 1990s.

SOUTH KOREA'S DEVELOPMENT STRATEGY

South Korea's first concrete economic development strategy was launched when Park Chung Hee assumed political power following the coup *d'etát* in 1961 and inaugurated the first five year plan in 1962. Before Park the South Korean government was led by the first president, Rhee Syungman, who lacked a clear vision of economic development, largely because he was preoccupied with taking over North Korea by force. During the period directly after the Korean War, the South Korean economy was heavily dependent on US aid. For instance during Rhee's presidency (1953–60)

South Korea received $2.3 billion in aid (approximately two thirds of South Korea's total imports), with 85 per cent coming from the USA. In the late 1950s US. economic aid to South Korea accounted for over 10 per cent of South Korea's GNP (Lie, 1998). The Rhee government was characterised by corruption and an inability to implement any viable economic policy. In April 1960 Rhee was ousted by a student-led popular uprising and replaced by Chang Myun. Well aware of the causes of Rhee's downfall, Chang made economic development the number one priority of the new government and vowed to clean up corruption within the government. However, owing to the lack of both external support and internal unity, Chang's economic development plan never materialised. Chang's second republic was short-lived – it only lasted about 10 months and was toppled by a military coup, led by Park and a group of graduates from the Korean Military Academy.

Park Chung Hee's Economic Development Strategy (1962–79)

Unlike his two predecessors, Park had a concrete economic development objective. His principal goal was to establish a self-reliant economy. Surprisingly his first five year plan did not include export-oriented industrialisation; it was essentially an extension of the Chang regime's five-year plan, which had emphasised import-substitution industrialisation (Lie, 1998). On the other hand Park was keenly aware of Japan's development success and was determined to adopt the Japanese model. A look at Park's background makes clear his reason for wishing to adopt this model. After graduating from teacher training school in Kyungsang province Park gained admission to the Japanese imperial military academy in Manchuria. He graduated top of his class and was sent to Tokyo for further training at the Tokyo Military Academy. He was then sent back to Manchuria and served in the Japanese imperial army until Japan surrendered to the Allied forces in 1945.

Manchuria was a testing ground for a wartime economy under military rule. The Japanese military ran the Manchurian economy according to a model developed in Japan, with a touch of military regimentation. The Japanese model was essentially in line with the model in which the state directs and utilises enterprises to serve national economic development by controlling finance. In the context of imperial Japan, the government was directly involved in planning and directing economic plans and distributing income. Park's exposure to the Japanese state's involvement in postwar economic development, especially in heavy industry, came to have a profound impact on Korea (Clifford, 1998).

When Park assumed the political leadership of South Korea in 1961 he put into practice what he had learned during the Manchurian years. First he set up an Economic Planning Board (EPB) with wide powers to draft over-all economic planning, control the national budget and implement plans. The role of the Ministry of Commerce and Industry (MCI, later the Ministry of Trade and Industry, or MTI) was further strengthened. The MTI was responsible for export promotion, import control, industrial development plans, investment application and trade licensing (Lansberg-Hart, 1993). Likewise the role of the Ministry of Finance (MoF), which was responsible for regulating and supervising all domestic and foreign financial institutions, was greatly strengthened.

Park's economic development strategy changed from import substitution to export orientation as the international environment became favourable for South Korean exports. There were two important external developments that induced the government to turn to export oriented industrialisation (EOI). First, South Korea normalised diplomatic relations with Japan in 1965, despite opposition from the South Korean public. Many South Koreans, remembering the brutal years of the Japanese colonial period and fearing renewed dominance by Japan, protested against the normalisation of relations. Nevertheless Park was determined to proceed and ruthlessly repressed the protesters. Diplomatic normalisation was significant to the South Korean economy for a couple of reasons. First, it received a quick infusion of capital ($800 million) from Japan,[1] which compensated for the fall in economic aid from the USA, and gained access to Japanese technology and capital. South Korean enterprises took over the production of some Japanese products and machinery used for lower value-added and labour-intensive production as Japanese enterprises moved into higher value-added and more capital-intensive production.

Second, South Korea's involvement in Vietnam provided a spur to light industry and exports. During the Vietnam War (1965–73), South Korea earned over $2 billion from a combination of military and civilian activities in Vietnam and increased its exports to Vietnam. Utilising its links with the USA during the war,[2] South Korea exported cement, fertilisers, petroleum products and consumer items such as textiles, shoes and plywood. The receipts from this represented approximately 19 per cent of South Korea's total foreign exchange earnings over the period.

By following Japanese companies in the product cycle and seizing business opportunities during the Vietnam War, South Korea changed its development strategy from import substitution to an export drive. More importantly, after a period of dormancy the industrialisation process took off. As can be seen Table 7.1, the average annual GNP growth rate during this period was 9.5 per cent and the average annual export growth

Table 7.1   GNP and Export growth rate, South Korea,
1962–80 (per cent)

	GNP growth rate	Export growth rate
1962	2.2	31.7
1963	9.1	61.1
1964	9.6	37.9
1965	5.8	45.8
1966	12.7	42.9
1967	6.6	34.0
1968	11.3	45.1
1969	13.8	35.4
1970	7.6	34.0
1971	8.8	28.5
1972	5.7	47.9
1973	14.1	95.9
1974	7.7	37.5
1975	6.9	10.8
1976	14.1	56.2
1977	12.7	28.6
1978	9.7	26.5
1979	6.5	15.7
1980	−5.2	17.1

Source: Bank of Korea.

rate was 44.4 per cent. Manufactured exports rose from 8 per cent of final demand in 1963 to 22 per cent in 1966 and 40.1 per cent in 1973. Employment in the production of goods for export accordingly rose from 6.4 per cent of total manufacturing employment in 1963 to 16.5 per cent in 1966 and 34.5 per cent in 1973 (Song, 1990). Park used the EPB and other state bureaucracies such as the MTI and MoF to shape and dictate the economic development process. Consequently the size and influence of these economic bureaucracies grew and strengthened.

State intervention was particularly pronounced in the financial sector. The government owned and controlled all five commercial banks, including the Bank of Korea (the central bank), all six special banks and two of the country's three major non-bank financial institutions. The state also introduced the exceedingly stringent Foreign Capital Inducement Law in 1962 to control foreign capital flows and access to foreign capital by the private sector. According to this law, all foreign loans had to be guaranteed by the government. Moreover the law forbade all overseas transfers of US$1 million or more that had not been approved by the government. By controlling finance, the state could exercise complete dominance over the business sector. Businesses could turn to the kerb market for capital, but this was not an attractive option as the interest rate in that market was exorbitantly high.[3] The implication was obvious; enterprises' business activities were moulded and directed by the state. Those firms that followed the directions of the state were rewarded with much-needed capital while those that were not willing to operate within the boundaries of the state's plan were abandoned to the kerb market (Lansberg-Hart 1993).

From 1965 economic policy in South Korea was dominated by the growth-first goal and the maxim was dynamic rather than static efficiency; this goal inspired 'supply side' intervention by means of planning, export promotion measures, credit allocation, control of access to foreign exchange, and industrial policy. What was achieved was mainly due to the greater role of state bureaucracies such as the EPB and MoF and the nationalisation of the banking system. South Korea's growth-first approach seemed to be working as the economy grew at an average rate of 9 per cent during the 1965–72 period. However the strategy also had a number of grave consequences.

First, in order to induce firms to concentrate on growth, the state had to adopt a low interest rate policy. However the holding of interest rates below their equilibrium level created excess demand for investable funds and the banks were forced to ration credit. In general, credit rationing favoured large firms – the established customers. The problem was exacerbated by the granting of concessionary loans by the state to favoured companies that complied with state policies and plans. Nonetheless these firms were not necessarily the ones that earned the highest rate of return on their investments. Hence credit rationing by government policy crowded out some higher-return investments – this would have been avoided if the interest rates had been allowed to perform their allocative function in the credit market. Moreover, credit rationing also provided the breeding ground for crony capitalism.

Second, the low interest policy generated excess demand for capital, resulting in high inflation. There were two negative consequences of this. First, inflation reduced the real value of debt for both debtor and creditor, which in effect redistributed real wealth from creditors to debtors. In South Korea, this kind of wealth redistribution always favoured big business enterprises over small and medium-sized enterprises as the former were the recipients of most concessionary and special loans.

Third, domestic savings were discouraged in this high-inflation environment as people had less incentive to keep their money in the bank. As a result the government had to rely on foreign borrowing to finance its industrialisation drive. This problem worsened as the state pursued its growth-first

Table 7.2   Inflation and Saving Rates,
South Korea, 1961–72

	Inflation Rate in CPI	Household Savings
1961	6.1	−0.97
1963	20.0	3.45
1964	29.8	0.18
1965	14.7	4.15
1966	11.2	1.38
1967	10.8	3.06
1968	10.4	7.45
1969	12.4	3.51
1970	16.2	3.17
1971	13.5	5.70
1972	11.5	8.98

Source: Bank of Korea.

strategy (Table 7.2). Fourth, its heavy reliance on foreign borrowing made South Korea vulnerable to external shocks, and as it was pursuing an export-oriented strategy its vulnerability to external shocks was doubled. It needed to earn enough foreign currency through trade to service its debts. If the external environment had become unfavourable (for instance if the environment in the foreign markets had become sour or if interest rates had risen suddenly due to a supply shock, such as an oil crisis), South Korea's industrialisation drive would have been jeopardised or halted.

South Korea's industrialisation drive entered its second stage in 1972. The third five-year plan (1972–76) was a watershed in the country's economic development. Park's first regime was faced with internal and external problems[4] and Park's response was to strengthen his authoritarian rule by promulgating the new Yushin Constitution[5] in 1972 and launching the Heavy Chemical Industrialisation (HCI) Plan. The HCI Plan, known as the 'Big Push', hardly came as a surprise as Park's aim from the beginning had been to develop a self-reliant economy. The HCI Plan called for the construction of heavy and capital-intensive industries such as iron and steel, shipbuilding, machinery, electronics and petrochemicals. Park hoped to reduce imports and produce higher-value-added exports to solve the country's balance of payments problems and achieve self-sufficiency. The plan was also motivated by the need to build up a defence industry as Park increasingly doubted the USA's commitment to defend South Korea.

The HCI Plan represented a strengthening of the state's intervention in the economy. A special Heavy and Chemical Industry Committee was created and took priority over the rest of the governmental institutions, bypassing the EPB and giving orders directly to the MoF and MCI (Clifford, 1998). The government once again gave concessionary loans and business licences to companies that were supportive of its plan. Businesses were induced to invest in heavy industry, which required about US$10 billion in investments, and big companies became even bigger. The HCI Plan laid the foundation for the emergence of gigantic conglomerates known as *chaebol*. The combined net sales of the top 10 *chaebol* rose from 15.1 per cent of GNP in 1974 to 30.1 per cent in 1978 and 55.7 per cent in 1981 (Song, 1990).

The state's growth-first strategy did not change; rather it was strengthened and given greater emphasis. For instance when the first oil shock hit the world economy and raised oil prices four fold, the general response in other countries was to slam the brakes on monetary policy in order to control inflation. South Korea, interested in growth only, did nothing about it. Domestic prices shot up 40 per cent in 1974 as M1 increased by 30 per cent. Consequently real GNP rose from an annual average of 9 per cent in the early 1970s to an average 10.8 per cent from 1975 to 1979 (Amsden, 1989).

In order to finance the ambitious HCI Plan the government borrowed heavily from foreign countries. Foreign borrowing was not the only option available – foreign direct investment (FDI) could have been utilised to finance part of the plan, but the government preferred foreign borrowing over foreign investment because it wanted to maintain domestic ownership of these industries. Foreign investment was not to play a significant role in financing economic development in South Korea until the 1990s. For instance foreign loans during the third five year plan (1973–76) amounted to US$5432.8 million whereas total foreign direct investment was a mere $556 million, only about 10 per cent of total foreign loans during the period. As South Korea insisted on foreign borrowing its foreign debt rapidly increased. In 1962 the total foreign debt was $157 million but it increased to $392 million in 1966 (at the end of the first five year plan), $2922 million in 1971 (at the end of the second five year plan), $10 533 million in 1976 (at the end of the third five year plan) and $20 500 million in 1979, the year in which Park was assassinated. Moreover, as the state encouraged businesses to borrow and expand, the debt–equity ratio (the sum of fixed and current liabilities expressed as a percentage of the firm's net worth) increased dramatically. By the end of 1979 the debt–equity ratio in manufacturing in South Korea had reached 488 per cent, compared with 167 per cent in Taiwan and 110 per cent in the USA (Scitovsky, 1986).

In sum the South Korean growth-first strategy during Park's tenure (1962–79) involved borrowing from abroad, using the proceeds to pay for oil and invest in new industrial plants, and using the plants to increase exports and foreign-exchange earnings. While South Korea did achieve its economic objective – the average annual GNP growth rate over the 18-year period was 9 per cent – domestic expansion created an inflationary pressure that negatively affected domestic savings. Thus the government had to borrow even more heavily from abroad to offset the shortage in domestic funds. The practice of foreign borrowing was intensified by the government's decision to limit direct foreign investment. With \$20.1 billion in outstanding debt by the end of 1979, South Korea ranked among the largest foreign borrowers in the world, trailing only Argentina, Brazil and Mexico. The government's utilisation of credit allocation, the government-controlled financial system, and the bolstering of prioritised and privileged industries did serve to achieve the goal of rapid growth, but it also helped to create giant conglomerates, which by the end of the 1970s had become too big to fail. Against this backdrop, South Korea entered a new political era.

Economic Policy During the Chun and Roh Regimes (1981–91)

Chun Doo Hwan seized political power in 1980 by means of a military coup and a bloody crack-down on a people's uprising in Kwangju. Unlike Park, Chun had neither a clear vision nor a concrete plan for economic development when he took power. However it was clear to him that if he squandered Park's legacy of economic growth he would not survive. Hence, he listened to the technocrats, who wished to restructure the high-growth, high-inflation economy into a more rational and stable one. The technocrats in the early Chun regime had two important goals: price stability by cutting the government deficit, limiting monetary growth and slowing wage hikes; and market liberalisation by selectively introducing measures to privatise and deregulate the national commercial banks and anti-*chaebol* measures to limit and check the *chaebol's* economic power.

The technocrats' first objective – price stability – was maintained throughout this period. Except in 1981, the inflation rate was kept under 10 per cent from 1981–91 (Table 7.3). Their second objective – market liberalisation – was only partially accomplished. In 1981 the government introduced a programme that included the privatisation and deregulation of the five national commercial banks, the ten provincial banks and all non-bank financial institutions. By the end of 1983 all five national banks and all financial institutions had been privatised. However privatisation

Table 7.3   GNP growth and inflation,
South Korea, 1981–91 (per cent)

	Real GNP Growth	Rate of Inflation, CPI
1981	6.62	11.3
1982	5.6	7.3
1983	11.9	3.4
1984	8.4	2.3
1985	7.0	2.5
1986	12.9	2.8
1987	12.8	3.0
1988	12.4	7.1
1989	6.8	5.7
1990	9.0	9.5
1991	8.4	9.7

Source: Bank of Korea.

and deregulation did not mean that the government had relinquished all power to the private sector; the state continued to influence the financial sector by reserving the right to appoint the management of the banks, set interest rates and loan allocation guidelines, and mandate policy loans. *De facto* the banking sector remained a government organ. Because the state saw control of the financial system as the most effective tool with which to discipline businesses, it constantly intervened in that sector. However this created problems. For instance when the economy slowed down in 1985 (the growth rate dropped from 11.9 per cent in 1983 to 8.4 per cent in 1984 and 7.0 per cent in 1985), the state-controlled Bank of Korea cut its interest rate from 6 per cent to 3 per cent and pumped 300 billion won in emergency low-interest loans to the banks in order to relieve the burden of their non-performing loans (Bae, 1995).

There were other notable changes. The majority of non-bank financial institutions came under the control of the *chaebol*. Although the government took a number of preventive steps, such as putting an 8 per cent ceiling on the ownership of shares of commercial banks and a 15 per cent ceiling on the ownership of provincial banks (ibid.), the *chaebol* found ways of gaining control over the newly privatised banks. By the end of 1989 the *chaebol* owned 25–35 per cent of the shares of the commercial banks and controlled about 63 per cent of the funds of security companies. The technocrats' hope of limiting the power of the *chaebol* failed miserably. Instead the privatisation and deregulation measures served to increase the *chaebol's* power to the point where they could challenge the influence of the government in the financial sector. The erosion of state power occurred not only because of the *chaebol's* challenge, but also because the South Korean state evolved in such a way that it came to resemble a racketeering state rather than a developmental one.

Economic development had not been on Chun's agenda when he took power and he quickly became tired of disciplining businesses – he became more interested in enriching himself, his family and his supporters by taking advantage of state–*chaebol* relations. During Chun's seven-year tenure as president he and his associates forced businesses to pay political contributions or quasi–taxes. The latter were estimated to range from 0.48 per cent to 0.85 per cent of the total annual sales of South Korean companies. In 1989 the average corporation spent 1.4 billion won (about $2 million) on quasi-taxes. This amount did not include unreported donations to Chun and his associates, which a conservative estimate placed at $4–5 billion over the eight years of his tenure (Clifford, 1998). Roh Tae Woo, who succeeded Chun, embezzled about the same amount of money while he was president.

Between 1986 and 1989, for the first time since long-term economic planning began in 1962 South Korea generated a large trade and current account surplus.[6] The economy grew at a phenomenal rate: 12.9 per cent in 1986, 12.8 per cent in 1987 and 12.4 per cent in 1988. This unparalleled economic boom was largely due to external factors. As the USA's and Western European countries' trade imbalance with Japan continued to deteriorate, five major industrial nations agreed artificially to reduce the strength of the US dollar in the September 1985 Plaza Accord (ibid.). At the same time interest rates and commodity prices, especially that of oil, were lowered. Since the won was loosely pegged to the dollar, South Korean exports became cheaper than competing Japanese exports in consumer electronics, steel, ships and cars. Moreover the cheaper oil prices and lower interest rates helped to produce a current account surplus and reduce foreign debt.

As the economy continued to grow at a record rate, South Korean businesses decided to increase their investment in new plants and production facilities. Although the government continued to loosen monetary policy after 1985, businesses wanted even more capital to take advantage of the economic boom. Concerned about inflation, the government would not allow companies to borrow capital from abroad so they increasingly turned to the stock market, which was also booming. Hence companies became more independent of the government as they became less dependent on banks for financing. Moreover South Korean companies, especially *chaebol*, started to invest abroad as domestic labour costs rose and the currency appreciated. This trend continued during Chun's and Roh's presidencies, when corrupt government had disastrous consequences. The cozy relationship between the state and businesses continued and state officials received bribes or kick-backs from businesses. Concessionary or special loans were given to those with special connections with the Blue House and the Ministry of Finance. Furthermore, since the state usually bailed out big companies in trouble, firms borrowed heavily and diversified their businesses recklessly. This practice resulted in dangerously high debt–equity ratios (Table 7.4).

In summary, the technocrats attempted to rationalise the economy by controlling monetary policy and implementing a deregulation and liberalisation programme in the financial sector in the early years of Chun's presidency. On the one hand this brought down inflation, which had been a chronic problem in South Korea. On the other hand the deregulation and liberalisation programme failed to control or limit the power of the *chaebol*. Or the contrary they became even more powerful as they were now able to influence the financial sector. Owing mainly to the 'three external lows' (low US dollar, low interest rates and low energy prices), the economy grew at a rapid rate – GNP growth averaged 9.3 per cent during the 1981–91 period. Although the government maintained a strong grip on the banking system its power eroded considerably as businesses started to rely on the stock market for financing and found new ways of avoiding the administrative guidelines. The state began to lose its autonomy as its officials, including two presidents, sought self-enrichment by accepting bribes from firms. Moreover firms utilised their cozy relationship with the state to obtain special concessions from banks and they recklessly enlarged their businesses with borrowed funds. All this put the South Korean economy in an extremely precarious position as it became highly leveraged and more vulnerable to an economic downturn (as more of the cash flow must be devoted to the interest payments) and disruptions in international capital markets.

Table 7.4   The *chaebols'* debt–equity ratio

Year/Month	Debt/Equity Ratio	
	Top Five Chaebol	*Top 30 Chaebol*
1988./12	314.8 %	239.9%
1992./3	442.2 %	361.1%

Source: Office of Bank Supervision and Examination.

Economic Crisis in 1997

Kim Young Sam's government attempted to shed the legacy of Park Chung Hee's top-down, state-led, and authoritarian development strategy and adopted the establishment of a free market system and deregulation as its major economic policy objective. As soon as Kim Young Sam assumed the presidency, he launched 'The Five Year (1993–97) Plan of New Economy'. The core of the new plan was to strengthen free market mechanisms by relaxing or repealing regulation and promoting incentive and participation. A series of economic reform measures was introduced and in May 1993, in order to promote competition among the banks, the government launched the 'Financial Sector Self-Regulation Program'. In June of the same year, the government also initiated a 'Foreign Currency and Capital Transaction Liberalization' program. In early August, in an attempt to bolster his new economic plan, Kim Young Sam announced an emergency decree outlawing the use of aliases in financial transactions. He also tried to clean up corruption by disclosing senior officials' assets; as a result, many government officials including three ministers, five vice-ministers, and the mayor of Seoul along with many others were forced to stepped down. Furthermore, the government put a few *chaebol* executives on trial for corruption. But, by the 1990s the *chaebol* had become too big and powerful to be checked by the government. They continued to dominate the South Korean economy,[7] and the fundamental pattern of corruption remains deeply ingrained in the country's political and economic culture (Clifford, 1998). Moreover, the government's attempts to deregulate, internationalise, and liberalise the economy in the context of a *chaebol* controlled economy only allowed them to take advantage of the situation. For example, the 1994 to 1996 period saw a burst of liberalisation tied to South Korea's bid for membership of the OECD. The *chaebol* and other private sector companies took this opportunity to binge on foreign borrowing. As a consequence, between 1994 and 1997 foreign debt tripled from $56.9 billion to $154.4 billion. Almost all the foreign borrowing was done by the private sector and more than half of the total debt was short term (Table 7.5).

International lenders preferred short-term lending to long-term lending because this gave them the option not to roll-over outstanding debts if they became too risky, so South Korean firms borrowed short-term funds but put them into long-term investments. This portfolio mismatch paved the way for the recent currency crisis, when foreign lenders suddenly decided not to roll-over their short-term liabilities as crises loomed in Thailand and Indonesia.

There were other factors that contributed to the South Korean financial crisis, including the problem of excess capacity or overaccumulation in the

Table 7.5   Total external liabilities, South Korea, 1993–97 (billion US dollars)

	1993	1994	1995	1996	1997*	1997
Total external debt	43.9	56.9	78.4	104.7	161.8	154.4
Medium and Long-term	24.7	26.5	33.1	43.7	72.9	86.0
Financial institutions	13.0	13.9	19.6	27.7	53.2	50.4
Private enterprises	7.9	9.0	10.5	13.6	17.6	17.6
Public sector	3.8	3.6	3.0	2.4	2.0	18.0
Short term	19.2	30.4	45.3	61.0	88.9	68.4
(% of total)	(43.7)	(53.4)	(57.7)	(58.2)	(54.9)	(44.3)
Financial institutions	11.4	19.4	29.7	39.0	63.1	43.8
Private and non-	7.8	11.0	15.6	22.0	25.8	24.6
financial sector						

*November.
Source: Bank of Korea.

East and Southeast Asia region. For example, between 1980 and 1991 Asia's share of world trade rose from 9 per cent to 15 per cent while the developed nations' share slipped from 72 per cent to 63 per cent. By 1994 more than half of all investments in developing countries was going to East and Southeast Asian countries (McNally, 1998). Private capital flows into Indonesia, Malaysia, the Philippines, South Korea and Thailand nearly quintupled between 1990 and 1996, soaring from $20 billion to $95 billion per year. The money pouring into these countries fuelled growth that was increasingly based on a pyramid-type, Ponzi-style asset market. Value went up because more money flowed in, attracting still greater capital inflows. Since assets had been purchased with borrowed funds, which had to be refinanced to support highly leveraged positions, some of the assets had to be liquidated to cover debts. As stock and property holdings were sold, panic spread. Currency flight followed as investors pulled out of these markets. In 1997 these countries experienced a net outflow of private capital of $20 billion. China's export drive, which was mainly based on cheaper labour costs, was another important factor in driving down the currency and equity markets. China's growing exports cut into markets, and regional productive capacity came to exceed the absorptive capacity of the global market.

In addition to these external factors, a main cause of the economic crisis in South Korea was its political–economic structure. The growth-first strategy, coupled with the government's preference for foreign borrowing over foreign direct investment, led to the further growth of the giant chaebol. As the chaebol's power increased and the government turned its eye to racketeering rather than development, the state's power eroded and the *chaebol* became too big to fail. Against this backdrop, the government continued to implement financial deregulation and liberalisation policies. The domestic financial deregulation process, begun in the early 1980s, neared completion in the 1990s and the country's borders were opened to short-term financial capital flows, thereby undermining the state's ability to control speculation against the won. In this deregulation process the *chaebol* began to dominate the financial sector and borrowed heavily when the government lowered the mandatory ratios on medium and long-term borrowing in 1996. When the Asian crisis erupted, there was a flight of investor capital from Asian markets and the South Korean economy was pushed to the verge of collapse as foreign banks refused to roll-over loans. Hence the crisis not stemmed only from outside factors such as overcapacity in the region or speculative attacks by hedge funds, but also from inherent problems in the South Korean economic structure. Now let us examine how Taiwan escaped the crisis.

TAIWAN'S ECONOMIC DEVELOPMENT STRATEGY

After the communist victory in mainland China in 1949, General Chiang Kai-shek moved his Kuomingtang (KMT) regime to Taipei. At first Chiang and his fellow mainlanders were not interested in the economic development of Taiwan because their primary objective was to take over the mainland. As the hope of this dimmed and US aid diminished in the 1960s,[8] Chiang turned his attention to economic development.

Taiwan's economic development strategy was quite similar to that of South Korea. In both countries, development was guided by state-led industrial policy, utilising credit allocation, regulated and differential interest rates, prioritised industries and technologies, coordination of investment plans, regulation of the labour market, high state spending on education and infrastructure, managed trade, controls over the movement of money capital into and out of the country, and regulation of inward and outward FDI (Crotty *et al.*, 1997). However there were subtle but crucial differences between the two strategies.

First of all, defeat in the mainland heavily influenced Chiang's economic policies in Taiwan. Unlike Park, who was more concerned with growth, Chiang's main concern was to control inflation and maintain stability, for he and the KMT leadership believed that runaway inflation had contributed to their loss of public support and eventual defeat at the hands of the communists. Hence in Taiwan, the Central Bank of China exerted a strong and ultraconservative influence on the economic bureaucracy (Field, 1995).

In order to maintain low inflation, the government was legislatively prevented from borrowing from the central bank. To maintain monetary stability, the government nationalised the banking system in Taiwan and took very tight control of the entire financial sector. The government's strong grip on the financial sector continued during the 1960s and 1970s. It was not until the mid 1970s that the government allowed the growth of a formal money market in short-term debt, and until 1991 private commercial banks were not allowed to operate in Taiwan, apart from a few small foreign banks and some non-bank financial institutions such as life insurance or trust and investment companies (Wang, 1998). Non-bank financial institutions such as insurance companies, trust funds and bill finance companies did not play an important role in the financial sector as they accounted for only 7 per cent of total financial claims outstanding by the late 1970s. Up to 1964 the total assets of government-owned banks were 71.3 per cent of the aggregate of all financial institutions in Taiwan. Even up to 1990 the government owned more than 50 per cent of 12 of the 16 domestic commercial banks (Liu, 1992).

The KMT government's institutionalisation of a credit-based, bank-led financial system blocked the development of security-type of financial instruments such as bonds and stocks. Furthermore, unlike their counterparts in South Korea, major banks in Taiwan were not strongly motivated to form security networks or engage in more intensive relational transactions with private firms, for three reasons: a significant proportion of most banks' loans were allocated to the government; most bank loans to the private sector were secured by collateral; and banks generally did not take equity positions in private enterprises. As a result of this tight regulation and control of the financial sector, traditional household networks became the major source of capital accumulation and security sharing. This reliance on traditional household networks for finance limited the size of Taiwanese companies to small and medium-sized firms. Because Taiwanese entrepreneurs pooled capital among themselves, family members, close relatives or intimate friends – as opposed to heavy subsidies and long-term security sharing from concentrated financial resources directly or indirectly supplied by the state, as in South Korea – the Taiwanese firms could not expand as much as those in South Korea. Moreover this reliance on traditional household networks for finance also limited the debt–equity ratio of private firms in Taiwan.

Another important distinction between the South Korean and Taiwanese economies was the longevity of the state's autonomy in Taiwan relative to that in South Korea. Whereas South Korean presidents and government officials received bribes and kick-backs from businesses, the KMT government managed to maintain autonomy. The KMT implemented a drastic 'party reform' in 1950–52 to remove corrupt elements and tighten party discipline. The party came to resemble a Leninist vanguard party: a single, 'democratic centralist' elite party, exercising leadership throughout the entire political system (Jacobs, 1978). This organisational structure, combined with the nationalists' extensive network of military and security agencies bent on rooting out corruption, collusion and communism, ensured that the state organs remained free from societal influences. However the most important factor in the state's autonomy was its financial independence. After the Second World War, most of the large, capital-intensive, technology-intensive industries were state-owned,[9] which prevented the top party leaders and their bureaucratic minions from becoming captives of potential private capitalist clients. In addition, most of the political refugees arriving from the mainland were military personnel or civil servants with no local property or family connections. The linguistic and cultural differences were substantial between the mainlanders and the natives of Taiwan. These differences compounded the subethinic division and gave the nationalist state a high degree of autonomy from Taiwanese society (Field, 1995).

Although Taiwan was ruled by mainlanders and the KMT, they were the numerical minority and faced a rapidly expanding private sector that was dominated by ethnic Taiwanese. Hence the KMT leadership introduced a division of labour that placed virtually all political power in the hands of the minority mainlanders and left the private sector to the local Taiwanese. Concerned that economic power might be translated into political power, the KMT leadership also introduced policies that limited economic concentration and promoted the equitable distribution of income.

This concern with equitable income distribution of was also influenced by the teachings of Sun Yat-sen, Chiang's predecessor. Sun, a revolutionary influenced by socialism, preached a doctrine that advocated the regulation of capital and the equalisation of land tenure, but without class struggle and granting a significant role to free enterprise (Gold, 1986). Sun's ideas had a significant influence on the KMT leadership, especially when they moved to Taiwan after their defeat by the communists.

These subtle but crucial differences gave rise to a very different industrial and financial structure in Taiwan. The KMT government's anti-inflationary policy, in fact a high-interest-rate policy, boosted capital accumulation and growth. Savings deposits accumulated very rapidly because of the substantial interest paid on deposits. The raising of interest rates also rendered investment a more efficient and more effective engine of growth. In South Korea, concessionary and special loans to favoured companies, credit rationing by banks and government policy crowded out investments that might have brought high returns if the interest rate had been the main factor limiting the demand for credit. In Taiwan, since credit was rationed mostly by interest rates rather than bank managers and government officials, it raised the average return on the total volume of investment, further accelerating growth (Scitovsky, 1986).

Furthermore the Taiwanese government was much less vigorous than its Korean counterpart in applying financial controls such as concessionary credit allocation and the use of tariffs and quotas as instruments of selective protection. Although exporters (who received a subsidised rate) and large enterprises (which could obtain bank loans) received favourable credit rates relative to other private sector borrowers, Taiwanese policymakers' fear of inflation, the private concentration of capital and accusations of favouritism meant that they were much more reluctant than their Korean counterparts to use preferential financial treatment – whether concessionary loan rates or direct financial bailouts – to foster the success of the few at the expense of the many (Field, 1995).

As a result of the policy of avoiding excessive consolidation of financial resources and the conservative approach to banking operations, Taiwanese firms had to rely on their own funds, small loans from a number of banks or money borrowed from relatives, friends and so on. This reliance on traditional household networks for financial help explains two important features of the Taiwanese industrial structure. First, the size of firms tended to be smaller since Taiwanese firms could not obtain large concessionary or special loans, unlike their South Korean counterparts. Second, the debt–equity ratio tended to be lower than in South Korea because banks were not willing to lend large amounts to individual firms and they could only pool so much of their money in traditional household networks.

Taiwan's financial and industrial structure had a number of important advantages. Since a major proportion of capital needed for investment was generated internally through domestic savings, Taiwan did not have to depend on foreign capital to finance domestic investment. In sharp contrast to South Korea, between 1971 and 1994 Taiwan financed its entire gross domestic capital formation out of domestic savings (Table 7.6). This of course reduced its vulnerability to foreign debtors and thus stabilized the economy. Also, under the constraints of the government's financial and industrial policies, Taiwanese firms had to conduct their financial and industrial operations in a highly flexible, widely diversified manner (Wang, 1998). The small-scale, flexible and informal household network groups became highly advantageous instruments in the implementation of so-called flexible specialisation, which eased the adaptation of the economy to changing circumstances.

Table 7.6   Gross national savings and gross domestic
investment in Taiwan, 1951–94 (percentage of GDP)

	Savings	*Investment*
1951–60	9.8	16.3
1961–70	19.7	21.9
1971–80	31.9	30.5
1981–90	32.9	21.9
1991–94	27.4	23.2

Source: UNCTAD data base.

Table 7.7   Debt–equity ratio of manufacturing firms
in South Korea and Taiwan, 1972–85 (per cent)

	South Korea	*Taiwan*
1972	313.4	—
1973	272.7	—
1974	316.0	91.5
1975	339.5	99.3
1976	364.6	100.4
1977	367.2	97.4
1978	366.8	92.8
1979	377.1	85.3
1980	487.9	82.5
1981	451.5	78.6
1982	385.8	78.1
1983	360.3	84.8
1984	342.7	110.1
1985	348.4	121.2

Source: Bank of Korea.

More importantly, unlike in South Korea, where the excessively large
conglomerates wielded a strong influence over government policy,
Taiwanese firms were not allowed to concentrate or consolidate their economic power or political power. Due to the KMT government's decision to
limit public lending to private firms, the debt–equity ratios of Taiwanese
firms were considerably lower than those of South Korean firms (Table 7.7).
As highly leveraged firms are extremely vulnerable to economic downturns
or other external shocks, the low debt–equity ratio of Taiwanese firms indicates economic robustness and stability. Finally, while South Korea
expressly blocked FDI, Taiwan welcomed it and FDI played an important

role in Taiwan's transformation into a newly industrialised economy. FDI not only contributed to capital formation but was also a crucial vehicle for technology transfer to Taiwan (Chowdhury and Islam, 1997).

These differences explain why Taiwan was able to avoid the contagion of the currency crisis of 1997 while South Korea was one of the main casualties. Nonetheless it is very important to point out again that no country could be safe if it was subject to the massive international capital outflow that took place in Southeast and East Asia in 1997. In 1996, the year before the crisis, there was a net flow of $93 billion to South Korea, Malaysia, Indonesia, Thailand and the Philippines, while in 1997 the net outflow was $12 billion – more than 10 per cent of the area's precrisis GDP. This would be equivalent to a change in net capital flows of $850 billion in the US economy, which would undoubtedly wreak havoc on the US financial markets (Crotty and Dymski, 1998). However it is also important to point out that all the countries hit by crisis had large foreign debts, especially South Korea. South Korea's outstanding foreign debt was around $160 billion in 1997 and about 55 per cent of the entire external debt was short term.

The whim of international investors may have triggered the Asian crisis in 1997, but as we have seen, South Korea was suffering from two major structural problems. Its economic stability increasingly weakened as its dependence on foreign borrowing continued. External pressure from powerful international agents such as the G7, the OECD, the IMF, the IBRD and transnational banks and corporations to deregulate the domestic financial markets and capital flows and reduce barriers to imports and FDI, together with the South Korean government's hasty decision to join the OECD, have loosened almost all controls on the financial institutions and eliminated the state's ability to control speculation against the won.

The South Korean government also lost its autonomy and failed to control the *chaebol* which became too big to fail and were able to exert considerable influence on the government's economic policies. The government, rather than directing and guiding businesses towards its developmental goals, began to resemble an agent of big business. For example in the 1990s the *chaebol*, in their thrust to invest in new capacity and new technology at home and abroad, allied themselves with external forces to pressure the government to hasten the pace of domestic financial market deregulation. In response, the Kim Young Sam government, consented to the establishment of 24 new merchant banks by 1996. The *chaebol* took significant ownership positions in many of these new banks and borrowed extensively from them. Furthermore, as the *chaebol* and the new merchant banks were also attempting to gain fuller access to foreign credit markets in order to take advantage of the lower global interest rates, which were about 50 per cent of South Korea's semiregulated rates, they pressured the government to liberalise – prematurely and excessively – short-term inward capital flows, bank loans and portfolio capital (Crotty and Dymski, 1998; Amsden and Eun, 1997). All this increased the fragility of the South Korean financial market and significantly reduced the government's ability to control and regulate international hedge funds, known as 'hot money'.

In contrast the Taiwanese government never lost its autonomy although significant liberalisation measures were introduced in the financial and industrial sectors, such as the privatisation of state-owned banks, easing restrictions on foreign banks and freeing interest rates. The government also lowered average real tariffs from 7.8 per cent to 5 per cent during 1986–91, freed the exchange rate and sought to shift output from exports and into domestic consumption (Kuo, 1990; Auty, 1997).

These deregulation and liberalisation measures did not signficantly change state–business relations because the government's penchant for controlling and regulating private capital remained intact. Banks in Taiwan are still very conservative in allocating loans to private enterprises, which they keep at arm's length due to the strict penalties that are imposed on bankers who fail to abide by rules such as limiting total loans to a single customer to 25 per cent of the bank's net worth. In the light of such regulations, private firms prefer to obtain financing through the informal kerb market (Wang, 1998). It is important to note that the state still occupies the 'commanding heights' in Taiwan. In order to restrict the expansion of business network groups, the government promulgated the 'Fair Trade Law' in 1992, which provides for the close monitoring of potential monopoly enterprises, including private firms with over US$40 million in annual sales, single businesses with a 50 per cent market share, three companies accounting for two thirds of a product's sales, or five firms with three-quarters of a particular market. However this law does not apply to state-owned enterprises that are deemed crucial to key economic policy (*Free China Journal*, 11 February, 1992).

THE EAST ASIAN DEVELOPMENT MODEL RECONSIDERED

South Korea and Taiwan were prime examples of the East Asian development model. Both countries can be characterised as a developmental state in which the government played a strategic role in taming domestic and international market forces and harnessing them to achieve national ends. Both countries also promoted a bank-based financial system under close government control. Finally, both countries emphasised trade as the primary means of economic development. These commonalties explain the phenomenal economic success of both countries for three decades.

However there were also important differences between them that explain why South Korea was affected by the currency crisis of 1997 while Taiwan remained largely unscathed. The key differences lie in how the respective governments utilised the financial institutions to achieve regime priorities. In South Korea economic growth took priority over everything else, so the state deliberately nurtured big business groups to facilitate this. The *chaebol* received concessionary and special loans (with low or even negative interest rates) and grew bigger, more concentrated and politically powerful. In Taiwan, the KMT regime's main objective when creating and commanding the repressive formal financial system was to maintain price stability and prevent the concentration of private capital. Taiwanese firms turned mainly to traditional household networks and informal kerb markets for financing, and as a result they tended to be small, fragmented and flexible.

These differences in development strategy had far more important consequences. In South Korea the growth-first strategy, especially during the big push period of the 1970s, inevitably resulted in high inflation. Consequently domestic saving suffered as in a high-inflation environment people have less incentive to keep their money in a bank. Therefore the government was compelled to seek investment funds abroad. Moreover the government consciously limited foreign direct investment in order to maintain full control over domestic enterprises. This decision to rely on foreign borrowing while restricting foreign investment had very serious consequences. Although foreign borrowing may provide a country with more autonomy than would be the case if it allowed foreign equity ownership, the South Korean economy became highly vulnerable to external shock. Ironically, when South Korea was caught up in the 1997 currency crisis and requested an IMF rescue package it virtually lost its economic sovereignty.

During the economic development process the *chaebol* became the main beneficiaries of the government's growth-first strategy. By taking advantage of their access to cheap and often risk-free financing, they were able to increase their size, diversify their products and enhance their international competitiveness. On the other hand, they became too big to fail and too powerful to control. When South Korea started to deviate from its status as a developmental state in the 1980s and 1990s, the *chaebol* took advantage of the situation and even pressured the government to accommodate their private interests.

In Taiwan, the leadership of the KMT government had learned a painful lesson from their defeat on the mainland. Chiang Kai-shek and other mainlanders regarded inflation as one of the main causes of their defeat and were determined to pursue an economic development strategy aimed at growth with stability. The KMT regime implemented economic policies designed to prevent inflation, financial instability and the overconcentration of private capital. Over the years, by keeping interest rates relatively high the government managed to maintain price stability and encouraged high private saving rates. This proved to be a sounder policy than the growth-first strategy of South Korea. Taiwan was not exposed to the vulnerability inherent in excessive foreign debt because investments were financed by domestic savings rather than foreign borrowing. This is the main reason why Taiwan avoided the contagion that swept through those East and Southeast Asian countries whose investments heavily depended on short-term foreign borrowing.

Unlike the South Korean state, which by and large became a captive of the *chaebol*, Taiwan remained a developmental state because of its financial independence from interest groups. In order to accommodate the large flow of mainlanders and consolidate its power, the KMT took over major industries and economic institutions in the early stages of its rule and over time developed a publicly owned industrial sector characterised by large-scale, capital-intensive or high-tech production technologies and monopolistic operations. This financial autonomy enhanced the state's strength and insulated the top government officials and other state bureaucrats from the influence of private capitalist clients.

Since the end of 1997, most research on East Asian economic development has focused on 'what went wrong'. Most neoliberal or neoclassical commentators assert that the roots of the Asian crisis lie in the incompatibility between the external global environment and most Asian countries' internal economic structures and policies. They also stress that market fundamentals should drive outcomes, and that state intervention can only worsen outcomes. Contrary to this view, other analysts argue that South Korea's continued reliance on foreign borrowing, especially short-term borrowing, was one of the fundamental causes of its economic crisis in the late 1990s. However this only explains the surface of the crisis. South Korea's decision to give growth greater priority than stability at the start of its economic development programme made the economy prone to high inflation, which negatively affected the domestic savings rate. As investment could not be financed through domestic savings, the government relied heavily on foreign borrowing to finance the industrialisation drive. As a consequence the economy became highly vulnerable to external shocks such as that which occurred in 1997.

Furthermore, contrary to the neoliberal view that too much government interference in the private sector and too much cronyism caused the crisis, the South Korean government's weakening in relation to the *chaebol*, precipitated the crisis. As we have seen, the *chaebol* became too big and powerful and eventually pressured the state prematurely and excessively to liberalise short-term inward capital flows in the mid 1990s. The preconditions for the crisis were created by the failure of the government to maintain its responsibility to monitor and control economic activity in the national interest.

The different outcomes of South Korea's and Taiwan's economic development in the late 1990s has taught us crucial lessons. First, stability should not be sacrificed to growth. When a developing country formulates an economic development strategy, stability should be one of the prime objectives. Second, as Peter Evans argues, an economic bureaucracy that is highly capable and closely connected to – but still independent of – the business community, is an essential institutional prerequisite for successful policy formulation and implementation (Evans, 1998).

Notes

1. $200 million in public loans, $300 million in grants and $300 million in commercial loans.
2. Over the eight years of the Vietnam War, South Korea sent over 300 000 soldiers and became the largest US-allied force after the South Vietnamese.
3. It was as high as 54 per cent during the 1966–70 period.
4. Park had become very unpopular. Despite his economic success as a result of the first and second five year plans and his extensive and well-funded political organisation, he only narrowly defeated Kim Dae Chung in the 1971 presidential election because there was growing dissatisfaction with his harsh authoritarian rule among students and the educated middle class. Foreign debt surged out of hand in the late 1960s and South Korea was forced to turn to the International Monetary Fund for help in 1971. In terms of security Park was unhappy about the withdrawal of nearly a third of the US forces on the peninsula in the wake of the Nixon doctrine. Moreover the world economy began to slow in the early 1970s and protectionism began to rise. For instance the USA pushed South Korea to sign a bilateral trade restraint agreement on textiles, which were South Korea's leading export item. In 1970 textiles accounted for 33 per cent of total manufacturing output, 32 per cent of manufacturing employment and 38 per cent of total exports. Textile exports to the USA alone accounted for 15 per cent of all South Korean exports (Woo, 1991).
5. The Yushin Constitution was essentially designed to make Park a dictator for life.
6. The trade surplus was $3.13 billion in 1986, $6.26 billion in 1987, $8.89 billion in 1988 and $.92 billion in 1989. The current account surplus was $4.62

billion in 1986, $9.85 billion in 1987, $14.16 billion in 1988 and $5.06 billion in 1989.

7. The top *chaebol* groups increased the number of individual companies within their fold by 150 in 1996 and were involved in 114 company mergers in the first nine months of 1997 (Yoon, 1997).

8. Total US military assistance to Taiwan over the period 1951–65 amounted to about US$2.5 billion. US economic and military aid accounted for about 4 per cent of Taiwan's GNP during this period.

9. The party-state has directed manufacturing activities in the following areas: electric power, heavy construction, petrol, petrochemicals, fertilisers, breweries, sugar, tobacco, aluminum, shipbuilding, steel, bus transportation and airlines (Wang, 1998).

References

Akyuz, Y., H. J. Chang and R. Kozul-Wright (1998) 'New Perspective on East Asian Development', *Journal of Development Studies*, special issue, pp. 4–36.

Amsden, A. (1989) *Asia's Next Giant: South Korea and Late Industrialization* (New York: Oxford University Press).

Amsden, A. and Y. D. Eun (1997) 'Behind Korea's Plunge,' *New York Times*, 27 November.

Auty, R. S. (1997) 'Competitive Industrial Policy and Macro Performance: Has South Korea Outperformed Taiwan?', *Journal of Development Studies*, vol. 33, no. 4, pp. 445–63.

Bae, Y. M. (1995) 'Finance in South Korea', in Korean Socioeconomic Conference (ed.), *Lecture on the South Korean Economy* (in Korean) (Seoul: Hanwool Economy series).

Bank of Korea (1970–98) *Annual Report* (Seoul: Bank of Korea).

Chowdhury, A. and I. Islam (1997) *Asia-Pacific Economies: A Survey* (New York: Routledge).

Clifford, M. (1998) *Troubled Tiger: businessman, bureaucrats, and generals in South Korea* (Armonk, NY: M. E. Sharpe).

Crotty, J. and G. Dymski (1998) 'Can the Global Neoliberal Regime Survive Victory in Asia?', *International Papers in Political Economy*, no. 3, pp. 17–29.

Crotty, J., G. Epstein and P. Kelly (1997) 'Multinational Corporations, Capital Mobility and the Global Neo-Liberal Regime: Effects on Northern Workers and on Growth Prospects in the Developing World', *Seoul Journal of Economics*, vol. 10, no. 4, pp. 297–337.

Cumings, B. (1987) 'The Origins and Development of the Northeast Asian Political Economy: Industrial Sectors, Product Cycles and Political Consequences', in F. C. Deyo (ed.), *The Political Economy of the New Asian Industrialism* (Ithaca, NY: Cornell University Press), pp. 44–83.

Deyo, F. C. (ed.) (1987) *The Political Economy of the New Asian Industrialism* (Ithaca NY: Cornell University Press).

Evans, P. (1995) *Embedded Autonomy: State and Industrial Transformation* (Princeton, NJ: Princeton University Press).

Evans, P. (1998) 'Transferable Lessons? Re-examining the Institutional Prerequisite of East Asian Economic Policies', *Journal of Development Studies*, special issue, pp. 66–86.

Field, K. (1995) *Enterprise and the State in Korea and Taiwan* (Ithaca, NY: Cornell University Press).

Glenson, W. (1979) *Economic Growth and Structural Change in Taiwan: The Post War Experience of the Republic of China* (Ithaca NY: Cornell University Press).

Gold, T. (1986) *Economic Development, Principles, Problems, and Policies* (New York: W. W. Norton).

Gold, T. (1988) 'Colonial Origins of Taiwanese Capitalism', in E. A. Winckler, and S. Greenhalgh, *Contending Approaches to the Political Economy of Taiwan* (New York: M. E. Sharpe), pp. 101–17.

Hsiao, F. and M. Hsiao (1996), 'Taiwanese Economic Growth and Foreign Trade', in J. Kuark (ed.), *Comparative Asian Economies* (Greenwich, CT: JAI Press).

Jacobs, N. (1978) *The Origin of Modern Capitalism and Eastern Asia* (Hong Kong: Hong Kong University Press).

Johnson, C. (1982) *MITI and the Japanese Miracle*, (Stanford, CA: Stanford University Press).

Johnson, C. (1987) 'Political Institutions and Economic Performance: the Government–Business Relationship in Japan, South Korea, and Taiwan', in F. C. Deyo (ed.), *The Political Economy of the New Asian Industrialism* (Ithaca, NY: Cornell University Press).

Lansberg-Hart, M. (1993) *Rush to Development. Economic Change and Political Struggle in South Korea* (New York: Monthly Review Press).

Lau, L. (ed.) (1986) *Models of Development: A Comparative Study of Economic Growth in South Korea and Taiwan* (San Franscisco, CA: Institute for Contemporary Studies Press).

Lie, John (1998) *Han unbounded: the political economy of South Korea* (Stanford, CA: Stanford University Press).

Liu, J. C. (1992) *An Economic Analysis of Postwar Taiwan* (Taipei: Jen-Jien Publishing).

Kuo, S. (1990) 'Liberalization of the Financial Market in Taiwan in the 1980s', in S. G. Rhee and R. P. Chang (eds), *Pacific-Basin Capital Markets Research* (Amsterdam: North-Holland).

McNally, D. (1998) 'Globalization on Trial: Crisis and Class Struggle in East Asia', *Monthly Review*, vol. 50, no. 4, pp. 1–14.

Office of Bank Supervision and Examination (Republic of Korea) (1987–1993) *Annual Report* (Seoul).

Onis, Z. (1991) 'Review article: The logic of the developmental state' *Comparative Politics*, vol. 24, pp. 109–26.

Scitovsky, T. (1986) 'Economic Development in Taiwan and South Korea, 1965–1981', in L. Lau (ed.), *Models of Development: A Comparative Study of Economic Growth in South Korea and Taiwan* (San Francisco, CA: Institute for Contemporary Studies Press).

So, A. Y. and S. W. Chu (1995) *East Asia and the World Economy* (Thousand Oaks, CA: Sage).

Song, B. N. (1990) *The Rise of the Korean Economy* (Oxford: Oxford University Press).

Stiglitz, J. (1994) 'The Role of the State in Financial Markets', in *Proceedings of the World Bank Conference on Development Economics 1993* (Washington, DC: World Bank).

UNCTAD (1997) *Trade and Development Report, 1997* (New York and Geneva: United Nations).

Wade, R. (1990) *Governing the Market: Economic Theory and the Role of Government in East Asian Industrialization* (Princeton, NJ: Princeton University Press).

Wade, R. and F. Veneroso (1998) 'The Asian Crisis: The High Debt Model vs. the Wall Street–Treasury–IMF Complex', *New Left Review,* no. 228 (March–April).

Wang, H. H. (1998) *Technology, Economic Security, State and the Political Economy of Economic Networks* (New York: University Press of America).

Woo, J. E. (1991) *Race to the Swift: State and Finance in Korean Industrialization* (New York: Columbia University Press).

World Bank (1993) *The East Asian Miracle: Economic Growth and Public Policy* (Oxford: Oxford University Press).

World Bank (1996) *Global Economic Prospects and the Developing Countries* (Washington, DC: World Bank).

Yoon, Jin-Ho (1997) 'IMF Bailout and Employment Crisis: the labour response'. Korean Confederation of Trade Unions, 11 December, 1997.

8 Dual Sources of the South Korean Economic Crisis: Institutional and Organisational Failures and the Structural Transformation of the Economy

Dongyoub Shin

THE POLITICO-ECONOMIC INSTITUTIONS AND CORPORATE ORGANISATIONS OF SOUTH KOREA: FROM CORE COMPETENCIES TO CORE RIGIDITIES

This chapter analyses the sources of the South Korean economic crisis and the current economic reforms. Many business scholars and practitioners have tried to figure out the causes of the economic crisis that swept through most Asian countries in 1997. Among the seriously damaged Asian countries, the case of South Korea, which used to be the world's eleventh largest trading country, has drawn special attention from students of Asian economic systems. Until the financial crisis in 1997 the South Korean economy had enjoyed miraculous growth. In the early 1960s South Korea was one of the world's poorest nations, but by the mid 1990s it had become a major competitor in many core industries, such as semiconductors, cars, ship-building, steel and electronics. The South Korean economic system was so highly praised that it was closely studied and ardently copied by many developing countries. South Korea was even acclaimed as 'the next giant' that would follow in the footsteps of Japan as a significant force in the world economy (Amsden, 1989). As late as the mid 1990s few anticipated the sudden collapse of the economy. So what went wrong?

There are various possible causes of the South Korean economic crisis, but this study focuses on structural problems at the institutional and

169

organisational levels. It is argued that while South Korea's politico-economic institutions and corporate organisations were the core instruments of the rapid growth during the earlier stages of economic development, they later became the main causes of the economic crisis. It has been suggested elsewhere that when there is an environmental change, an organisation's core competence can become ineffective and turn into a core rigidity that obstructs the organisation's adaptive change (Leonard-Barton, 1995). This chapter will show how the institutional and organisational factors that had served as the core competencies of the South Korean economy later became the core rigidities that hindered adaptation to the changing environment and eventually caused the economic crisis of 1997.

Particular emphasis is placed on the interaction between South Korea's politico-economic institutions and the large business organisations called *chaebol* as the main cause of both the rapid growth and the 1997 crisis. The interaction between institutional environments and organisational actors is a central research area in institutional organisation theory (Meyer and Rowan, 1977; DiMaggio and Powell, 1983). Institutions are taken-for-granted rules and contexts for action (DiMaggio and Powell, 1983). Since economic actors try to maximise their interests within the constraints of taken-for-granted institutional factors such as laws, regulations, practices and norms, politico-economic institutions significantly affect the performance of an economic system (North, 1990).

As well as serving as external constraints, institutions define the structures of incentives and opportunities that organisational actors can take advantage of (Williamson, 1975; North, 1990; Milgrom and Roberts, 1992). Therefore, while effective institutions can facilitate a high performance by economic actors by providing appropriate incentives and opportunities and reducing transaction costs, ineffective ones seriously hold down the level of performance of economic actors by imposing unnecessary constraints, incurring high transaction costs and displaying internal inconsistencies and vulnerability. Neither the rapid growth nor the recent crisis of the Korean economy can be properly explained without a clear understanding of the interactions between institutional dynamics and organisational dynamics.

The second section of this chapter discusses the politico-economic institutions that orchestrated the rapid economic growth during the 1960s and 1970s, while the third section looks at the organisational characteristics of the *chaebol*, which served as the main corporate engines behind that growth. An understanding of the institutional and organisational dynamics during the growth period is crucially important because these same dynamics later became the fundamental cause of the economic crisis. In the fourth section the institutional and organisational failures that caused the economic crisis in 1997 are systematically analysed. It will be argued that both the politico-economic institutions and the *chaebol* failed to adapt to the environmental changes in the mid 1980s. Instead the *chaebol* continued their old ways of doing businesses due to organisational inertia, whereas the government displayed institutional confusion by implementing ill-prepared, uncontrolled and inconsistent institutional changes. Further damage was inflicted on the economy by the misalignment between the politico-economic institutions and the *chaebol*. The fifth section discusses the structural transformation of the South Korean economy since the crisis. Finally, the concluding section examines the outcomes of and the problems with the government's economic reforms.

THE POLITICO-ECONOMIC INSTITUTIONS OF SOUTH KOREA DURING THE HIGH-GROWTH PERIOD

The miraculous economic growth of South Korea has been widely studied by business scholars and practitioners. There are numerous statistics that testify to this growth. For instance, exports increased from mere US $3.5 million in 1946 to $136 billion in 1996 (*Korean Economic Review,* 23 October, 1998). GNP per capita rose from about $100 in the early 1960s to more than $10 000 in the mid 1990s. In 1995 Korea was the world's eleventh largest trading country, the fifth largest producer of cars, the second largest ship-builder and the largest producer of semiconductors (Song, 1997). The two main engines behind this unprecedentedly rapid economic growth were Korea's unique politico-economic institutions and the *chaebol*.

The Birth of Developmental Dictatorship

The economic growth of South Korea often referred to as 'the miracle of the Han river', started after Park Chung Hee seized control of the country in 1961 and assumed the presidency. At the time of the military coup there was virtually no modern industry in South Korea. The development of modern industries had been deliberately suppressed and natural resources had been stripped by the Japanese occupation forces throughout the colonial period (1910–45). Further damage had been inflicted on the national economy by Korean War, which had completely destroyed the industrial facilities during the period 1950–53. During the volatile period between the end of Japanese occupation in 1945 and the military coup in 1961, the government, led by President Rhee Seung Man, had been unable to lead the country towards modernisation and industrialisation. Instead the corrupt and incompetent administration had been concerned only with the maintenance of political power and had consequently been overhauled by the student revolution in 1960. Then came the military coup led by General Park Chung Hee in 1961.

Unlike most dictators with a military background, Park was highly successful in the area of economic development. Based on a powerful coalition between authoritarian politicians and technocrats, Park systematically implemented economic development measures and effectively mobilised the limited national resources throughout his 19-year rule. Rapid economic growth, however, was inevitably accompanied by the complete loss of political democracy. Park ruthlessly persecuted all those who opposed his policies or challenged his power. As a result Park's presidency, which ended with his assassination in 1979, was characterised by numerous antigovernment rallies and the imposition of marshall law. That is why the Park era is often referred to as the period of 'developmental dictatorship' (Shin, 1994).

Building Institutions for Rapid Economic Growth

In order to industrialise the economy, Park set up powerful politico-economic institutions to ensure tight government control over economic organisations such as companies, banks and government agencies. To this end he relied mainly on the following three government bodies: the Ministry of Commerce and Industry, the Ministry of Finance and the Economic Planning Board. The Ministry of Commerce and Industry was responsible for guiding corporate activities such as entry into a particular industry. If the government did not want a certain company to do business in a particular industry, it had the legal right to prevent it from entering. With the Bank of Korea under its jurisdiction, the Ministry of Finance was responsible for fiscal and monetary policies. Since it controlled all the South Korean banks, no company could obtain a bank loan if this was against the government's wishes. Therefore the government had the discretionary power to ruin or support companies and actively exercised this power to align corporate activities with its economic policies. In other words the government played the role of a pseudo market that sorted out fit and unfit companies.

The following agendas lay at the heart of Park government's economic policies: the nurturing of export-oriented industries, the buliding up of heavy industry, the provision of cost advantages to South Korean companies based on the control of labour, the protection of domestic markets from foreign competition, and the concentrated allocation of limited national resources to a small number of *chaebol*. Exports were at the very centre of Park's economic agenda. He aided and rewarded companies that brought in dollars by exporting goods to foreign markets (Kim, 1997), and he provided generous financing and export subsidies to companies with the potential to make money in overseas markets. Park's obsession with exports is well illustrated by the fact that he did not miss a single monthly export promotion meeting during his 19-year rule. The export-oriented economic policy was an inevitable choice for the rapid economic development of South Korea, which had a small domestic market, and Park's policy contributed significantly to the early internationalisation of South Korean firms.

Unlike in most other developing countries, the development programme was centred on heavy industries such as steel, cars, ship-building, petrochemicals and electronics. Park poured a vast amount of resources into heavy industries that many economists predicted would never become a significant competitive force in international markets, for example the Pohang Integrated Steel Company (POSCO), founded in 1968. Although there was literally not a single person in South Korea who had seen a blast furnace at the time of its construction, POSCO went on to become the world's largest and most efficient steel mill in the 1990s (Innace and Dress, 1992).

In order to provide South Korean companies with cost advantages in overseas markets the Park administration ensured an abundance of cheap labour by ruthlessly suppressing labour movements and preventing labour unrest. Although the quality of domestic labour was one of the world's highest (South Korea had a very high literacy rate), most workers were paid only minimum wages (Shin, 1994). Labour activists were stigmatised as communists and were arrested. As a result companies enjoyed the benefits of cheap, high-quality labour with little serious labour unrest during the Park era.

The domestic markets were strongly protected by the government, and since there was little preexisting industry, first-movers were able to gain a virtual monopoly or oligopoly status in these markets. The only constraint was the government's veto over market entry. Since the government explicitly favoured export-oriented companies, those first-movers had to demonstrate their willingness and ability to export to overseas markets. Thus many companies exported their products at lower than cost price, the losses being compensated by high prices in the domestic markets, where they enjoyed near monopoly status. In other words consumers were actually subsidising these export-oriented companies. Due to the success of this under-pricing practice, coupled with the fact that labour was cheap and technological capabilities immature, competing at the lower end of international market remained the primary strategy of South Korean firms' for a considerable time.

Since there were very limited financial resources for economic development, the government ensured that they were allocated efficiently by distributing them to a small number of large corporations that showed the potential to become viable competitors in the international market. These corporations enjoyed various favours, such as special financing, subsidies for the importation of capital goods and the exportation of products, and monopoly status in the domestic markets. Thus began the era of the *chaebol*, large conglomerates with highly diversified business activities. As long as they conformed to the government's guidelines the *chaebol* were strongly supported by the government, at the cost of small and medium-sized firms, the rural sector, workers and domestic consumers. The politico-economic institutions set up by Park performed splendidly and contributed to the unprecedentedly rapid economic growth of South Korea by systematically orchestrating the activities of all corporate and financial organisations.

THE ROLE OF THE *CHAEBOL* AS THE CORPORATE ENGINE OF ECONOMIC DEVELOPMENT

The Governance Structures of the *Chaebol*

As mentioned above, the government relied heavily on the *chaebol* as the main corporate engine of its economic development project. Due largely to the *chaebol*'s superb performance, the South Korean export industry grew from scratch into a major world force in semiconductors, ship-building, steel and cars in less than twenty years. In order to understand why the *chaebol* were so effective we need to look briefly at their organisational dynamics (the organisational characteristics of the *chaebol* are analysed in detail in Shin and Kwon, 1999).

A *chaebol* is a group of large companies operating in diverse and mostly unrelated industries, usually under the ownership and control of a single family. Until the 1997 crisis the economic landscape of Korea was dominated by a small number of *chaebol*. For instance the 30 largest *chaebol* accounted for more than 70 per cent of GNP from the mid 1970s (Shin, 1994). The head of a *chaebol* family held the title of chairman (*Hoejang*), which was an informal position without legal basis. The chairman had almost unlimited power within the group, and without consulting anybody he could found new companies, disband existing ones, enter new business areas and appoint or fire the CEOs of member companies, regardless of business feasibility. Most *chaebol* chairmen had their own office and personal staff, usually referred to as the office of planning and coordination (OPC).

The OPC was the most powerful unit within the *chaebol* and tightly controlled all the activities of the member companies. The owner–chairman's plans and wishes were translated into concrete business plans and implemented by the OPC. The original function of the OPC was to assist the chairman's decision making by acting as a think-tank and collecting and analysing data on the member companies. Later its functions expanded to include most major strategic decisions and much of managerial decision making.

Unlike in large firms in the West, there was no governance mechanism to monitor or sanction the managerial behaviour of the chairman and the OPC. The board of directors in a *chaebol* company was composed only of internal executives so these executives were responsible for monitoring and evaluating their own credibility and accountability. Moreover, since there was neither a legally guaranteed right for minority shareholders to call a general meeting of shareholders nor an organised agent to whom minority shareholders could delegate their votes, the annual shareholders' meeting did little more than ritualistically approve the chairman's and OPC's decisions.

The member companies of a *chaebol* group were tightly controlled and managed in a highly centralised manner by the chairman and the OPC as if they were a single organisation. In order to examine empirically the degree of centralisation of *chaebol* groups, the author and a colleague (Shin and Kwon, 1999) measured the distribution of decision-making power between the headquarters (that is, the chairman and the OPC) and the member companies according to a scale that ranged from 1 (decisions are made solely by the headquarters), to 7 (decisions are made solely by the member company). In between were various degrees of joint decision making.

The results showed that the headquarters made most of the strategic decisions and a significant proportion of the managerial decisions for the member companies. More specifically, the headquarters made the following types of decision almost free of input from the member companies: the formation of joint ventures and mergers and acquisitions by member companies (1.37 on the seven-point scale), the appointment and replacement of top managers of the member companies (1.40 on the scale) and the expansion of business areas (1.60 on the scale). With regard to managerial decisions the ratings were as follows: changes in the organisational structure of the member companies (2.45), determining financing methods (2.76), budgetary decisions of the member companies (2.97), determining target areas and R&D investment (2.97), strategic planning within existing business areas (3.25) and the hiring and firing of employees (3.27). Thus the survey clearly indicated that the member companies were governed by headquarters in a highly centralised manner, so centralised in fact that even decisions on resource exchanges between member companies were made solely by the owner–chairman and the OPC and the member companies were seldom involved in the decision-making process.

The explanation of the degree of power enjoyed by the owner–chairman and his office lies in the ownership structure of *chaebol*. Lim's (1997) pioneering work sheds some light on this. The corporate control of a *chaebol* by the owner–chairman was maintained through two types of internal shareholding: direct shareholding by the owner and his family and corporate shareholding among the group's member companies. The owner and his family held shares in a few key companies, which in turn held shares in other member companies. The member companies not only held each others' shares but also guaranteed each others' loans and debts, which enabled them to obtain the external financial resources needed for their relentless expansion. As a result the average debt–capital ratio among the 30 largest *chaebol* exceeded 500 per cent in the mid 1990s (Lim, 1997; Kim, 1998).

The Corporate Strategy of the *Chaebol*:
Expansion through Diversification

The corporate strategy of the *chaebol* is well illustrated by their in derogatery nickname: 'octopus companies.' From their birth in the 1960s, until the mid 1990s, when the economic crisis started to emerge, the *chaebol* consistently pursued a diversification strategy. According to the strategic management literature, diversification is pursued for various reasons, such as obtaining new sources of profits, reducing risk, achieving economies of scale and scope, securing the supply of new production factors, gaining new competencies and using existing competencies in new ways (Ansoff, 1965; Rumelt, 1974; Porter, 1985; Barney, 1997; Collis and Montgomery, 1997). If effectively implemented, diversification can contribute significantly to firm performance (Weston and Mansinghka, 1971; Levitt, 1975).

Most of the *chaebol* engaged in unrelated diversification, that is, they relentlessly expanded their size by continually entering new industries with little technological commonality. For example major *chaebol* such as Samsung, Hyundai and Daewoo entered a wide range of unrelated industries such as electronics, computer hardware and software, telecommunications, petrochemicals, cars, ship-building, construction, hotels and tourism, trading, department stores and so on.

Conversely, the dominant strategic trend among the world's leading companies during the same period was increasing specialisation in a few closely related business areas for which they had core competencies and withdrawal from peripheral business activities (Shleifer and Vishny, 1994). It has been repeatedly shown that, of the two types of diversification strategy, related diversification is generally superior to unrelated diversification in terms of firm performance (Rumelt, 1974; Palepu, 1985; Varadarajan, 1986; Robins and Wiserma, 1995). Most of the competitive advantages that a diversification strategy can provide, such as synergy generation, economies of scale and scope and the full exploitation of existing competencies, apply only to related diversification. Despite this the *chaebol* consistently pursued an extremely unrelated diversification strategy.

There are a number of competing explanations for the *chaebol*'s choice of strategy. In the strategic management literature it is argued that the core benefit of unrelated diversification is risk reduction under environmental uncertainty (Galbraith *et al.,* 1986; Amit and Livnat, 1988). Thus, one could argue that the main reason for the *chaebol*'s choice of strategy was the existence of a high degree of environmental uncertainty and risk. In other words, specialising in a few business areas was too risky as the *chaebol* did not possess strong technological capabilities in any area and the business environment surrounding them was extremely volatile and unpredictable. However this line of reasoning bears the danger of becoming a self-fulfilling prophecy. If a company chooses to diversify into a wide range of unrelated business areas because it lacks accumulated technological competence in any particular business, that decision will prevent the future accumulation of specialised competence. As a consequence, widely diversified firms will stay that way forever.

Lim (1997) offers an alternative explanation from a corporate finance perspective. He argues that unrelated diversification was adopted by the *chaebol* not because of business risk, but because of financial risk – that unrelated diversification was an efficient means of managing the risk portfolio of the owner's personal assets. According to this explanation, by investing his assets in a wide range of unrelated businesses the owner of a *chaebol* was less likely to lose a significant proportion of his assets than would be the case if he invested in a few specialised areas (ibid.).

However it is argued here that the extreme degree of unrelated diversification engaged in by the *chaebol* can be fully understood only by also taking into consideration the idiosyncratic environment of South Korea during the high growth period. Thus it is maintained that the motives for unrelated diversification in South Korea were quite different from those of US corporations in the 1960s (Shleifer and Vishny, 1994). During the high growth period the South Korean economy was in what might be called an 'industrial vacuum.' Modern industry simply did not exist in most business areas. Thus even if it had little technological competence a firms could make a profit merely by being the first to enter an industry. All that was needed was the ability to mobilise financial resources and some degree of managerial capability. Since the *chaebol* were the only organisational actors to have these two attributes at the time, they were able to enjoy a virtual monopoly in a wide range of industries. However it should be stressed that the *chaebol* had to rely increasingly on external financing as their internal resources were limited.

Environmental Conditions and the Competitive Advantages of the *Chaebol*

Why were the *chaebol* such an effective corporate engine in the rapid economic growth of South Korea? What exactly were the sources of their competitive advantage? Most studies fail to explain specifically why and how the *chaebol* were able to become so internationally competitive in such a short time, for example they seldom go further than emphasising government subsidies or the entrepreneurial ability of *chaebol* founders such as Lee Byung-Chull of Samsung and Chung Ju-Young of Hyundai (Amsden, 1989; Steers *et al.*, 1989; Steers, 1998). In contrast it is maintained here that the fundamental explanation of the *chaebol*'s strong performance lies mainly in their organisational dynamics. In other words, the *chaebol* were able to achieve such an outstanding performance and rapid growth because their particular organisational characteristics fitted nicely into the environment that prevailed during the high growth period.

It is generally agreed that the heyday of the *chaebol* was roughly the 20-year period between the mid 1960s and the mid 1980s. In line with the Park government's guidelines, embodied in a series of five year economic development plans, the *chaebol* transformed South Korea from an agricultural society into a modern industrial economy by indiscriminately entering all types of industry during the 20-year period. However it is very important to understand the environmental conditions that supported this rapid expansion and outstanding performance.

Many of the environmental conditions were discussed earlier in this chapter, but to recap, the developmental government of President Park Chung Hee strongly supported the *chaebol* as the main organisational weapon for its national economic development project. Because of the limited national resources the government provided cheap financial resources only to a small number of large *chaebol* in order to create an industrial infrastructure as fast as possible. Furthermore, so that the *chaebol* would have cost advantages in international markets the government ensured an abundance of cheap, high-quality labour by suppressing labour movements. The domestic markets were strongly protected from foreign competition so the *chaebol* enjoyed near monopoly status. Most of all, there was a huge industrial vacuum in most business areas that the *chaebol* could easily fill without much competition. As a result of the interaction between these environmental conditions and the organisational advantages of the *chaebol*, they were able to expand rapidly by entering whatever business areas were available. However it was *chaebol*'s organisational abilities that enabled them to utilise these environmental conditions effectively. The following three organisational factors should be particularly stressed: resource mobilisation, economy of scope, and safety-net effects.

First, the *chaebol* were highly effective in gathering together the resources needed to enter new businesses. As explained earlier, a *chaebol* was able to draw in a significant amount of resources from its member companies based on its highly centralised governance mechanism cross-subsidisation, cross-shareholding and internal trading. Moreover the *chaebol* had advantages over non-*chaebol* companies in the acquisition of external resources based on mutual payment guarantees between member companies (Kim, 1998). In the absence of such internal and external resource-pooling systems, a non-*chaebol* company either had to rely on its own resources, which were often limited, or obtain external resources, which usually took a long time to negotiate and contract.

Second, unlike non-*chaebol* companies, the *chaebol* enjoyed economies of scope through the sharing of competencies and resources among member companies. In addition to risk reduction, economy of scope is considered to be a main advantage of diversified companies (Chandler, 1962, 1977; Collis and Montgomery, 1997). By sharing competencies and resources across different businesses, diversified firms could reduce their total costs. There are numerous examples of the advantages that arise from economies of scope. For example when the Samsung *chaebol* set up a new member company, it normally used the facilities and human resources of existing member companies until the new company became self-sufficient. Another salient example is integrated trading companies, which most *chaebol* established in the 1970s as international trading agencies for all member companies.

Third, probably the *chaebol*'s greatest competitive advantage compared with non-*chaebol* companies was the safety-net effect, whereby a *chaebol* member company could overcome a temporary crisis by obtaining help from the other members of the group. For example, if a member company faced a temporary competitive threat and was unable to deal with it by itself because inexperience or lack of maturity prevented it from competing independently, its sister companies dealt collaboratively with the problem by providing financial resources and other aid to the stumbling company. Of course this type of resource provision was not voluntarily offered by the sister companies, but dictated by the group headquartes. Had it not been for the existence of such safety nets the *chaebol* would not have been able to enter risky new markets or stay in business in highly competitive markets. For instance, when faced with growing competition from the *chaebol* in the 64K DRAM and 256K DRAM memory chip markets in the mid 1980s, the then dominant Japanese semiconductor manufacturers staged a fierce price war, dumping their models at less than a half of the South Korean producers' costs in order to get rid of the new competitors at an early stage. However the strategy failed to have the desired effect. While many US producers, all of which were independent companies, were forced out of the market, the South Korean companies were able to ride out the price war because of the financial cushion provided by their sister companies, under the direction, of course, of the powerful headquarters (Kim, 1997).

THE FALL OF SOUTH KOREAN POLITICO-ECONOMIC INSTITUTIONS AND CORPORATE ORGANISATIONS

Environmental Changes in the Mid 1980s and the Unfolding of the Economic Crisis

In early 1997 the South Korean economy started to show signs of being in serious trouble. It was reported that the economy had incurred a $20 billion trade deficit the previous year. A number of major *chaebol*, such as Hanbo, Sam-Mi, Jinro, Haitai and Kia, went bankrupt in 1997, and the crisis began to accelerate from the autumn of that year. The credit rating of Korea by S&P was downgraded by six steps from AA− in early October 1997 to B+ (unsuitable for investment) in December (*Korean Economic Review*, 14 February 1999). The won exchange rate, which used to hover around 800 won per US dollar, fell to 1300 won per dollar in November. The government quickly depleted most of its foreign currency reserve in order to defend the value of the won, but in vain. The foreign currency reserve decreased from $33 billion to $7.2 billion that month. The South Korean Stock Exchange index, which had passed the 1000 point mark, plummeted to 450, the lowest in ten years. Foreign creditors started to recall their loans, but South Korean companies and financial firms did not have sufficient liquid resources to pay them back. The South Korean economy was on the verge of collapse by the end of November 1997.

On 27 November, the government applied for $55 billion emergency loan from the IMF – the largest bailout in the IMF's history – but even after this deal was signed the crisis continued. The exchange rate fell even further to as low as 1964 won per US dollar in early 1998. Two months into the crisis about 7000 small and medium-sized firms went bankrupt

(*Korean Economic Review*, 23 December, 1998). The Korean Stock Exchange index sank to 280 in early 1998 and the unemployment rate, which stood at about 2 per cent before the crisis, exceeded 8 per cent in late 1998. In the 1998 fiscal year the annual economic growth rate was minus 6 per cent and GNP per capita, which had exceeded $10 000 in 1995, fell to $6500. More than 75 per cent of the population admitted that their wealth had substantially decreased after the crisis (ibid., 13 October, 1998). Of the 30 largest *chaebol*, 11 were virtually bankrupt.

What went wrong with these highly effective institutions and organisations? What caused the downfall of the Korean economy in 1997, which was referred to as the greatest national disaster since the Korean War? By and large there are three competing explanations of the crisis. Some blame the *chaebol* for their endless expansion, based on external financial resources, while others point to the incompetence of the government in dealing with the crisis. Still others – from a more radical camp – consider that the economic crises in Korea and other Asian countries were an inevitable consequence of worldwide neoliberalism, which had consistently forced unprepared developing countries to open their financial and trade markets. It is submitted here that it was the combined effect of all three factors that caused the crisis. In other words the crisis can be properly understood by focusing on the interaction among the *chaebol*, the politico-economic institutions and the changing environment. Of course neoliberalism should be counted as an important environmental factor. Here it is argued that the economic crisis was a result of South Korea's failure to make adaptive changes to its politico-economic institutions and corporate organisations in order to deal with the new environmental factors. What were the environmental changes that made these once-powerful institutions and organisations stumble so seriously?

The critical period seems to have been the mid 1980s, when the economy was simultaneously faced with the following environmental changes: the opening of domestic financial and product markets as a result of pressure from other countries; the democratisation of South Korea and the consequent sharp increase in labour costs; challenges from less developed countries such as China and other Southeast Asian countries, which were armed with much cheaper labour and other production factors; the organisational maturation and rapid globalisation of the *chaebol*; the industrial shift towards products with high added value such as semiconductors and computers; and the worldwide trend towards corporate restructuring and intensified competition. All these changes took South Korea by surprise and imposed a whole new competitive environment on the economy that was qualitatively different from the previous environments, in which

South Korea's politico-economic institutions and corporate organisations had been able to perform competently.

An antigovernment movement swept the entire nation and gave birth to a new, democratically elected government in 1987. Unlike the previous governments of Park and Chun, both of whom had seized power by military coup, the new government of Roh Tae Woo was not able to suppress labour movements or hold labour costs at the minimum level. As a result the average wage level in South Korean firms increased sharply during the late 1980s.

Great damage to the traditional cost advantages of South Korean firms was inflicted by the entry of China and other Southeast Asian countries – such as Indonesia, Malaysia, Thailand and Vietnam – to the international business scene in the late 1980s. Blessed with much lower labour costs, these countries started to encroach into low-end markets that were traditional strongholds of South Korean firms. Thus, whether they liked it or not, South Korean firms had to make the transition to mid and high-end markets.

However the competitive dynamics in the mid and high-end markets were very different from those in low-end markets. In low-end markets competition was based mainly on low prices rather than state-of-the-art technological innovations or high quality, therefore firms did not have to develop technological capabilities and could rely on technologies that had been developed by more advanced firms quite some time ago. Also, as these firms were not located at the technological frontier, the environment tended to change relatively slowly and the firms did not develop the organisational flexibility required for rapid environmental adaptation. Instead, managerial attention focused on tight and centralised control of all corporate activities in the interests of cost efficiency (Perrow, 1967, 1986).

On top of all this, in the 1980s the global business environment underwent a turbulent paradigm shift. What is often referred to as 'the new competition', based on the continuous improvement of quality and technological innovation, rapidly spread and became widely institutionalised in the mid 1980s (Best, 1990). Under the new paradigm, competitive advantage based on a single product or technological innovation became unsustainable. Instead firms were faced with 'hyper-competition', in which the only way to achieve a sustainable performance was continually to generate new competitive advantages (D'Aveni, 1994). The worldwide trend towards restructuring, reengineering, outsourcing and downsizing that began in the mid 1980s can be interpreted as an adaptive response to this change in the competitive environment. Thus South Korean firms not only had to move to new markets, they also had to deal with a paradigmatic change in these unfamiliar markets.

Another critical change in the mid 1980s was the opening of the South Korean financial and product markets, primarily in response to increasing pressure from foreign countries. The setting up of the World Trade Organisation made it even more difficult for the South Korean government to protect its domestic markets. Thus firms that used to enjoy near monopoly status in domestic markets had to compete against foreign firms even in their home base. This also meant that they could no longer charge low prices in international markets by overpricing the goods they sold in domestic markets. However a much greater threat to the South Korean economy was posed by the opening of the financial markets to foreign investors, which can be seen as a double-edged sword. On the bright side, South Korean firms now had access to much more diverse and efficient sources of finance. But at the same time the economy became highly vulnerable to fluctuations in the international environment and the behaviour of foreign investors.

It should be pointed out here that the environmental changes in the mid 1980s were not cumulative but discontinuous, and each environment was sharply distinct from the preceding one (Tushman and Anderson, 1986; Tushman *et al.*, 1986). In other words, they were not the result of the improvement, adjustment or intensification of existing competitive dynamics.

Hence, the environmental changes in the mid 1980s forced South Korea to compete in whole new areas and in completely different ways. Moreover these changes were competence-destroying in the sense that they destroyed the effectiveness and utility of the institutions and organisations that had been the core competencies of the South Korean economy during the high growth period (Utterback, 1994). In order to compete effectively in the new environment the economy needed to create new competencies by making significant adaptive changes. However, as we shall discuss later, the economic actors of South Korea did not change their course, which I believe was the central reason for the 1997 crisis.

Organisational Inertia and the Failure of the *Chaebol*

The main problem with the *chaebol* during the transition period in the mid 1980s was their organisational inertia. Despite the environmental changes they did not change their corporate strategies and governance structure, rather they enhanced them. For instance, although it is generally perceived that the unrelated diversification gradually decreased with the maturation of the *chaebol*, it in fact accelerated during the decade running up to the 1997 economic crisis in terms of both the number of member companies and the number of product groups (Shin, 1998). The average number of business areas in terms of two-digit SIC codes among the 30 largest *chaebol* increased from 16.0 to 18.8 during the period 1987–96, and among the five largest *chaebol* they reached 29.6 in 1996, a year before the economic crisis emerged (Hahn, 1997).

Another interesting finding is that the degree of centralisation in the *chaebol* also increased during that decade. Contrary to the general perception that their highly centralised structure became increasingly decentralised with organisational maturation, a 10-year panel study found the reverse to be true (Shin *et al.*, 1999).

The present author believes that this organisational inertia among the *chaebol* was significantly responsible for the economic crisis. First, their unrelated diversification strategy inevitably involved the dispersal of limited resources, which in turn prevented the accumulation of advanced technological and organisational competencies. As discussed earlier, the lack of accumulated competencies did not pose a serious competitive problem in low-end markets where the *chaebol* could compete on cost advantages. However, in the new environment, in which the main criteria in the competitive game were technological innovation and high quality, the *chaebol* were unable to compete against foreign firms that were highly specialised in a few interrelated business areas.

Instead of abandoning their unrelated diversification strategy the *chaebol* attempted to solve the problem by obtaining further external resources. Since domestic financial resources were limited the *chaebol* lobbied the government to open up the financial markets so that they could freely borrow cheap capital from foreign investors. This wish was granted and the financial markets were opened in 1994. Thereafter the *chaebol* not only borrowed heavily within South Korea, but their foreign branches borrowed even more aggressively abroad. While foreign borrowing by *chaebol* headquarters was monitored by the government, the direct finance obtained by their foreign branches was not and this form of borrowing increased rapidly. Thus when foreign investors withdrew in the run-up to the crisis, most *chaebol* were faced with a serious liquidity problem.

A serious side effect of the *chaebol*'s excessive diversification and chronic overinvestment was the devastation of the South Korean financial sector. Since the member companies of a *chaebol* offered cross-payment guarantees for one another and they were more reliable borrowers than small and medium-sized firms, South Korean banks willingly provided them with loans. Other reasons why the banks were still lending a large amount of money to stumbling *chaebol* in the mid 1990s were their sunk costs and government pressures. By the mid 1990s the *chaebol* had accumulated such huge bank debts that if they went bankrupt the banks would go bankrupt with them. In order to avoid this they had to lend even more to the already debt-ridden *chaebol*.

Another factor was the government's wish not to cause an economic panic by letting huge *chaebol* go bankrupt, which might have a devastating effect on South Korea's credibility in international markets and influence the results of the forthcoming presidential election. Hence, the government exerted pressure on the banks to provide more loans to troubled *chaebol*. When a number of major *chaebol*, for example Hanbo, Kia, Haitai, Jinro and New Core, finally went bankrupt in 1997, most Korean banks fell into serious trouble too and a number of major banks, such as Cheil Bank and Seoul Bank, were virtually bankrupted.

Second, the highly centralised governance structure of the *chaebol* did not fit the new competitive environment either. During the earlier stages of their corporate evolution, when they were competing in low-end markets based on cost advantages, central control over the member companies was necessary to the efficient utilisation of limited resources. However, in the rapidly changing and unpredictable competitive environment, organisational flexibility became crucial. That is, subsystems needed greater autonomy so that they could make quick local adaptations (Weick, 1976; Orton and Weick, 1990). In this regard the *chaebol*'s highly centralised governance structure became a liability (Shin *et al.*, 1999).

Besides, when a firm contains diverse functions and business activities within its boundaries the costs of planning and coordination can easily exceed the benefits from economies of scope (Williamson, 1985; Perrow, 1986). Thus, according to the strategic management literature (Chandler, 1962, 1977; Collis and Montgomery, 1997; Barney, 1997), as the extent of a firm's unrelated diversification increases, the degree of decentralisation should also increase. This is a logical conclusion because it is impossible for a small number of top managers at company headquarters to possess adequate information on and competencies in a wide range of unrelated business areas. However, contrary to this common-sense managerial axiom, the *chaebol* strengthened their centralised governance mechanisms, the inevitable results of which included slow decision making, low adaptive capability and high bureaucratic costs.

Institutional Confusion: Deregulation and the Opening of Capital Markets

To understand the logic behind the accusation that the incompetence of the government was to blame for the economic crisis, we have to look at the political changes that took place after the assassination of President Park in October 1979. Immediately after Park's death another military strongman, Chun Doo Hwan, seized power through a military coup and the subsequent massacre of hundreds of civilians in the southern city of Kwang-Ju in 1980. Even more authoritarian than his predecessor, Chun violently repressed all antigovernment forces, including opposition parties and labour and student movements.

The continued suppression of labour movements meant that South Korean firms continued to enjoy their competitive advantage based on low labour costs during Chun's seven-year rule (1980–87). During this period, government control over the *chaebol* strengthened and Chun even forced the *chaebol* to donate companies to the government or swap member companies between them. If a *chaebol* was unwilling to comply with the government's requests, the latter did not hesitate to use brutal coercive power. For example the Kukje Group, then the sixth largest *chaebol*, was completely dissolved and put of business because of its uneasy relationship with Chun government.

Although Chun maintained basically the same politico-economic institutions established by Park, the developmental aspects of Park's economic policy faded to a considerable degree during Chun's rule, due primarily to the maturation and growth of the *chaebol*, which by that time had gained their own momentum. Thus the main thrust of the government's policy was not to support the *chaebol*, but to control and guide them. In addition, as the Chun government had a serious legitimacy problem within Korea, it tried hard to gain foreign support by implementing economic policies favoured by the USA, such as partial market opening. As a result, while labour costs remained low, other sources of the *chaebol*'s cost advantages, such as the protection of domestic markets, significantly weakened. Nonetheless, the economy enjoyed another big boom in 1985 thanks to the so-called 'three lows phenomenon' – the simultaneous arrival of low oil prices, low interest rates and a low US dollar, which enabled South Korean firms to export a huge volume of products to international markets (Song, 1997).

Because of ongoing and vehement antigovernment action by students, workers, politicians and ordinary civilians, the weakened government of President Chun had to reintroduce democratic elections in 1987. Violent labour disputes were sweeping the nation at that time and the government was unable to quash the workers' demand for fair wages and better labour conditions. In particular the fierce strikes at the Hyundai factories in the summer of 1987 clearly showed that the *chaebol* and the government could no longer suppress labour activists just by harassing them. Wages subsequently rose rapidly in most industries, and so even cheap labour was removed as a source of competitive advantage. The governing style of President Roh Tae Woo, who was elected in the 1987 presidential election, was very different from that of his predecessors. In terms of economic policies, the Roh era is best characterised by the uncontrolled deregulation of economic activities and the unprepared opening of financial and product markets.

Unlike Park and Chun, Roh seldom intervened in the business activities of the *chaebol*. For instance in 1990 he removed the controls on land use in green belts, the development of which the previous governments had strictly prohibited. In 1992 he implemented an import liberalisation plan and opened the Korean stock market to foreigners. Roh's successor, Kim Young Sam, who was inaugurated in early 1993, extended the policies of deregulation and market opening by declaring *Sekyehwa* (globalisation) in November 1994, geared to the establishment of a completely open market economy compatible with the Anglo-American economic model. The government not only completely opened the domestic capital market to foreign investors, but also fully deregulated loan financing by South Korean corporations and financial companies in foreign capital markets. With the opening of the product and financial markets, South Korean firms that formerly competed for exports quickly began to compete for imports and rushed to attract as much foreign capital as possible. In particular the *chaebol*, which were still strongly expansion-oriented, rushed for cheap foreign loans in both domestic and overseas capital markets. As a consequence the domestic product markets became completely exposed to foreign competition and the economy became heavily dependent on foreign capital.

* * *

With the arrival of Roh government in 1988, then, the era of authoritarian and developmental government virtually ended. It is contended here that the policies of rapid deregulation and market opening by Presidents Roh and Kim resulted in institutional confusion which eventually became a source of the 1997 economic crisis. There are two reasons why these policies unintentionally caused institutional confusion. First, as discussed above, the *chaebol* retained both their policy of diversification and their highly centralised governance structure until the outbreak of the economic crisis in late 1997. When the government lifted the restrictions on capital markets the *chaebol* rushed to acquire for foreign capital for their expansion projects, most of which were commercially unfeasible. Consequently, as the size of the *chaebol* grew between the mid 1980s and mid 1990s, their profitability paradoxically fell.

According to an empirical study of the economic value added (EVA: net operating profit after taxes minus the cost of capital) of 570 non-financial firms listed on the Korean Stock Exchange between 1992 and 1996

(Kim *et al.*, 1998), only 27 per cent had a positive EVA. In other words, almost three quarters of the listed Korean companies generated insufficient operating profits to cover their external capital costs, which means that most South Korean firms were destroying value rather than creating it (Kim, 1998). In an advanced open market such destructive behaviour is controlled internally by corporate governance mechanisms such as boards of directors or externally by market discipline. Unfortunately in South Korea neither of these existed to prevent the uncontrolled expansion of the *chaebol*.

As explained earlier, all *chaebol* board members were inside executives and there were no institutional means for minority shareholders to express their concerns. Therefore the managerial processes in *chaebol* were completely without transparency and accountability, and very little crucial information was disclosed to outsiders. Although the chairman had almost unlimited power within the group he was not legally responsible for his decisions. A market for corporate control, such as mergers, acquisitions and hostile takeovers, did not exist. Thus with government regulations lifted, the *chaebol*'s highly risky pursuit of expansion based on borrowed foreign capital was unstoppable until the 1997 economic crisis. It is argued here that one of the causes of the Korean economic crisis was the hasty implementation of deregulation and capital market opening when no institutional mechanisms existed to countervail the high risks inherent in a deregulated and open economy.

The second type of institutional confusion was caused by the vast array of inconsistencies among economic policies. An institution is structured as a complex network of interrelated components, such as laws, policies, rules, norms and patterns, consistency among which is crucially important for the generation of good performance (DiMaggio and Powell, 1983; Zucker, 1983; North, 1990). The economic policies of Roh and Kim were riddled with inconsistencies, which generated a state of institutional confusion. For instance both exerted pressure on formally deregulated South Korean banks to provide huge loans to a number of troubled *chaebol*. As a result many banks were suffering serious credit problems at the outbreak of the economic crisis.

The most salient examples of this are Cheil Bank and Seoul Bank, both of which went bankrupt as a consequence of the loans they were forced to provide to problematic *chaebol*, such as the now defunct Hanbo Group. Because of his illegal involvement in bank loans for Hanbo Steel, Kim Hyun Chul, son of President Kim, was sentenced to imprisonment in early 1997, which crippled the credibility and political power of the Kim administration. With the presidential election scheduled for December 1997, the arrest of his son not only made Kim a lame-duck president, but also fatally affected his ability to handle the economic crisis that started in September that year.

A more serious inconsistency in the government's economic policies lay in the relationship between its capital market policy and its exchange rate policy. While the government implemented various policies to liberalise the capital markets, such as opening financial markets to foreign investors and relaxing controls on currency flow, it continued to exert tight control over the exchange rate. This type of inconsistency also existed in other developing countries that have suffered an economic crisis, such as Mexico and Thailand. This odd mix of mutually contradictory policies can work fine if the government-imposed currency value is similar to its market value. However, if there is a significant gap between the two values, speculative currency flows, such as short-term capital and hedge funds, may precipitate a currency crash (Kim, 1998).

Despite the falling profitability of South Korean firms in the 1990s the government chose not to devalue the won, the accumulated effects of which eventually caused the crash of the won in the 1997 crisis. Even in the midst of the crisis the government refused to devalue the won, partly because of the negative effect this might have on its chances in the presidential election, scheduled for December. Instead the government wasted $25 billion of its foreign exchange reserve in November in a vain attempt to defend the value of won. This futile act virtually depleted the foreign exchange reserve, and as a consequence the won was devalued by more than 50 per cent, which in turn doubled the foreign debts of South Korean organisations, which were still competing to borrow whatever foreign capital was available. Now the confused government had no other option but to go for the largest bailout in the history of IMF.

THE STRUCTURAL TRANSFORMATION OF THE SOUTH KOREAN ECONOMY SINCE THE CRISIS

After the inauguration of President Kim Dae Jung in February 1998 the new government immediately started work on the structural transformation of the economy. At his inauguration Kim declared that he would create the necessary politico-economic institutions for a truly free market system by allowing autonomous decision making in economic organisations, minimising government intervention and deregulating most business activities. The central tenet of the various reform policies was the undoing of the institutional and organisational problems discussed in this chapter. The reform agenda included the restructuring of the financial sector, letting the value of the currency be determined by the market, restructuring government agencies related to economic affairs, the prohibition of cross-subsidisation and mutual payment guarantees between *chaebol* member companies, the dissolution of the *chaebol*'s offices of planning and coordination, the forced reduction of the *chaebol*'s debt–captial ratio to 200 per cent of capital, a reduction in the extent of *chaebol* business areas and the establishment of a tripartite coalition between labour, management and the government.

The Reform of the Financial Sector

Since one of the direct causes of the economic crisis was the crippled financial sector, which had been unable properly to monitor and control the *chaebol*'s excessive diversification and chronic overinvestment, it naturally became one of the first targets of the new government's reform programme. The government duly broke the old unwritten rule about the inviolability of banks by forcing troubled banks either to offer themselves for sale to foreign investors, to merge with each other or to go bankrupt. Moreover all the banks were required to increase their BIS ratio to 8 per cent by the end of 1999.

Subsequently five relatively small banks – Donghwa, Dongnam, Daedong, Kyungki and Chungcheong – had to declare themselves bankrupt. Of the seven largest banks, only two – Jutaek Bank and Kookmin Bank – were considered to be financially healthy; the two most problematic banks – Seoul Bank and Cheil Bank – were sold to foreign banks; and Hanil Bank and Sangup Bank were merged to become Hanbit Bank. The Foreign Exchange Bank was able to stay alone by attracting an equity investment of 350 billion won from the Komertz Bank of Germany. Mergers between smaller banks or between smaller ones and larger ones were also strongly encouraged. For instance three major deals were signed between Hana and Boram, Choheung, Chungbuk and Kangwon, and Kookmin and the Long-Term Credit Bank.

The second financial sector, which had not been controlled directly by the Bank of Korea until the crisis, was also heavily restructured by the government. The government closed down 16 integrated financial services firms (*Chong-Kum-Sa*), 10 lease companies, eight security companies, 22 insurance companies and two investment banking firms. In the process the government had to spend 31 trillion won on the restructuring of banks and 12 trillion won on the restructuring of the second financial sector.

The central organisational apparatus of the financial sector reforms was the Financial Supervisory Board (FSB), which was installed on 1 April

1998 as a government agency with virtually unlimited power over the financial sector. The FSB was created by integrating the following previously separate government agencies: the Bank Supervisory Institute, the Security Supervisory Institute, the Insurance Supervisory Institute and the Credit Management Fund (*Chosun Ilbo*, 1 April 1999). The FSB was bestowed with a wide range of powers over all types of financial organisation. For instance, it was given the power to replace the top managers of banks. The FSB is the government's main organisational weapon to enforce the highly problematic deals between the *chaebol*, which will be discussed shortly. Since most of the banks to which the *chaebol* owe a large amount of outstanding debt are heavily dependent on government subsidies for their restructuring, they are willing to exert pressure on the *chaebol* at the FSB's request. For this reason, some observers of the South Korean economy have strongly criticised the FSB as representing the resurrection of the government-controlled financial sector of the developmental period (ibid.).

The Restructuring of the *Chaebol*'s Financial Structure

Immediately after taking office in February 1998 the new government introduced various *chaebol* reform policies, which focus on improving the *chaebol*'s financial structure, transforming their governance structure and restructuring their business areas. The most fundamental of these is the financial restructuring of the *chaebol*, because, if thoroughly implemented as planned, it will dissolve the foundation of the *chaebol* structure described earlier.

First, the government ordered the *chaebol* to reduce their debt–capital ratio from over 500 per cent of their capital to less than 200 per cent. This was to be achieved by the end of 1999 by selling some of their member companies and assets or attracting foreign investment (*Korean Economic Review*, 16 December 1999). Otherwise their outstanding debts would be recalled immediately by the banks at the government's request. As a consequence, further expansion based on external financial resources has become impossible. The sale of even profitable companies to foreign investors has been strongly encouraged by the government. In order to make South Korean companies attractive to foreign investors the government and banks have offered various incentives, such as debt reduction and tax exemption. Foreign investors have indeed rushed to buy them at bargain prices, and many once-profitable companies, such as Daehan Jungsuk, the world's largest tungsten producer, and Hansol Paper have been sold in this way.

Second, the government prohibited both cross-investment and mutual payment guarantees between *chaebol* member companies, and all existing mutual payment guarantees must be cleared by the end of March 2000 (ibid., 8 April 1999). Therefore the *chaebol* not only lost their ability to mobilise internal resources, they also lost a means of attracting external resources. Hence the complex web of ownership networks within *chaebol* groups will soon disappear.

Third, internal trading between the member companies was prohibited by the government, which gave the Korean Fair Trade Commission full authority to monitor trading between member companies of the same *chaebol* and to take heavy punitive measures in the event of infringement. On 26 March 1998, the LG Group announced that transactions between its member companies would henceforth be made only if the companies concerned considered it beneficial to both parties. This strongly testifies to the former prevalence of internal trading, the sole purpose of which had been to subsidise other member companies (ibid., 27 March 1998).

Fourth, in order to make monitoring by external investors and regulatory agencies easier, the government ordered the *chaebol* to present consolidated financial statements for all the companies in their corporate control for the fiscal year 1999. While this would make their corporate finances much more transparent, the cost of producing consolidated financial statements for dozens of member companies would be enormous.

The Transformation of the *Chaebol*'s Governance Structure

The dismantling of the unique governance structure of the *chaebol* explained earlier in this chapter, was also one of the early aims of the government's reform policies. *Chaebol* owners were required to assume formal CEO status with full legal responsibilities. Thus unlike in the past, the owner–chairman of a *chaebol* group can now be held legally accountable for all his managerial decisions. Then the *chaebol* were required to appoint board members from outside the group and end the situation where all-insider boards consisting of top executives of *chaebol* companies monitored and audited their own managerial behaviours.

The government also introduced the legal right for minority shareholders possessing more than 1 per cent of a company's stocks to call a general meeting of stockholders. Coupled with this legal amendment was strong pressure from the so-called 'minority shareholder activists'. Starting with the 1997 general meeting of the stockholders of Cheil Bank to debate its problematic loans to the now defunct Hanbo Steel, minority shareholder activists fiercely confronted top executives of major *chaebol* on a wide range of managerial decisions. Minority shareholder activism has received a mixed response. Those in favour argue that it not only protects the rights of minority shareholders, but also contributes to the improvement of firm performance by preventing owners and executives from pursuing their individual interests rather than the firm's interests (Chamyo Yondai, 1999). Those against argue that it may discourage reasonable risk-taking by executives, which is crucial for the achievement of above-normal returns (*Yonsei Business Review*, 15 April 1999). Regardless of the pros and cons, minority shareholder activism has become a force for *chaebol* owners and executives to reckon with. For instance, at the general meeting of shareholders of Samsung Electronics in February 1999, Samsung executives agreed to most of the requests of minority shareholder activists and decided to institute an interim dividend system and a regulatory mechanism for internal trading, and to grant shareholders the right to recommend outside board members.

The most controversial one of the *chaebol* reform measures was the government's demand for the immediate dissolution of the offices of planning and coordination (OPC). As discussed earlier in this chapter, the OPC was the core body that sustained the owner–chairman's highly centralised control of the diverse member companies. For instance, the OPC arranged and coordinated internal trading and cross-subsidisation among member companies, which the government deemed to be the *chaebol*'s main structural problem. However, the *chaebol* argued that the government was overlooking the crucial functions of the OPC in the effective coordination of member companies, such as rapid decision making, synergy generation and the creation of new business opportunities (*Chosun Ilbo*, 8 February 1998; *Joong-Ang Ilbo*, 9 February 1998).

The *chaebol* also argued that they needed their OPCs to implement the restructuring measures that the government was demanding. The dismantling of their OPCs was problematic for the *chaebol*, particularly since the holding structure was not legally allowed in Korea. There have been many debates on the desirability of the holding structure, but most law makers are opposed to the idea of allowing the *chaebol* to establish holding companies, and through these to exercise formal control over their member companies. Many observers of the South Korean economy, including law makers, were worried that legalisation of the holding structure would justify and enhance the *chaebol*'s advantages based on internal trading, mutual payment guarantees and cross-subsidisation. However, the *chaebol* maintained that, given the unique ownership structure of *chaebol*, it would be practically impossible to manage the diverse member companies without some kind of centralised coordination mechanism. Hence they insisted that if their OPCs were to be terminated in line with the government's policy, then the creation of holding companies should be legally allowed. Eventually all the *chaebol* surrendered to the government's pressure to dismantle their OPCs by the end of March 1998. Based on the logic that the effective management of diverse companies would be impossible without a coordination unit, the *chaebol* looked for suitable alternatives to the OPC, such as establishing an association structure among member companies or delegating OPC functions to a core company in which the owner–chairman would take up the position of CEO (*Chosun Ilbo*, 8 February 1998). For instance the LG group announced that, along with its OPC, it would dismantle all its group-level decision-making units, such as the strategic planning committee and the human resource committee, and institute a lower-level, interfirm cooperation mechanism, primarily for information exchanges between member companies. The board of directors of each member company would have autonomous decision-making authority, and each company would have complete autonomy in CEO selection and strategic decision making (*Korean Economic Reveiw*, 27 March 1998). However it remains to be seen whether the closure of the OPCs will really transform the *chaebol* into a cooperative interfirm structure based on truly autonomous decision making.

Big Deals and the Restructuring of the *Chaebol*'s Business Areas

The most problematic of the new government's economic reform measures was the so-called 'big deal policy', which involved massive swaps of companies and business lines between *chaebol* groups. In order to force the *chaebol* to concentrate on a few specialised business areas, the government identified a number of industries that were covered by too many *chaebol*, including such core industries as cars, semiconductors, electronics, petrochemicals and aerospace. For instance, the government demanded that swaps be made between Samsung Motors and Daewoo Electronics and that LG Semiconductors should be taken over by Hyundai Semiconductors.

The 'big deal' policy was heavily criticised by the *chaebol*, economists and even some government officials (Kim, 1998). For example Bae Soon-Hun, the minister of information and telecommunications, had to resign after he expressed his disagreement with the swaps between Daewoo Electronics and Samsung Motors. The forced merger between LG Semiconductors and Hyundai Semiconductors was fiercely resisted by the LG Group, which was required to sell its equities to Hyundai. LG protested that the value of LG Semiconductors was actually greater than that of

Hyundai Semiconductors (*Korean Economic Review*, 25 December 1998). It was also pointed out that this takeover of LG Semiconductors by Hyundai Semiconductors was inconsistent with the government's big deal guidelines, which clearly prescribed that relatedness among business areas was a core criterion. The LG Group reluctantly agreed to hand over its semiconductor business only after the government threatened to take strong punitive measures, such as the early recall of its bank loans and the prohibition of future loans (ibid., 29 December 1998).

The rationale behind the government's big deal policy was that the *chaebol* could not be trusted to reduce their overdiversified business areas and excess capacities, which had posed a heavy burden on the competitiveness of the South Korean economy. However some considered that the government's role in the economic reforms should be confined to the establishment and enforcement of a truly free market system, and hence the restructuring of the *chaebol*'s business areas should be left to the discipline of market mechanisms (Kim, 1998). Some even voiced the criticism that the big deal policy was based on government-centred economic reasoning that was basically the same as the economic logic of the developmental period (ibid., 14 October 1998).

CONCLUSION: OUTCOMES AND DILEMMAS OF THE ECONOMIC REFORMS

Throughout this chapter, it has been argued that South Korea's politico-economic institutions and corporate organisations have had both positive and negative effects on the economy. While these institutions and organisations served as the main engines of rapid economic growth until the mid 1980s, they were also responsible for the economic crisis of 1997. It is submitted that the politico-economic institutions and corporate organisations served the South Korean economy as a core competence in the 1960s and 1970s but became a core rigidity that hindered the economy's adaptation to the changing environment in the late 1980s and 1990s. In other words the economy fell into the same competence trap that had caused the sudden failure of once-outstanding organisations during discontinuous environmental changes in which the utility of their competencies abruptly disappeared (Utterback, 1994; Leonard-Barton, 1995).

Since the economic crisis South Korea has made various attempts at structural transformation, geared to realigning of its politico-economic institutions and corporate organisations with the new competitive environment. However the results have so far been mediocre, at best. On the plus side the credit rating of the South Korean economy by S & P, Moody's and Pitch IBCA was upgraded to 'suitable for investments' at the end of 1998 (*Korean Economic Review*, 14 February 1999). Also, the average debt–capital ratio of the 30 largest *chaebol* fell from 518.9 per cent at the end of 1997 to 379.8 per cent on 1 April 1999 (KFTC, 1999). However, by the end of 1998, the debts of the five largest *chaebol* had increased by about 13 trillion won compared with the end of 1997 (one US dollar was roughly equivalent to 1200 South Korean won at the end of 1998). In particular the debt of the Daewoo Group had increased by 17 trillion won and that of Hyundai Group by 10 trillion won, whereas Samsung, LG and SK had significantly reduced their debts during this period. Dissatisfied with the *chaebol*'s debt–reduction performance, President Kim announced that the government requirement that the *chaebol* reduce their debt–capital ratio to 200 per cent by the end of 1999 would not be renegotiated (*Korean Economic Review*, 6 April, 1999).

The profitability of the *chaebol* has not significantly improved either. Although the average sales of the 30 largest *chaebol* increased by 7.1 per cent in 1998, their net losses had increased by 16 trillion won compared with 1997 and amounted to 19 trillion won (KFTC, 1999). According to another report on the profitability of 584 listed companies, the average return on equity was minus 20.4 per cent in 1998 (*Joong-Ang Ilbo*, 6 April, 1999). These statistics testify that the *chaebol* have not completely discarded their old way of doing business, that is, expansion at the cost of profitability. The reform of their governance structure has not been satisfactory either. Although their OPCs were officially dismantled, virtual OPCs have been maintained for the coordination of member companies by delegating this function to one of their core companies. Furthermore the owner–chairmen are still exerting a powerful influence over their member companies.

The area of greatest government dissatisfaction concerns the big deal policy. Although the *chaebol* reluctantly agreed to conform to the government's guidelines, by March 1999 not a single deal had been signed. For instance the Samsung Group was still hesitating about taking over debt-ridden Daewoo Electronics, while the Daewoo Group was still trying to beat down the takeover price of Samsung Motors. In the negotiations between the LG and Hyundai Groups agreement could not reached about the proper price for LG Semiconductors. In order to put pressure on the deadlocked negotiations, President Kim declared that the government might apply 'Workout' – forced restructuring preceded by the removal of corporate control from the owners – to large *chaebol* that failed to keep their promises about these deals (*Chosun Ilbo*, 15 April 1999; *Dong-A Ilbo*,

15 April, 1999). This resulted in the LG and Hyundai Groups agreeing on the price of LG Semiconductors on 23 April, 1999 (*Chosun Ilbo*, 23 April 1999).

Careful consideration of the 1998–9 reform processes reveals two types of fundamental dilemma: the government's role in structural transformation, and the tradeoff between the resolution of the existing structural problems and the construction of new competencies. With regard to the first dilemma, the government has had to intervene actively in the economic activities of the *chaebol* and banks in order to facilitate the transformation of the South Korean economy from a government-centred system to a free market system. Some argue that the government should lead the process of economic restructuring, or at least during the transition period, whereas others insist that the government is turning back the clock to the government-centred economy of President Park (*Chosun Ilbo*, 1 April, 1999).

The second and more important dilemma is the tradeoff between the resolution of the existing institutional and organisational problems and the construction of new competencies. Going back to the earlier point about the shift of Korean institutions and organisations from core competence to core rigidity, what the Korean economy most urgently needs is the building of new competencies. However the measures implemented since the economic crisis seem to have concentrated on the removal of core rigidities rather than the building of new core competencies. Many observers question whether the South Korean economy will be able to compete in the future without the developmental government and the unique advantages of the *chaebol* structure (*Korean Economic Review*, 18 December 1998). Although it is widely agreed that the worst of the economic crisis is over (ibid., 23 February 1999), it has yet to be seen whether South Korea can rise again in the world economy by building new competencies. In other words the recovery of the South Korean economy will depend on whether Korea can effectively build post-developmental politico-economic institutions and post-*chaebol* corporate organisations that can offer as new competitive advantages and core competencies in a borderless world market characterised by hypercompetition (D'Aveni, 1994).

References

Amit, R. and J. Livnat (1988) 'Diversification and Risk Return Trade-Off', *Academy of Management Journal*, vol. 31, pp. 154–66.

Amsden, A. (1989) *Asia's Next Giant: South Korea and Late Industrialization* (Oxford: Oxford University Press).

Ansoff, I. (1965) *Corporate Strategy* (New York: McGraw-Hill).

Barney, J. (1997) *Gaining and Sustaining Competitive Advantage* (Reading, Mass.: Addison-Wesley).

Best, M. (1990) *The New Competition* (Cambridge, Mass.: Harvard University Press).

Burns, T. and G. Stalker (1961) *The Management of Innovation* (London: Tavistock Press).

Business Week (1998) 'Samsung: A Korean Giant Confronts the Crisis', 23 March, pp. 14–18.

Chamyo Yondai (1999) *On Chaebol Reforms* (Seoul: Chamyo Yondai Press) (in Korean).

Chandler, A. (1962) *Strategy and Structure* (Cambridge, Mass.: MIT Press).

Chandler, A. (1977) *The Visible Hand: The Managerial Revolution in American Business* (Cambridge, Mass.: The Belknap Press of Harvard University Press).

Cho, D. (1986) 'Diversification Strategies of Korean Firms', in H. Lee and K. Jung (eds), *Structures and Strategies of Korean Companies* (Seoul: Bumunsa) (in Korean), pp. 207–32.

Cho, D. and M. Huh (1998) 'A Study on Mechanisms and Economic Performance of Diversification', Unpublished manuscript.

Christensen, C. M. (1997) *The Innovator's Dilemma* (Boston, Mass.: Harvard Business School Press).

Chung, K., H. Lee, and K. Jung (1997) *Korean Management: Global Strategy and Cultural Transformation* (New York: Walter de Grutyer).

Clifford, M. (1998) *Troubled Tiger: Businessmen, Bureaucrats and Generals in South Korea* (Armonk, NY: Sharpe).

Collis, D. and C. Montgomery (1997) *Corporate Strategy* (Chicago, Ill: Irwin).

D'Aveni, R. (1994) *Hyper-Competition: Managing the Dynamics of Strategic Maneuvering* (New York: Free Press).

DiMaggio, P. (1992) 'Nadel's Paradox Revisited: Relational and Cultural Aspects of Organizational Structure', in N. Nohria and R. Eccles (eds), *Networks and Organizations: Structure, Form, and Action* (Boston, Mass.: Harvard Business School Press) pp. 118–42.

DiMaggio, P. and W. Powell (1983) 'Iron-Cage Revisited: Institutional Isomorphism and Collective Rationality in Organizational Fields', *American Sociological Review*, vol. 48, pp. 147–60.

Dyer, J. and H. Singh (1997) 'Relational Advantage: Relational Rents and Source of Interorganizational Competitive Advantage', Working Paper (Wharton School, Pennsylvania State University).

Galbraith, C., B. Samuelson, C. Stiles and G. Merrill (1986) 'Diversification, Industry R&D Performance', *Academy of Management Proceedings*, 46th annual meeting, pp. 17–20.

Glassman, R. (1973) 'Persistence and Loose Coupling in Living Systems', *Behavioral Science*, vol. 18, pp. 83–98.

Gomes-Casseres, B. (1994) 'Group versus Group: How Alliance Networks Compete', *Harvard Business Review*, July–August, pp. 62–74.

Gomes-Casseres, B. (1996) *The Alliance Revolution* (Cambridge, Mass.: Harvard University Press).

Goulder, A. (1960) 'The Norm of Reciprocity: A Preliminary Statement', *American Sociological Review*, vol. 25, pp. 161–78.

Granovetter, M. (1985) 'Economic Action and Social Structure: The Problem of Embeddedness', *American Journal of Sociology*, vol. 91, pp. 481–510.

Granovetter, M. (1994) 'Business Groups', in N. Smelser and R. Swedberg (eds), *The Handbook of Economic Sociology* (Princeton, NJ: Princeton University Press), pp. 453–75.

Hahm, S. D. and L. C. Plein (1997) *After Development: The Transformation of the Korean Presidency and Bureaucracy* (Washington, DC: Georgetown University Press).

Hahn, D. (1997) 'A Study on the Ownership Structure of the 30 Largest Business Groups in Korea', unpublished manuscript, Yonsei University (in Korean).

Hamel, G. and Y. Doz (1989) 'Collaborate with Your Competitors and Win', *Harvard Business Review,* January–February, pp. 133–9.

Hamilton, G., W. Zeile and W. Kim (1990) 'The Network Structure of East Asian Economies', Working Paper (Davis, CA, Department of Sociology, University of California).

Hatori, T. (1989) 'A Comparison of Business Groups Between Korea and Japan: A Focus on Ownership and Management', in H. Lee and K. Jung (eds), *Structures and Strategies of Korean Companies* (Seoul: Bumunsa) (in Korean), pp. 149–203.

Innace, J. and A. Dress (1992) *Igniting Steel: Korea's POSCO Lights the Way* (Huntington, NY: Global Village Press).

Jarillo, C. (1995) *Strategic Networks* (Oxford: Butterworth).

Johnston, R. and P. Lawrence (1988) 'Beyond Vertical Integration: The Rise of the Value-Adding Partnership', *Harvard Business Review,* July–August, pp. 94–101.

Kanter, R. M., B. Stein and T. Jick (1992) *The Challenge of Organizational Change* (New York: Free Press).

KFTC (Korean Fair Trade Commission) (1999) *Report on the 30 Largest Chaebol Groups* (Seoul: KFTC). (in Korean).

Kim, E. H. (1998) 'Globalization of Capital Markets and the Asian Financial Crisis', *Journal of Applied Corporate Finance,* vol. 11, no. 3, pp. 30–9.

Kim, E. H., M. K. Kim and J. Yi (1998) 'Economic Value Added of the Listed Companies', *The Korean Stock Exchange Report*, pp. 98–101 (in Korean).

Kim, L. (1997) *Imitation to Innovation* (Boston, Mass.: Harvard Business School Press).

Lawrence, P. and J. Lorsch (1967) *Organization and Environment: Managing Differentiation and Integration* (Boston, Mass.: Harvard Business School Press).

Leonard-Barton, D. (1995) *Wellsprings of Knowledge* (Boston, Mass.: Harvard Business School Press).

Levitt, T. (1975) 'Dinosaurs among the Bears and Bulls', *Harvard Business Review,* Janauary–February, pp. 41–53.

Lim, U. (1997) 'Ownership Structure and Family Control in Korean Conglomerates: Cases of the 10 Largest Chaebols', working paper (Seoul: Yonsei Business School).

March, J. and J. Olsen (1989) *Rediscovering Institutions* (New York: Free Press).

March, J. and H. Simon (1958) *Organizations* (New York: Wiley).

Meyer, J. and B. Rowan (1977) 'Institutionalized Organizations: Formal Structures as Myth and Ceremony', *American Journal of Sociology,* vol. 83, pp. 340–63.

Meyer, M. and L. Zucker (1989) *Permanently Failing Organizations* (Newbury Park, CA: Sage Publications).

Milgrom, P. and J. Roberts (1992) *Economics, Organizations and Management* (Englewood Cliffs, NJ: Prentice-Hall).

Miyashita, K. and D. Russell (1994) *Keiretsu: Inside the Hidden Japanese Conglomerates* (New York: McGraw-Hill).

Nishiguchi, T. (1993a) 'Governing Competitive Supplier Relations', working paper (Boston, Mass.: MIT-IMVP).

Nishiguchi, T. (1993b) 'Supplier and Buyer Networks', working paper (Boston, Mass.: MIT-IMVP).

North, D. (1990) *Institutions, Institutional Change and Economic Performance* (Cambridge: Cambridge University Press).

Orton, J. D. and K. Weick (1990) 'Loosely Coupled Systems: A Reconceptualization', *Academy of Management Review*, vol. 15, pp. 203–23.

Palepu, K. (1985) 'Diversification Strategy, Profit Performance, and the Entropy Measure', *Strategic Management Journal*, vol. 6, pp. 239–55.

Perrow, C. (1967) 'A Framework for the Comparative Analysis of Organizations', *American Sociological Review*, vol. 32, pp. 194–208.

Perrow, C. (1981) 'Markets, Hierarchies, and Hegemony', in A. Van de Ven and W. F. Joyce (eds), *Perspective on Organization Design and Behavior* (New York: John Wiley & Sons), pp. 371–86.

Perrow, C. (1984) *Normal Accidents: Living With High-Risk Technologies* (New York: Basic Books).

Perrow, C. (1986) *Complex Organizations: A Critical Essay* (New York: Random House).

Perrow, C. (1991) 'A Society of Organizations', *Theory and Practice*, vol. 20, pp. 725–62.

Perrow, C. (1992) 'Small Firm Networks', working paper (New Haven, Conn. Yale University).

Pfeffer, J. and G. Salancick (1978) *The External Control of Organizations: A Resource Dependence Approach* (New York: Harper & Row).

Piore, M. and C. Sabel (1984) *The Second Industrial Divide: Possibilities for Prosperity* (New York: Basic Books).

Porter, M. (1985) *Competitive Advantage* (New York: Free Press).

Powell, W. (1990) 'Neither Market nor Hierarchy', *Research in Organizational Behavior*, vol. 12, pp. 295–336.

Powell, W. and L. Smith-Doerr (1994) 'Networks and Economic Life', in N. Smelser and R. Swedberg (eds), *The Handbook of Economic Sociology* (Princeton, NJ: Princeton University Press), pp. 368–402.

Robins, J. and M. Wiserma (1995) 'A Resource-base Approach to the Multibusiness Firm', *Strategic Management Journal*, vol. 16, pp. 277–99.

Rumelt, R. (1974) *Strategy, Structure and Economic Performance* (Cambridge, Mass.: Harvard University Press).

Selznick, P. (1942) *The Organizational Weapon* (New York: McGraw-Hill).

Selznick, P. (1949) *TVA and the Grass Roots* (Berkeley, CA: University of California Press).

Shin, D. (1994) 'Contradictory Institutional Pressures and Loose Coupling', *PONPO Research Series*, no. 203.

Shin, D. (1998) 'The Corporate Strategy and Governance Structure of Korean Chaebols', in Joong-Ang Management Institute (ed.), *Beyond Survival* (Seoul: Joong-Ang University).

Shin, D. and K. Kwon (1999) 'Demystifying Asian Business Networks: The Hierarchical Core of Interfirm Relations in Korean Chaebols', in F. J.

Richter (ed.), *Business Networks in Asia: Promises, Doubts and Perspectives* (Westport, CT: Quorum Books).

Shin, D., D. Suh and D. Lee (1999) 'The Evolution of the Korean Enterprise Systems: A 10 Year Panel Study of Large Korean Firms', working paper (Seoul: Yonsei University).

Shleifer, A. and R. Vishny (1994) 'Takeovers in the 1960s and the 1980s: Evidence and Implications', in R. Rumelt, D. Schendel, and D. Teece (eds), *Fundamental Issues in Strategy* (Boston, Mass.: Harvard Business School Press).

Song, B. (1997) *The Rise of the Korean Economy* (Oxford: Oxford University Press).

Steers, R., Y. Shin and G. Ungson (1989) *The Chaebol: Korea's New Industrial Might* (New York: Harper & Row).

Steers, R. M. (1998) *Made in Korea: Chung Ju Yung and the Rise of Hyndai* (London: Routledge).

Stinchcombe, A. (1990), *Information and Organizations* (Berkeley, CA: University of California Press).

Tolbert, P. and L. Zucker (1983) 'Institutional Sources of Change in the Formal Structure of Organizations: The Diffusion of Civil Service Reform', *Administrative Science Quarterly*, vol. 28, pp. 22–39.

Tushman, M. and P. Anderson (1986) 'Technological Discontinuities and Organizational Environments', *Administrative Science Quarterly*, vol. 31, pp. 439–65.

Tushman, M., W. Newman and E. Romanelli (1986) 'Convergence and Upheaval: Managing the Unsteady Pace of Organizational Evolution', *California Management Review*, vol. 29, pp. 1–31.

Utterback, J. (1994) *Mastering the Dynamics of Innovation* (Boston, Mass.: Harvard Business School Press).

Varadarajan, P. (1986) 'Product Diversity and Firm Performance', *Journal of Marketing*, vol. 50, pp. 43–57.

Von Hippel, E. (1988) 'Cooperation between Rivals: The Informal Trading of Technical Know-How', *The Sources of Innovation* (Oxford: Oxford University Press).

Weber, M. (1958) *The Protestant Ethic and the Spirit of Capitalism* (New York: MacMillan).

Weick, K. (1976), "Educational Organizations as Loosely Coupled Systems", *Administrative Science Quarterly*, vol. 21, pp. 1–19.

Weston J. and S. K. Mansinghka (1971) 'Tests of the Efficiency Performance of Conglomerate Firms', *Journal of Finance*, vol. 26, pp. 919–36.

White, H., S. Boorman and R. Breiger (1976) 'Social Structure from Multiple Networks I.: Blockmodels of Roles and Positions', *American Journal of Sociology,* vol. 81, pp. 730–80.

Williamson, O. (1975) *Markets & Hierarchies: Analysis and Antitrust Implications* (New York: Free Press).

Williamson, O. (1983) 'Credible Commitments: Using Hostages to Support Exchange', *American Economic Review*, vol. 73, pp. 519–40.

Williamson, O. (1985) *Economic Institutions of Capitalism* (New York: Free Press).

Williamson, O. (1991) 'Comparative Economic Organization: The Analysis of Discrete Structural Alternatives', *Administrative Science Quarterly*, vol. 36, pp. 269–96.

Williamson, O. (1993) 'Calculativeness, Trust, and Economic Organization', *Journal of Law & Economics*, vol. XXXVI, pp. 453–502.

Williamson, O. (1996) *Mechanisms of Governance* (Oxford: Oxford University Press).

Woodward, J. (1965) *Industrial Organizations* (New York: Oxford University Press).

Yoshino, M. and U. Rangan (1995) *Strategic Alliance* (Boston, Mass.: Harvard Business School Press).

Zucker, L. (1976) 'The Role of Institutionalization in Cultural Persistence', *American Sociological Review*, vol. 42, pp. 726–43.

Zucker, L. (1983) 'Organizations as Institutions', *Research in the Sociology of Organizations*, vol. 2, pp. 1–47.

Zucker, L. (1986) 'The Production of Trust', *Research in Organizational Behavior* (Greenwich, CT: JAI Press), pp. 53–111.

9 The Malaysian Model: Governance, Economic Management and the Future of the Development State

Subramaniam S. Pillay

INTRODUCTION

Before the Asian economic crisis, Malaysia was regarded by many as a remarkable success story (World Bank, 1993). After gaining independence in 1957 it transformed itself from a primary commodity-producing nation into an economy driven more by the production and exportation of manufactured goods. This was done in the context of a complex, multiethnic population representing 'a microcosm of Asia, with the three largest communities in its heterogeneous population – Malays, Chinese, and Indians – representing samples of Asia's three most populous countries – Indonesia, China and India' (Leete, 1996, p. 1). The annual growth rate of Malaysia's gross domestic product (GDP) averaged more than 8 per cent over the period 1988–97. This high growth rate was achieved in a relatively benign inflation environment. Much of this economic progress was credited to the unique Malaysian development model, which is often associated with Mahathir Mohamad, the current prime minister of Malaysia. This model is a variant of the highly touted East Asian development model, which forms a common thread in the various chapters of this book.

However the Asian economic crisis of 1997 exposed some of the weaknesses in the political economy of Malaysia. This in turn dented the image of the development model. Thus the main objectives of this chapter are (1) to examine the pattern of economic development of Malaysia, especially under the administration of Prime Minister Mahathir Mohammed; (2) to review the principal features of the economic crisis and its consequences; and (3) to evaluate the response of the Malaysian government to the crisis.

The rest of the chapter is divided as follows. In the next section, a brief background of the history and politics of Malaysia is presented. In the third section we shall examine the main patterns of the economic development of

Malaysia between independence in 1957 and 1981. We have chosen 1981 as the dividing line since that was the year in which Mahathir became the prime minister of Malaysia. The fourth section continues the discussion of the patterns of economic development, but this time under Mahathir's administration. This will bring us up to the beginning of the crisis, which is the topic of the fifth section. In the sixth section the government's response to the crisis and its effectiveness will be evaluated. In the seventh and final section we shall briefly discuss the future prospects of the Malaysian economy.

HISTORICAL BACKGROUND

In many countries, developments on the economic front cannot be separated from political influences. In Malaysia this relationship is arguably more intense than in many countries due to the institutionalisation of multiethnic politics. Therefore it is important for readers to be acquainted with the history and politics of independent Malaysia. Accordingly this section provides a thumbnail sketch of its political history.

Malaysia is located at the centre of Southeast Asia and is made up of two distinct parts: peninsular Malaysia, which includes 11 states, contains about 80 per cent of the population and occupies about 130 000 square kilometres; and Sabah and Sarawak, which are located on the northern part of the island of Borneo and occupy 200 000 square kilometres. The current population is estimated to be about 22 million.

Ethnic Evolution

Under British colonial rule, peninsular Malaysia was administered separately (as the Federation of Malaya) from the states of Sarawak and North Borneo (as Sabah was then known). Of the three main ethnic groups living in peninsular Malaysia (the Malays, Chinese and Indians), the Malays, most of whom are Muslim, are officially and culturally recognised as indigenous. The Chinese and Indians are seen as immigrants, although over 90 per cent of them are actually Malaysian-born and would regard Malaysia as their motherland.

Chinese immigration into Malaysia became substantial at the turn of the nineteenth and twentieth centuries due to the discovery of large deposits of tin. The British encouraged large-scale migration from southern China so as to have an adequate labour supply in the tin mining industry and related services. Another wave of immigration took place in the 1930s.

Indians – mainly from the southern provinces of India, particularly Tamil Nadu – were brought is in large numbers by the British to provide labour for the new rubber plantations at the beginning of the twentieth century. The Indian subcontinent was also the source of semiprofessional, semiskilled and unskilled staff for the British administration in Malaysia. Thus the main roads and railways were built on the backs of Indian workers brought in under the indenture system (Sandhu, 1969).

Independence and the Formation of Malaysia

Immigration was stopped in the mid 1950s. The large-scale immigration of non-Malays in the first half of the twentieth century was largely a British colonial decision and the Malay population was not really consulted. As a result the Malays developed a high degree of insecurity about being outnumbered in their own homeland. In the quest for independence, the citizenship status of non-Malay residents and the position of Malays in the constitution became important issues. Compromises were struck and independence was obtained on 31 August 1957. At that time, the ethnic composition was 49.8 per cent Malay, 37.2 per cent Chinese, 11.1 per cent Indian and 2.0 per cent others. The Malays' feeling of insecurity was one of the key factors in enshrining the special position of the indigenous or bumiputera community and the accompanying affirmative-action-type policies in the constitution of independent Malaya.

In 1963 the British colonies of Singapore, Sarawak and Sabah joined Malaya to form the enlarged Federation of Malaysia. Due to subsequent political disagreements, Singapore separated from Malaysia in 1965. The introduction of Sabah and Sarawak into the federation increased the ethnic complexity of the nation. There are many indigenous groups in Sabah and Sarawak but the population is generally classified into three broad groups: Muslim bumiputera, non-Muslim bumiputera and the Chinese community. Since the late 1950s, one of the most significant demographic changes has been the relative decline in the population growth rate of the Chinese community in Malaysia. By 1991 their proportion in peninsular Malaysia had declined to less than 30.0 per cent compared with 37.2 per cent in 1957.

Politics in Malaysia

Naturally politics in Malaysia is dominated by ethnic considerations.[1] Most political parties are organised along ethnic lines. In the first election, held in 1955, the Alliance Party – a coalition of three ethnic parties: the United Malay National Organisation (UMNO), the Malayan Chinese Association (MCA) and the Malayan Indian Congress (MIC) – won a resounding victory. It won 51 of the 52 seats in the self-governing legislative council of pre-independent Malaya. This coalition negotiated for independence in 1957 and won the next three elections, held in 1959, 1964 and 1969. However there was a considerable erosion of support for the Alliance in 1969 and a communal riot broke out on 13 May 1969, three days after the election. It resulted in a few hundred deaths, and many of the victims were Chinese Malaysians. Parliament was suspended and emergency rule was instituted for the next two years.

A modicum of democracy was restored in 1971. One of the political casualties of the poor performance of the Alliance Party and the subsequent riot was the first prime minister, Tunku Abdul Rahman, who was eased out of office in 1971. The deputy prime minister, Tun Abdul Razak, took over. He expanded the Alliance Party by persuading a number of opposition parties to join the coalition and renamed it the Barisan Nasional (BN) or National Front. The BN has been in power since then by comfortably winning all subsequent general elections, with a more than two-thirds majority in parliament. In short the people of Malaysia have been under the same ruling party since independence in 1957.

There have been smooth changes in political leadership. As mentioned above, the first prime minister resigned in 1971. His successor, Tun Abdul Razak, remained in office until his death in 1976. He was replaced by Tun Hussein Onn, who retired in 1981 and was succeeded by the current prime minister, Mahathir Mohamad. They were all presidents of UMNO, the main and dominant partner in the BN. UMNO itself is a well-organised party with an extensive following among the grassroots. Elections to all party positions are held every three years, although the president is rarely challenged. Patronage using government largesse has been one of the main lubricants of the well-oiled UMNO machinery.

ECONOMIC DEVELOPMENT PRIOR TO 1981

At the time of independence Malaysia was a successful economy that depended on two strategic primary commodities – tin and rubber.[2] It was the world's largest producer of tin from the early part of the twentieth century until the mid 1980s (Pillay, 1990). During the same period it was also the largest producer and exporter of natural rubber, and even today it is the third largest supplier of rubber. Basically the country was a small open economy with a capitalist system dominated by large British firms in the tin, rubber and banking industries. Most of the small and medium-scale operations in the tin and rubber sectors were owned by Chinese Malaysians, who also controlled a large part of the wholesale and retail sector.

The Malays were mainly involved in subsistence agriculture, focusing on rice farming. Some were employed in the colonial government service. The Indians worked mainly in the plantations or in government service. There were very few industries as the British saw the rich colony of Malaysia as a market for goods produced in British factories (Jomo, 1988).

After independence the government decided to adopt a development model that would encourage import substituting industrialisation (ISI) by offering very attractive tariff protection for such industries. This was not very successful because of the relatively small population base, which prevented many industries from operating efficient economies of scale. A second feature of the development model was a very successful, large-scale, state-funded development programme focusing mainly on the provision of education, health and basic amenities such as water and electricity for rural residents. This in fact laid a solid foundation for the availability of a well-educated labour force two decades later.

A third feature of the model was agricultural diversification within the plantation industry. Instead of relying only on rubber, efforts were made to diversify into oil palm and later cocoa. This again was very successful and Malaysia became the largest producer and exporter of palm oil in the mid 1970s, and it continues to hold that position even now. This success was mainly due to the very efficient, globally competitive plantation sector, although government incentives and encouragement played a role too. With the incorporation of Sabah and Sarawak, petroleum and tropical timber also became important elements of the export economy. In short, from 1957 to 1969 the economy was still based on primary commodities, although the number of commodities had increased. Industry was very limited. In 1970 the manufacturing sector accounted for 13.1 per cent of GDP and 11.9 per cent of exports, and only 11.4 per cent of the labour force was involved in that sector. In general, unemployment was increasing because employment opportunities were not expanding as rapidly as the growth of the labour force.

The New Economic Policy

The 1969 communal riots underlined the urgent need for economic reforms, and in response the New Economic Policy (NEP) was introduced. The two main objectives were to reduce poverty regardless of ethnicity and to reduce the economic imbalance between the various ethnic communities.

From the beginning it was clear that state resources were going to be used for programmes specifically aimed at helping the bumiputeras. An important element of the NEP was to expand the economic cake so that the bumiputera community would have a larger share of the economic pie.

A major reversal took place in industrialisation policy. Now the focus was on encouraging foreign investors to set up export-orientated industries (EOI) in specially created free industrial zones (FIZ). The latter were mainly located in the northern state of Penang and around Kuala Lumpur. The timing could not have been better because it coincided with the rise of globalisation in the electronics industry. Due to the very low weight-to-value ratio of semiconductor products, the more labour-intensive parts of the manufacturing process could be done in low-labour-cost countries. Malaysia was one of the early entrants into this global division of labour. Multinational corporations, mainly American, were given tax and other incentives to locate their factories there. Among the earliest investors in the Malaysian FIZs were such well-known firms as Hewlett-Packard, Intel, Motorola, Texas Instruments, Robert Bosch and AMD.

Globally, the 1970s were characterised by major economic upheavals as a result of the oil crisis. The price of crude oil quadrupled in 1973–74 and by the end of the decade it was almost ten times higher than it had been at the beginning of the decade. Many countries in both the developed and developing world went through economic stagnation, with high inflation giving rise to the new economic term 'stagflation'.

Fortunately for Malaysia, major petroleum and natural gas deposits were discovered near the existing oilfields in Sarawak, as well as in Sabah and the east coast of peninsular Malaysia. A national petroleum company, Petronas, was set up and became an important contributor to export earnings, and more significantly to the national treasury. The commodity price booms in the latter half of the 1970s also helped the federal government to obtain the resources required for the implementation of the NEP.

Politically, the launch of the NEP was very popular with the Malay community, but the non-Malays became very apprehensive about the sharp reduction in the proportion of non-Malays being admitted public universities and recruited into the public sector. This discriminatory policy created a groundswell of unhappiness among non-Malays and ethnic polarisation increased within Malaysian society.

In summary, when Mahathir took office in 1981 the economic prospects looked very bright, with forecasts of petroleum prices hitting US$100 per barrel by the end of the century. Furthermore the country was becoming industrialised and the rural development programmes of the earlier decades were bearing fruit in terms of producing a well-educated, trainable labour force.

ECONOMIC DEVELOPMENT UNDER THE MAHATHIR REGIME

The Look East Policy

As soon as Mahathir came to power he introduced major changes to Malaysia's economic policies, which were subsumed under the catchy slogan 'the Look East policy'. This urged Malaysians to adopt the Japanese and Korean models of economic development, where the state plays a crucial role in the drive for industrialisation. (Excellent reviews and critiques of the policy can be found in Edwards, 1975; Jomo, 1985; Jomo and Tan, 1999.)

Politically, the model advocated a trade-off between economic growth and democracy, following the lead of Korean strongman Park Chung Hee. Economically, the state sponsored a massive programme of heavy industrialisation, focusing on the steel, cement and car industries, which were ringed by a wall of tariff and non-tariff barriers. This industrialisation drive can be labelled as the second round of ISI. Help was sought from Japan and Korea and there was much anti-Western posturing, especially against Britain.

If the economic performance of these new industries are measured objectively they can be seen as massive failures. There are many reasons for this. Firstly, the timing could not have been worse. The external demand for primary commodities and electronics slumped due to the global slowdown of the mid 1980s. This led to a recession between 1985 and 1987 in Malaysia, sharply curtailing the demand for steel, cement and cars. Secondly, the state-sponsored companies were run very inefficiently due to corruption, cronyism and lack of experience. It was a good example of state failure. Thirdly, the chosen industries had many strong competitors regionally and globally. Thus these large Malaysian firms faced shrinking domestic demand and could not compete in the export market either.

The 1985–87 Recession

As can be seen from Table 9.1, which provides macroeconomic data for the period 1981–90, the recession affected Malaysia severely. Export earnings suffered a massive contraction, with commodity prices plunging to unprecedented lows due to lower demand in the developed countries. Workers were laid off. The government was unable to engage in counter-cyclical spending due to its earlier investment in heavy industry. This investment had been financed by external borrowing. In the early 1980s, given its petroleum resources, banks had lined up to lend to Malaysia.

Table 9.1 Selected economic indicators, Malaysia, 1981–90

	1981	1982	1983	1984	1985	1986	1987	1988	1989	1990
Real GDP (% change)	6.9	6.0	6.2	7.8	-1.2	1.2	5.4	8.9	9.2	9.7
Inflation (% change)	9.7	5.8	3.7	3.9	0.3	0.7	0.3	2.5	2.8	3.1
Unemployment (%)	4.7	4.6	5.2	6.3	6.9	8.3	8.2	8.1	7.1	6.0
3-month inter-bank offer rate (%)	10.6	9.1	8.0	9.8	8.2	9.2	3.2	3.7	5.4	6.5
RM/US$ (average)	2.3	2.3	2.3	2.3	2.5	2.6	2.5	2.6	2.7	2.7
Gross national savings (% of GNP)	26.1	25.0	28.0	30.7	27.5	27.4	33.5	32.8	29.7	30.7
Gross investment (% of GNP)	36.3	39.1	40.4	36.0	29.7	27.8	24.7	27.5	30.3	32.9
Govt. budget surplus (% of GNP)	-21.8	-20.9	-16.4	-13.2	-4.7	-10.1	-4.9	-1.6	-2.0	0.2
Current account (% of GNP)	-10.1	-14.1	-12.4	-5.3	-2.1	-0.5	8.9	5.5	0.7	-2.2
Money supply – M3 (% of GNP)	68.4	74.3	78.9	80.6	91.1	106.9	100.3	94.4	101.0	104.2

So when the recession hit, Malaysia had exhausted its borrowing capacity. The high global interest rates caused by the Reagan administration's economic policies in the USA made debt servicing a heavy task for the new industries.

By 1988 the economy had bottomed out. Meanwhile some market-oriented reforms were introduced and government budgets were slashed. Commodity prices slowly recovered. However, what really spurred economic recovery was the massive inflow of Japanese and Taiwanese foreign direct investment in the subsequent five years. This was prompted by the appreciation of the yen, triggered by the G7 countries through the so-called Plaza Agreement of 1985.

Economic Recovery

Almost all of these new investments were channelled into the FIZs and were geared for exports. This second round of EOI fuelled a sharp increase in the economic growth rates of Malaysia, as well as those of Thailand, Singapore and Indonesia. Real GDP grew at more than 8 per cent per year. This growth reduced the urgency for continued economic reforms. In the domestic economy, increased emphasis was placed on the privatisation of existing and new government projects and the expansion of investment in non-tradable infrastructure and the real property sector. The problem with privatisation was that, even more than before, projects were awarded without transparency and open tendering to UMNO-linked companies (ULCs). The award of the 869 kilometre north–south highway privatisation project to United Engineers Malaysia Berhad (UEM), one of the key ULCs, was a typical example (Lim, 1987, and Jomo, 1995, provide comprehensive analyses of Malaysia's privatisation programme).

Consequences of the Economic Boom

First, the boom virtually eliminated the unemployment problem and resulted in a significant increase in per capita income. In fact one of the major problems in the mid 1990s was the labour shortage, particularly in terms of skilled workers, as public investment in technical education had not kept pace with the demand for such skills. Second, the plantation industry also faced a labour shortage as more and more plantation workers were migrating to urban areas where higher-paying factory jobs were available. This problem was partially solved by importing foreign contract workers, mainly from Indonesia and Bangladesh. One consequence of this move was that the repatriation of foreign workers' income reduced the value added by the plantation sector to the Malaysian economy. It also depressed wages for Malaysian unskilled workers.

Third, the infrastructure and construction projects resulted in a massive increase in demand for loans from local financial institutions. Because many of these projects were awarded without competitive lending to ULCs, they were overpriced, thus lowering capital productivity. They also resulted in excess capacity in many key industries, such as telecommunication, commercial and industrial real estate and high-rise apartments. There was also a form of Dutch disease in the sense that the boom in the non-tradable sector drove up wages and other input costs. This in turn raised operating costs for the EOIs, thus eroding their competitiveness. In fact in 1996, growth in manufactured exports stagnated while current account deficits increased rapidly.

Fourth, this period also coincided with an inflow of foreign portfolio investment (FPI) into the Kuala Lumpur Stock Exchange. This inflow helped to finance the rapidly rising current account deficit and the expansion of the non-tradable sector, that is, construction and infrastructure projects. This situation was not sustainable in the long run.

The overall effect of the economic boom was that it tended to create a false sense of security and a sense that there was something unique about the Asian model of growth. Numerous books and articles by Asians and others debated the superiority of the East Asian development model. Some of these are cited and discussed in other chapters in this book. In the midst of this euphoria, Krugman (1994) suggested that the so-called Asian miracle was simply a result of rapid growth in capital and labour, somewhat similar to what had happened during the Stalinist era in the Soviet Union. This aroused much controversy and even indignation in the region. However if one examines the evidence carefully there may be some element of truth in Krugman's assertion. In Malaysia, for example, the inflow of foreign capital plus local capital obtained from the high savings rate combined with foreign and local labour to account for most of the growth. Much of the technology was embedded in foreign direct investment. Thus it can be argued that growth due to the endogenous total factor productivity was limited.

On the sociopolitical front, rapid economic growth lowered ethnic tensions. In particular the Chinese community became less unhappy because of the liberalisation of education through the establishment of private (many of them profit-orientated) colleges that offered joint degree programmes with foreign universities. New public universities were also established during this period. Thus more educational opportunities became available not only for bumiputera students but also for non-bumiputeras.

The growth also contributed to the expansion of the Malay middle class. This, together with the increasing proportion of Malays in the population due to their higher birth rate, led to the solidification of Malay pre-eminence in Malaysian politics. Thus the Malays too felt more secure about their socioeconomic and political position in the country.

On the other hand, rapid urbanisation and an excessive focus on materialism alienated a segment of the rural population. This was exacerbated by the neglect of the subsistence agriculture sector under Mahathir's administration. As noted above, his focus was on mega-projects and large-scale industrialisation.

All in all, however, the economic boom led to a strong sense of pride among Malaysians as well as respect and support for Mahathir, as reflected in the 1995 elections (Pillay, 1995). However the weaknesses that were submerged during the euphoric period became exposed when the Asian economic crisis hit the shores of Malaysia in July 1997.

THE ECONOMIC CRISIS AND ITS CONSEQUENCES

At the onset of the crisis the Malaysian economy had a bifurcated manufacturing sector. One of the segments was vigorous, internationally competitive, export-oriented and largely owned by foreign multinational corporations. This segment mainly focused on electronics and semiconductor products. The other was the import-competing segment, which concentrated mainly on cars, steel, cement and other heavy industries. This segment required heavy protection and subsidies to continue operating. Malaysia also possessed a globally competitive primary commodity sector, producing crude petroleum, natural gas, palm oil, rubber and timber. The non-tradable sector (construction, infrastructure, transport and telecommunication services) had also grown rapidly during the Mahathir era. The ringgit had become overvalued due to the large inflows of footloose foreign portfolio investment in the 1990s. With the unofficial pegging of the ringgit to the US dollar, it became even more overvalued when the US dollar started to appreciate against most other currencies in the mid 1990s. This, then, was the economic setting in Malaysia when the Asian economic crisis hit the country in the second half of 1997.

The causes of the Asian economic crisis have been the subject of much debate and controversy in the earlier chapters of this book and elsewhere (for example Montes, 1998; Krugman, 1998; Radelet and Sachs, 1998). The main issue is whether the crisis was caused by currency speculators and hedge funds or by the misalignment of economic fundamentals. The causes of the crisis in Malaysia in particular have also been widely discussed (for example Jomo, 1998; Lim, 1998; NEAC, 1998; Rasiah, 1998). Whatever the causes, the punishment suffered by the affected Asian countries was vastly out of proportion to the alleged mismanagement of the economy.

The Economic Effects of the Crisis

The extent of the immediate effects of the crisis in Malaysia can be seen in the collapse in the value of both the currency and the share prices listed on the Kuala Lumpur Stock Exchange (KLSE). The ringgit depreciated from around RM2.50 per US dollar in July 1997 to about RM4.80 per US dollar at its worst point in January 1998. Although it recovered somewhat after that, it was hovering around the RM4.00 mark when its value was pegged at RM3.80 per US dollar on 2 September 1998, when capital controls were imposed. This represented a 38 per cent depreciation. The economic impact of such a massive depreciation was quite critical, especially for businesses that depended on imported inputs for their production. Worse still was the volatility in the exchange rate during the period, which made business planning and decision making very difficult.

But more importantly, for the majority of the population the psychological shock of seeing the value of the national currency being decimated was traumatic. The stability and strength of the currency had been an achievement that the BN government had claimed credit for in the past. From the time that the ringgit was floated after the collapse of the Bretton Woods system in the early 1970s, it had strengthened from its fixed rate of RM3.00 per US dollar to as much as RM2.20 and had never returned to the RM3.00 level until the crisis. It is a safe bet to say that before 1997 virtually no Malaysian would have imagined a RM3.00 rate, let alone a RM4.00 rate.

Stock prices took an even more severe beating. The benchmark KLSE composite index, which had averaged around 1077 points during June 1997, collapsed to almost half that value in November 1997. The lowest monthly average was during August 1998, when it averaged 303 points. The extent of the collapse was even more dramatic in the second board index, which represents the smaller capitalised and more speculative companies. Here the index dropped by more than 90 per cent and many individual shares lost more than 95 per cent of their value during the 15-month period commencing July 1997. Many middle- and upper-class Malaysians had some part of their savings invested in the stock market, either directly or indirectly through unit trusts (mutual funds). The negative effects of such a dramatic erosion of wealth were stagnation in consumption spending and a sharp decline in investment, which in turn led to a sharp contraction in GDP, as shown in Table 9.2.

Real estate prices also dropped. Commercial property prices fell by as much as 50 per cent but the decline in residential properties was less severe. Nevertheless, for a generation of Malaysians who had been brought up on the maxim that one can never lose if one invests in real property, the slump was a real shock.

As can be seen in Table 9.2, GDP contracted by 7.5 per cent in 1998, the worst performance ever since independence in 1957. In 1999 the economy was expected to expand by 3–5 per cent. The only bright spot in the economy was the increase in exports. All the other components of GDP contracted sharply.

Unemployment did not rise as much in Malaysia as in other recession-hit countries. The most severely affected sector was the construction industry, where the vast majority of workers were foreign, mainly Indonesians and Bangladeshis. They bore the brunt of the employment effect as many of them lost their jobs and had to return to their home countries.

Inflation, as measured by the consumer price index, increased from 2.7 per cent in 1997 to 5.3 per cent in 1998, the highest rate of inflation since 1982. The major contributor to this rise was the 9.8 per cent increase in food prices. This affected lower income groups more than others. Nevertheless the sharp contraction in the consumption and investment components of GDP partly offset the imported inflation arising from the depreciation of the ringgit. Thus the inflationary impact was not as severe as originally feared.

The Social and Political Impact

In terms of wealth erosion, the crisis affected the middle and upper classes disproportionately more than the working class because of the collapse in the value of financial and real assets. Many middle-class Malaysians were angry and confused. This was in sharp contrast to the earlier feeling that Malaysia was invincible in its relentless stride towards the goal of attaining developed country status by the year 2020. This goal had been popularised by Mahathir using the catchy slogan 'Vision 2020' throughout the 1990s. The sense of devastation was particularly acute among young working

Table 9.2 Selected economic indicators, Malaysia, 1991–98

	1991	1992	1993	1994	1995	1996	1997	1998
Real GDP (% change)	9.5	8.9	9.9	9.2	9.8	10.0	7.5	−7.5
Inflation (% change)	4.4	4.7	3.6	3.7	3.4	3.5	2.7	5.3
Unemployment (%)	5.6	3.7	3.0	2.9	2.8	2.6	2.6	3.9
3-month interbank offer rate (%)	7.6	8.1	7.2	5.1	6.1	7.2	7.8	9.4
RM/US$ (average)	2.8	2.6	2.6	2.6	2.5	2.5	2.8	3.9
Gross national savings (% of GNP)	30.0	33.1	34.7	34.4	35.3	38.5	39.4	41.9
Gross investment (% of GNP)	39.3	37.1	39.8	42.5	45.7	43.7	44.8	34.8
Govt. budget surplus (% of GNP)	0.4	−1.4	0.4	1.9	3.2	4.2	6.6	−1.8
Current Account (% of GNP)	−9.3	−4.0	−5.1	−8.2	−10.4	−4.7	−6.1	14.0
Money Supply – M3 (% of GNP)	108.4	113.9	127.0	126.1	134.3	146.7	138.6	141.1

Malaysians – those in their twenties and early thirties – as they had never experienced an economic slowdown in their working lives. Jobs had chased after them and job-hopping, accompanied by a rapid rise in salary, was the norm in the booming years. The situation was somewhat similar in Thailand, but less intense. How did Malaysians react?

Initially they rallied around the leadership of Mahathir, who was equally if not more shocked and angry at the scale of the devastation. His much-vaunted East Asian development model, or more specifically the unique Malaysian development model, appeared to lie in tatters. Once he realised that the crisis was not going to be over quickly, he, just like his Western critics, began to look for scapegoats. While the mainstream Western media laid the entire blame on the corruption, cronyism and nepotism seen as inherent in the Asian way of doing things, he blamed Western speculators and shortsighted fund managers for causing the crisis. Mahathir's relentless attacks made him the symbolic Asian spokesman against the 'evil' and 'greedy' West. There was widespread admiration and support for his stand against the West.

At times he hinted at a conspiracy by Western nations to bring down Asia because they were worried about the economic ascent of Asian nations. In speeches to local audiences he claimed that the West was jealous of the success of Malaysia and other East Asian nations. He singled out George Soros, the well-known hedge fund operator, and even called him a 'moron', while Soros replied that 'Dr Mahathir was a menace to Malaysia'. Every time Mahathir made a controversial statement the value of the ringgit and the KLSE composite index dropped. And after a while Mahathir's utterances started to affect the value of other regional currencies and stock markets due the contagion effect. Mahathir still persists with his views. This is demonstrated by the following extract from a report in the *Singapore Business Times* (1 September 1999) on his National Day speech, which captures the style and substance of his attacks on the West:

In office since 1981 and Asia's longest-serving elected leader, Dr Mahathir made no mention of election dates in a state-of-the-nation address late on Monday. Instead, he urged Malaysians to defend the country's sovereignty and reject attempts by foreign powers and media to 'colonise' the country's economy and politics. 'We have been colonised for more than 400 years. We have been independent for only 42 years and we are not willing to allow this to be taken away with the advent of globalisation … we must defend our independence,' he said. Dr Mahathir frequently rails at unspecified 'foreign enemies'. He has blamed the Asian financial crisis which began in 1997 on foreign speculators and accuses the liberal Western media of eroding Asian traditional values.

The crisis also started to expose differences between him and his deputy, Anwar Ibrahim, both in style and substance. The markets responded positively to Anwar's actions and conciliatory statements, in contrast to those of Mahathir. These growing differences eventually resulted in a serious political crisis within UMNO, the dominant party of the ruling BN coalition. Fourteen months into the economic crisis, Anwar was dismissed from the cabinet on 2 September 1998. The next day he was unceremoniously thrown out of the party. Three weeks later he was arrested under the Internal Security Act (ISA), which provides for detention without trial. In his first night in detention, he was allegedly physically assaulted by the inspector-general of police, the highest ranking police officer in the country. The public discovered his injuries more than a week later. (*Aliran Monthly*, Oct. 1998, p. 40).

Anwar was later charged and convicted for attempting to use his office to block an investigation into alleged homosexual activities involving him. The conduct of the trial raised grave doubts among many Malaysians and human rights groups elsewhere about the operation of the legal system in Malaysia. Anwar was sentenced to six years in prison. His request for bail after he was initially charged was disallowed. The whole episode divided the nation, especially the majority Malay community, as never before. There has been a sea change in the political climate in Malaysia.[3]

POLICY RESPONSES BY THE MALAYSIAN GOVERNMENT

Before we discuss policy responses it is important to note that, in general, one's response to a crisis is conditioned by one's prior beliefs on the causes of the crisis. If one takes the initial IMF view that the Asian economic crisis occurred mainly because of structural weaknesses in the affected countries, then the recommended policy options will attempt to address these real or imaginary weaknesses. On the other hand, if one believes that the crisis was caused by external forces, then the policy options will differ. Thus Malaysia's response was conditioned by the view of those who made economic policy decisions at that point in time. This partly explains the series of reversals in policy since the crisis began. Here it is argued that many of the responses, especially in the initial period, appear to have made the economic situation worse. Our analysis of the government's response can be divided into three phases.

Phase 1: Shock, Anger and Denial (July 1997 to November 1997)

When the defence of the Thai baht was abandoned on 2 July 1997 the Malaysian authorities were not too worried as it was seen as a local problem confined to Thailand. When the currency speculators focused their attention on the peso, rupiah and ringgit, the initial response was to defend the currency. After suffering losses amounting to a few billion ringgits in less than a fortnight, Bank Negara Malaysia (BNM), the central bank of Malaysia, wisely gave up and allowed the ringgit to float.

Given the centralisation of power that had taken place during the Mahathir era, the policy makers took their cue from Mahathir as to the causes of the crisis. As we saw in the previous section, there was shock followed by anger. The blame was placed entirely on external forces, that is, rogue speculators and foreign fund managers. Many of Mahathir's words and policy actions are understandable given this world view. We shall highlight the main ones below. Firstly, in August 1997 the KLSE, under Mahathir's orders, arbitrarily announced that the one hundred stocks that make up the KLSE composite index had been declared 'designated' stocks, that is, they had to be traded on a ready basis. This was aimed at (foreign) speculators, who were alleged to be artificially depressing share prices by short-selling shares. The move backfired as investors panicked and liquidated more of their holdings, further depressing the composite index. This policy was reversed within a few days, thus damaging the credibility of the authorities.

Secondly, on 3 September 1997 Mahathir announced that the government was planning to set up a RM60 billion fund to support the falling stock market by purchasing shares from Malaysians at a premium while discriminating against foreign shareholders. He must have reasoned that it was perfectly legitimate to use public funds to counteract what he believed was foreign short-selling, which was undermining the economy. But foreign portfolio investors saw it as yet another attempt to bail out companies that were linked to UMNO and the regime's cronies. Around the same time the authorities threatened the use of the Internal Security Act and other draconian laws to detain anyone suspected of sabotaging the economy, including financial analysts and journalists writing unfavourable reports on Malaysia. In the eyes of investors it confirmed their suspicion that the authorities had something to conceal. Naturally all this led to another depreciation of the ringgit and a further decline in the composite index.

Thirdly, in a speech in Hong Kong on 20 September 1997 Mahathir argued that 'currency trading is unnecessary, unproductive and immoral' and called for it to be stopped and made illegal. He repeated this view in an interview with a Hong Kong newspaper the following day. This was seen as signalling an imminent ban on forex trading in Malaysia. As Jomo (1988, p. 19) puts it:

> Despite subsequent denial and clarification by Deputy Prime minister and Finance Minister Anwar Ibrahim, the market reaction was swift and painful, pushing the ringgit to a new low – which can only be explained by market sentiment, rather than any serious reference to economic fundamentals. Subsequent Mahathir remarks in faraway Chile on the last day of September plunged the ringgit to a new all time low, casting a long shadow halfway round the world on the Malaysian financial sector the next morning.

During this third quarter of 1997 the ringgit had depreciated by 27 per cent and the composite index had dropped by more than 30 per cent. But worse was yet to come.

The fourth example that can be cited was the reaction to the 1998 budget, which was tabled in parliament on 17 October 1997. The budget did try to reassure the market that the government was seriously trying to handle the crisis. Large-scale projects were deferred, corporate tax was reduced from 30 per cent to 28 per cent and government spending was cut by 2 per cent. Fiscal surplus was projected to increase in 1998. Disclosure requirements on non-performing loans were improved and increased provisions for doubtful debts were mandated. Yet the market was not convinced of the government's efforts to reform the economy, in part due to the erosion of its credibility and what Montes (1998, p. 29) describes as a problem of definition of the term 'economic fundamentals':

> Private asset managers appear to associate 'fundamentals' with factors that support the one-year to year-and-a-half stability of key asset prices, especially exchange rates. Economists and public officials would probably think of 'medium-term' in terms of 3 years and look on fundamentals more in terms of the impact of asset prices on real economic variables, such as output growth, exports, and employment.

This may explain why policy makers often view analysts' excessive focus on the short term as irrational.

The fifth and final example is also the most controversial. On 17 November 1997, United Engineers Berhad, an UMNO-linked company that owns the highly profitable North–South Toll Highway concession, announced that it had purchased a 32.6 per cent stake in its parent company, Renong Berhad (another UMNO-linked company) at a premium to the market price. UEM had borrowed RM2.4 billion to finance the purchase. Lim (1998, pp. 130–6, 172–7) provides a detailed and probing analysis of this episode. Apparently, 12 days before that the authorities had quietly granted a waiver to UEM in respect of extending a general offer to the remaining shareholders. The whole deal appeared to have been engineered to use the cash-rich UEM to save Halim Saad, the chairman of Renong, from the deep debt problems he was then facing. In the process the rights of minority shareholders in both Renong and UEM were completely disregarded.

The impact of this scandalous episode was swift and massive. In three days the composite index dropped by 19.6 per cent from an already low 667 points to a new five-year low of 536.6 points. It was perceived as a bailout for Halim Saad, who was regarded as a close associate of the powerful former finance minister, Daim Zainuddin. To arrest this sharp decline, Anwar Ibrahim announced that the waiver granted earlier would be withdrawn. The subsequent eight-week period of indecision by the authorities before they announced that Anwar's decision had been overruled made things worse by providing further evidence of the growing rift between Anwar and Mahathir.

In the realm of economic and financial management by the Malaysian government, this episode was undoubtedly the single biggest contributor to the erosion of credibility of the authorities. Ironically, the strongly adverse market reaction might have strengthened Anwar's position, at least temporarily, within the cabinet. Thus began the second phase, with Anwar trying to exercise greater control over the economy.

Phase 2: Acceptance (December 1997 to May 1998)

To reassure the market, Anwar introduced additional fiscal measures on 5 December 1997 for the 1998 budget. These included an 18 per cent across-the-board reduction in spending and the cancellation of some mega-projects. Interest rates would be allowed to go up and credit was to be tightened. These measures were initially welcomed by the market and the move was labelled as an IMF-style austerity programme without IMF loans. This major reversal of policy may have been partly due to Anwar's perception that Malaysia's economic problems were due more to domestic weaknesses and less to external factors. However it was pointed out by some that such highly deflationary measures would cause a severe recession (Pillay, 1998). These measures might have been appropriate if they had been introduced before the crisis arrived. With currency and asset price devaluation then in progress, the contractionary monetary and fiscal policies just accelerated the downward spiral of the economy. This somewhat tarnished Anwar's image as an able finance minister.

To be fair to him, two things can be said in his favour. First, once he realised the severity of the looming economic contraction, in April 1998 he began to take steps to ease the situation with further budgetary measures. Second, and more importantly, Mahathir and his supporters within the party and government continued with actions that undermined Anwar's policies. For example the creation of the National Economic Action Council (NEAC), which would have broad-ranging powers, and the appointment of the UMNO treasurer and former finance minister, Daim Zainuddin, as its executive director, clearly undermined Anwar's authority in economic matters. This was confirmed when Daim was able to get the appropriate regulatory body to overrule Anwar's decision on the UEM–Renong deal. In February 1998 Petronas, the national oil company, which is the direct responsibility of the prime minister's department, announced the proposed purchase of a number of ships belonging to a Malaysian company called Konsortium Perkapalan Berhad. The controlling shareholder of this company was Mirzan Mahathir, who happened to be the eldest son of the prime minister. Investors interpreted this (correctly, I believe) as another classic case of a bailout of cronies and family members.

All these actions caused the currency to spiral downwards, eventually reaching its lowest value of RM4.88 per US dollar in early January 1998. The currency and stock markets enjoyed a temporary boost in the next two months due to improved market sentiments and reaction to the relentless seven-month decline. By this time it was clear the economy was contracting faster than expected and changes were needed.

Phase 3: Regaining Control (from June 1998)

After six months of deflationary policies, the sharp economic downturn appeared to be threatening not only the debt-ridden crony companies but also other relatively healthier firms. There was much political pressure, especially from the Malay business community, to reverse the earlier policies. In June 1998, in the crucial annual UMNO delegates' conference, Mahathir's policies were criticised by a number of party officials who were seen as Anwar's allies. They stated that Malaysia had a serious problem of corruption, cronyism and nepotism – the slogan used successfully by the anti-Suharto movement in Indonesia. Mahathir prevailed in the meeting and from that point onwards the rift between him and Anwar appeared to be irreconcilable.

Soon after that the NEAC, which had been set up in January 1998, announced a national economic recovery plan. More importantly, Daim was brought into the cabinet as a minister with special functions. It was clear that Anwar was being marginalised. Fiscal and monetary policies were completely reversed. Public spending was increased substantially and the budget deficits were to be financed by the domestic sale of bonds. Monetary policy was eased, with interest rates coming down rapidly. The statutory reserve requirement for banks was lowered from 13.5 per cent in February 1997 to 4 per cent by September 1998, thus injecting more than RM30 billion into the banking system.

These measures began to put pressure on the exchange rate. To overcome this problem, on 1 September 1998 capital control measures were introduced. This was the most controversial of all the policy responses by the NEAC, and it was no coincidence that it was introduced a day before Anwar was dismissed from the cabinet. The governor of Bank Negara and his deputy resigned, apparently because they did not agree with the capital controls. The most important features of the new policy were as follows. Firstly, the ringgit would not be freely convertible outside Malaysia. Its value was pegged at RM3.80 per US dollar. Trade and foreign direct investment flows would not be obstructed. Portfolio investors would not be allowed to repatriate their funds for a period of 12 months after investment. This rule was subsequently amended to allow the repatriation of capital brought in before 15 February 1999, subject to a graduated levy or exit tax based on the duration of the investment.

The effects of the capital control measures have been the subject of much debate. While the government claimed that it had been a major success, others argued that its side effects would be felt for a long time to come, as distortions to market forces would almost certainly create problems for the economy in the long run. Paul Krugman, during a visit to Malaysia in August 1999, stated that the controls had been introduced too late. He saw no further need for them since the instability had abated. A positive result of the pegging of the ringgit was that it brought exchange rate stability for many importers and exporters. Nevertheless they were still exposed to exchange risks with respect to the currencies of major trading partners such as Singapore, Japan and Europe. The ringgit – at the rate of RM3.80 per US dollar – was perceived to be undervalued. This had provided a competitive edge to Malaysian exports, as reflected in the strong trade surplus.

To deal with the banking crisis, three special agencies were set up. According to the BNM (1998, p. 228), Danaharta was established in June 1998 to remove non-performing loans from financial institutions so that they could resume their lending activities and thus support economic recovery. By August 1999 it had taken over most of the non-performing loans in the banking system. Danamodal was established two months later to recapitalise financial institutions whose capital base had been eroded. Both these bodies worked very rapidly and ameliorated problems in the banking sector that were caused by the crisis. The Corporate Debt Restructuring Committee was set up in July 1998 to facilitate negotiations between borrowers and lenders on restructuring corporate debt. So far it has been successful only in a few cases.

FUTURE PROSPECTS

There are two extreme views on the future prospects of the Malaysian economy. Government spin doctors and supporters claim that Malaysia will make a strong V-shaped recovery in the next few years, achieving the precrisis high economic growth rates and low inflation. They also claim that all this will be due to the able, decisive and visionary leadership of Mahathir. On the other hand, many critics, both foreign and domestic, claim that while there has been a mild recovery in Malaysia, as well as all over East Asia, it is more due to the vagaries of external demand and currency-depreciation-induced competitiveness. In the long run only countries such as South Korea, Singapore and Thailand, which have introduced genuine reforms in their financial and real sectors, will emerge stronger, while Malaysia's economic recovery will be more in the form of a stretched U. They urge Malaysia to be more serious about its efforts at corporate restructuring, financial reforms and more general reforms of its economic and political institutions in order to set it on the path of sustainable recovery.

It is also instructive for us to note again that the Malaysian economy, as we have seen in earlier sections, has some strong positives: a globally competitive commodity-producing sector, a globally competitive export-oriented manufacturing sector, a high savings rate, a desirable demographic profile with an expanding middle class and a large pool of trainable workers, and reasonably effective government machinery.

However, if we examine the details of recent economic recovery the evidence appears mixed. As noted in earlier sections, there have been some reforms in the financial sectors but new problems have arisen. Credit for the productive economic sectors (agriculture and manufacturing) is not expanding fast enough due to the lack of demand for credit. Instead credit expansion is increasing for the purchase of real estate as well as shares and other securities. This may be setting Malaysia up for another asset bubble.

Much of the recovery can be attributed to a robust increase in external demand in the electronics sector (semiconductors and other computer-related products). This is due to the continued global strength of that sector, but if there is a cyclical downturn in electronics in the next couple of years the recovery is likely to slow down.

The other reason for the current recovery is the massive increase in public-sector spending, especially on infrastructure expansion. Malaysia can already boast of having some of the best physical infrastructure in the region, and further investment could lead to diminishing returns. Again this would not be sustainable *ad infinitum*. Foreign and domestic bond issues are funding the fiscal expansion. Sooner or later Malaysia will reach its borrowing limit, and in order to continue its fiscal pump priming it may have to resort to printing money, which would sow the seeds of inflation. Eventually this would erode the competitiveness that was gained by the depreciation of the ringgit.

Another drain on the economy is the protected, import-substituting manufacturing sector, which is still not globally competitive. The crisis has exposed its weaknesses and shielding it from genuine restructuring will definitely cause allocational inefficiencies in the economy.

The uncertain political climate also impinges on investment decisions. Many investors, both foreign and domestic, are concerned about the Anwar saga – with its revelations of the abuse of state power – and the alienation of a large segment of Malaysian society from the regime. This and other uncertainties can be erased only by a further general election. Although Mahatir Mohamad won yet another election in November 1999, this does not make his policies right, and it does not guarantee the country a stable and prosperous future. The choice is clear. Do Malaysians want to retain the authoritarian regime or would they prefer an open, transparent, social democratic government? I believe that sustainable recovery will not be possible if the current regime remains in power.

However this does not mean that the economy would face imminent collapse. For all its weaknesses, the regime is not as venal as the regimes of Marcos in Philippines and Suharto in Indonesia. It has also delivered some economic benefits to a sizeable section of the population, particularly the politically important Malay community through patron–client relationships. Given that it took a few decades to dislodge the Marcos and Suharto regimes, it is not inconceivable that the Mahathir regime may be around for some time to come.

Acknowledgements

I would like to express my gratitude to S. Sharmila and S. Vanmala for helping me with the typing of this chapter. I would also like to thank Frank-Jürgen Richter for his patience and encouragement while the chapter was being written.

Notes

1. For a more detailed account of Malaysian politics see Means (1991) and Milne and Mauzy (1978).
2. There are many detailed analyses of colonial and post-colonial economic developments, for example Jomo (1998), Gullick and Gale (1986) and Lim (1973).
3. Most of the regional media (for example CNN, *Asiaweek*, *Far Eastern Economic Review* and the *Asian Wall Street Journal*) gave extensive coverage to the Anwar saga. Among Malaysian sources, the *Aliran Monthly* and the website www.freemalaysia.com are excellent for their critical analysis of the political crisis.

References

Bank Negara Malaysia (1998) *Annual Report 1998* (Kuala Lumpur: Bank Negara Malaysia).

Edwards, C. B. (1975) 'Protection, Profits and Policy: An Analysis of Industrialisation in Malaysia', PhD thesis, University of East Anglia, Norwich, UK.

Gullick, J. and B. Gale (1986) *Malaysia: Its Political and Economic Development* (Petaling Jaya: Pelanduk Publications).

Jomo, K. S. (ed.) (1985) *Malaysia's New Economic Policies* (Kuala Lumpur: Malaysian Economic Association).

Jomo, K. S. (1988) *A Question of Class: Capital, the State, and Uneven Development in Malaya* (Singapore: Oxford University Press).

Jomo, K. S. (ed.) (1995) *Privatizing Malaysia: Rents, Rhetoric, Realities* (Boulder, CO: Westview Press).

Jomo, K. S. (1998) 'Foreword', in Lim Kit Siang, *Economic and Financial Crisis* (Kuala Lumpur: Democratic Action Party).

Jomo, K. S. and K. W. Tan (eds) (1999) *Industrial Policy in East Asia: Lessons for Malaysia* (Kuala Lumpur: University of Malaya Press).

Krugman, P. (1994) 'The Myth of Asia's Miracle', *Foreign Affairs*, November/December.

Krugman, P. (1998) 'What Happened to Asia?', mimeo (Cambridge, Mass.: Massachusetts Institute of Technology).

Leete, R. (1996) *Malaysia's Demographic Transition: Rapid Development, Culture, and Politics* (Kuala Lumpur: Oxford University Press).

Lim, D. (1973) *Economic Growth in West Malaysia, 1947–70* (Kuala Lumpur: Oxford University Press).

Lim Kit Siang (1987) *The $62 Billion North–South Highway Scandal* (Kuala Lumpur: Democratic Action Party).

Lim Kit Siang (1998) *Economic and Financial Crisis* (Kuala Lumpur: Democratic Action Party).

Means, G. P. (1991) *Malaysian Politics: The Second Generation* (Singapore: Oxford University Press).

Milne, R. S. and D. K. Mauzy (1978) *Politics and Government in Malaysia* (Singapore: Times Book International).

Montes, M. F. (1998) *The Currency Crisis in Southeast Asia,* updated edition (Singapore: Institute of Southeast Asian Studies).

NEAC (1998) *National Economic Recovery Plan: Agenda for Action* (Kuala Lumpur: National Economic Action Council).

Pillay, S. (1990) 'Performance of the World Tin Market: Effects of the International Tin Agreements, 1956–85', PhD thesis, University of British Columbia, Vancouver, BC, Canada.

Pillay, S. (1995) 'Election 95: Barisan Wins Big – Why?', *Aliran Monthly,* vol. 15, no. 4, pp. 3–11.

Pillay, S. (1998) 'Addressing the Crisis: Rethinking Policy Response', *Aliran Monthly,* vol. 18, no. 1, pp. 2–5.

Radelet, S. and J. Sachs (1998) 'The Onset of the Asian Financial Crises', working paper (Boston, Mass.: Harvard Institute of Development Studies).

Rasiah, R. (1998) 'The Malaysian Financial Crisis: Capital expansion, cronyism and contraction', *Journal of the Asia Pacific Economy,* vol. 3, no. 3, pp. 358–78.

Sandhu, K. S. (1969) *Indians in Malaysia: Immigration and Settlement, 1786–1957* (London: Cambridge University Press).

World Bank (1993) *The East Asian Miracle* (New York: Oxford University Press).

10 Suharto's Tax on Indonesia's Future

Hilton L. Root

The collapse of Suharto's Indonesia offers many lessons about the nature of economic development and the role that development assistance can play in facilitating economic change. This populous, resource-rich country was the flagship model of assisted development (Cole and Slade, 1996; Jomo, 1998; Root, 1996a; Root and Campos, 1996; Schwarz and Paris, 1999; Winters, 1996). The World Bank endorsed the Indonesian model with $25 billion over three decades. International investors interpreted the World Bank's enthusiasm to lend as a sign that Indonesia was a prime investment environment. Foreign investment peaked at $18 billion in 1996.

Then something went terribly wrong. In November 1997 the currency plummeted, losing about 80 per cent of its value against the dollar. Per capita income fell from $1300 to $340, wiping out several decades of economic progress. Even after the IMF managed to get its wish list of reforms included in its loan package, the rupiah continued to collapse.

THE ERA OF RAPID DEVELOPMENT

The depth of Indonesia's problems surprised international monetary officials, who had been very proud of Indonesia's accomplishments under Suharto. There was much to be proud of. As Indonesia's economy grew, poverty fell. Various indicators of progress, such as electrification, a phone service and paved roads, gave a strong impression that the benefits of growth were being broadly shared.

The first three five-year development plans were almost exclusively dedicated to rebuilding infrastructure and developing the rural sector. The first plan emphasised rural and agricultural development, self-sufficiency in rice production and modernised irrigation facilities. The second and third five-year plans, buttressed by the oil boom, prioritised rural infrastructure. The emphasis continued to be rice production, expanding physical and social infrastructure – roads, bridges, schools, health facilities – and promoting human resource development through universal primary education.

By the late 1970s the government's development programmmes had begun to show significant results. From a high of 60 per cent in 1970, the proportion of the population in poverty dropped to 28.6 per cent in 1980. Income inequality steadily contracted, with the Gini index declining from 0.40 in the late 1960s to 0.30 in the late 1980s.

An expenditure programme, INPRES, which institutionalised a formula for allocating revenues among various levels of government (central, provincial, district and village), was introduced to reduce interregional disparities. It provided flexible direct subsidies to equalise the infrastructure of all provinces. (Today INPRES has many critics, such as the inhabitants of oil-rich Riau, who claim that their province has not prospered from the $3 billion in oil revenues it provides to Jakarta each year.)

Indonesia was different from other oil-exporting nations because it used oil revenues to create income-generating opportunities for the rural poor rather than for pure transfers. Unlike in South Asia and Latin America, the immediate goal was not improving the distribution of income but rather the promotion of growth. The outcome was improved productive capabilities, greater access to markets and enhanced human capital.

WHAT PRICE GROWTH?

On the merits of its poverty-reduction record Indonesia was held up as a model, allowing for general forbearance of its poor performance in other areas of development administration. Compared with other resource-rich countries, Indonesia channelled more of its oil revenue into productive activities. However, compared with other East Asian countries, Indonesia's leaders did little to overcome the basic weaknesses in its investment environment (Root, 1996a, c). Property rights protection was the weakest in the region, as was the quality of the bureaucracy. The World Economic Forum consistently ranked Indonesia's business environment below the fiftieth percentile among a group of 14 newly industrialised countries. Transparency International ranked Indonesia as one of the most corrupt of the 50 countries in its annual ratings. As a result, private investment as a share of GDP was lower in Indonesia relative to other high performers, although the private investment ratio was higher than in oil-rich Nigeria or Venezuela.

Transparency has rarely been a factor in resource-based development. Property rights were weak during the California gold rush and in the early days of oil exploration in the USA. But other sectors of the US economy were transparent and rule-bound, so private markets developed in a broad range of industries and services. This was not so in Indonesia.

The quality of Indonesia's civil service resembled that of other countries that had not developed successfully. Indonesia's development programmes succeeded when they enjoyed direct and constant supervision by the president; but without direct supervision, failures in implementation were common. An example is Indonesia's failure to implement privatisation in 1996–97 because government agencies were unable credibly to organise auctions. Most of Indonesia's four million civil servants were part of the political party Golkar and were selected for political loyalty, allowing Golkar to crush its rivals. The civil service provided an important part of the voting population and it campaigned in the villages to mobilise support for the party. Their reward was the ability to collect bribes while supervising government projects. Demoralisation was commonplace for want of a well-defined, competitive career path with a reward for a job well done. Corruption was hard to avoid because civil servants had to pay a tax to foundations controlled by the president.

The central government forced districts to accept village administrators chosen by the nation's official party. With no accountability to the people they governed, answering only to Jakarta, these 'little Suhartos' in the villages could buy and sell village land. Many reputedly bribed their way into office and recouped their expenses by misusing village funds and fraudulently resolving land conflicts.

When Transparency International ranked Indonesia among the most corrupt countries in the world, Indonesian officials retorted, 'How can you argue with our consistently high growth rates?' There are several reasons why corruption in Indonesia did not seem to deter business. The country's growth was based largely on resource extraction, so it did not have to stake its name on providing a transparent business environment. Corruption allowed elite business interests to trample on the rights of rural society and thereby exploit forests and mineral wealth without having to succumb to the niceties of the law or due process. The system of corruption was highly centralised so that redundant extraction could be eliminated and people at the top could ensure that bribe payers had their informal agreements enforced. As a result, investors found the business environment as conducive to profit-making as the reputable and legalistic Singapore. In effect, profit margins in Indonesia were among the highest in the world, despite the corruption, because a lack of legalism allowed for unmitigated resource extraction and exploitation of labour.

High growth rates justified indifference to mismanagement, allowing multilateral donors to disregard poor governance, as reflected in rampant corruption, an outdated commercial code and an inept judicial system. Never a harsh word was heard from the two principal powers and donors in the region – both Japan and the USA highly valued the *status quo* in Indonesia. Japan had an eye to cheap natural resources and the increasing consumption of its industrial products. Since most of the deals were secured through networks, personal ties and political connections, Japan did not see any reason to encourage a change in leadership that might place those deals in jeopardy. The USA wanted stability in Indonesia because of the country's strategic importance as an anticommunist bastion during the Vietnam War, and sees it now as a counterweight to China's military strength in the region.

Indonesia had another charm to endear its donors. The technocrats who liaised with international donors were highly regarded and held their positions for long periods of time. Hence the country embodied the donor ideal of economic policymaking without politics (Liddle, 1996; Kingsbury 1998; Vatikiotis, 1998). Responsible macroeconomic management – including stringent controls on the budget, depreciation and currency convertibility – resulted from technocratic counsel. Inflation fell from triple-digit levels in the 1960s to single-digit levels in the 1980s. With inflation and poverty levels going down and the currency stabilised, the economy could absorb huge flows of funds from donors who were anxious to justify high levels of lending.

Two crises occurred that allowed Suharto to signal his commitment to technocratic solutions, even when close political allies were involved. In 1975 the state-owned oil company failed to meet its foreign debt obligations, and in 1982 oil prices collapsed. In both cases Suharto relied upon technocratic counsel to get the economy moving. Requiring only the consent of the top leadership, effective macroeconomic policies did not necessitate wholesale reform of the bureaucracy. The microeconomy was in the hands of the generals; technocrats managed the macropolicies and thus did not threaten the dissemination of spoils.

However reforms only took place during periods of economic crisis, when the flow of financial resources was threatened. Changes had to be prompted by product or factor markets. Internal discipline was lacking. The technocrats' advice was valued when their ideas were needed to get out of a crisis, but no process existed for continuous innovation on the basis of internal feedback mechanisms.

In any society, informal decision-making processes do much of the work of filtering or framing issues, generating a range of alternative solutions and placing new issues on the table. Indonesia had none of the advantages of informal social processes. As a society dominated by one decision maker, it lacked the ability to identify or resolve issues in order continuously to upgrade the policy environment. In Suharto's Indonesia, social agreements could be achieved in only one direction. Those outside the small decision-making hierarchy at the top had no way to signal their agreement or put their issues on the agenda. With decisions only being made at the top, social habits of political persuasion were irrelevant.

Unlike East Asia's high performers, Indonesia had practically no organised coalitions that were part of the decision-making matrix with power to influence government policy (Root, 1996b, c). The high-performing East Asian countries developed a governance framework in which alternatives could be articulated. Business councils met with the top political leadership to shape fiscal and trade policies as well as to monitor bureaucratic performance. Similar decision-making bodies were not allowed to flourish in Suharto's Indonesia. Informal organisations risked censure and sanction; even random conversations between individuals could result in punishment. With criticism silenced, friends of the regime were able to obtain funding for their projects even when market sense was absent. Inefficiencies in the allocation of resources, numerous white elephants and inefficient, mismanaged state-run industries all reflected the lack of accountability of those at the top and the absence of informal processes or networks at the bottom. Major investment decisions reflected the interests of a single clique, ultimately a single family. In politics, coalition dynamics that might enrich policymaking were absent, the scholarly debate in Indonesia's universities was frozen; its think tanks could address issues only obliquely. It was virtually impossible to obtain an objective assessment of the costs to the economy of any particular economic regulation.

Without durable economic institutions to establish clear rules, two routes to wealth existed, both of them informal: team up with the Chinese or sign up with the president's family. A system of informal business relations evolved in which the economically experienced ethnic Chinese ran the businesses, and the politically dominant military used its clout to secure regulatory arrangements and its muscle to ensure a compliant labour force. Owners ensured a docile labour force by keeping military commanders on the boards of firms (to which they contributed no managerial expertise). This lucrative partnership left many senior officers financially secure. The approximately six million ethnic Chinese eventually came to dominate the business of the archipelago. Although they made up only 3.5 per cent of the population, they controlled more than 70 per cent of the non-landed wealth, 68 per cent of the top conglomerates, 80 per cent of total assets of the top 300 conglomerates and nine of the top 10 private sector groups. Nevertheless their assets were trivial compared with those acquired by the president's family.

Because of the state's inability to ensure functioning markets, the ruling family had vast leeway to extract value from any proposed economic activity. With the legal system and commercial codes unable to sustain modern business transactions, investors depended on administrative or executive discretion. The result was corruption and opportunism. To overcome the government's inability to enforce rules, businesses relied on connections with some important agent of the state, such as the president's family. Would-be investors needed the political muscle of the Suharto family and their cronies to enforce property rights, overcome regulatory uncertainty and ward off rampant bureaucratic malfeasance and graft in the civil administration. Although their involvement in a deal created value for these potential investors, much of their wealth simply came from using the family name to gain access to state bank credits and government concessions.

The president's empire included toll roads, satellite communications, broadcasting, car factories, power projects, domestic airlines, taxi services and water utility trading ventures. The state-owned oil company alone had 143 contracts with firms controlled by the president's family. In many of these areas the family injected little management expertise or capital; they simply made it possible for friends to get government contracts and licenses. Since multinationals needed a local partner, the partner of choice was the Suharto family.

Jealousy was building up against both the Chinese and the Suharto family, but it was liberalisation that unleashed its expression. With resentment stewing, liberalisation heightened tensions.

THE DECLINE OF SUHARTO'S AUTHORITY

Indonesia's friends believed they had won a significant debate on how to help Indonesia. They secured more than $50 billion in assistance by convincing members of the international community concerned with economic policy that economic security must be established before political order could be reformed. But were they merely restating the assumptions that caused the country's economic collapse? They perpetuated several misleading myths.

Myth One: Popular Unrest Brought Down Suharto

Suharto followed a global trend and opened up the Indonesian economy in the mid 1980s. To gain greater access to foreign funds, he undertook a tax reform and liberalised trade and the financial market. Previously a complex licensing regime had determined access to the market, making investors dependent on political connections. By depriving Suharto of many of those powers, liberalisation created economic interests that he could not control and which grew to resent his domination of the economy. As a result his authority began to decline. By 1995, loose talk about Suharto's personal grip on the economy started to circulate, even among trusted advisers whose lips had been sealed earlier. Discontent among the elite nurtured the student movement.

During the riots preceding Suharto's resignation, eyewitnesses reported that looters were being ignored by the military. Many even observed the army withdrawing as the rioting spread and asked why the army did not act sooner to restore order (Aspinall *et al.*, 1999).

The army was going through an internal tug-of-war that escalated into a purge by General Wiranto shortly after Suharto departed. A unified elite could have easily suppressed the fledgling student movement. However, as the president's authority began to collapse, members of both the military and the technocracy defected, wanting to distance themselves from the regime. Suharto was the last one to know about the desertion of his troops.

Financial donors hoped that by giving the government some breathing room they could improve the welfare of the population. They failed to understand that Suharto's government owed little to the people in the streets. Infighting among elites fuelled the unrest. After the fall of Suharto new problems of collusion, nepotism and corruption surfaced as the politicians, bureaucrats and generals jockeyed to protect and even expand their empires. Many well-connected business groups espoused a position of economic nationalism in order to justify the return of protectionist policies. Indonesia's elites were concerned with protecting the spoils of three decades of monopoly, privilege and corruption, not on extending economic opportunities to Indonesia's poor. Upon taking charge in 1967, President Suharto emphasised shared growth to deter communism's strength throughout the archipelago. In the 1980s, with communism eliminated and tight control over the military established, Suharto increased his share of the take, leaving only crumbs for other members of his coalition, especially the military. Liberalisation reduced their once lucrative role as facilitators. With democracy and all institutions of accountability crushed, Suharto was able to divide the spoils among an increasingly smaller inner circle. Support for liberalism had its roots in the desire by those left out of the circle to overturn Suharto.

Now there is talk of the need to curtail the expansion of the international financial system or to subject cross-border capital flows to some kind of international governance. This is unfortunate. In the absence of institutions to make leadership explicitly accountable for economic performance, reform has come from the international financial markets. The capital market imposed the discipline that the internal control systems lacked. By buying into the myth that Indonesia can be stabilised economically without political reform, financial donors are contributing to the source of the problem: the unaccountable political leadership.

Myth Two: The Problems Could Not be Foreseen

Believing that Indonesia was on a sound path to development, financial donors pointed to unexpected circumstances to explain Indonesia's collapse. Unexpected circumstances are a fact of life, and all leaders face crisis; but some respond more successfully than others. Indonesia failed to respond to its economic challenge because its political system was frozen.

In fact the same unexpected circumstances that created catastrophe in Indonesia were prevalent throughout East Asia. Foreign lenders found local borrowers using pegged local currencies. The borrowers were willing to arbitrage relatively low foreign interest rates against higher local rates to make short-term loans. This resulted in the situation where a proliferation of intermediaries with funds to lend were chasing the few good projects. But Indonesia's banking sector, the region's most politicised, was also the weakest. Political opportunism allowed two kinds of abuse to develop in Indonesia's banking system. First, accountability was notoriously flouted so that funds could be channelled to friends of the regime. Non-performing loans to regime cronies accounted for much of the total private debt. A list of bad debtors, leaked in 1994, revealed that eight of the top 22 borrowers at the state banks were behind on 40 per cent of their loan repayments. Suharto's children and their associates were high on the list of delinquent borrowers. Second, internal corruption within the banking system was tolerated. Loan supervisors would typically collect 10–15 per cent of a loan upfront as a kickback. In both cases projects were not chosen on their economic merits. Adverse selection resulted in the funding of highly risky projects or of projects enjoying political protection. Banks did not become skilled at assessing the risk of particular investments because such skill was unnecessary.

Myth Three: Economics, not Politics, was the Source of the Problem

It was due to arrested political development that Indonesia's reforms were not credible. After the resignation of Suharto, active political figures carried baggage from the past; promising, capable young leaders were not available. Suharto's personally chosen successor, Habibie, having grown up in the Suharto household, was virtually a son. Twenty of 36 ministers of the reform cabinet had served in Suharto's last administration; many represented the same political interests that had blocked reform in the past, and they had the most to lose from future liberalisation or tighter supervision of the banks. With few options for multilaterals to depend on other than the existing power structure, the promised reforms lacked credibility. Investors, shunning an Indonesia that was run by the same individuals who had blocked change in the past, returned to Thailand and South Korea, where elected governments with new faces were committed to reform. Political failure was why Indonesia's problems surpassed those of its neighbours.

New leaders were elected in Thailand and South Korea in late November and December, 1997 respectively. Both of the new governments announced a series of far-ranging reforms in their first few months of power, which encouraged the marketplace to strengthen and stabilise their currencies. The marketplace, by contrast, did not view Indonesia's commitment to reform as credible without political change. The currency continued to fall even after Suharto relinquished power to Habibie in late May.

Myth Four: Prosperity can be Restored without Major Political Reform

The collapse of Indonesia's economy offers the donor community a clear example of how development assistance can postpone necessary domestic institutional and political reform. But history offers many useful lessons from analogous situations that can lend perspective to events in Indonesia.

Consider a financial crisis that occurred in 1787 in highly centralised, autocratic, old regime France. With the crown's finances shrouded in secrecy, a credit default spiral unfolded following a rumour that a private financier was bankrupt. Although the economy seemed healthy the government finances collapsed. In fact the French kingdom's credit structure was highly analogous to that of Indonesia under Suharto in several ways. The French crown's financial intermediaries capitalised on their own reputations by engaging in short-term overseas borrowing and lending this money to the crown at higher interest rates. With currency stability guaranteed by the sovereign, France became a haven for Europe's savings. But when doubts emerged about the solvency of the system there was no IMF to step in and provide breathing space. To avoid bankruptcy, the crown had to convoke an assembly of national representatives, who demanded political reforms in exchange for higher taxes. The political reasons for the French financial crisis were rectified through an extensive institutional overhaul that improved the accountability of the government to the citizens. France's complete political transformation included modern property rights and a public debt, helping transform a non-industrial, impoverished nation of peasants and lords into a major industrial power.

When the English monarchy ran out of funds twice during the seventeenth century it had to make political concessions to the parliament, which gained control over the purse strings of the government. The parliament demanded an annual budget from the king that anticipated all receipts and expenditures, so that it could predict and control spending. A funded public debt resulted, with the parliament holding much of that debt. As in France, a political settlement allowed the nation to exit a financial crisis with enhanced financial capacity.

By contrast, with the IMF stepping in, Indonesia has no incentive to design institutions that bind the interests of its elite to the welfare of the state. Instead Indonesia's citizens are now taxed by an international body they do not elect. As a result, Indonesia's future is more likely to resemble that of two other Cold War relics. Strategic allies of the West during the Cold War, Pakistan and the Philippines have the most reactionary social structures in their respective regions and the highest levels of debt to multilateral lenders. These nations have elected governments with representative bodies that are not accountable for the nation's fiscal performance. Just a few families, which rarely pay taxes, continue to dominate the economy; extreme inequality flourishes, and endemic corruption prevents long-term investment strategies.

However Ayub Khan's Pakistan was the donor showcase of the 1960s; the Philippines of Marcos was the flagship borrower of the 1970s; both featured high growth through donor-assisted borrowing. Both regimes were celebrated for being technocratic autocracies, yet their economies were and continue to be controlled by oligarchs who prosper by plundering governmental resources – much of which is borrowed in the name of the ruler – while contributing little capital of their own to the nations' industrial foundations. Loans to private individuals for pet projects that make little economic sense have been available through political contacts. Rich foreign friends bankrolling a compliant elite has made permanent beggars of both countries. The ability to roll over existing debts has helped them to avoid reforming the system towards public accountability. The resulting massive debt overhang has reduced the development prospects of both nations, making it virtually impossible for their economies to recover.

Will Indonesia join the cohort of nations that have become perpetual international beggars rather than link its citizens' private interests to collective responsibility for the nation's finances (Forrester, 1999)? The IMF bailouts imply that the nation must bear the burden of debt to pay for the loot of its leaders. Indonesia's situation could become the greatest case of debt overhang in history, as the entire banking system may have to be refunded to pay for the poor investment decisions of its leaders. Unable, then and now, to subject its leaders to accountability for effective governance, a country that might have been a giant is destined to become permanently crippled, able to provide prosperity to only a small segment of its population. Is this the future that Indonesia's friends had in mind?

References

Aspinall, E., H. Feith, and G. van Klinken (1999) *The Last Days of President Suharto* (Clayton Australia: Monish Asia Institute).

Cole, D. C. and B. F. Slade (1996) *Building a modern financial system: The Indonesian experience* (Cambridge: Cambridge University Press).

Forrester, G. (1999) *Post Soeharto Indonesia: Renewal or Chaos* (Leiden and Singapore: Institute of Southeast Asian Studies).

Jomo, K. S. (1998) *Tigers in Trouble: Financial Governance Liberalisation and Crisis in East Asia* (New York: St Martins Press).

Kingsbury, D. (1998) *The Politics of Indonesia* (Oxford: Oxford University Press).

Liddle, W. R. (1996) *Leadership and Culture in Indonesia Politics* (Sydney: Allen and Unwin).

Mann, R. (1998) *Economic Crisis in Indonesia: The Full Story* (Dublin: Gateway Books).

Root, H. and J. E. Campos (1996) *The Key to the East Asian Miracle: Making Shared Growth Credible* (Washington, DC: The Brookings Institution).

Root, H. (1996) *Small Countries, Big Lessons: Governance and the Rise of East Asia* (London: Oxford University Press).

Root, H. (1996a) 'Tensions Underlie Indonesia's Success', *The Asian Wall Street Journal,* 18 April.

Root, H. (1996b) 'Indonesia: Political Insecurity Linked to a Sense of Injustice', *International Herald Tribune*, 1 August.

Root, H. (1996c) 'Indonesia: Success is Threatened for Lack of a Modern State', *International Herald Tribune,* 2 August.

Schwarz, A. and J. Paris (eds) (1999) *The Politics of Post Suharto Indonesia* (Washington, DC: Council on Foreign Relations).

Vatikiotis, M. R. J. (1998) *Indonesian Politics Under Suharto: The Rise and Fall of the New Order*, 3rd edn (London and New York: Routledge).

Winters, J. A. (1996) *Power in Motion: Capital Mobility and the Indonesian State* (Ithaca, NY: Cornell University Press).

11 ASEAN's Position in the New Asian Order after the Economic Crisis – Management Strategies of Singapore: 'Present Pain for Future Gain'

Ha Huong

INTRODUCTION

From the early 1990s until 1996 the Asian economic boom was seen as a remarkable phenomenon in world economic history. Many books and articles were devoted to the rapid economic growth and tremendous achievements of the five 'Asian tigers' – Japan, Hong Kong, Taiwan, South Korea and Singapore. At the same time the membership of ASEAN increased from the six founder members (Malaysia, Philippines, Thailand, Indonesia, Singapore and Brunei) to nine with the admission of Vietnam in 1995 and Laos and Cambodia at the end of 1998. But then came the economic crisis. The recession started with the collapse of the foreign currency market in Thailand, insupportable foreign debt in Indonesia, the decline in the electronics market in Western countries, which affected the domestic market of Singapore, and political instability in Malaysia, Indonesia and the Philippines.

THE NEW ASIAN ORDER

Since the economic crisis a new order seems to have emerged in Asia. With the collapse or partial collapse of the five Asian tigers, China has been given greater consideration as a potential market in Asia. It has also been viewed as one of the strongest competitors of ASEAN in terms of military strength, nuclear weapons and political strategies. One of the factors in strengthening the position of China in Asia was the visit by the US president in 1997, opening a new page in the diplomatic history between the two countries. Even the tiny Pacific kingdom of Tonga cut its ties with Taiwan in order to set up a new diplomatic relationship with China. The handover of Hong Kong in 1997 has further increased the economic potential of China. Hong Kong has continued its economic activities and maintained its relative political stability.

Japan recently announced that it was nearing economic recovery – 'the financial crisis is about to be over and the rate has returned to its pre-crisis level' (AFP, 1999), but this is yet to be confirmed and other economic indexes have still not reached the expected level. Although Japan has been strong economically, it is not a potential contestant in terms of military strength when compared with China. Thus Japan may not become a major threat to ASEAN with regard to national security and military conflict. However it is a significant threat to ASEAN in terms of trade. On the other hand China is a big threat not only to ASEAN but also to other countries in terms of military strength. If China can gain more back-up from the USA it will certainly have more chance of consolidating its power.

While economic and military strength play an important role in classifying countries into various groups, information technology (IT) plays the main part in restructuring the world order. Since the advent of the IT revolution, high-tech devices and advanced technological methods have been applied in business, international trade, education, international relations, the armed forces and all dimensions of daily life. This is causing a dramatic change in social structure at both the national and the international level. There are two major groups: those with IT knowledge and skills and those without such knowledge and skills. Those who possess IT skills are similar to the capitalists of the nineteenth century. They can use IT as means of production to generate income and wealth as well as to control other activities. Those without IT skills can be compared to the proletariats, who had no means of production and were exploited by the capitalists. Their modern-day counterparts will be eliminated from the labour market sooner or later because of lack of competencies. This is the case in Indonesia, Vietnam, the Philippines, Cambodia and Laos, where IT and high-tech are considered to be too luxurious in the development of the countries. This can also be applied to other ASEAN countries (except Singapore) in terms of expanding market share with the use of advanced technology, such as electronic commerce.

Given this scenario, ASEAN obviously plays a secondary role in the international arena. The loose coalition between the member countries and the limited cooperation between ASEAN and other economic groups is evidenced by the low volume of trade with the USA and the EU. ASEAN only accounted for only 1–2 per cent of total EU trade in 1987, while '16.5% of its imports and 15.7% of its exports' went to the EU (Curry, 1984). Likewise, ASEAN does little business with the Middle East, South America and Africa. In addition, ASEAN depends heavily on the reabsorption of imports from Japan (Chua, 1999) and Western countries.

The new Asian order (mainly South and Southeast Asia) is depicted in Figure 11.1. Japan, China and Russia occupy the three main positions, forming a triangle with the USA, the IMF and the World Bank at the core. Due to time and information constraints, Russia will not be discussed in this chapter. The trade relationship between the EU and Japan is stronger than between the EU and ASEAN – in 1989 exports from the EU to Japan amounted to US$677 825 million while EU exports to ASEAN totalled just US$14 807 million (Tan *et al.*, 1992). Although APEC was set up as long ago as 1991, it has yet to prove itself as an economic unit.

The main ties are between the USA and China, the USA and Japan, and the USA, Japan and China. These ties give Japan great advantages in terms of rescuing its economy. China will have a greater opportunity to reform its economy if it opens its market more widely, relaxes political control and complies with international human rights laws.

Thus China and Japan will be the main actors in Asia in terms of international trade and international relations. China ranked second in a recent GDP growth forecast (*The Economist*, 16 January 1999). Hong Kong may become the gateway to Northeast Asia and will be Singapore's main competitor in terms of liberalisation of the banking and financial sectors (Chua, 1999). Singapore will consolidate its position as a financial and banking centre rather than an operation site, with the main focus on Southeast

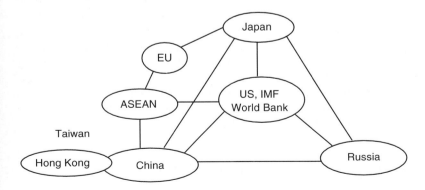

Figure 11.1   The new Asian order after the economic crisis

Asia. Singapore also has a strong technological base and invests heavily in R&D, which will contribute a great deal to its economic growth rate. If it is able to recover quickly, South Korea may be given the same rank as Singapore and Hong Kong. Otherwise it will join the rest of the ASEAN countries, which will be at the bottom of the rank due to their economic and political vulnerability. In addition they depend heavily on international aid and lack experts able to function competently in the international environment. Moreover the ASEAN countries may fall deeper into economic crisis if they continue to practice protectionism since they cannot just export and import to one another (Chua, 1999). Within this ASEAN group there are two sub-groups.

The first sub-group consists of Thailand, the Philippines, Brunei and Malaysia, where there are optimistic signs of recovery. With abundant oil and a small population, Brunei has been less affected by the regional crisis. Thailand's response to the regional crisis has been widely admired abroad because of the special efforts made by Prime Minister Chuan and his coalition government to stabilise the currency market. So far, President Estrada is managing to rule the Philippines with international support. Malaysia has applied a fixed exchange rate system, which could help to revalue the ringgit and control its outflow. However this can only be a short-term solution. Under foreign pressure, in early 1999 Malaysia announced a relaxation of monetary policy that enabled investors to take money out of Malaysia following a 30 per cent tax payment (*The Straits Times*, 6 February 1999). By showing its willingness to comply with international requirements, Malaysia might gain the support needed from international communities to boost its economy.

The second sub-group comprises Vietnam, Indonesia, Laos and Myanmar. With its tight political and economic controls and strong party protectionism, Vietnam can hardly integrate totally into the region in terms of economic development and policy making. Indonesia will not be able to recover without international assistance, and racial and ethnic clashes are driving away Chinese entrepreneurs and foreign investors. The more social unrest there is, the more the economy and people will suffer. In Myanmar, political infighting among the political parties for power and personal gain is the main hindrance to international trade and relations.

ASEAN: HINDRANCES AND CHALLENGES

ASEAN has a tremendous pool of manpower (more than 400 million people), plenty of land and abundant natural resources, such as oil, water, sea-food and so on. Nonetheless the member countries are still classified as developing or newly industrialised economies. To understand the challenges for ASEAN in the coming years, we should consider the following main points.

Firstly, ASEAN is not strongly integrated due to conflict among the member countries. At the national level, national leaders cannot achieve a consensus that would help them to gain bargaining power at the international level. If the ASEAN countries cannot settle their own disputes and solve their own problems, how can they manage to speak with one voice and gain a strong stake in the international arena? This situation is worsened by the superpower practice of throwing oil on the fire – the more conflicts there are among the ASEAN countries, the more that powerful countries can gain by selling weapons and consolidating their upper hand in the international chess game.

Thus ASEAN can hardly be seen as a big happy family as it cannot even achieve internal agreement. On the contrary, the individual countries tend to seek help and advice from outsiders. For example relations between Malaysia and Singapore soured because of water and air quality issues. Then Malaysia refused to borrow from Singapore, and turned to Japan for help. The ASEAN countries are doing little to help Indonesia with its economic reconstruction and recovery, so the IMF, the World Bank and of course the USA have become the main rescuers. Also, what is ASEAN doing to help newcomers such as Vietnam, Laos and Myanmar to integrate into the group? What is ASEAN doing to help Cambodia to settle its internal disputes? Surely refusing to allow Cambodia to join the group is no solution.

Obviously an opening has been provided for a foreign force or alliance to intervene in or influence domestic affairs. The question of whether foreign powers should play any role in the dismissal of leaders and the calming of social unrest should be further examined. Although the student movement in Indonesia is extremely strong it does not have clear objectives or strong, identifiable leaders. Thus, who have really stood behind all of these protest movements? In case of Malaysia, former Deputy Prime Minister Anwar was once the right-hand man of Prime Minister Mahathir. If Anwar had not been a good partner, then Mahathir would not have appointed him as his deputy. So what really happened behind the political scenes? Another hot issue is the dispute over Spratly Island. Among those who lay claim to the territory are five ASEAN members: Vietnam, Malaysia, the Philippines, Indonesia and Brunei. If these countries perceived themselves as a bloc or family they would reach agreement among themselves, which would obviously give them more bargaining power in their disputes with China and Taiwan.

Secondly, the lack of trust among member countries should be considered. As mentioned above, Malaysia accepted a loan from Japan rather than neighbouring Singapore. The Philippines turned to the USA for assistance in consolidating its armed forces. Indonesia is helped by the IMF and others rather than member countries. As world history shows, once you open the door to outsiders there are two possibilities: if they are friends they will help you to overcome your problems; if they are enemies there may be big trouble and much spilt milk to cry over. Nobody is altruistic enough to help freely without thinking of their interests. Only mutual understanding and mutual benefits can neutralise these adverse effects.

Not only are solidarity and unity missing from ASEAN, but also the formation of APEC has diverted its objectives. Some of the stronger member countries have favoured a coalition with powerful APEC members. As a result ASEAN may not form the core of APEC, as initially intended. Unlike the EU, which has reached the last stage of economic integration currency union, ASEAN is only in the third phrase. Although it was agreed at the APEC summit of November 1998 that AFTA should be put in place by 2002 rather than 2003, the likelihood of this happening is questionable.

Thirdly, the crisis of leadership in ASEAN has contributed to the economic crisis and political instability. Personal interest and ambition do not make leaders. It is certain that the relevant authorities knew about the foreign debts accumulated by the private sector, but they failed to take action until tragedy occurred. The dense network of roots spread so far and so wide that you could not cut one root without affecting the others. Apart from Singapore, which has had a strong and continuous government, other countries in the region have faced leadership crises in terms of strong protest by political opponents in Thailand and the Philippines and political opponents and the people in Indonesia and Malaysia. It is natural for opposition parties to make trouble for the ruling parties, but if the ruling parties are capable enough they can at least gain the support of their people.

Another concern is the competence of governments. In Indonesia, have the people at last found a president who can help them to overcome the recession? With regard to the Philippines, so far President Estrada has received optimistic reviews and some support, but will he and his cabinet be able to improve the economic growth rate and do better than previous presidents, or will he end up like his predecessors? Will he be able to get a stake in the international political world? In Thailand, although it seems that the coalition government of Prime Minister Chuan Leekpai is working well, his leadership has been challenged by opponents.

Fourthly, it seems that ASEAN leaders lack the ability to predict. A broad outlook and the ability to respond promptly to emergencies are not sufficient. There is a need for strong teams of capable and competent governmental officials with sufficient managerial experience and technical knowledge to lead their countries. At the moment ASEAN has to rely on international experts, specialists and consultants to assist it in most of its important projects and plans. Exchanging ideas and assisting each other to generate wealth for the world is necessary since there are strong ties among nations and markets. However, too much dependence on external factors or outsiders is not the best way to tackle problems since all countries have their own historical, political, social and economic characteristics.

Fifthly, protectionism is extensive in ASEAN. If the ASEAN countries want to defend their economies, regional protectionist measures should be applied rather than national ones. At the moment individualism and self-interest are the norm, for example ambitious Singapore wants to be the America of Southeast Asia, with the National University of Singapore as the Harvard University of Asia; and proud Vietnam insists on the supremacy of the communist party. Thus collective interest and benefits are a secondary concern.

Finally there is a miscellany of causes that contribute to regional instability. Here we should look at a combination of economic, social and political factors to analyse the situation of ASEAN. The lack of democracy, freedom, human rights and transparency is a major feature of public policies and affects the economic growth and social order of the ASEAN countries. In addition the personal interests of power-hungry politicians and other top leaders mean that collective interests are placed low on the agenda. Also, corruption, weak law enforcement and high crime rates undoubtedly deter foreign direct investment.

Although it seems that ASEAN does not have an optimistic future, some member countries can sustain their economic activities, including Singapore, which has designed new management strategies for the twenty-first century.

THE MANAGEMENT STRATEGIES OF SINGAPORE: PRESENT PAIN FOR FUTURE GAIN

Singapore, one of the five Asian tigers, was least affected by the economic crisis and is likely to recover first. In order to understand the factors that have helped Singapore to achieve its goals, this section will examine its particular strengths and opportunities, as well as its weaknesses and problems.

Strengths and Opportunities

Political Stability

One of the strengths of Singapore is that the government really wants to help the people. Other strengths are strategic position, small population and long-term rule by one party – the People's Action Party (PAP). The political map of Singapore has changed little since 1966, and the push and pull factors have remained more or less the same. This political stability provides Singapore with considerable advantages compared with other countries.

Singapore can achieve its goals faster and easier because the opposition parties are very weak and the government can do whatever it likes. There is no democracy or 'guided democracy' as in the case of Indonesia and elsewhere. Instead, as Chalmers (1992) notes, Singapore is a strong city state where 'the policy-making processes [are] increasingly shaped by domestic class forces'.

Racial and Ethnic Harmony

Another strength is racial and ethnic harmony. Singapore did experience turbulence in the 1960s and early 1970s, when racial riots and communist-inspired demonstrations were a daily occurrence (Souza, 1999). However, unlike Indonesia, where racial disharmony has become significant, the Singapore government introduced policies to normalise relations between the ethnic groups, namely public housing policy, recruitment policy and language policy.

Management Strategies

Singapore has adopted a system of strategic management in order to generate greater opportunities. Table 11.1 summarises these short-term and long-term strategies.

Fiscal and Monetary Policies   The cutting of interest rates in accordance with the lower interest rates in the USA and other countries was aimed at stabilising the economy and the foreign currency market. The fixed exchange rate system has been applied in Malaysia and shows some signs of raising the value of the Malaysian ringgit and stabilising the currency market in the region. However this is just a short-term solution.

Cutting Business Costs and Assisting Local Entrepreneurs to Increase their Investment   By dividing salaries into variable elements (bonuses, overtime, Central Providing Fund, or CPF) and fixed elements (wages),

Table 11.1 Strategic management in Singapore

Major strategies	Key measures
Short term	
Fiscal policy	• Cut indirect tax by cutting 10 per cent of CPF contribution
Monetary policy	• Lower interest rates to increase investment
Exchange rate system	• Floating exchange rate
Business costs	• Cut wages to decrease business costs
Investment policy	• Provide incentives to entrepreneurs
International competition	• Comply with international standards, such as copyright law, quality control regulations, environmental law, etc.
Long term	
Human resource policy	• Invest in education and attract foreign talent
	• Invest in educational projects such as the IT master plan for primary to junior high schools
	• Create a safe and sound business environment
Political stability	• Strict control on the opposition parties' activities
	• Maintain a 'clean' government, free from corruption
	• Control on the media and other communications
	• Cooperate strongly with pressure groups such as the NTUC (trade union)
Financial policy	• Invest in the financial and banking sectors
	• Relax control on the financial sectors, e.g. foreigners can be involved in the stock markets
Emphasis on R&D	• Invest increasingly in R&D projects through the National Computer Board and Singapore One (the national IT highway)
Economic policy	• Create jobs and assist local entrepreneurs
Development of service industries	• Promote tourism and other service industries

Source: Adapted from Lindenberg (1993).

the government has helped employers to cut their business costs. For example the CPF was cut by 10 per cent and salaries were reduced by 10–15 per cent, depending on the company in question or rank in the case of civil servants. Singapore does not want to become a welfare state, hence there is no unemployment benefit or other financial assistance, apart from reduced prices on 15 basic goods in NTUC (trade union) supermarkets. Retraining schemes have been launched to assist employers to retrain their employees, and to help redundant workers upgrade their computer, business or professional skills.

Local businessmen can seek assistance from the government in terms of document processing and favourable business conditions. The government has also helped entrepreneurs to promote their businesses and increase their international competitiveness by setting up electronic commerce through Singapore One – the national IT highway.

Tightening the Labour Market Job vacancies are offered to Singaporean citizens or permanent residents before they are opened to foreigners. However Singapore relies heavily on foreign talent and many foreign experts and specialists are recruited by MNCs. In addition, small and medium-sized enterprises in Singapore tend to recruit foreigners from traditional labour markets such as China and India in response to the high turnover of Singaporean employees in their companies. These migrant workers usually receive less pay and have less favourable working conditions than their Singaporean colleagues.

Investment in Social Infrastructure Education receives heavy investment at all levels. Realising the importance of human resources in the development of the country, Singapore has a policy of equipping the younger generations with both general education and professional education to meet the demands of the labour market at both the national and the international level. An IT master plan for the educational sector has been in effect since 1995 to provide students with relevant IT skills. In addition, people are encouraged to continue studying, for example by joining retraining schemes and similar programmes.

Weaknesses and Problems

Naturally Singapore does have some weaknesses and problems. For example there is a tendency towards excessive pride and overambitiousness. *Kaisu* (wanting to be the best, afraid of losing face) is a very commonly used word among young Singaporeans. They are ambitious to become a New Yorker in Asia, their universities will become the Harvard of Asia and so on. They have a right to be proud of all of their achievements in the past, but overambitiousness can lead to subjectivity and racial separation.

Another problem is the lack of space and time to be personally productive and creative. Singaporeans are proud of their high productivity at work, but they have to work 10 or more hours a day and even at weekend so there is little time for personal creativity. This may be acceptable in the short term, but in the long term, without a foreign labour force, will Singaporeans be able to achieve what they want?

In addition, tight control even on people's private lives may lead to the 'crowding out' of manpower. People do not have enough space to breathe and be creative. In other developing countries there are world-class engineers, scientists and academics, but it is hard to find a world-class Singaporean scientist, even though Singapore's GDP per capita is ranked among the top ten in the world.

Moreover labour relations are not always good in Singapore. Better understanding between employers and employees would be a good foundation for long-term relations and benefits. A brain drain may take place in the near future if talented foreigners feel that they are not being fairly treated and their work is not properly recognised. Obviously Singapore has to rely heavily on foreign talent, but on the other hand it has introduced policies to restrain the movement of foreign labour. As a result, if these people can find better jobs and better living conditions elsewhere, they will not hesitate to emigrate to countries where there is greater freedom and democracy.

Last but not least are the five Cs – car, cash, credit, condominium and certificate which people struggle very hard to possess rather than attending to traditional, cultural and basic human values, such as benevolence, solidarity, assistance and reciprocity. The latter should be fostered and developed. Moreover racial separation is observable in Singapore, especially in the case of foreign workers, who may suffer discrimination in terms of wages, refusal of permanent resident status, holidays and so on.

While the East can meet the West, the East cannot duplicate the West. In any case duplication is not a good strategy – modification is a better method.

CONCLUSION

Although we should not be too pessimistic about the future of ASEAN, it is too early to be optimistic. The ASEAN members will have to achieve consensus at the national level before they can confidently articulate their views with one voice at the international level. Solidarity should be consciously pursued in order to consolidate this loose integration. In addition, in the age of information technology ASEAN will have to work hard to catch up in respect of advanced technology, as well as become more competent in terms of political policy and international trade. Moreover a social infrastructure should be considered and developed to meet the basic requirements of the people. It will be a difficult and painful process for ASEAN to realise these goals.

References

AFP (1999) 'Japanese Crisis is Almost Over, Says Mr. Yen', *The Straits Times*, 30 January.

Chalmers, I. (1992) 'Loosening State Control in Singapore: The Emergence of Local Capital as a Political Force', revised version of a paper prepared for the Asian Studies of Australia conference.

Chua, Lee Hong (1999) 'SM on Prospects for Recovery', *The Straits Times*, 30 January.

Curry, R. L. Jr (1984) 'A Case for Further Collaboration between the EU and ASEAN', *ASEAN Economic Bulletin*, November.

Lindenberg, M. (1993) 'Key Concepts for Understanding national Strategy', speech at MPP Program at the NUS.

Souza, L. de (1999) 'S'poreans should not Take Tranquillity for Granted', *The Straits Times*, 30 January.

Tan, Kong Yam, Mun Heng Toh and L. Low (1992) 'ASEAN and Pacific Economic Co-operation', *ASEAN Economic Bulletin*, March.

12 China's Economic Growth and Transformation: Effects on the World Economy

Wolfgang Klenner

INTRODUCTION

Asia often comes up with surprises. During the Second World War and in the 1950s and 1960s, in spite of their own deep-rooted cultures and societies Asian nations became battlegrounds for ideological conflicts that had originated in Europe. Marxism versus capitalism became the crucial paradigm that split the whole region and even nations. Later on the East and Southeast Asian countries, which according to conventional development theory could not be expected to achieve overwhelming development success because of their lack of material resources, embarked one after another on a remarkable growth path, leaving countries richly endowed with resources, such as Brazil, far behind.

More recently there was another puzzling development: many of China's Asian neighbours that had achieved impressive economic success – which some time ago had motivated China to emulate their development concept, transform its economy and open up to world markets – suddenly faced financial disaster. China however, which only a short time ago seemed to be prone to political and economic turmoil, is enjoying rather stable conditions, at least for the time being. The political transition after Deng Xiaoping to a new leadership, which many observers thought would be a difficult process, took place rather smoothly. Moreover, contrary to the expectations of those Western-trained economists who tend to give credit only to 'pure' economic systems, China's mixed economy – which is still much less market oriented than the Japanese economy was in the early 1950s – is working quite well.

Even more surprising is the fact that China has experienced an enormous economic bubble but has nevertheless survived. Speculative investment has taken place in the island of Hainan, where even in small villages high buildings have been constructed between ricefields, and northwards along the coast to Shandong province and beyond. Much of this investment has proved unproductive – it has not resulted in increased output or better products. It is financed by banks on the basis of private connections, or via triangular debts, whereby companies provide each other with resources on a credit basis. Whilst China has experienced very similar or even worse developments than the rest of Asia, surprisingly they have not led to a crash. On the contrary, the currency has remained stable, the GDP growth rate is about 8 per cent, there is almost no inflation, foreign reserves stand at more than US$130 billion and for more than four years there has been an export surplus.

How can this be explained? China's financial stability is obviously due to the specific 'China mix', whereby economically unreasonable credit chains are cemented by personal ties between entrepreneurs and their friends in the banking system, the administration and the party organisation. Moreover financial flows between China and the outside world are almost entirely restricted to inward investment in material assets within China. Foreigners only have very limited access to China's financial assets. They are expected to invest in specific production projects that cannot be easily liquidated should rumours arise of liquidity problems in the country. Finally the Chinese government, when making use of foreign loans, has quite successfully balanced short-term credits with long-term credits.

This specific China mix is, from a theoretical point of view, not at all the best solution. It results in enormous misallocations and hence a waste of manpower and material resources. But in view of what has been observed in Korea, Thailand, Indonesia and other Asian countries, it is certainly not that bad for China, or not at the moment. But how might China's growing economy, which is only 'half transformed' and only partly opened, affect the world economy? We shall attempt to find answers to this question by looking at (1) China's role as a hub of economic growth, (2) its ability to control business cycles, (3) its exchange rate policy, (4) its ability and willingness to establish market rules and competition within its borders and promote market rules worldwide, and (5) its policy of attracting foreign capital and fostering exports on the other hand, and discouraging capital exports and imported commodities and service on the other.

ECONOMIC GROWTH

There was a famous slogan during the Cultural Revolution: *Duo kuai hao sheng di* (more, faster, better and more economically). These goals were never realised during the Cultural Revolution, in spite of the mobilisation of millions of people for economic and political purposes. Now, since the changes to the overall economic system, most of these goals are about to be realised. For almost a decade China produced roughly 10 per cent more products and services each year than it did the year before. Furthermore the variety and quality of products increased tremendously. Finally, the cost of inputs was reduced with the result that total factor productivity increased. It is not only Paul Krugman (1994) who questions the increases in factor productivity in Asian countries. Total factor productivity has always been something of a statistical dummy, that is, it is a matter of belief. However it is difficult to explain China's economic growth and the increase in the variety and quality of its products just by additional inputs of labour and capital.

As a result of this improved economic performance, public welfare has also improved substantially, although more than 100 million people still face the harshness of poverty. Conversely a few clever and lucky people, sometimes with fathers in high-ranking positions, have taken much more than their fair share.

As a consequence of China's integration into world markets, benefits have accrued outside China as well. Consumers in Western countries enjoy Chinese products at low prices. Entrepreneurs investing in China are able to earn profits, though quite a few Western firms have yet to reach break-even point. Because of growing competition from Chinese firms, Western companies are being forced to do better than before – which supposedly is not appreciated by themselves but is a bonus for the consumers of their products.

Certainly, China's economic development does not constitute the kind of economic growth that will place the world on a higher growth path. We expect an economic leader to develop new technologies and to apply existing technologies to new fields. Nothing of this can yet be observed in China as it is still in the process of catching up, importing technologies and applying well-established technologies in order to reform its outdated production system (Klenner, 1999).

However, in a world of slow growth, stagnation and recession even conventional growth is extremely helpful. The European continent shows no prospect of breathtaking economic growth for the time being. The economic development that can be observed in Latin America is still fragile. Many East and Southeast Asian countries, which for more than a decade were the motor of world growth, have subsided into financial turmoil, their currencies even temporarily disappearing from the world trading lists. Under these conditions conventional growth is helpful in a material sense because it means that China is able to absorb imports from other countries, thereby stimulating production abroad and providing new export opportunities. In a psychological sense it nourishes the idea of more than a billion consumers waiting for the specific product of a foreign firm – a dream that lies deep in the hearts of quite a few Western entrepreneurs. But much will depend on the steadyness of this growth. In this regard, comparisons of countries at different stages of development usually reveal that when a country in the low-income range ventures along a growth path, the growth rate of GDP rises as per capita income increases, but at a certain point it begins to decline again (Ezaki, 1995). One important explanation of this is that labour productivity rises from a low level in low-income countries to a comparatively high level in middle-income countries but decreases in higher-income countries (Oshima, 1995). Assuming that this finding is an 'empirical law' and taking into consideration the fact that incomes are comparatively low in China, labour productivity should grow, which will help to sustain steady growth.

This conclusion, however, requires a few qualifications. Productivity increases and economic growth in lower-income countries are usually spurred by increased industrial production. The decline in overall labour productivity in well-off countries is generally due to structural changes, whereby the employment share of service-related industries increases and that of the manufacturing sector declines. The important point here is that productivity in the service sector is usually below that in the production sector. For decades China, in line with the Stalinist development model, neglected services and now urgently requires additional capacities in this sector. The service sector therefore has to grow substantially faster than in other countries at a comparable level of development but without a history of socialist planning. The struggle to overcome past hurdles will probably render China's productivity growth relatively low in comparison with countries that are able to allocate most of their resources to the manufacturing sector. After this restructuring has taken place, China's labour productivity should increase according to the 'empirical law' described above.

The assumption that productivity in the service sector is below that in the production sector could be questioned. Certainly, specific services such as the restaurant sector hardly allow innovations. But we have to keep in mind that the forces that contribute to increased productivity stem from competition. Manufacturing enterprises increase their productivity because of competition – their products usually have to compete with those of other countries. Certain branches of China's service sector, however, are providing services that do not face international competition and very often not even competition at the national level. It could be argued that in these cases productivity might rise if protective measures were removed. Banking and insurance, for instance, have been subject to very little national and international competition. Hence even in the service sector there is potential for productivity gains, eventually resulting in a smaller decline in overall productivity than can be expected in countries with long-established market systems.

The opportunity for future productivity gains and hence economic growth can also be found in China's state sector. In general, growth in manufacturing has been high among private firms and township and village enterprises but low among state enterprises – although not as low as might be concluded from the flood of negative assessments of the state sector (Ishikawa, 1997). If China succeeds in putting the fundamentals right in this sector, productivity gains and additional economic growth should be possible. Finally, China's inland provinces, which still lag far behind the coastal areas, could become economic growth centres when the economic dynamics in eastern China are inhibited by infrastructural overload and rising wages and property prices. As is well known, transfer mechanisms – usually associated with foreign direct investment, trade and official development assistance – have been important components of the catching up process in less developed countries. Japanese economists refer to this as the 'flying geese concept' (Adachi, 1985; Ezaki, 1995). The basic idea is that countries that receive capital, know-how and other resources from industrialised countries are usually able to achieve relatively high economic growth rates and to advance technologically. As a consequence, step by step they are placed in a position to export capital and know-how to even less developed countries, and so on. It seems that this kind of transfer mechanism contributed considerably to the economic development that took place in East and Southeast Asia. China, too, has profited from such transfers, that is, from capital and know-how from Hong Kong, Taiwan, Japan, the USA and Europe (Klenner, 1999). It has also become obvious that a similar process is taking place *within* China, in that the private and collective sectors in the coastal provinces have reached the stage where they can transfer capital and know-how to inland provinces, thereby spurring China's overall growth and productivity.

Another question is whether China will be able to mobilise the capital required for further economic growth. In view of the change from labour-intensive to capital-intensive production and the wide array of infrastructure projects, enormous amounts of capital will be needed. Obviously China's own savings will not be sufficient to finance its future capital and technological needs. But the high savings rate (approximately 40 per cent) and the fact that China's investment rate did not stagnate when it opened its doors to foreign capital – as happened in some countries enjoying capital transfers – but instead increased, indicates that savings have not been substituted by capital imports and China seems to be in a rather good position to make full use of its opportunities as an industrial newcomer. Hence the important preconditions for a certain steadiness of economic growth can be assumed to be satisfied and this will also have a positive effect on the world's economic growth.

BUSINESS CYCLE

There are two aspects to a country's ability to control business cycles: its ability to control its own business cycle, which benefits the rest of the world when that country is large as China; and the extent to which a country is willing to cooperate with other nations in order to stabilise world economic growth state.

Several requirements have to be met before a country can control its own business cycle, but in this chapter only the three most important ones will be scrutinised. First, the country must possess appropriate monetary and fiscal tools. Formally, China has taken the necessary steps to introduce some of the modern tools of monetary policy such as a discount rate policy, an open market policy and a minimum reserve requirement. However there is no proper fiscal policy and the national tax system and budget are in a disastrous state.

Second, there should be sufficient experience in applying these tools. For example policy makers should know the extent to which changing the discount rate by one percentage point will affect firms' demand for investment. However the problem is that previous experience is only useful if conditions remain the same, or at least do not change fundamentally. But China introduced modern monetary instruments only very recently. Since then its economic system has been transformed in various steps and in batches in order to make way for market mechanisms. So far it has had virtually no useful experiences to help identify which investment functions and so on are available for applying the modern instruments.

Finally, there should be a broad framework that forces enterpreneurs to act and react in the right way when monetary and fiscal changes are introduced by the country's policy makers. This framework does not exist for state-run enterprises. For instance an interest rate rise of even 5 percentage points will hardly affect firms' demand for capital as long as they are able, because of their soft budget, to tap financial resources from administrative channels.

Since it is unable to meet the necessary requirements for applying modern monetary and fiscal instruments, China has had to resort to credit rationing. This usually means a stop–go policy, killing bad as well as good investment projects when credit limits are tightened, and giving leeway both to desirable and to less desirable investments when they are loosened. In the last few years there has been a definite 'stop' policy, with rather drastic results as far as individual citizens are concerned. Millions of migrant workers have lost their jobs in construction works. Millions of workers in state-run firms have been laid off. Quite a few workers older than 40 years have been forced into early retirement, receiving pensions that very often amount to just 30 per cent of their previous income. They might have been happier if they had been allowed to stay in the flats provided by their enterprise. From a macroeconomic point of view, however, the application of credit brakes within the last two or three years has resulted in a rather soft landing (Fan, 1999) – contrary to the expectations of many observers, including the present author. So far China's policy makers have proved to be willing and to a certain extent able to control China's business cycle.

Another question is whether China is willing to cooperate with other nations in order to stabilise world economic growth. It has to be acknowledged that this kind of cooperation is extremely rare, even among rich industrialised nations, and there are very few examples of countries being prepared to pull other economies out of a slump by increasing imports if this role runs counter to their own interests. In view of China's limited ability to control its business cycle for its own sake it will hardly be surprising if it makes little contribution at the international level. However its decision not to devalue its currency, for the time being, in the light of the financial turmoil of its neighbours can by judged as an important sign of its willingness to cooperate at the regional or worldwide level to help alleviate the structural problems of other nations. This brings us to the next point, China's currency policy.

CHINA'S CURRENCY POLICY

A leading economy is that which can provide the world with an international currency that central banks and individuals are willing to keep as reserves and firms use to denominate their imports and exports.

It goes without saying that China is unable to provide an international currency. The renminbi does not even have status and weight of the currency of a smaller Western country. However only a few years ago the renminbi was an international pariah – even mainland Chinese banks in Hong Kong refused to exchange it for Hong Kong dollars. Now, after the unification of exchange rates, the Chinese currency is gaining international respect step by step and many of the economic fundamentals supporting it are quite impressive. As mentioned before, China's foreign currency reserves are very high, and if Hong Kong's reserves were added (which of course should not be done) they would be enormous. The volume and structure of its foreign debt is not sufficient to arouse fear among its foreign creditors. Foreign investment accounts for more than US$150 billion. China has been successful in promoting exports and controlling imports, which from the point of view of the principles of free trade is deplorable, as will be outlined below, but it could be called a positive factor as far as the stability of the currency under the present conditions is concerned.

Moreover the exchange rate is basically stable as a result of the continuing trade surplus. Nevertheless a devaluation of the renminbi is being considered. Because of the drastic devaluation of currencies of competitors such as Korea, Thailand and Indonesia, Chinese officials are asking themselves how long China will be able to perform well on world markets when the products of Korea and other Asian nations become cheaper. On top of this, investors planning to set up plants in China are urging that, if the Renminbi is to be devalued, this should be done as soon as possible in order to save their new investments from devaluation.

However there are strong arguments against devaluing the renminbi, the most important of which is China's desire to establish the renminbi as a solid international currency that is worthy of the trust of its trading partners. Another point is that present investors do not want their Chinese assets to lose value and may lobby against devaluation. For the time being the government seems to be in favour of sticking to the present exchange rate. There can be no doubt that this is primarily because it serves China's own interests and goals, but by leaving the exchange rate unchanged China will help to reduce the burden of Korea and other Asian neighbours.

MARKET RULES

In a world economy based on market mechanisms, nations are expected to help establish and strengthen the international framework for workable competition. Since the Chinese economy lacks appropriate market and enterprise structures and its entrepreneurs hardly behave according to market rules, it is making no visible contribution to the free trade system.

It could be argued that China's move from a planned economic system towards a mixed economic system is already progress. However it should be noted that Chinese policy makers are hardly impressed by smaller and highly specialised Western companies who have had to face stiff competition for decades and adjust to the new market conditions. Quite the reverse – they are impressed by big corporations such as Mitsubishi and Siemens and the Korean *chaebol* (even if quite a few of them are facing enormous problems at the moment). In their eyes, big is beautiful – and China does have gigantic state-run companies. Thus most of China's economic policy makers do not share the Western paradigm of competition, rather they are fascinated by size.

There is some kind of privatisation of China's state-run firms in the offing and the possibility cannot be excluded that this will result in the creation of independent enterprises. However one should not be surprised if these enterprises maintain close links with the administration and continue to rely on the government coffers. In this event, foreign competitors will have to face gigantic Chinese firms that enjoy state backing, state subsidies and huge economies of scale because of the size of the Chinese market. It would be difficult to see this kind of 'China Inc.' as consistent with free trade.

TRADE POLICY

As is well known, for a while communist China cut itself off from the outside world. There was a period of self reliance lasting more than a decade, during which time China mobilised its own resources, mostly poorly qualified manpower, in the mistaken belief that it would be able to overtake the industrialised world. However from the end of the 1970s it began to follow a more conventional development approach by opening up the country to trade with the West and trying to attract foreign capital, modern technology and Western managerial know-how. By that time, socialist planning had provided China with a rather solid industrial base, which in spite of all its problems seemed to be more comprehensive than that of many other East and Southeast Asian nations when they started to integrate into world markets.

A liberal economy should allow a large degree of freedom in respect of imported and exported commodities, services, capital and labour. In China, however, the importation of commodities and services is discouraged, whereas exports are decisively fostered. While imports of capital are highly welcome, capital exports are kept under strict control. As far as the importation and exportation of labour is concerned, the degree of freedom is virtually zero. How does all this affect the world economy? In order to answer this question we shall look at the impacts on industrialised and less industrialised countries.

China's policy of attracting capital from industrialised countries is highly appreciated by Western enterprises and governments – it was not so long ago that Western politicians and bankers travelled to China in order to convince its leaders that using foreign capital and starting a 'growth cum debt' process was not the 'sin' that China's extremely conservative governments had long perceived it to be. The opening of China to foreign capital provided opportunities for rent-seeking capital, which can be profitable for all partners. In fact it has been quite successful for China (Zeng *et al.*, 1997), but not always for China's foreign partners. The share of joint ventures in China's exports rose from 1.1 per cent in 1985 to 31.5 per cent in 1995 *(The Economist*, 8–14 March 1997, p. 10). Foreign direct investment constituted about 10 per cent of China's total accumulated capital. It might be argued that such a low percentage does not justify these transfers being given so much attention. Indeed their role might sometimes be overemphasised. However it should be noted that foreign investors – by struggling with local administrations, which very often do not understand modern production and business methods – can help to create the necessary conditions for local businesses to thrive, thereby increasing the total productivity of the recipient country. Hence even a small percentage of foreign investment in total capital accumulation can have beneficial effects that go far beyond its size. It goes without saying that these effects are supported by credits to governments and firms, official development assistance (ODA) and other official flows. Of the less developed countries receiving foreign direct investment, China has been the main recipient. Moreover, or at least in 1995, it was also the main recipient of official development finance (Radke, 1999). In view of these facts it is understandable that China is regarded as a serious competitor by other less developed countries, who also want to profit from FDI and official development finance.

There is a general consensus that FDI usually increases intra-industry trade (Wakasugi, 1997). This is the case even when the input structures in the investing country and the country receiving the FDI are similar – a finding that goes against traditional international trade theory, which argues that countries with different patterns of factor endowment specialise in production that is best suited to their factor endowment. However it is evident that product differentiation is an important driving force, so countries conduct trade in industrial goods even if their input structures are similar. This is just a more theoretical view of the simple fact that firms, having moved their production bases abroad, develop regional procurement networks (Sakurai, 1995) even if certain limitations are imposed on them by local content requirements or other restrictive measures on trade. The development of China's international capital and trade flows seems to support these findings, or at least it would be rather difficult to use these figures to support the thesis that FDI hinders trade increases.

Japan, the USA and Europe have each contributed 5–10 per cent of foreign direct investment in China since 1988. A substantial proportion has been contributed by enterprises in Hong Kong, Taiwan and Macao (Chen and Wong, 1995; Kwan, 1990; Tang, 1995). But China does not only attract capital from industrialised countries – wealthy Chinese industrial groups in Southeast Asia, have invested in China too. In the latter case, Southeast Asian nations that were eager to attract foreign capital to build up their infrastructure and create production capacities had to face the fact that national capital was flooding abroad, thereby deepening their capital bottleneck. In this regard quite a few observers in Southeast Asia began to admire the entrepreneur owners of South Korea's *chaebol*, who in spite of attractive investment opportunities abroad, chose to invest within Korea in order to build up the national economy.

Comparable ambivalent effects have resulted from China's specific link between commodity exports and imports of foreign capital. This has not caused much of a headache for entrepreneurs and policymakers in highly industrialised countries, but it has caused problems for China's less developed neighbours. In the global economy, international entrepreneurs aim to extend their networks by establishing, for example, regional centres in the USA, Europe and Asia. When they establish their Asian centre in a specific area they usually attempt to supply other Asian countries with commodities from this centre. This means that if a multinational company invests in China, other countries in Asia, for instance Indonesia, will not only fail to receive any investment from this company, but can also expect it to try to sell its Chinese-made products in Indonesia. This might make Southeast Asian nations think twice about opening up their markets to each other.

CONCLUSION

We have obtained a rather mixed picture of the effects on the world economy of China's half-liberalised economic system and partially opened economy. In principle the extension of the free market and a higher level of international exchange should help to alleviate many of these problematic effects.

But China should by aware that failure to coordinate each of its steps in this direction could quite easily result in a disaster comparable to that recently suffered by China's neighbouring countries, where liberalisation took place without adequate care being taken of market requirements. Bailing out China would be much more costly for the IMF and the world economy than the measures taken to support Thailand, Korea and Indonesia. In order to move ahead, China will have to introduce a wide array of supportive measures such as regulations for financial supervision and competition, social networks to help to those unable to produce commodities for sale on the market, adequate industrial relations and so on.

References

Adachi, Fumihiko (1985) 'Trade, Growth and International Economic Conflicts' in *International Economic Conflict Discussion Paper* no. 21 (Economic Research Center, Faculty of Economics Nagoya University).

Chen, Edward K. Y. and Teresa Y. C. Wong (1995) 'Economic Synergy: A Study of Two-Way Foreign Direct Investment Flow between Hong Kong and Mainland China', in *The new wave of foreign direct investment in Asia* (Tokyo: NRI Nomura Research Institute Ltd, ISEAS Institute of Southeast Asian Studies, Tokyo Club Foundation for Global Studies), p. 243.

Ezaki, Mitsuo (1995) 'Growth and Structural Changes in Asian Countries', *Asia Economic Journal*, vol. 9, no. 2, pp. 113–35.

Fan Gang (1999) 'Kefu xindai weisuo yu yinhang tixi gaige', *Jingji Yanbjiu*, no. 1, pp. 3–8, 52.

Ishikawa, Shigeru (1997) China's 'open door' and internal development in perspective of the twenty-first century', in Fumio Itoh (ed.), *China in the Twenty-First Century: Politics, Economy, and Society* (Tokyo, New York and Paris; United Nations University Press), pp. 48–71.

Klenner, Wolfgang (1999) 'Japan's Economy – Coping with Structural Changes in East and Southeast Asia', *Economic Research Center Discussion Paper* no. 108 (Economic Research Center School of Economics Nagoya University).

Krugman, Paul (1994) 'The Myth of the Asian Miracle', *Foreign Affairs*, vol. 73, no. 6, pp. 62–78.

Kwan, C. H. (1990) 'The Emerging Pattern of Trade and Interdependence in the Pacific Region, Nomura Research Institute, Ltd', *Tokyo Club Papers*, no. 4, Part 2 (Tokyo: Tokyo Club Foundation for Global Studiews) p. 121.

Oshima, Harry T. (1995) 'Trends in Productivity Growth in the Economic Transition of Asia and Long-Term Prospects for the 1990s', *Asian Economic Journal*, vol. 9, no. 2, pp. 88–112.

Radke, Detlef (1999) *Private Kapitalzuflüsse nach China. Konsequenzen für die öffentliche Entwicklungsfinanzierung* (Berlin: Deutsches Institut für Entwicklungspolitik).

Sakurai, Makoto (1995) 'East Asian trade and investment policies', in Toshihiko Kawagoe and Sueo Sekiguchi (eds), *East Asian Economies: Transformation and Challenges* (Tokyo: Center for Asian and Pacific Studies, Seikei University, ISEAS Institute of Southeast Asian Studies), pp. 172.

Tang, K. Y. (1995) 'Hong Kong's Economic Relations with China', in *New Economic Partners: Dynamic Asian Economies and Central and Eastern European Countries* (Paris: OECD), p. 49.

Ueda, Kazuo (1998) 'Ajia Kiki o Keiken shite', in *Kaigai Tôshi Kenkyûjo hô* (Nihon Yushutsunyû Ginkô Kaigai Tôshi Kenkyûjo) no. 5, pp. 4–25.

Wakasugi, R. (1997) 'Missing factors of intra-industry trade: Some empirical evidence based on Japan', in *Japan and the World Economy 9* (Dordrecht: Elsevier), pp. 353–62.

Zeng Wuyi, Mo Sanxin and Zhang Hongcheng (1997) 'Woguo liyong waizi xiaoguo de hongguan fenxi', *Tongji Yanjiu, Beijing*, no. 4, pp. 3–8.

13 Governance, Fertility Transition and Economic Development: Cross-Country Evidence – East Asia and the Case of China

Yi Feng, Jacek Kugler and Paul J. Zak

INTRODUCTION

Prior to the onset of the Asian financial crisis in July 1997, East Asian countries had made tremendous strides in economic growth, raising real per capital income levels and improving living standards. Between 1960 and 1990 the economy grew by 542 per cent in Taiwan, 563 per cent in Hong Kong, 638 per cent in South Korea and 610 per cent in Singapore. Among the four newly exporting countries (NECs) in East Asia, during the same period the economy grew by 55.7 per cent in the Philippines, 209 per cent in Indonesia, 261 per cent in Malaysia and 280 per cent in Thailand.[1] Despite the current need for financial market reform, these countries have positive factors that can contribute to long-term growth, including human capital, an export-oriented economy, a propensity to save, entrepreneurship and a demographic change that is poised for growth.

This chapter focuses on the determinants of demographic transition, which is regarded as a source of economic development. Fertility has been found to affect economic growth. For instance, following an increase in population, a proportion of the nation's capital will be used by new workers, thus reducing the previous capital–labour ratio, which results in a decrease in the steady-state level of per capita output (Barro, 1997). Furthermore, when fertility rises, resources have to be diverted from the production process to the rearing of children. In addition, an increase in childbirth increases the cost of education, thus reducing the quality of education (Behrman and Taubman, 1989) and leading to a reduction in human capital stock. All these phenomena – a decrease in the steady-state level of per capita output, a reduction in production capital and a deterioration in the quality of education – result in a decline in economic growth. Statistically, it has been found that, in a reduced form, the effect of fertility on growth is negative (Barro, 1997), which is consistent with the three channels mentioned above, through which fertility may have an adverse effect on economic growth.

Empirically, East Asian nations showed a decline in fertility rates over the period 1970–95 (Figure 13.1). Hong Kong and Singapore experienced a fertility reduction of 71 per cent and 69 per cent respectively, followed by Thailand (68 per cent), South Korea (66 per cent), Indonesia (53 per cent), the Philippines (43 per cent) and Malaysia (38 per cent). Fertility in Taiwan was already low at the beginning of this period and dropped further to 1.75 per cent in 1995.[2] As will be discussed later in this chapter, the conditions in East Asia favour a rapid demographic transition.

It is important to identify the systemic determinants of population growth so that demographic conditions favourable to growth can be created. In this chapter, we argue that governments can increase economic growth by effecting a smooth demographic transition. As the strengths and qualities of governments vary, nations follow different paths in their demographic change and economic development.

The second section of this chapter discusses a political theory of fertility transition. The third section specifies a model to test the implications generated by the theoretical construct. The fourth section analyses cross-country data on demographic changes. The fifth section focuses on a case study of China. The sixth section concludes the chapter with policy implications relevant to policy making with a view to maintaining the growth momentum by overcoming negative demographic factors.

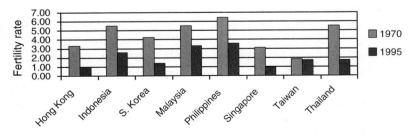

Figure 13.1   Fertility rate reduction in Pacific Asia

WHY SHOULD POLITICAL INSTITUTIONS MATTER?

The literature has so far produced two main approaches to examining the determinants of fertility change. The modernisation thesis argues that fertility reduction is a response to aspects of the modernisation process. For instance Thompson (1929) and Notestein (1945) propose that societies with increasing socioeconomic development will experience a decrease in the death rate followed by a reduction in the birth rate. Some empirical studies lend support to this general relationship between development and demographic change (Coale, 1975; Demeny, 1989; Bongaarts, 1992). The modernisation approach has inspired studies that link specific modernisation policies or social conditions to demographic transition. For instance Cowgill (1949), Kirk (1971), Nam and Philliber (1984) and Bongaarts (1992) look into the timing of changes and specific factors in modernising societies undergoing demographic change. Meanwhile Sinding *et al.* (1994), Freedman (1994), Camp (1993) and Bongaarts *et al.* (1990) examine specific policies aimed at changing the pattern of fertility through family planning, health, education and the empowerment of women. Furthermore Schultz (1989) and Barro and Lee (1994) show that fertility decreases as the result of economic prosperity connected with the advancement of female education.

In contrast, recognising the role played by the political system and government in demographic transitions, the political institutionalisation thesis maintains that it is the political system and governance that makes a difference in demographic transitions. Arbetman *et al.* (1997) refocus political analysis away from policy and towards structural determinants of fertility. They maintain that strong governments that are capable of controlling their population and extracting resources can effectively reduce the fertility rate as a result of not only the direct effects of policy planning programmes but also the spill-over effects of other government policies. Such policies include internal security, infrastructure projects, urbanisation, public health and education. Thus the policies of a government can have an indirect, often *unintended,* inhibiting effect on fertility growth. In similar vein, Ness and Ando (1984) and Midgal (1988) posit links between a strong society and a decline in population. Organski *et al.* (1984) show that regardless of policy preferences, a substantial reduction in the fertility and mortality rates takes place in societies where the political costs are low. Rouyer (1987) demonstrates that, in the case of India, the same population planning policy will reduce the fertility rate under a strong government but fail to achieve its goal under a weak one. Wolf (1986) and Coale and Freedman (1993) maintain that strong and effective government intervention in China has played a key role in reducing the high fertility level.

While we agree with Knodel and van de Walle (1979) that fertility declines take place under a wide variety of social, economic and demographic conditions, we believe, as Organski *et al.* (1984) argue, that any theoretical explanation has to start with political institutions. Chen and Feng (1996) and Feng and Chen (1996) discuss three fundamental political conditions for economic growth and socioeconomic development: political instability, political polarisation and government repression, which condition and constrain an individual's economic decision to invest in reproducible capital in the marketplace. Economic activity (a function of the accumulation of reproducible capital) will also increase or decrease as a function of instability, polarisation and repression. As Feng (1999) points out, however, political repression tends to have an indirect effect on the economy, while the effects of political instability and polarisation are direct and immediate. Therefore this chapter emphasises political instability and polarisation as the two main channels through which politics affects fertility transition and economic growth.

We argue that fertility decisions are not intrinsically different from choices about investment and consumption. The household, like the investment agent, examines the current and future political environment and evaluates information about political instability and polarisation when it decides what number of children to have or what amount of goods to consume. Political instability associated with political violence contributes to a rise in fertility rates, directly and indirectly. As the probability of children being killed increases with political violence, and as more children die from poor sanitation and lack of medical services because of political instability, the insurance incentives of parenthood rise. Such decisions can also be made *ex post* – that is, when young lives are lost in political violence, immediate replacement becomes an urgent need. The effect of this is the well-known postwar baby boom phenomenon that frequently compensates for the casualties of war (Organski and Kugler, 1980). In addition, political uncertainty reduces the opportunity cost of raising children. By disrupting the production process and lowering the value of earnings, the relative cost of fertility is reduced, making child rearing a more attractive option than before.

In addition to political instability, political polarisation also instils uncertainty into the market place and the decision making of investors and consumers alike. Polarisation is defined as the difference between the ruling party and its opposition in their policies for managing the economy and running the government. A large difference between the government and its opposition implies that the country may undergo a drastic change of course, keeping the probability of a government transfer as constant. Uncertainty generated by political polarisation will reduce the opportunity cost of having children, as growth under political polarisation decreases (Chen and Feng, 1996). This argument is consistent with Arbetman *et al.*'s (1997) suggestion that governments that are capable of controlling their population and extracting resources can effectively reduce the fertility rate through the spill-over effects of other government policies. Such policies may include internal security, infrastructure projects, urbanisation, public health and education. In the context of this chapter, capable government implies that the conflict between the government and its opposition is minimal and effective polarisation is reduced. Similarly, Zak *et al.* (1998) hold that a low political-capacity environment makes production more costly, thus reducing wages, which in turn raises fertility.

Fertility can be reduced through population planning programmes, female educational and employment opportunities and urbanisation and migration from the countryside (Bongaarts *et al.*, 1990; Camp, 1993). We propose that such a reduction in the fertility rate can be accelerated under a capable government and further enhanced by a stable political system. Under such conditions the government can improve educational facilities, provide adequate healthcare and institute laws and policies that increase both economic and political career opportunities benefiting women, and allow a choice of family planning.

In sum, we argue that political uncertainty causes the fertility rate to rise because political instability increases the probability of child mortality in the presence of worsening social conditions. Under such uncertainty, parents' preference tilts toward raising additional children as insurance. Additionally, the opportunity cost of having children decreases as the value of earnings decreases in the presence of political instability and violence. For the same reason, a weak and incapable government cannot succeed in reducing fertility, even if it has formulated a sound birth control policy.

This chapter focuses on political instability and government capacity as indicators of the strength of political institutions, which varies substantially according to national, social and political attributes. They capture non-economic differences in the environment for economic production and human reproduction. In addition to the modernisation thesis of fertility, the political environment provides a powerful alternative interpretation of fertility transition. Along with economic determinants, political institutions can have a pronounced effect on fertility decisions.

STATISTICAL SPECIFICATION

This section examines the operation and measurement of political instability and government capacity. It is impossible to have a viable long-term economic development programme, including population control, under a weak government or an unstable political system.

Total Fertility Rate

The dependent variable is the total fertility rate (TFR). The data are from the Global Data Manager 3.0 (World Game Institute, 1997). This analysis examines cross-country fertility patterns for the years 1970, 1992 and 1995, which are the only years for which the data set has substantial observations for the fertility variable.[3] To alleviate the endogeneity problem, lagged values are used for the independent variables – political instability, government capacity and real GDP per capita.[4] Crude birth rates (CBR) are used to check consistency in the estimation as well as to deal with the endogeneity problem.

Political Instability

Political instability is latent in the social and political system of a country. Feng (1997) distinguishes between unconstitutional government change, major constitutional government change and minor constitutional government change. He finds that unconstitutional government change (such as a military coup) has a pronounced negative effect on economic development. It is this type of government change that is utilised in the empirical testing.

Political instability is measured using a limited dependent variable model. The probability of government change is a function of (1) economic variables measuring the recent economic performance of the government (for example previous levels of inflation, consumption and income), (2) significant political events that may signal an imminent government change (for example riots, assassinations, general strikes or revolutions), (3) political structures indicating systemic stability (for example an effective state executive, parliamentary responsibility and an effective legislature), and (4) dummy variables grouping countries according to their continents so as to control for systemic effects not explained by the model. From the fitted values of a logit model using pooled, time-series, cross-national data, the probability of an unconstitutional government change for each country in any given year during the period 1951–89 is estimated. We expect political instability to have a positive effect on the total fertility rate.

Political Capacity

A government's political capacity, as defined by Organski and Kugler (1980) is measured by its ability to tap into the human and material resources of society. This indicates the degree of effective polarisation in the country. As taxes indicate governmental presence, political capacity is measured by the government's ability to collect taxes. Governmental operations depend on resources extracted from the population and cannot survive in the absence of such resources. Without some form of tax revenue there can be neither national unity nor state control. Failure to impose and extract taxes is one of the essential indicators of the government's inability to obtain and maintain support (ibid.). In this study we utilise the relative political extraction (RPE) measure developed by Arbetman and Kugler (1995), based on the difference between the *observed* taxation level in a country and the *expected* taxation level, determined by economic factors. A country of high political extraction presupposes a strong and capable government that is likely to implement its policy effectively. We postulate that government capacity has a negative effect on the total fertility rate.

Figure 13.2 presents a snapshot of the political determinants of fertility transition in seven East Asian countries. In terms of political capacity, the governments of six of these countries can be classified as 'strong', the exception being that of Thailand, which tends to extract about 30 per cent less from society than might be expected on the basis of its economic conditions.

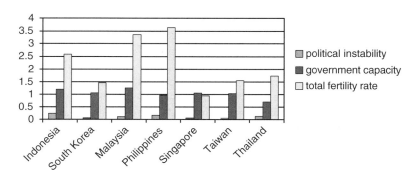

Figure 13.2   Fertility and politics in Pacific Asia, 1985–95

In terms of political stability, Singapore, South Korea and Taiwan are noted for their stable political systems and the low probability of unconstitutional government change, which is conducive to a low fertility rate. In contrast, political instability in Indonesia, the Philippines, Malaysia and Thailand is relatively high. Perhaps it is no coincidence that these politically unstable societies have high fertility rates compared with Singapore, South Korea and Taiwan.

However it can be argued that economic development and cultural or religious preferences also determine the fertility rate in these countries. The Roman Catholic Church remains predominant in the Philippines, Islam is the principal religion in both Indonesia and Malaysia, and Buddhism is popular in China. This line of argument requires that the political variables – political instability and government capacity – be controlled by economic and other systematic variables, including religion. Therefore several control variables are included in the model to test the political determinants of fertility transition. The following is a discussion of their effect on fertility and its measurement.

Gross Domestic Product Per Capita

Real GDP per capita is included in the estimation of fertility change to control for the modernisation effect. There is ample theoretical and empirical evidence to show that variations in income affect fertility. Thompson (1929) and Notestein (1945) propose that societies undergoing socioeconomic development will experience a decrease in the death rate followed by a reduction in the birth rate. Empirical studies lend support to this general relationship between development and demographic change (Coale, 1975; Demeny, 1989; Bongaarts, 1992). The GDP data in this chapter are from the Penn World Tables (Mark 5.6), which adjust national income levels according to the purchasing power parity standard, thus avoiding the complications caused by foreign exchange rates. We expect that a higher level of real GDP per capita will be associated with a lower level of fertility.

Religion

Among the religious factors, we include the percentage of the population belonging to the Roman Catholic,[5] Islamic[6] and Buddhist religious denominations.[7] Lesthaeghe (1983) asserts that differences in fertility levels and their speed of change are related to differences in religious beliefs and practices in terms of the degree of secularism, materialism and individualism.

Wetherell and Plakans (1997) have found that fertility followed different patterns among the Protestants, Eastern Orthodox, Catholic, Raskolnik and Jews of Riga, Latvia, during the period 1867–81. Religious affiliation is determined by self-identification and is not limited to those who consider themselves religious or members of a church, mosque or temple. The data were obtained in censuses, opinion polls and surveys and the source is Global Data Manager 3.0 (World Game Institute, 1997).

Region

While religion may influence the onset and spread of fertility decline *independently* of socioeconomic conditions (Knodel and van de Walle, 1979), cultural differences are clearly observed through regional differences that contribute to separated fertility regimes (Coale and Watkins, 1986). It can be argued that regional differences that include, but are not limited to, religious factors have a fundamental impact on fertility choice. In order to capture regional effects we use dummy variables to control for Latin America, Sub-Saharan Africa and East Asia.

STATISTICAL RESULTS

The results of cross-country regressions based on the statistical model discussed in the preceding section largely support the political model of fertility change.

The two policy variables – political instability and government capacity – have the expected signs. While political instability has a positive effect on fertility, the impact of government capacity on fertility is negative. These results demonstrate that political institutions do matter in determining the trends of fertility. The effects of political institutional variables become more pronounced when controlled by religious and regional variations. This result indicates that in the cross-country data, the predicted effects of political instability and government capacity on fertility become more precise when stratified according to the religious or regional groups than without control for them. The level of development is found to have a negative effect on fertility, which is consistent with the modernisation thesis.

Among the control variables, Buddhism and Catholicism have a negative effect on fertility but Islam has a positive effect. As these dummy variables may just represent substantial regional variations and not necessarily substantial religious content (for example Islam is correlated with Africa,

Catholicism with Latin America and Buddhism with East Asia), the religious variables are replaced with a regional dummy. While Africa has a positive effect on fertility, East Asia and Latin America appear to have an adverse effect, with the African and East Asian effects more pronounced.

Finally, when the religious variables are combined with the regional dummy variables, Islam and Africa remain positively related to fertility, while both Buddhism and East Asia contribute to a reduction in fertility. Catholicism and Latin America become statistically insignificant. Buddhism might be a proxy for the Chinese population in a country. It has been found in various studies that people of Chinese origin seem to have been more willing to practice birth control than those of other ethnic origins in the same country (Noor Laily *et al.*, 1985; Tan and Soeradji, 1986; Gastardo-Conaco and Ramos-Jimenes, 1986). Wang *et al.* (1995) and Zhao (1997) also find that the Chinese have a tradition of deliberate birth control.

The total fertility rate represents the average stock of children for women in their reproductive years. Therefore its use as the dependent variable has endogeneity implications. The right-hand side variables may have occurred before or overlapped with fertility. The effect of both political instability and government capacity on the birth rate is very strong. While the former boosts the number of new births, the latter depresses it.

Standardised coefficients (beta coefficients), which indicate the change in the dependent variable in terms of standard deviations, given one standard deviation change in the independent variable, is further illustrated. As standardised coefficients take into consideration the variation of the independent variables in the model (equal to the parameter estimate multiplied by the standard deviation of the independent variable and divided by the standard deviation of the dependent variable), they provide clues about the usefulness of the explanatory variables. Although both political instability and government capacity have lower beta coefficients than GDP per capita, they do add to the predictive power of the model, based upon both their variation and their causal impact on the birth rate. The replication and confirmation of the results strengthen the relevance of the political model in explaining fertility and births.

It should be noted that the cross-country evidence discussed so far on the effect of political institutions on fertility and the birth rate only deals with the direct effects of political instability and government capacity, keeping the level of economic development fixed. It is plausible, however, that political institutions affect economic development, which in turn influences fertility trends. For instance it has been found that political instability has a pernicious effect on economic growth,[8] lowering the level of development and increasing the birth rate. Therefore, in addition to their direct effects, political institutions may affect demographic trends *indirectly* through their effect on economic development.

CHINA: A CASE STUDY

We now turn to a detailed exploration of fertility in mainland China, a frequent subject of case studies given the attention to and debate on China's policy of one child per family. In the literature, there are four views on fertility transition in China. According to Zhao (1997), cultural elements have played a critical role in the success of the government's family planning programme. 'These elements are the traditional values concerning the relationship between state, family, and individual, and the related social norms. In contrast to Western countries where individualism has its origin, the interests of the state and the family were strongly emphasized in historical China' (ibid., p. 731). Wu and Jia (1991) and Zou (1993) likewise argue that Chinese people take the government's family planning programme seriously and willingly adhere to it because of cultural norms. Although traditional Chinese values regarding the relationship between the state and the family may strengthen the hand of state intervention, we argue that the political decision to act is vital to fertility decline.

From a traditional demographic transition perspective, King Whyte (1984) dismisses the existence of specifically Chinese characteristics in the fertility trend and attributes its rapid decline to the universal process of modernisation. He suggests that government and culture are irrelevant and argues that industrialisation, urbanisation and other forms of modernisation – all part of the worldwide industrial revolution and transformation – are responsible for the success of birth control in China. Likewise Lavely and Freedman (1990) consider that the rising levels of health, education and urbanisation in China might have initiated a fertility transition in urban areas with little government intervention. Nonetheless they find a conundrum: 'It is more difficult, however, to explain the precipitous subsequent declines in both urban and rural areas and the rapid rise in family planning among illiterate rural women by appealing to these developmental factors' (ibid., p. 366). Again, while we agree that modernisation contributes to fertility decline, we argue that the exclusion of political factors leads to misrepresentation of the process of fertility decline.

A third view of China's fertility transition is offered by Coale (1984), Chen (1984) and Poston (1992), who focus on a social demographic explanation of demographic transition in China. According to them, the significant drop in the total fertility rate in China between the late 1950s and the early

1960s was caused by the famine that took place during and immediately after the Great Leap Forward campaign. This period is noted for serious subfecundity as well as disruptions to the normal patterns of married life. The marked increase in the total fertility rate in the early 1960s occurred in conjunction with the economic recovery in China. It was also due to 'the restoration of normal married life, ... an abnormally large number of marriages and ... the unusually small fraction of married women who were infertile because of nursing a recently born infant' (Coale, 1984, p. 57). Alternatively it has been argued that 'the political climate of the 1950s and the 1960s was generally favorable to high fertility. The socioeconomic system, characterized by the "iron rice bowl," encouraged large families by making childbearing easier. For an individual family, the cost of bringing up a child might have been even lower than before' (Zhao, 1997, p. 753). Our argument is that fertility transition in China should be examined in a broader perspective than the short timeframe of the Great Leap Forward and a general theory such as ours should be tested on a long-run trend in order to have meaningful results.

Finally, Wolf (1986) challenges the modernisation thesis by emphasising the role played by the Chinese government in birth control and comparing the fertility patterns in Taiwan and China. While the trend of the former is gradual and seems to be irreversible, the trajectory of the latter seems 'erratic as a barometer chart tracing the changes preceding and following a series of violent storms' (ibid., p. 103). Taiwan's success in birth control appears to be more in line with the modernisation process, whereas China's is largely determined by politics. Wolf finds that two factors have contributed to China's fertility decline: 'The first is the great prestige enjoyed by the central government in Peking. The second factor is the penetration of village society by the national bureaucracy' (ibid., p. 114). To strengthen his argument, Wolf draws an analogy between India and China.

Birth control programs like those initiated in the early 1960s and 1970s would have had no more chance of success in China than Indira Gandhi's ill-fated efforts in India. As in India, the resistance would have barricaded itself behind the walls of village solidarity;. The Chinese program succeeded where the Indian program failed because the great collectivization program of the 1950s had already leveled those walls, putting the government in firm control of the communities they once sheltered.

(ibid., p. 114)

In contrast to the sociological interpretation of the fertility increase in the early 1960s, Wolf ascribes the rise in China's fertility and birth rates in 1962–63 to a 'superhuman effort demanded of the population' during the years of the Great Leap Forward.

Figure 13.3 shows China's total fertility rates at the national, rural and urban levels for the years 1950–90,[9] which seems to confirm the social demographic pattern summarised by Poston (1992) for China's fertility rates during the late 1950s and the early 1960s. The rise in 1962 was immediately followed by a decline when the first government-initiated birth control programme was launched, but in the 1966–68 period the rate rose in response to the chaos and lack of government control associated with the onset of the Cultural Revolution (1966–76). The rate subsequently dropped rapidly until the late 1970s, when it levelled off.

An alternative interpretation of fertility change in China can be offered, based on variations in political instability and capacity. The People's Republic of China was founded in 1949 after decades of civil war between the nationalists and communists, as well as the eight-year war with Japan. After assuming power the new government was involved in a series of wars, including the Korean War (1950–53) and the border war with India (1962). Meanwhile the Great Leap Forward (1957–60) ended in a severe economic crisis with major political consequences. 'Overworked and hungry populations began to turn against party cadres – apathy, disobedience, and even instances of insurrection spread in rural areas' (Townsend, 1980, pp. 115–16). Ideological indoctrination declined in 1961–62 and political victims of the anti-rightist movement attempted to rehabilitate themselves. The socialist education movement during 1962–64 attempted to mobilise

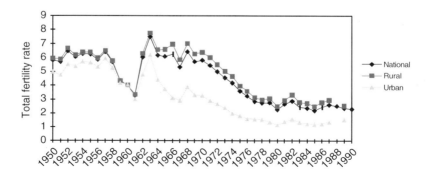

Figure 13.3   Total fertility rate in China, 1950–90

the nation, leading to the Cultural Revolution, which unleashed enormous political instability. As has been emphasised in this chapter, the birth rate tends to increase in the presence of political uncertainty and social upheaval. It is observed that the rise in the fertility rate in China occurred largely in tandem with an increase in political instability, which peaked in 1960 and 1968 in our data. Since the 1971 inauguration of a strict birth control policy, political stability and government capacity have played an increasingly important role in the success of the programme.

We have already reported cross-country evidence of the effects of political stability and government capacity on birth reduction. A case study of China will shed additional light on the political mechanisms of fertility transition. This section conducts two statistical tests. One is on time series data for China's total urban and rural fertility rates from 1950–90; the other is on cross-provincial birth data for 1989. The choice of years and the dependent variables are determined by the availability of data.

Family planning is a dummy variable that takes the value of one for the year 1971 onwards and zero otherwise. We have chosen 1971 as the starting year for the family planning programme because China's fertility rate was at a high level between 1949 and 1971 (with the exception of the late 1950s and the early 1960s), when the Chinese government voiced its determination to launch an official programme to control births (see Wolf, 1986; Zheng, 1995, pp. 238–9). This choice is also consistent with Figure 13.3, which shows that fertility in China started to fall evenly from the early 1970s, in contrast with the 1960s, when the pattern was uneven and fluctuating.

The inclusion of the family planning programme dummy variable is particularly important in the Chinese case. We argue that there is a difference between policy content and political efficiency. The success of a policy depends not only on the relevance and soundness of the policy in question, but also on the efficacy and efficiency of the government, as well as political stability. If the policy itself is enough to reduce fertility in China, then it is unlikely that government capacity or political instability will matter once the policy is announced. If, however, government capacity or political instability remains significant in its impact on fertility, even during the period of the family planning programme, then we have evidence that political institutions are important to successful policy.

The regression analysis uses autoregression, which corrects for various orders of serial correlation that tend to inflate statistical significance in time series data. The dependent variables in three regressions are the total fertility rate in rural areas, the total fertility rate in urban areas and the national crude birth rate. The statistical results, using Chinese time-series data, are highly consistent with those of our previous cross-country comparison. Political instability has a boosting effect on the total fertility rate in both rural and urban areas, as well as on the crude birth rate. Extractive capacity has a dampening effect on fertility and the birth rate. The years in which the political system was stable and government remained strong are associated with the years in which better results in birth control were achieved, even during the family planning period. A government can devise a birth control programme, but it requires a stable political environment and a strong government to ensure its success.

As expected, the dummy variable for the family planning programme tends to have a negative effect on fertility and the birth rate, though it is statistically significant only in the case of the birth rate. This result is not surprising. As the total fertility rate indicates the total number of children born to an average woman, this variable may not be sensitive to contemporaneous policy. The government-imposed programme has tended to be more effective in urban areas than in rural ones. One explanation of this is that urban Chinese are politically mobilised through their work units (*danwei*). 'By making employees not only economically but also socially and politically dependent on their work units, the regime in China gains full control over employees' lives' (Shi, 1997, p. 14). In order to ensure the success of its family planning programme, the government has had to increase its extractive capacity in the countryside. The policy would not work in the Chinese countryside but for the political stability of the country and the political capacity of the government. We have evidence that the policy itself is not sufficient for the success of birth control; the political environment matters too.

We further estimate the cross-province pattern of crude birth rates in 29 provinces and municipalities in China in 1989. Three dependent variables are estimated: the crude birth rate, the percentage of second births per person, and the percentage of third or more births, all at the provincial level. The policy variable in the equation is government capacity. As unconstitutional government change may occur only at the national level in China, it is not feasible to employ the concept of political instability at the provincial level. Local governments do not change or experience political crises in the same way as the central government does.

However government capacity does apply to the local level as provincial governments differ in their strength of governance. The provincial governments have gained political power in the process of economic liberalisation, and stronger provincial governments have been able to extract more from their populations and concede less to the central government. Prime (1992) has developed a measure of tax effort for all provinces and municipalities in China, except for Tibet, Taiwan and the recently established municipality, Chongqing. We utilise her operationalisation of government capacity at the provincial level in our cross-province analysis. The data for the independent variables are from Prime (ibid.) and the birth data are from the Department of Population Statistics (China State Statistics Bureau, 1990).

Even at the provincial level, the effect of government capacity on the birth rate remains negative and statistically significant. The effect is particularly pronounced with regard to second and multiple births. For provinces where the local government is strong, the percentage of second and multiple births is significantly reduced. As in all the other regressions presented in this chapter, provincial income per capita has a negative effect on the birth rate and is statistically significant in all three situations. At the provincial level, government capacity remains effective in reducing births, though economic incentives can also achieve the same end.

CONCLUDING REMARKS

This chapter has shown that politics matter in fertility transition, which is an important source of long-term economic development. In particular we have argued that political instability and political capacity are crucial factors in fertility change. The evidence from the cross-country data supports the argument that political instability serves to raise the fertility rate and strong government political capacity helps to lower the fertility rate. The time-series analysis also provides evidence in support of our theory, though we also find that output per capita is conducive to birth reduction.

The policy implication of our study is that fertility policy initiated and carried out under a stable political system and a capable government has a better chance of success than under an unstable political system and a weak government. The difference in the outcome of the family planning programmes in India and China attests to this point. Stable political systems and capable governments can thus prompt sustained growth by effecting the desired fertility transition. Such an approach is more effective than the alternative path of development characterised by the modernisation process, in which the reduction in births and the growth of the economy are simultaneous.

Organski *et al.* (1984) show that over the modernisation trajectory, the highest political costs of building up the political system occur at two extremes: when there is a low level of development and once the society is fully developed.[10] The implication is that transitional economies require an efficient and stable political system in order to achieve fertility reduction and thus accelerate their economic growth. Such economies might include Taiwan, South Korea, Hong Kong and Singapore in the 1970s and 1980s, and mainland China, Thailand, Malaysia, the Philippines and Indonesia at the moment.

This chapter has examined the trend of demographic change in the light of a theoretical construct and has tested the hypotheses generated by the model. Fertility transition has played a unique role in the development of Asian economies, laying the foundation for long-term growth in the region. In order to ensure the success of their development programmes, Asian countries should maintain a consistent population policy that contributes to an improvement in human capital and the quality of the labour force. Stability in population growth has a positive long-term effect on marketplace activities and business practices, thus promoting economic development in individual nations and the world.

Acknowledgements

This research was partially supported by the National Science Foundation (SBR-9730474). We thank Marina Arbetman and Zhongwei Zhao for their helpful comments and for making data available; Ismene Gizelis, Antonio C. Hsiang and Hui Zhang for their assiduous efforts in data collection; and Natalia Maric for editorial assistance. Yi Feng would like to thank the Fletcher-Jones Foundation for a faculty research grant which facilitated this research.

Notes

1. The source is Summers and Heston's (1995) cross-country data on GDP per capita based on international prices.
2. The Taiwan fertility data were obtained from World Bank (1993, p. 69); the initial year is 1985. The data for all the other countries were derived from United Nations figures via The World Game Institute (1997).
3. In addition to the problem of time-series analysis (see Barro, 1997, pp. 36–42), the absence of fertility data for other years renders panel data analysis impossible.
4. Average values for the ten years preceding the value of the fertility variable.
5. Roman Catholics include non-Latin rites.
6. Islam includes Sunni, Shi'a, Ismaili and Ahmaddiyah.
7. It is expected that a large Catholic or Muslim presence in the population will lead to higher fertility in a nation. In this context Catholicism is important in that it rejects contraceptive devices, while Islam may exert an effect on fertility through the promotion of marriage at a young age.
8. For instance see Barro (1991), Alesina *et al.* (1996) and Feng (1997).

9.　The birth rate data for the chart were obtained from the *China Statistical Yearbook* (China State Statistic Bureau, 1993). China's national, rural and urban fertility rates are based on the following: for the period 1950–82, China Population Information Center (1984); 1982–90, statistics from the Planning and Statistics Department of the State Family Planning Commission of China – the rates for 1982–88 are based on the 1988 'Two-per-Thousand Population Sampling Survey on Fertility and Contraceptive' released on 7 April 1991, and those from 1989–90 were based on the population sampling survey conducted by the Planning and Statistics Department of the Family Planning Commission of China in October 1992. The above data are summarized in Yao and Yin (1994).

10.　In less developed countries the organisation of political structures is difficult because so few in the population are organised for political purposes and awards are too small to give. In developed societies where political consolidation has been achieved, the government must overcome organised opposition to its new policy initiatives.

References

Alesina, Alberto, Sule Ozler, Nouriel Roubini and Phillip Swagel (1996) 'Political Instability and Economic Growth', *Journal of Economic Growth,* vol. 1, pp. 189–212.

Arbetman, Marina and Jacek Kugler (1995) 'The Politics of Inflation: An Empirical Assessment of the Emerging Market Economies', in Thomas D. Willett, Richard C. K. Burdekin, Richard J. Sweeney and Clas Whilborg (eds.), *Establishing Monetary Stability in Emerging Market Economies* (Boulder, CO: Westview Press), pp. 81–100.

Arbetman, Marina, Jacek Kugler and A. F. K. Organski (1997) 'Political Capacity and Demographic Change', in Marina Arbetman and Jacek Kugler (eds), *Political Capacity and Economic Behavior* (Boulder, CO: Westview), pp. 193–220.

Banks, Arthur S. (1971) *Cross-National Time-Series Data* (Cambridge, Mass: MIT Press).

Barro, Robert J. (1991) 'Economic Growth in a Cross-section of Countries', *Quarterly Journal of Economics,* vol. 106, pp. 408–43.

Barro, Robert J. (1997) *Determinants of Economic Growth* (Cambridge, Mass: MIT Press).

Barro, Robert J. and Jong-Wha Lee. (1994) 'International Comparison of Educational Attainment', *Journal of Monetary Economics,* vol. 32, pp. 363–94.

Behrman, Jere and Paul Taubman (1989) 'Is Schooling "Mostly in the Genes"? Nature–Nurture, Decomposition Using Data on Relatives', *Journal of Political Economy*, vol. 97, pp. 1425–46.

Benson, Michelle and Jacek Kugler (1998) 'Parity of Political Resources and Domestic Conflict', *Journal of Conflict Resolution,* forthcoming.

Bongaarts, J. (1992) 'The Supply Demand Framework for the Determinants of Fertility', Working Paper no. 44 (New York: Research Division of the Population Council).

Bongaarts, J., W. P. Mauldin and J. F. Phillips (1990) 'The Demographic Impact of Family Planning Programs', *Studies in Family Planning,* vol. 21, pp. 299–310.

Camp, S. L. (1993) 'Population: The Critical Debate', *Foreign Policy,* vol. 90, pp. 126–44.

Chen, Baizhu and Yi Feng (1996) 'Some Political Determinants of Economic Growth', *European Journal of Political Economy*, vol. 12, pp. 609–27.

Chen, Shengli (1984) 'Fertility of Women during the 42-year period from 1940 to 1981', In China Population Information Center, *Analysis of China's National One-per-Thousand Sampling Survey* (Beijing: China Population Publishing House), pp. 32–58.

China Population Information Center (1984) *Analysis of China's National One-per-Thousand-Population Fertility Sampling Survey* (China Population Information Center).

China State Statistics Bureau, Department of Population Statistics (1990) *China Population Statistics Yearbook 1990* (Beijing: Science and Technology Press).

China State Statistics Bureau (1993) *China Statistical Yearbook* (Beijing: China Statistics Press).

Coale, Ansley J. (1975) 'The Demographic Transition', *The Population Debate: Dimensions and Perspectives,* vol. 1 (New York: United Nations).

Coale, Ansley J. (1984) *Rapid Population Change in China, 1952–1982* (Washington DC: National Academy Press).

Coale, Ansley J. and Ronald Freedman (1993) 'Similarities in the fertility transition in China and three other East Asian populations', in Richard Leete and Iqbal Alam (eds), *The Revolution in the Asian Family* (Oxford: Clarendon Press), pp. 208–238.

Coale, Ansley J. and Susan Cotts Watkins (eds) (1986) *The Decline of Fertility in Europe* (Princeton, NJ: Princeton University Press).

Council for Economic Planning and Development, Republic of China (1997) *Taiwan Statistical Data Book 1997* (Taipei: CEPD).

Cowgill, C. P. (1949) 'The Theory of Population Growth Cycles', *American Journal of Sociology*, vol. 55, pp. 163–70.

Demeny, P. (1989) 'World Population Growth and Prospects', Working Paper no. 4 (New York: Research Division of the Population Council).

Feng, Yi (1997) 'Democracy, Political Stability and Economic Growth', *British Journal of Political Science*, vol. 27, pp. 391–418.

Feng, Yi (1999) Democracy, Governance and Economic Performance: Theory, Data Analysis, and Case Studies, manuscript (Claremont, CA: Claremont Graduate University).

Feng, Yi and Baizhu Chen (1996) 'Political Environment and Economic Growth', *Social and Economic Studies*, vol. 45, pp. 77–105.

Freedman, L. P. (1994) 'Family Planning as an Instrument of Empowerment', *International Family Planning Perspectives*, vol. 20, pp. 31–3.

Gastardo-Conaco, Ma. Cecelia and Philar Ramos-Jimenes (1986) *Ethnicity and Fertility in the Philippines* (Singapore: Institute of Southeast Asia Studies).

King Whyte, M. (1984) *Urban Life in Contemporary China* (Chicago: University of Chicago Press).

Kirk, Dudley (1971) 'A New Demographic Transition?', in *Rapid Population Growth* (Washington DC: National Academy of Sciences).

Knodel, J. and E. van de Walle (1979) 'Lessons from the Past: Policy Implications of Historical Fertility Studies', *Population and Development Review*, vol. 2.

Kugler, Jacek and Marina Arbetman (1997) 'Relative Political Capacity: Political Extraction and Political Reach', in Marina Arbetman and Jacek Kugler (eds), *Political Capacity and Economic Behavior* (Boulder, CO: Westview) pp. 11–46.
Lavely, William and Ronald Freedman (1990) 'The Origins of the Chinese Fertility Decline', *Demography*, vol. 27, 357–67.
Lesthaeghe, R. (1983) 'A Century of Demographic and Cultural Change in Western Europe: An Exploration of Underlying Dimensions', *Population and Development Review*, vol. 9.
Midgal, J. S. (1988) *Strong Societies and Weak States: State–Society Relations and State Capacities in the Third World* (Princeton, NJ: Princeton University Press).
Nam, C. B. and S. G. Philliber (1984) *Population: A Basic Orientation* (Englewood Cliffs, NJ: Prentice-Hall).
Ness, G. and H. Ando (1984) *The Land is Shrinking: Population Planning in Asia* (Baltimore, MD: John Hopkins University Press).
Noor Laily binti Dato Abu Baker, Tan Boon Ann, Tey Nai Peng and Rohani Abd. Razak (1985) *Ethnicity and Fertility in Malaysia* (Singapore: Institute of Southeast Asia Studies).
Notestein, F. (1945) 'Population, The Long View', in T. W. Schultz (ed.), *Food for the World* (Chicago, Ill.: University of Chicago Press), pp. 36–57.
Organski, A. F. K. and Jacek Kugler (1980) *The War Ledger* (Chicago, Ill.: University of Chicago Press).
Organski, A. F. K., Jacek Kugler, Timothy Johnson and Youssef Cohen (1984) *Birth, Death and Taxes: Political and Economic Transition* (Chicago, Ill.: University of Chicago Press).
Poston, Dudley L. Jr (1992) 'Fertility Trends in China', in Dudley L. Poston Jr and David Yaukey (eds), *The Population of Modern China* (New York: Plenum Press).
Prime, Penelope B. (1992) 'China's Fiscal Reform: A Cross-Provincial Analysis', Working Paper (Washington, DC: Center for International Research, Bureau of the Census).
Rouyer, A. (1987) 'Political Capacity and the Decline of Fertility in India', *American Political Science Review*, vol. 81.
Schultz, T. Paul (1989) 'Returns to Women's Education', PHRWD background paper 89/001 (Washington, DC: World Bank, Population, Health, and Nutrition Department).
Scotese, Carol A. and Ping Wang (1995) 'Can Government Enforcement Permanently Alter Fertility? The Case of China', *Economic Inquiry,* vol. 23, pp. 552–70.
Shi, Tianjian (1997) *Political Participation in Beijing* (Cambridge, Mass.: Harvard University Press).
Sinding, S., J. Ross and A. Rosenfield (1994) 'Seeking Common Ground: Unmet Need and the Demographic Goals', *International Family Planning Perspectives*, vol. 20, pp. 23–8.
Tan, Mely G. and Budi Soeradji (1986) *Ethnicity and Fertility in Indonesia* (Singapore: Institute of Southeast Asia Studies).
Thompson, W. S. (1929) 'Population', *American Journal of Sociology,* vol. 34, pp. 959–75.

Townsend, James R. (1980) *Politics in China,* 2nd edn (Boston, Mass.: Little, Brown).

Wang, Feng, James Lee and Cameron Campbell (1995) 'Marital fertility control among the Qing nobility: Implications of two types of preventive checks', *Population Studies,* vol. 49, pp. 383–400.

Wetherell, Charles and Anderjs Plakans (1997) 'Fertility and Culture in Eastern Europe: A Case Study of Riga, Latvia, 1867–1881', *European Journal of Population,* vol. 13, pp. 243–68.

Wolf, Arthur (1986) 'The Preeminent Role of Government Intervention in China's Family Revolution', *Population and Development Review,* vol. 12, pp. 101–16.

World Bank (1993) *World Population Projections: Estimates and Projections with Related Demographic Statistics* (Baltimore, MD: John Hopkins University Press).

World Game Institute (1997) *Global Data Manager 3.0: The Source of Global Statistics on Your Personal Computer* (Philadelphia, PA: World Game Institute).

Wu, Canping and Shan Jia (1991) 'Chinese Culture and Fertility Decline', *China's Population Science,* vol. 5, pp. 7–12.

Yao, Xinwu and Yin Hua (1994) *Basic Data of China's Population* (Beijing: China Population Publishing House).

Zak, Paul, Jacek Kugler and Yi Feng (1998) 'Endogenous Growth, Fertility and the Migration of Productive Factors', Working Paper, (Claremont, CA.: Claremont Graduate University).

Zhao, Zhongwei (1997) 'Deliberate Birth Control under a High-Fertility Regime: Reproductive Behavior in China before 1970', *Population and Development Review,* vol. 23, pp. 729–67.

Zheng, Xiaoying (1995) *China's Female Population and Development* (Beijing: Beijing University Press).

Zou, Qingfeng (1993) 'China's Family Planning and the Chinese Culture', in D. Bing, S. Lim and M. Lin (eds), *Asia 2000: Modern China in Transition* (New Zealand: University of Waikato Printery), pp. 92–107.

Part Three
Strategic Responses of Asian Firms

14 Successful Strategies in Post-Crisis Asia

Usha C. V. Haley

INTRODUCTION

Asia's rapid economic growth, previously the principal attraction for foreign direct investment, now appears to be a hallmark of the past. Local companies are suffering along with multinational companies (MNCs). In Thailand, real-estate agents are selling noodles on the street. Indonesia, once home to more than 240 banks, will probably retain less than five. The Philippines has already lost a national airline and is struggling to resuscitate it. Yet increased market openness and other structural and regulatory changes in the wake of the crisis have created a new set of opportunities for companies. This chapter examines some of the strategies employed by companies that appear to be winning in the new Asian economic, social and political environment.

An Andersen Consulting survey of more than 70 MNCs operating in Asia found that the financial crisis has 'shifted the shoreline' of market dynamics in the region, prompting companies to revamp their business strategies and aggressively pursue opportunities for expansion in new markets (Burrell, 1999). However the survey also found that rapid responses appear to be the key to success for companies seeking to exploit these openings, with major MNCs such as GE Capital, Unilever, British Telecom and Coca-Cola already investing billions of dollars in the region. As Haley *et al.* (1998) have argued, MNCs often freeze when operating under the uncertain conditions of Asian business environments. Yet as Alan Salter, Andersen Consulting's managing partner for strategy in the Asia-Pacific region, stated, 'Those who recognize the shift in the shoreline and have the boldness to act will find the opportunities are enormous' (Burrell, 1999).

For MNCs, the Asian markets' new strategic dynamics (Burrell, 1999) include building market share while competitors are weak, regionalisation to diversify local market risks and build critical mass, exploitation of market liberalisation and foreign investment rules, and adoption of new technologies to gain competitive advantages and create more efficient production and distribution networks. In the wake of financial reforms brought about by gross mismanagement and corruption (ibid.), some local companies are also parlaying their transparency in operations as a managerial technology to garner legitimacy and symbolic as well as substantive benefits from stakeholders. This chapter explores the winning strategies of two companies in Asia's changed environment – Unilever in Indonesia and the local Asia Commercial Bank (ACB) in Vietnam.

We first explore the back-to-basics market-expansion strategy followed by the foreign MNC, Unilever. Next we sketch the deliberate strategy of normal operations and transparency followed by the ACB in Vietnam. Finally, based on these case studies, we make some recommendations for MNCs and local companies operating in post-crisis Asia.

UNILEVER, A SUCCESSFUL FOREIGN MNC

As the economic crisis crushes Asia's middle classes, some MNCs are shifting their sights from urban malls to tin-roofed shops such as those lining the roadside in Mesuji, a small, one-lane village in Indonesia, five hours by bus from the nearest city. Tiny sachets of Unilever's Sunsilk and Clear shampoos dangle from the eaves of shops. At just 250 rupiah apiece (3.3 US cents), Unilever has targeted the single-use packets at poorer consumers who cannot spend their weekly wages on bottled shampoo. In one open-air stall a blue and yellow banner advertises Unilever's new, minisized Lifebuoy soap. The motto, in Indonesian, reads: 'With a price you can afford' (Karp, 1998).

Unilever is building market share in Indonesia with an aggressive strategy for inexpensive, miniature products. Unilever's secret: it sells affordable products everywhere. This strategy has worked for Unilever in developing rural markets in places such as Africa and India for decades. In implementing this strategy, Unilever is applying lessons learned from developed markets when economies sink: consumers need to make their purchases in tiny quantities, so distribution networks spring up to sell for example, loose cigarettes or single eggs. In contrast Unilever's rival, US consumer-goods giant Procter & Gamble (P&G), has continued to stock the larger, more expensive bottles, even in Mesuji. 'A half-dozen dusty bottles of P&G's Pantene, at 5000 rupiah each, have been sitting untouched on a back shelf for more than two months', said shopkeeper Sukaini (McDermott and Warner, 1998).

Unilever started operating in Thailand in 1932 and in India and the islands that now form Indonesia a year later. The explosion of supermarkets and shopping malls in Asia distracted many MNCs, including Unilever, from their traditional main market, the rural majority. 'We were all too much focused on that urban middle class. We saw Bangkok and thought the rest of Thailand and Asia was just like it', said Ralph Kugler, chairman of Unilever Thai Holdings 'To really get to Asian consumers, we must leave the cities' (ibid.).

Since the Asian economic crisis hit, Unilever has been getting back to basics. Its aims now include the production of high-quality goods affordable to poor people, earning a tiny margin on broad-based sales and building a consumer base that will stay loyal as it grows more affluent. Simultaneously the company is including modern markets and marketing in its strategic endeavours. 'We now span 1000 years of retailing evolution' said East Asia president André Van Heemstra, 'from global customers like supermarkets to distributors on foot selling a single bar of soap at a time' (ibid.).

Unilever is following a systematic price-cutting strategy in Asia. For example, to slash packaging costs in Indonesia, Unilever is selling Sunsilk shampoo in plastic bags instead of bottles with expensive four-colour printing; it has also introduced bulk containers of its Blue Band margarine, Sariwangi tea and Sunlight laundry detergent so that customers can buy the amounts they can afford. Similarly, from the Vietnamese Mekong Delta to metropolitan Manila, Unilever has stretched its usually exclusive distribution networks to reach villages such as Mesuji, seeking to obviate wholesalers and the commissions they add to products' retail prices.

Sleepy villages such as Mesuji, once considered backwaters and off the marketing track, now offer welcome stability to Unilever. The collapse of Indonesia's economy and currency have sent the nation's average annual per capita income plunging to an estimated US$260 in late 1998 from US$1000 in late 1997. Yet even as riots rip Jakarta, Mesuji has changed little. Prices have risen, but the village's basic economy has remained roughly the same: people have become poorer, but not much poorer than before the crisis; and some people have actually become richer. For example, while petrol prices have more than doubled since the crisis, farmers are now paid in dollars for their harvest. With the rupiah worth just a quarter of its value a year ago, those dollars stretch farther for the farmers, increasing their earnings and purchasing power substantially in Mesuji.

Unilever's sales have steadily increased in Indonesia since the economic crisis, fuelled by an aggressive campaign to expand reach. Unilever's distributor for the district, including Mesuji, has indicated that in the first half of 1998 sales were more than double what they had been a year ago. Because of raging inflation (in October it hit 79 per cent) Unilever doubled the price of its premium-brand Lux soap, but the per unit sales volume rose for some products as well. In July 1998 the distributor delivered 312 cartons a week of Rinso laundry detergent, three times the average of the previous year. He also doubled to 408 the number of small stores, pavement stalls and corner shops his sales people covered. From across Indonesia, such independent but exclusive distributors send national sales manager Hanafiah Djajawinata detailed data on the 290 000 retail outlets (or half of Indonesia's total outlets) they visit each week – four times their range in 1985 and about six times what analysts estimate constitutes the reach of other MNCs such as PepsiCo and Nestlé (ibid.).

At Unilever's headquarters in Jakarta, Hanafiah can locate every new outlet – and every prospective one – on hundreds of pages of multicoloured transparencies held in a set of giant ring binders. The transparencies slip over a map of the country, with each sheet marking different types of retail outlet. Together they account for every supermarket and farmer's market in the nation. The sales data fed to headquarters helps Unilever with its difficult logistics task. Distribution became particularly challenging in 1998 as Indonesia's economic crisis spawned riots, directed in part against the Chinese minority, who control most of the country's logistics and retail industries (Haley *et al.*, 1998). Unilever's 265 mostly Chinese distributors did not escape the riots. Several fled their homes and two saw their warehouses torched. But unlike other MNCs, Unilever backed its Chinese distributors and retailers. It paid for hotel rooms and lent them money to restock Unilever products. Consequently it retained all its distributors in the country, increased their loyalty and dependence and kept their products available for the masses.

Unilever has extended its Asian strategic model from India, where its subsidiary Hindustan Lever is one of the country's biggest and best-known MNCs. India has some of the world's biggest cities, but Unilever approaches the country as one giant rural market. It uses small, cheap packaging, lots of bright signs and numerous distributors driving, cycling and walking through the subcontinent selling Unilever products (Jordan, 1999). Hindustan Lever makes India's best-selling face lotion, 'Fair & Lovely', which is so pervasive that men advertise for 'Fair & Lovely' brides. 'In the past we never looked to India as an example because we thought they were backward', said Unilever's national sales manager in Indonesia. 'Now India is an inspiration to me' (ibid.).

Unilever's increased market share in Indonesia is proving profitable. Profits at PT Unilever Indonesia, listed on the Jakarta stock exchange, rose 55 per cent in the first half of 1998 on a sales growth of 54 per cent, although the growth of its rupiah earnings appear negligible when translated into dollars. However there are signs that Unilever's quest for market share may have reached the point of diminishing returns: new outlets are harder to find and reach and some executives have started to worry about the incremental costs of expansion. Furthermore, foreign competitors, particularly P&G, are appearing at Unilever's heels. The national sales manager has expressed his concern about P&G's expansion campaign: 'They're not only good now in the supermarkets, but they're getting better in the traditional markets' (ibid.). P&G's shampoo sells for only 50 rupiah more in Indonesia than Unilever's. Local competitors are also surfacing at the lower end of the pricing spectrum. For example consumers in Mesuji can purchase packets of Tancho, a locally made powdered shampoo, for 50 rupiah each. To compete with the local competitors on price, Unilever reduced the size of its sachets from seven millilitres to six millilitres. Unilever's strategic campaign in Asia will have to incorporate some of these tradeoffs between price, volume, perceived quality and increased market share.

THE ASIA COMMERCIAL BANK, A SUCCESSFUL LOCAL COMPANY

Banking in Vietnam is generally opaque. Freewheeling entrepreneurs with little interest in bookkeeping manage the typical Vietnamese bank with private shareholders, or joint-stock banks, while communist party members with connections manage most of the government-owned banks. Among Vietnam's beleaguered financial institutions, the ACB appears to be an exception: it makes a healthy profit. The ACB's secret? It is a relatively transparent company.

Transparent bookkeeping, qualified staff and strict lending policies together constitute an innovative way of doing business in Vietnam. The ACB is one of the very few joint-stock banks with a clean bill of health from an independent auditor, Ernst & Young. The bank follows strict guidelines for lending. Its management team has financial training and business experience. By contrast few of the country's other 52 joint-stock banks release earnings reports, and many hide their shareholders' names. While the ACB has voluntarily submitted to independent audits since 1995 – well ahead of foreign shareholder involvement at the end of 1996 – other joint-stock banks only began their audits in 1998, by government decree. Indeed the ACB is one of only two Vietnamese banks to have foreign shareholders.

Relative transparency – standard in most other countries but nearly non-existent in Vietnam – has earned the ACB a flood of praise. In 1997 an international finance magazine declared the ACB the best bank in Vietnam, and Western Union named it 'agent of the year'. Even the State Bank of Vietnam called the ACB the 'safest and most effective' private bank in the country – a rare tribute from a central bank to a private institution. With steady profit growth, despite a tough business environment, and with its rivals struggling, this private bank – less than half the size of Vietnam's state-owned banks – has the potential to become one of Vietnam's leading financial institutions, according to foreign investors and banking experts. The Mekong Project Development Facility, one of the International Finance Corporation's investing arms, is negotiating long-term lending deals with the bank. The ACB is one of very few Vietnamese banks to have the capital base (the biggest among private banks), credit facilities and balance sheet necessary for long-term project financing (Marshall, 1998).

Strict loan guidelines have helped the ACB to avoid some financial pitfalls. Loan decisions at many other Vietnamese banks often involve little or no due diligence. As a result, bad debts among private banks hovered around 20 per cent after the economic crisis, while the ACB's audited annual report for 1997 revealed that only about 4.8 per cent of its loans were overdue – one of the reasons why bank rating agency Thomson BankWatch considered the ACB to be one of the best banks in Vietnam. On a peeling wall in the ACB's threadbare Hanoi branch, a large bulletin board reminds tellers of the bank's stringent lending rules. Loan applicants must provide financial statements, credit history and properly valued collateral. These credit controls severely limit the number of ACB customers. Often in Vietnam, a connection with the director of a private bank is sufficient to secure a loan, and Vietnamese bankers blame widespread lending to friends and relatives for the unpaid letters of credit that have plagued local banks since the crisis (Haley, 1999). In 1997, by contrast, the ACB earned 11 billion dong in international settlement fees, or 23 per cent of the bank's pretax profits. The ACB's letters of credit are paid on time as light manufacturers of exported sea products and plastics, which generate a steady flow of foreign currency, constitute the majority of the ACB's trade finance customers (Marshall, 1998).

The ACB's net profits are growing, according to the few audits available in this sector. The bank earned 28.9 billion dong ($2.1 million) in net profits for 1997, up 4.7 per cent from 27.6 billion dong in 1996. Pretax profits rose 30 per cent to 48.5 billion dong in 1997 from 37.2 billion dong a year earlier, and the bank's shareholders predicted that pretax profits would rise an additional 20–30 per cent in 1998. By contrast, net profits fell by more than half at the Vietnam Export & Import Commercial Joint-Stock Bank (Eximbank), and by more than a third at the Vietnam Maritime Commercial Stock Bank (one of the better joint-stock banks). Even the strongest foreign and foreign-invested banks are just holding steady, and many local banks are selling assets to pay outstanding debts rather than building up their businesses.

In Vietnam's post-crisis financial environment the ACB's profit growth, while small, 'is very impressive', according to Mark Whitehead, chief representative of Jardine Pacific (Vietnam), one of the ACB's shareholders (ibid.). (Jardine holds a 7 per cent stake in the bank. The LG Group of South Korea and two foreign-investment funds hold the remaining 19 per cent of the bank's foreign equity.) It was the ACB's transparency that first attracted Hong Kong-based Jardine. Whitehead recalls that when Lam Ho ang Loc, the ACB's director of operations, flew to London for a lunch meeting with Jardine three years ago to solicit investment he was 'very open about bad debt'. While the bank does not openly espouse transparency as bank policy, Davenport and other foreign investors credit Loc for the bank's honesty. A devout Buddhist, Loc has chosen people with similar values to work under him (ibid.).

Yet in churning, government-dominated Vietnam the ACB faces many external uncertainties. The central government has yet to determine how to handle an estimated $137 million in overdue loans at joint-stock banks. A government plan to merge failing joint-stock banks with healthy ones may force the ACB to acquire debt-ridden competitors, a move that could reduce its capital of approximately $25 million.

The ACB's 1997 annual report showed signs of a very rapid expansion in its loan portfolio. In 1997 outstanding loans topped one trillion dong, 62 per cent higher than in 1996, suggesting that short-term loans were turning into longer-term, higher-risk ones. Loans nearly doubled in that year. In 1997 the ACB also diversified into loans for state-owned enterprises, which are notorious for not repaying on time. The net profits from a 74 per cent increase in loans in 1997 rose a mere 4.7 per cent. 'That percentage is not meaningful', said Huynh Quang Tuan, the ACB's Hanoi branch manager. Loans rose only $4 million compared with 1996 – not such a sharp rise, considering the bank opened in 1993 and was building a loan portfolio from scratch. Credit activities, the bank's core business, constituted about 65 per cent of its pretax profit in 1997 (ibid.). With 26 per cent of its equity in registered capital – cash injected by shareholders – the ACB has better cover than many Western banks. If, for example, all the bank's borrowers were to default, the bank would have enough capital to write off almost half of them. The ACB's foreign shareholders provided this hefty increase in capital early last year, enabling the bank to expand more quickly.

For the next two years the ACB plans to reduce its lending activities and plough more capital into expanding its services and improving its infrastructure. The bank already has become the first Vietnamese member of Visa and Mastercard, and one of Western Union's first Vietnamese agents. It also plans to become one of the first securities companies in Vietnam. Vietnam's much-delayed stock market will not be a source of much profit until many years after it opens, but the ACB plans to diversify into Vietnam's shallow and undeveloped financial market.

The ACB also is investing in computerisation – aiming by 2000 to connect branches electronically in a move that will enable the bank to monitor all activities from its head office. It is also increasing staff training in everything from treasury management to securities dealing. Unusual for Vietnam, in 1997, 377 of its 576 employees had university and postgraduate degrees. According to Tuan, 'we are only good because we know we are still bad. We are not professional yet' (ibid.).

RECOMMENDATIONS

This chapter has described two Asian companies' diverse and successful strategies in the post-crisis environment. Unilever has sought to expand market share through a return-to-basics strategy, followed by other MNCs. For example the ABN Amro Bank, another Dutch giant, recently opened four branches in remote Indonesian provinces but avoided urban areas where other foreign banks were closing branches. Ford Motors is building open-air dealerships in rural Thailand. Ford constructs these dealerships cheaply, and rice and sugar-cane farmers, potential customers who would feel awkward in Bangkok's posh, air-conditioned showrooms, feel comfortable in them. Similarly, advertising giant Ogilvy & Mather's Thai office has sent senior creative executives to northern provinces to talk to rural consumers about purchasing decisions.

As the Anderson survey indicates (Burrell, 1999), the toppling of competitors has created new opportunities for MNCs to expand in Asia. Opportunities exist for MNCs that can act rapidly and make decisions with little information that strategists would consider valid. Yet as Haley *et al.* (1998) indicate, MNCs from developed countries often balk at making strategic decisions with softer information and what they consider insufficient analysis. Clearly MNCs that do act, such as Unilever, can create winning strategies in the new post-crisis environment.

In contrast the local company, the ACB, has sought to establish legitimacy and to enhance reputation by adopting transparent policies and Western management techniques. Haley (1991) discusses how companies seek to establish legitimacy with key stakeholders through symbolic behaviours. In Asia, legitimacy and professionalisation have become key issues for local companies, especially those wishing to attract foreign investors. Backman (1999) calls insufficient transparency the Asian disease. He argues that whenever a single family or network dominates a web of public and private companies, opportunities arise for off-balance-sheet guarantees and asset shifting, resulting in a loss of confidence by major investors, especially foreign investors. Foreign investor confidence has become a major point of contention in cash-starved, post-crisis Asia. For example the CP Group of Thailand, one of the most successful local network companies, is suffering from just such a loss, with foreign brokerage houses recommending against the purchase of its stock, despite the CP's new debt-control policies and controlled expansion (Biers *et al.*, 1999). In the absence of a transparent structure, investors will not feel comfortable with or be able to gauge the extent of the CP's restructuring or reforms.

As hinted in the quote from the ACB's Tuan in the previous section, transparency and Western-style operations may often fall short of Western standards in Vietnam and other Asian countries; consequently one can assume that in these countries, the symbolic values for foreign investors may equal or exceed the substantive benefits. Table 14.1 indicates the perceived degree of corruption in various Asian countries.

Table 14.1   Perception of corruption in Asia, 1998[*]

	Ranking (out of 85 countries)	Score
New Zealand	4	9.4
Singapore	7	9.1
Australia	11	8.7
Hong Kong	16	7.8
Japan	25	5.8
Malaysia	29	5.3
Taiwan	29	5.3
South Korea	43	4.2
China	52	3.5
Philippines	55	3.3
Thailand	61	3.0
India	66	2.9
Pakistan	71	2.7
Vietnam	74	2.5
Indonesia	80	2.0

[*] 10 = very clean, 0 = very corrupt.
Source: Transparency International, survey published in September 1998.

Transparency as a means of establishing reputation and assuring foreign investors is probably more important in countries where corruption is perceived as rife, such as Vietnam. Consequently local companies that strive to appear professional may appeal more to foreign investors in these countries.

References

Biers, D., M. Vatikiotis, R. Tasker and P. Daorueng (1999) 'Back to school', *Far Eastern Economic Review*, 8 April.

Backman, M. (1999) *Asian Eclipse: Exposing the Dark Side of Business in Asia*, (New York: John Wiley).

Burrell, S. (1999) 'Asia dances to a new beat', *Sydney Morning Herald*, 28 May.

Haley, G. T., C. T. Tan and U. C. V. Haley (1998) *New Asian Emperors: The Overseas Chinese, their Strategies and Competitive Advantages* (Oxford and Boston: Butterworth-Heinemann).

Haley, U. C. V. (1999) *Strategic Management in the Asia Pacific: Harnessing Regional and Organizational Change for Competitive Advantage* (Oxford and Boston: Butterworth-Heinemann).

Haley, U. C. V. (1991) 'Corporate contributions as managerial masques: Reframing corporate contributions as strategies to influence society', *Journal of Management Studies*, vol. 28, no. 5, pp. 485–509.

Jordan, M. (1999) 'Indian toothpaste war is fought with a familiar, winning smile', *Wall Street Journal*, 15 April.

Karp, J. (1998) 'Hindustan Lever Ltd', *Wall Street Journal*, 26 October.

Marshall, S. (1998) 'ACB stands out in Vietnam for being a sound bank', *Wall Street Journal*, 4 December.

McDermott, D. and F. Warner (1998) 'Secret of Unilever's success is affordable, single-use packs', *Wall Street Journal*, 23 November.

15 New Development Model for a Post-Matured Japanese Industrial Sector

Yoshiya Teramoto and Caroline Benton

INTRODUCTION

The Japanese economy, and in particular the industrial sector, recovered spectacularly after the devastation of the Second World War by focusing on improvements in product quality and production efficiency. The *kanban* system of manufacturing, just-in-time delivery, quality control and total quality management have been the rallying calls for manufacturers over the last half century. Although the concept of scientific management was born in the USA, the enthusiasm for improving production technology has been so strong among Japanese industrial corporations that they are now recognised as world leaders in this area. Even the annual Deming Prize, which is awarded for quality control and is named after the famous American statistician and quality expert, was born in Japan.[1]

These efforts of the industrial sector to increase efficiency and reduce waste and product deficiencies have been aimed at perfecting the method of bringing a product or service to the market. However, in the age of the global economy and the Internet, this conventional Japanese business philosophy, which emphasises incremental improvements in product quality, production methods and distribution, is no longer sufficient. Both corporations and consumers now have access to global knowledge, products and services and are looking for unique value.

Armed with abundant information, corporate customers and consumers alike are empowered and increasingly sophisticated. Industries can no longer survive and compete on product quality and efficiency alone in the post-matured Japanese market with a GDP per capital of over $35 000, in which non-essential items account for over a 50 per cent of household expenditure and over 50 per cent of current high school graduates go on to earn a university or college degree. They must switch from an industrial development model that stresses how to supply products/services efficiently to one that focuses on what kind of value to create and offer.

This chapter therefore provides a synopsis of the evolution of past development models for industries, presents case studies of emerging successful models in Japan, discusses emerging types of model and discusses the implications for Asian countries. An analysis of the business models of Nintendo, the Japanese television animation industry and Suzuki Sogyo, a pioneer in printing technology, will be presented to address these points.

THE EVOLUTION OF DEVELOPMENT MODELS

Businesses and industries emerge and evolve over time with continuous advances in technology, products and services. This section traces the evolution of various industrial development models and discusses how they related to the environment of their times.

In the 1730s, the development by Englishman John Kay of the flying shuttle for weaving cotton led to other textile-related inventions and helped to usher in the first industrial revolution, which transformed the British economy from one comprised of cottage industries to one characterised by factories and mass production methods. In the eighteenth century, textile manufacturing was the leading high-tech industry, and the demand for cotton was great. To exploit this opportunity, corporations grew cotton in the British colonies on land that had been taken forcibly. The harvest was shipped to Britain, to be transformed into textiles for global export. Working conditions were extremely harsh for both the colonial population and the British working class.

This colonial development model became outdated as the British Empire declined and steam gave way to electricity as the main source of power. Colonies regained their independence and corporations could no longer exploit the working class or former the colonies. The discovery of electromagnetic induction by Michael Faraday gave birth to the electric generator and more powerful and efficient machines, leading to the second industrial revolution. American industrial corporations began to develop hierarchical models based on the concept of scientific management fathered by Fredrick Taylor and the assembly line method of mass production created by Henry Ford.

In the context of the hierarchical American development model, labour was tightly controlled and regulated in the early part of the twentieth century under conditions that would not be condoned in this day and age. This development model was refined and modernised as corporations increased in size and Western society became more employee-friendly, and is still predominant throughout the world in industries that mass produce products or services. IBM and the big three US vehicle manufacturers were representative of corporations or hierarchically structured industries that emphasised rigid organisational structure and tightly controlled business processes to achieve maximum management efficiency.

With the tremendous advances in information technology and the ensuing growth of knowledge-centred businesses, such as those involved in software development, multimedia, high-tech financing and consulting, a new industrial model that is focused on networking highly skilled individuals and companies has emerged. The rigid, hierarchical structure of conventional US industries was not suited to the needs of these emergent businesses because it stifled creativity and knowledge growth. A new model – which the authors call the Silicon Valley model – is used by these businesses because they are grounded in the talents and expertise of professionals, who are given the freedom to optimise their expertise within the framework of corporate policy and strategy.

The aim of the Silicon Valley model, which is particularly prominent in the software industry, is to maximise creativity and knowledge enhancement. It is based on a non-hierarchical networking among professionals with specialised technological ability and knowledge who can be brought together from inside and outside a company on a project by project basis. This model is thus fluid and flexible in terms of human resources; the required skills and talents are regularly recruited when needed through a variety of methods, for example using salaried, free-lance or contracted employees, or offering stock options to entice employees to bet on the future of a start-up company. Microsoft, Cisco Systems and Industrial Light Magic (the computer graphics and multimedia firm of filmmaker George Lucas) all create value with this flexible development model.

These three different types of development model for industry can be analysed and characterised in terms of their business area, content and context. The concept of business area is self-explanatory and refers to the major products/services offered by leading industries. Content is the technology and resources that comprise an industry's products and services. For example retort packaging technology is the content of many of Ajinomoto's processed foods, while micronising technology is that of Sony's audio visual products. Context is slightly more complex and denotes the positioning or meaning of a product's or service's value. In other words, the value of products and services change under a different context. Nuclear energy, for instance, has different positionings in military and civilian settings.

As shown in Table 15.1, the business area of these models have become increasingly complex with the evolution of industries and businesses. The business areas of the major British industries in the eighteenth and nineteenth

Table 15.1   Characteristics of the different development models

	British colonial model	Hierarchical US model	Silicon Valley model
Business area	Commodities and resources such as cotton, sugar	Steel, vehicles, mainframes etc.	Personal computers, software, network businesses etc.
Contents	Closed in terms of their resources and technology	Closed in terms of their resources and technology	Open in terms of their resources and technology
Context	Closed	Open functionally	Open functionally

centuries were commodities, natural resources and other simple products, while conventional US industries today produce hardware-based products (for example mainframes, vehicles and steel). In contrast Silicon Valley companies focus on information and knowledge-centred products and services (for example personal computers, Internet businesses and multimedia).

The contents (that is, resources and technology) that characterise these different development models also differ, as shown in Table 15.1. British industries that traded in commodities sought out relatively simple products that were not integrated into others. The contents of these models can be categorised as closed, because the technology and resources used in the products were uncomplicated and rarely linked to those of other businesses.

Similarly the technology and resources of products produced by conventional US companies are relatively closed and the products are more or less stand-alone – they are complete in and of themselves (Teramoto, 1999; Richter and Teramoto, 1996). The competitive advantage of these companies is high quality and cost performance. In contrast Silicon Valley businesses compete by offering information and knowledge-centred products that are integrated, and thus can be created only through networking and collaboration among skilled professionals, suppliers and third parties.

In terms of context, the products of the leading British colonial businesses were functionally closed. Cotton, other commodities and fabric did not have a wide range of functions and their meanings did not vary significantly. In contrast the products and services of the typically hierarchically structured US and flat Silicon Valley industries are open in terms of their context, as they have a diversified range of applications. For example cameras and personal computers have different functions when used in a medical or a home environment.

The Japanese information technology industry has been trying to emulate the Silicon Valley model to encourage innovation and knowledge under the guidance and support of the government. In spite of their efforts, the Japanese version of Silicon Valley has not been very successful, due to historical factors and different industrial fundamentals, such as less reliance on the mid-career recruitment of professional employees, lack of venture capital and vertical *keiretsu* relationships, which are not conducive to new independent businesses. Also, relatively fewer young adults appear to be entrepreneurial, possibly due to the harmonious and group-centred Japanese education system, in which 'the nail which sticks out, gets hammered'.

Since the end of the Second World War, the development of the Japanese economy and industries has been led by the state, in particular the all-powerful government ministries such as the Ministry of Finance and Ministry of International Trade and Industry. In this 'capitalist development state' the government bureaucracy worked in close coordination with politicians and the top representatives of leading businesses to guide and nurture industries. The strong ties among these groups, as shown by the exchange of personnel through the *amakudari* system and the mutual holding of stocks among *keiretsu* companies, allowed them to collaborate and jointly work towards the goal of transforming Japan into a modern economy from the ashes of the postwar devastation.

However this model is not highly conducive to the creation of new knowledge and independent venture businesses, since there is little interaction among the very territorially minded ministries; without the synergy generated through the interplay among different industries it is difficult to develop real breakthroughs in technology and products. Also, these three groups have a vested interest in preserving their own *status quo* and cannot work together to initiate significant change and knowledge-based innovations that might affect their delicate power balance.

Rather, individual industrial players and new independent businesses should take the initiative and provide the energy for the development of new knowledge-centred businesses, as this will give them more freedom to exercise their creativity and expertise for the creation of new value, which is not supported by the rigidity of the government-led industrial model. In a post-matured market with excess supply, new demand must be created by industries and companies as they have the best access to consumers/customers, and not by the preplanned policies of the government. After discussing successful cases of Japanese businesses in the following section, the authors will suggest a newer model for Japanese industries.

PIONEERING SUCCESS

Nintendo

Nintendo, the video game manufacturer that gave the world Mario Brothers, Game Boy and Super Nintendo, is a leader in the global retail video-game industry, which is estimated at over 15 billion dollars. The company manufactures and markets both the hardware and software for its video-game systems. The former is made up of outsourced parts such as microprocessors and many of the latter are developed by third party partners (thus the company has only slightly over 1000 employees). Table 15.2 shows Nintendo's performance from 1994–99. Sales and profits declined for three years after peaking in 1993 at 634 billion yen and 166 million yen, respectively, because its 16-bit video-game machine (Nintendo Entertainment System) was in the declining stage of its life cycle and consumers were waiting for the next-generation product. Demand for the product had been satisfied, and Sony and Sega began to grab sales and eat into the company's market share with their newer products. In 1997, however, Nintendo was able to recover sales with the introduction and launch of its video-game system Nintendo 64, the first 64-bit home video-game system. (Over the last two years, however, Nintendo has been challenged again by the global success of Sony's Playstation.)

Part of Nintendo's success is due to its ability to network with partners beyond its organisational boundaries, including character suppliers and third-party game developers. In its home page the company states, 'But even these dedicated resources [referring to its product development team] aren't enough. In a connected world, success also is determined by connections to outside resources. We're building these bridges on two central

Table 15.2   Recent trends in Nintendo sales/income
(consolidated) (million yen)

	Net sales	Rise/fall (%)	Net income	Rise/fall (%)
1994	485612	–	52653	–
1995	415240	−14	41661	−21
1996	353754	−15	59871	44
1997	417593	18	65482	9
1998	534646	28	83696	28
1999	572840	7	85817	3

Source: Nintendo.

foundations: partners capable of creating dramatic new play experiences and partners best equipped to help deliver the message to our target audience.' In its annual report it also acknowledged the importance of its business partners with the following statement: 'It is becoming increasingly more complex for developers in our industry to create new, breakthrough video game software. A broader range of talent, more time, and larger budgets are required to produce a hit game.'

Two of Nintendo's famous partners are Walt Disney and Lucasfilms, from which the company licenses characters. More importantly, the company has a network of third-party partners that develop software. For its current hit product Nintendo 64, 127 games have been marketed since the product launch in 1996, of which only 23 were developed in-house by Nintendo. The remaining 103 games were produced by third-party partners, including Hudson, Konami, Bottom up and ASCI.

Another very important factor in Nintendo's success has been its ability to build up its business on the tradition, wisdom and culture that it has accumulated since its foundation. Nintendo, whose roots go back to 1889, was founded as a manufacturer of *hanafuda* cards, an old Japanese game using cards that depict nature-related identities (a boar, a deer, a butterfly, the moon and so on). The company was founded in Kyoto, the cultural and historical centre of Japan, a fact that undoubtedly helped it to integrate the essence of Japanese entertainment culture into its business. As with its game software, Nintendo relied on a network of partners, including suppliers of beautiful *washi* (Japanese paper) for the cards and boxes, and artists to draw the pictures.

The company also expanded early into the Western game business and was the first domestic manufacturer to produce Western style playing cards (1902). Thus the company has a long history in the Japanese and Western game and entertainment businesses, from which it was able to build an underlying base for its digital game systems. Although analog games (playing cards) and digital games (home video games) are very different products, the essence of entertainment in human nature is unvarying. Nintendo's association with Walt Disney also goes back many years – to 1959, when it licensed Disney characters for playing cards, creating a boom in Japan. Partly due to the success of these character playing cards, the company went public and was listed on the second section of the Osaka and Kyoto Stock Exchanges in 1962.

Other breakthrough and pioneering products that the company created and launched in Japan were the first domestic toy product with electronic technology (1970), a laser clay-shooting system that became a major national pastime (1973), a video-game system using electronic video recording (1975), a video game with a microprocessor (1975) and a coin-operated video-game system using microcomputers (1978).

This series of hit products developed by Nintendo, starting with the *hanafuda* cards, shows that the company was able to exploit its competitive advantage and enlarge its business by integrating its accumulated cultural background and wisdom in entertainment with electronic and digital technology, and by networking with external partners.

Animation

Animation is another success story of Japanese industry. Starting with the works of Osamu Tetsuka, the author of 'Astro Boy' and 'Jungle Emperor Leo', Japanese modern animation programs have had wide global appeal and have been exported to Western and Asian countries. The latest Japanese animation to become a global hit is 'Sailor Moon', a program that revolves around the antics of a group of young schoolgirls who have been given special powers to fight the evil forces that are threatening the world. A quick search of Yahoo! USA came up with over 200 fan pages dedicated to the program and its various characters.

The success of Japanese animation is due to the distinctive attraction of elaborately created story lines and characterisations. Unlike Western comics and cartoons, many Japanese animation programs have rich and complex plots and finely defined characters that appeal to many adults as well. 'The Princess-Mononoke', an animation program created by Hayao Miyazaki, is about a young warrior princess who fights against a group of rogue traders trying to clear a forest to exploit its resources. She risks her life to protect the environment and its inhabitants, which include forest fairies, while winning over some of the traders through her impassioned efforts.

So distinctive is Japanese animation that the term *anime* has been incorporated into the English language to refer to this medium. In contrast Western animation programs are mainly simple and targeted at children. 'Road Runner' is one such cartoon. Every episode is a variation of a chase between a hungry coyote and a sly and clever road runner. Bugs Bunny, Donald Duck and Felix the Cat are other examples of Western cartoons. The recent animated movies produced by Walt Disney (Beauty and the Beast, The Hunchback of Notre Dame and so on) are exceptions in that they appeal to a wider age group, a fact that contributed to the success of these films and helped the company achieve a leap in sales.

The emphasis on an elaborate story line in Japanese animation can be traced back to the country's culture of storytelling. The twelfth-century Heian period's *emakimono* stories (scrolls of pictorial stories), with their intricate drawings and plots, are said by Isao Takahata, a famous animation director, to be one of the most influential factors in Japanese animation (*Hokuriku Chugoku Shimbun*, Yukan, 10 June 1999). *Emakimono* creators used storytelling techniques to add dynamism and these are applied in Japanese animation today, including the depiction of changes in space within one scene by using a cloud or bubble to illustrate another location, the illustration of movement with flowing lines and an indication of time progression by using multiple drawings of the same character or item in one scene. Takahata also states that if one rolls the *emakimono* scrolls in a manner that allows 60 centimetres of drawings to be viewed at a time, one gets the impression of a wide camera span.

In summary, it can be said that the global success of the Japanese animation industry is due to the fusion of Japan's storytelling heritage with high-tech animation technology. During Osamu Tetsuka's time, animation programs were produced using state-of-the-art analog technology, while recent animators such as Hayao Miyazaki and Hideaki Anno, creator of the Evangelion series,[2] are using sophisticated computer graphics to depict their stories and fantasies.

Suzuki Sogyo

Suzuki Sogyo, a medium-sized corporate group located in Shizuoka prefecture, is an example of success through the fusion of tradition with modern technology. The group has over 500 patents and has pioneered various industrial innovations. The company's business model, which it calls a balloon model (Figure 15.1),[3] is based on a network of group companies, each established for different technological innovations. Although some of the company's products have been developed in cooperation with

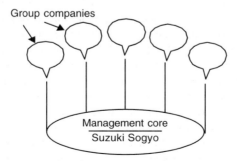

Figure 15.1   Suzuki Sogyo's balloon business model

other larger corporations for reasons of finance and market coverage, the company's strategy is to hold on to patent rights and intellectual property (*Nikkei Shimbun*, December 1995).

In 1974 Motoyasu Nakanishi, who at the time was chief engineer, developed a three-dimensional printing process that allows for printing on curved surfaces. This printing process, which is currently being sold by Cubic Co., a Suzuki Sogyo group company, uses water pressure to transfer ink to the target item from film that melts in water. This technology is used in the finishing of car dashboards, home electronic appliances, furniture and similar products, and is licensed by over 50 companies in 17 countries.

When developing this technology, Nakanishi envisioned being able to print on the curved surface of an egg. He had spent several years trying to develop the process without any breakthrough, until the day he was using a fountain pen and bottled ink. After dipping his pen into the ink, one drop of ink splattered onto a piece of paper, leaving a dispersed pattern that reminded him of the *suminagashi* design of his wife's *yukata*, or summer kimono. *Suminagashi*, which can be literally translated as the flow of ink, is a Japanese method of dying patterns by pouring ink onto water (or drawing with ink on water) and laying a piece of fabric over this to develop intricate designs (marbled, circles, waves and so on). Nakanishi was able to develop his three-dimensional printing process by integrating the craftsmanship of *suminagashi*, which involves using water as a printing medium, with modern-day printing technology.

Another innovation of the Suzuki Sogyo group is a silicon gel used for shock and vibration absorption and packaging. This use of silicon gel was first proposed by NASA but the suggestion was subsequently dismissed because of the product's instability and high cost. Suzuki Sogyo developed the gel for commercial use in 1984 and brought it to the market under the brand name Alpha Gel.[4] Currently the product is marketed by Sigel Incorporated, a group company, and is used in athletics shoes, electronic appliances and other items for shock and vibration absorption.

Nakanishi was also the main force behind the creation and development of Alpha Gel. His idea for developing NASA's silicon gel into a commercial product for shock and vibration absorption was born out of the method in which eggs had been packaged in Japan in the past. Before the advancement of transportation and packaging know-how, eggs had been placed in containers that were filled with the husks of rice. In sufficient quantity, these tiny husk particles had served to absorb shock in a similar manner to the way in which the silicon particles of Alpha Gel work today.

The success of Suzuki Sogyo can also be attributed to the company's focus on meeting market needs by fusing high technology with traditional

Japanese wisdom using elements of nature.[5] Nakanishi stated that in determining what to develop, it is important first to identify what would be a useful and widely welcomed innovation (*Nikkei Shimbun*, 21 May 1999). Once this is determined, the technology is found to realise the idea.[6]

A NEW DEVELOPMENT MODEL: FUSION OF THE OLD AND THE NEW

The manner in which a corporation produces value for its customers is contingent upon its environment. It is proposed that in the post-matured market, new knowledge is the key to value creation and corporate success. Alvin Toffler (1990) suggests that after physical power and economic power, knowledge power is essential to achieving an advantage. Japanese corporations must not merely copy the Silicon Valley model, because then they would be only followers and would miss the opportunity to capitalise on their inherent wisdom. Rather, in order to meet the challenges of the global, knowledge-centred environment, Japanese corporations must take advantage of their country's long history of commerce and craftsmanship and its cultural heritage. This will lead to a competitive advantage that cannot be easily copied by other advanced countries.

First it is necessary to define the characteristics that make knowledge-based resources so important in today's business context: (1) they are capable of repeated use by numerous people without wear and tear; (2) they are difficult to transfer unless codified; (3) their meanings and value depend on the context of usage; and (4) they are fragile and can be easily changed or adapted (Teramoto *et al.*, 1999).

The first of these characteristics refers to the fact that, unlike tangible objects, there are no physical limits to the number of persons who can use a knowledge-based resource or the number of times that it can be reused. If a company's knowledge and expertise can be used effectively in multiple applications, a company can achieve increasing returns on scale, since by definition there is less need for capital investment with the networking of knowledge.[7] For example specialised knowledge in derivatives can be used repeatedly and simultaneously by numerous financial experts to build credit or equity portfolios. This fact is evident in licensed and patented technologies such as Suzuki Sogyo's 3-D printing process, which is used throughout the world by corporations in various fields.

The second characteristic – knowledge transfer – relates to the fact that complex knowledge-based resources such as intellectual property are difficult to pass on (unlike tangible items) unless they are codified in a

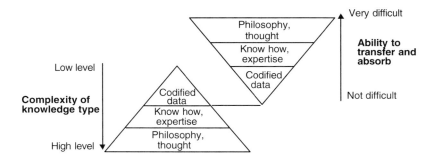

Figure 15.2   Transferability of knowledge types

manner that can be easily understood (Figure 15.2). The financial savvy of top fund managers and the taste sensitivities of master chefs are not easily written or stored in a manner that can be used for transfer, giving the creator and holder of the knowledge an advantage. In order to achieve the transfer of complex types of knowledge, it is important that the receiving partner is actively involved in the business or enterprise through shared experiences, joint ventures, codevelopment of technology and so on.

The third characteristic implies that the meaning and positioning of a certain knowledge-based resource differ according to the context of its usage, including who uses it and for what purpose, and why and how it is used. The Internet and aerodynamics were initially developed for military usage, but are now being used in the civilian sector for very different purposes. A contextual shift for a knowledge-based product/service, however, is not easy to achieve, but it can be promoted by the transfer of human resources from one functional unit to another, or by networking with corporations from a different field.

Knowledge-based resources are also flexible in that they are never in their final form, but are constantly changing and added to by innovations and discoveries. By increasing and furthering knowledge, new value can be created; the development of penicillin marked the start of antibiotic technology and led to the production of Vancomycin and similar medication. Nintendo's 16-bit home video-game system was once leading-edge technology, but has since been superseded by the company's 64-bit machine, which will undoubtedly be replaced by even faster game systems in the future.

These characteristics are what give power to the holder of the knowledge-based resource. A corporation can create a variety of proprietary and unique products and services by developing its expertise and technology, as these can be used multiply, are difficult to transfer outside the organisation, have different meanings depending on the context, and can be transformed. There are basically three ways for a corporation to develop its knowledge: it can expand the scope of its existing knowledge, extend the depth of its current knowledge or edit its present knowledge. Expanding the scope of knowledge is the extension of expertise into surrounding areas, such as when the technology used for freezing raw food commodities (for example meat, seafood) was refined and applied to prepared dishes (for example noodle dishes and fried rice). Extending the depth of knowledge is the vertical advancement of current knowledge in the current direction. Improving the audio quality of a CD player or increasing the effectiveness of safety features in a car constitute increased knowledge depth.

The evolution of Nintendo's game business from *hanafuda* cards to home video games is a case of knowledge expansion and extension. Extending its entertainment business from *hanafuda* cards to Western cards to digital games entailed expanding into other areas of the entertainment business, or knowledge expansion. The advancement of video games from a 16-bit system to a 64-bit system was achieved by extending the depth of the existing technology. The 64-bit machine plays similar game software as the older system, but with greater speed and richer visual effects.

Modern Japanese animation was developed by expanding the scope and extending the depth of the storytelling tradition and wisdom. The use of techniques that were developed in the Heian period to illustrate dynamic action in television animation is representative of extending knowledge into overlapping areas. Animators have also extended the depth of their animation capabilities by using modern-day filming technology.

Editing knowledge is slightly more complex than the first two methods and refers to the rearrangement of existing knowledge to create new value. In other words, current expertise/data/information is reviewed in a different context and given fresh meaning in order to develop original technology, products or services. The adoption of digital technology to make smart products such as refrigerators with microprocessors is an example of editing accumulated knowledge to make product advancements.

In the case of Japanese corporations, in a country with a long history of commerce,[8] craftsmanship and culture, the fusion of accumulated wisdom and tradition in these areas with leading edge technology is an example of knowledge editing to produce a competitive advantage. Suzuki Sogyo's incorporation of *suminagashi* printing and packaging techniques with modern technology for industrial innovations is a case of knowledge editing. The use of a water medium for printing was given fresh contextual meaning

Table 15.3   Proposed development model for Japan

	New development model
Business area	The fusion of traditional culture, technology, craftsmanship and high-tech
Contents	Open in terms of their resources and technology
Context	Open functionally and chronically; greater tendency to incorporate elements of nature

when it was transformed from a technique for printing fabric into an industrial process for printing three-dimensional items.

At the beginning of this section it was proposed that the fusion of tradition and wisdom with modern-day technology will allow Japanese corporations to develop a unique knowledge, which is an essential source of power for generating a competitive advantage in this post-matured market. In terms of the framework of the development models discussed in the second section, this model for Japanese industries can be analysed as shown in Table 15.3. The business area of this model includes products and services that are made from this fusion. The content (technology and resources) of the model is open, similar to that of the hierarchical US and flexible Silicon Valley models. The context of the model, however, differs in that it is open functionally and chronically; the value of the products and services of this model changes by functional application, and is created through the integration of past wisdom.

Also, Japanese businesses have always tended to incorporate objects of nature into their products and services. For example Nintendo's *hanafuda* cards depict the moon and deer, while many of Suzuki Sogyo's innovations incorporated traditional techniques using elements of nature (*suminagashi* was conducted in rivers). In contrast many modern Western businesses have a tendency to view elements of nature as consumables to exploit.

CONCLUSION

The evolution of industry is a core aspect of a country's economic development. In this chapter the authors have proposed that, in the post-matured market of Japan, a new development model that fuses wisdom and modern technology could create new knowledge for Japanese corporations that would enable them to compete against their European and US counterparts. Japanese companies will not be able to survive in the global environment by merely following the hierarchical US model or the flexible

Silicon Valley model because this would prevent them from producing distinctive value. Japan has a written history that dates back nearly 1800 years, and the wisdom that has accumulated over that time should be tapped in order to produce products and services that cannot be matched. In contrast, US and European businesses are grounded in the industrial revolution.

Like Japan, other Asian countries (for example China, Korea and Thailand) have deep-rooted traditions and wisdom that can be merged with modern-day innovations and technology to produce distinctive products and services. In China, a college student who was brought up in a family of calligraphy masters developed the country's first word-processing software with Chinese characters. India, which has a long history of mathematical discoveries (including the concept of zero), has been able to nurture a strong software industry through its mathematical heritage and the expertise of expatriates returning from the USA and Europe. The wisdom accumulated in countries with a long history should not be wasted but expanded, extended and edited to create new value. In this manner the rich base of intangible knowledge-based resources will not be lost, but can be used to produce a competitive advantage.

Notes

1. Subsequent to the Deming Prize, the Malcom Baldridge Quality Award was established in the United States in 1988 for quality management, and the Japan Quality Award was set up by the Japan Productivity Center for Socio-Economic Development (also for quality management) in 1996.
2. Evangelion is an animation series with a huge international following. It has an extremely complex storyline of mankind's battle with alien angels in the year 2015.
3. Figure 15.1 is meant to indicate that the individual companies are independent and help to support the group as a whole, but that the validity of the group will not be sacrificed if one company faces difficulties.
4. NASA used this product in a 1992 space shuttle flight to protect fertilised eggs for experimental purposes.
5. Another example is the biodegradable, corn-based packaging medium that Suzuki Sogyo developed in cooperation with Nippon Gousei Kagaku and Hitachi Butsuryu in 1995.
6. Nakanishi has said that most hints for a new technology can be found in standard textbooks used in junior high and high school (in particular, science-related textbooks), and in traditional wisdom.
7. In contrast, operation-based products and services (for example television sets and other conventional home appliances) exhibit decreasing returns on scale, as greater investment is needed with increased volume.

8.   Japan had the first futures market. Rice was traded during the Edo period (mid-seventeenth century) in a futures market.

References

Hokuriku Chunichi Shimbun (1999) 'Anime No Rutsu Ha Emakimono' (The Roots of Animation Are Found in Animation), 10 June.

Nikkei Sangyo Shimbun (1995) 'Suzuki Sogyo Group – Dokusou Gijutsu De Bunsha Keiei' (Suzuki Sogyo Group – Unique Technology and Group Company Management), 5 December.

Nikkei Sangyo Shimbun (1999) 'Tokkyo Senryaku De Chusho Kigyou Funto Chu, Hikara Gijutsu Ni Ohte Chumoku – Suzuki Sogyo, Taisei Purasu' (Medium-sized Corporations are Competing Based on their Patent Strategies), 21 May.

Richter, F. J. and Y. Teramoto (1996) 'Population Ecology versus Network Dynamics: From Evolution to Co-evolution', in F. J. Richter (ed.), *The Dynamics of Japanese Organizations* (London: Routledge), pp. 151–66.

Teramoto, Y. (1990) *Network Power* (Tokyo: NTT Shuppan).

Teramoto, Y. (1999) *Power Innovation* (Tokyo: Shin Hyoron).

Toffler, Alvin (1990) *Power Shift* (New York: Bantam Books).

16 Restructuring Asian Network Groups: Managing Around Core Competencies as a Way Out of the Crisis

Frank-Jürgen Richter and Usha C. V. Haley

INTRODUCTION

The Asian Network Groups' Legacy

Many scholars, particularly Western ones, have described theoretical links between Asian industrial patterns and the competitiveness of Asian firms. These scholars hold that the Asian economies exhibit continuous innovation and growth by linkages across, rather than within, specific industrial borders (Chen and Hamilton, 1991; Gerlach, 1992; Haley and Haley, 1999; Haley *et al.*, 1998; Richter and Teramoto, 1996; Richter, 1999b; Sako, 1992; Scher, 1997). Thus, by carefully combining resources located within and outside organisations, Asian firms have steadily advanced innovation across industrial spectrums and formed network groups such as the *keiretsu* in Japan, the *chaebol* in Korea and the overseas Chinese businesses in Southeast Asia.

Network groups have guided the transformation of Asian economies from an agricultural to an industrial base. Until the early 1990s investors were lining up to buy into Asia's rapid growth. Network groups then constituted the investment vehicles of choice: these groups had access to the politically powerful. They were involved in numerous economic sectors, which made their stocks proxies for national economic growth; and they were perceived as leaders of their country's industrial development. The top six Japanese *keiretsu*, the top five Korean *chaebol* and the top ten overseas Chinese businesses in Southeast Asia still control a very large proportion of key economic sectors. Although firms in the West may have a monopolistic hold on some product lines, the Asian network structures, and these networks' relative economic powers, distinguish the competitive patterns in Asian economies from those in the West. Because of their unique characteristics, the networks also face unique challenges and questions in post-crisis Asia.

The West is also reevaluating network groups. Following the success of the Asian network groups and the management philosophies they spawned, network-type exchange relationships proliferated in the USA and Europe (see Dunning, 1997). Politicians, scientists and managers called upon their home companies to acquire network strategies in order to reduce the apparent setback in Asia. The Asian economic crisis, however, destroyed many of the myths surrounding the mighty network groups and Western managers are returning to their own particular strengths.

Ersatz Capitalism Under Siege

The network groups are currently facing a serious crisis of confidence. Economists are increasingly arguing that the Asian economic crisis is a legacy of these groups. Market failure has assumed centrality in the groups' economic rationale: the inability of market mechanisms to achieve maximum efficiency and encourage growth when confronting economies of scale nurtured the network groups. Similar conditions have led to monopolies in the advanced economies and the elimination of competition from late starters. If the objectively based decisions of marketplaces have such predictable shortcomings, the argument runs, then the subjectively based decisions of government agencies or key individuals could improve market outcomes.

Researchers often describe the linking of Asian firms into network groups as 'ersatz capitalism' (Dunning, 1997; Gerlach, 1992; Yoshihara, 1988). This Asian model of industrial society is influenced little by Western economic liberalism or Marxism. Ersatz capitalism is capitalism without capitalists because the interests of those involved must be balanced to maintain long-term stability. The region's entrepreneurs and managers have often focused on amassing wealth, based on personal contacts and networking, rather than stressing shareholders' interests. Understanding the chasm between the Western and Eastern versions of capitalism is important now that policymakers and investors are debating the modes of globalisation.

The negative effects of ersatz capitalism have manifested themselves in wasted resources when non-market choices have resulted in faulty decisions, such as when the Japanese Ministry of Trade and Industry (MITI) invested in an analog-based, high definition television system and Indonesia invested in the national car industry. Further effects are obvious in the structural imbalances arising from an overemphasis on export industries, whose excess capacity has burgeoned by arbitrarily picking winners.

In post-crisis Asia, politicians are proposing that individuals and individual firms should take the initiative in the drive for reconstruction and regeneration. Western skeptics abound (for example Hall, 1998; Henderson, 1998), but Asian observers argue that many influential regional actors are no longer willing to toe the monolithic line (for example Shin and Kwon, 1999; Teramoto, 1999; Tezuka, 1997). While Asians still greatly value the tradition of internal cooperation, strident demands for transparency are emerging. Most of the reforms aim to unravel the tight networks of collaboration and reciprocity among government agencies, financial institutions and industrial companies and to institute US-style market mediation practices.

The large number of network forms and the variety of their approaches has made Asia a dynamic competitive arena where intensive rivalry exists. Although the networks' strategic intents appear to be similar in all these forms of business, the bases for competitive advantages differ considerably. Asian firms cut across a huge range of management philosophies, from the *keiretsu* to the *chaebol*, as do the overseas Chinese businesses and, more recently, the Chinese state-owned enterprises. In addition, Asian network groups include firms from different industries and value levels that are organised horizontally as interlinked firms in different industries and vertically as extensive subcontracting pyramids, often in manufacturing or construction. The following section investigates the network groups of Japan, South Korea, Southeast Asia and China.

JAPANESE *KEIRETSU*

The Myth of Japan Inc

Just as most Japanese describe themselves in terms of their place in a network of relationships rather than as individuals, Japanese firms define their roles and status through their relationship with other firms rather than as stand-alone organisations. Most of the larger firms are affiliated with other firms to form *keiretsu*, whereby firms maintain long-standing business ties with each other, sometimes – but not always – cemented by the mutual ownership of shares.

The *zaibatsu* were the ancestors of the *keiretsu*. The *zaibatsu* consisted of huge groups of family businesses combining interests in all major industries.

Even after their dissolution following the Second World War, the ties and linkages continued in a weaker form as *keiretsu*. The typical *keiretsu* is organised around a financial institution, a general trading company (*sogo shosha*) and manufacturing firms in wide cross-section of industries. The best known *keiretsu* are Mitsubishi, Mitsui and Sumitomo.

Terms such as 'Japan Inc' and 'Japanese bashing' explicitly and implicitly acknowledge the tight links between the Japanese administration and the Japanese economy and the conspiratorial system in which they are perceived to function. Commentators note that these tight links have harmed the established Western industrial nations and that only political pressure can remedy the situation. To Westerners, the interaction between administrations and economies represents a disguising of the political system, as the indirect tax mechanisms are difficult to decipher. As Hall (1998) notes, the rest of the world has a major stake in Japanese decisions to include foreigners selectively or exclude them systematically: this is all too clear in the negative term 'Japan Inc.'

Many see the *keiretsu* as an organisational form for advancing Japanese interests at the cost of outsiders, especially non-Japanese competitors. Foreign companies do indeed have difficulty establishing themselves in the Japanese market (Lasserre and Schütte, 1995; Richter, 1999b). The connections between the Japanese companies are complex and non-transparent and seem to leave foreigners out in the cold. Yet although the *keiretsu* function as key gatekeepers, the impenetrability of Japan does not necessarily imply a conscious blockade of foreigners.

Although some Japanese firms still enjoy record profits, an increasingly large number of firms appear to be underperforming in today's crisis environment. In particular the financial sector, seems to be on the verge of collapse. In addition, domestic prices are too high, the government spends too much and the system that built Japan's export powerhouse appears to be crumbling. The continued Japanese recession has led many observers to conclude that Japan now faces an extended period of near-zero economic growth. As a consequence, researchers and policymakers are debating whether the *keiretsu* are still the ideal form of industrial organisation within the Japanese economic framework.

Keiretsu Perestroika

Japan's *keiretsu* are reorienting themselves and developing new and innovative forms of interfirm relations in order to overcome the recent economic turmoil. Part of Prime Minister Obuchi's action plan, the Big Bang package of measures, is the proposal to tear up much of the red tape that is constraining the financial institutions, which constitute the core of the *keiretsu*. These measures include the lowering of brokerage commissions, allowing banks and securities companies to engage in each others' lines of business and dissolving the barriers to foreign competition. However observers such as Hall (1998) and Godement (1999) are pessimistic about real changes taking place in the institutional frameworks where economic decisions are taken.

In manufacturing and trading, Japanese firms are streamlining and restructuring their network organisations. Cross-*keiretsu* mergers and acquisitions have become quite fashionable. Mitsubishi and Mitsui, for example, two of Japan's largest trading companies, have begun talks on allying their steel businesses in order to increase their profitability. The talks may lead to the merger of their coil production facilities and consolidation of their steel distribution.

In the early 1990s Toyota took steps to reduce the dependency of its supplier firms (Richter and Wakuta, 1993). The dependency between firms and their suppliers has been a traditional and essential feature of supply relations in Japan, and the focus of scholarly inquiry among Japanese Marxist economist in relation to its exploitative nature. For example Marxist scholars have written of monopoly capital exploiting smaller supplier firms (Sako, 1992). Yet Toyota has allowed its suppliers to supply competing firms: Toyota gave the firms within its production network permission to supply 30 per cent of their turnover to competing firms such as Nissan, Mitsubishi Motors and Honda. Toyota and Nissan, the two largest firms in the Japanese car industry, now purchase parts and components from each other's suppliers. Both firms had previously distanced themselves from one another and avoided potential cooperation agreements. Denso, Toyota's biggest supplier, supplies most of the other Japanese car manufacturers, especially Nissan.

Toyota also began to examine its production network with the goal of removing all overheads in manufacturing and delivery. It asked its suppliers to examine the possibility of bilateral cooperation, even mergers. Some of the smaller firms in the Toyota group have indeed followed the merger route, so that the number of supplier firms has decreased. Suppliers from different production networks have sometimes banded together for partial cooperation: for example Toyota's Koyo Seiko entered into an R&D agreement with Nissan's Atsugi Yunisha in the area of power-steering elements.

Recently, Toyota again changed its network strategy. In response to the shakeup of the global car industry, including the Daimler–Chrysler merger, Toyota is strengthening its group ties. Together with Daihatsu and Hino Motors, Toyota is targeting a combined 40 per cent domestic share, up from the current figure of about 37 per cent. Anticipating a further intensification of global competition, Toyota aims to carry out radical cost-cutting efforts and speed up its decision-making process. Adopting a holding-company structure is one important measure, targeted at increasing its shares in Daihatsu, Hino and its key suppliers, Denso and Aishin. Once the restructuring into a holding company is completed, Toyota will look more like a wholly integrated US corporation than a typical Japanese *keiretsu*.

Innovative solutions have been found within the industry. The Japanese car manufacturers overcapacity is about 30 per cent, with Nissan and Mitsubishi Motors hit worst. Fearing labels such as 'defeatist' or 'tractor', in the past Japanese executives have not shared Wall Street's merger fever, so the recent cases of corporate takeover have been important hallmarks in Japanese economic history. For instance the French car maker Renault has acquired an equity stake in Nissan and the German supplier Bosch is now controlling Zexel. Further acquisitions may be the next step in the *keiretsu perestroika*: the *keiretsu* may dissolve by hooking up with Western multinationals.

Internal restructuring, however, is only one facet of the process: a real *keiretsu perestroika* needs a deep rethinking of the pillars of Japan's success story – life-time employment, the main bank system and cross-shareholdings, to mention just a few. The crisis of *keiretsu* system poses economic as well as value dilemmas.

KOREAN *CHAEBOL*

The Rise and Fall of the *Chaebol*

As in Japan, firms in South Korea are organised into network groups: the *chaebol*. The term *chaebol* means 'financial clique', but researchers and managers often use it to describe large business groups that were originally created by talented entrepreneurs, are largely family controlled and spread over many different industries. In 1997 the top five *chaebol* – Hyundai, Samsung, Daewoo, LG and SK – accounted for 32 per cent of all corporate sales in South Korea, 29 per cent of assets and 30 per cent of debts (Kang, 1997). Samsung alone accounted for 28 per cent of all South Korean exports in 1997. The *chaebol* produce a wide range of products and services. Superficially the *chaebol* seem very similar to the *keiretsu*, but substantial differences exist. Unlike the *keiretsu*, the founding families still dominate the Korean *chaebol*. Furthermore the South Korean government played a major role in the development of the *chaebol* by directing scarce capital, limiting foreign investment, assisting in foreign technology licensing and protecting home markets.

The *chaebol* are an offspring of South Korea's forced industrialisation. In the 1960s the South Korean government identified talented, export-oriented entrepreneurs and systematically aided them by granting import licenses, preferential credit, tax advantages and domestic protection. With liberal financial policies and astute financial engineering based on cross-equity exchanges and high leverage, the *chaebol* were able to sustain average growth rates of about 30 per cent a year during the 1970s and the 1980s.

When the Asian crisis descended the *chaebol*'s debts were huge, their profits slender and their operations vast and ill-focused, threatening their survival. The Samsung group, for example, controls 61 subsidiaries across 10 industries, ranging from electronics to newspapers. All the subsidiaries share an intricate web of cross-shareholdings and overlapping commercial relations that are very difficult to untangle. Some of the core firms, such as Samsung Electronics and Heavy Industries, have even formed mini-*chaebol* within the larger corporate structure. Samsung Electronics has about 100 affiliates of its own around the world. Shin and Kwon (1999) contend that Samsung has been overstretched and had begun to reevaluate its businesses well before the financial crash in 1997; the crisis and government pressure have only expedited this reevaluation and restructuring. In particular the ongoing credit crunch has highlighted the urgency of reducing debt.

From Inertia to Change

Many observers hope for a reform of the *chaebol* into slimmer, more profitable firms and the emergence of a free market where small firms can compete. With this goal in mind, South Korea aims to tame the *chaebol* by cutting off credit to some of their ailing subsidiaries. All poorly performing firms face liquidation unless they merge or engineer a turnaround under new ownership. By getting rid of these ailing firms, the government hopes to free banks from the burden of financing firms with little hope of survival.

These measures can be seen as a government warning to the *chaebol* to put their houses in order. Because of the *chaebol*'s dominant role in the South Korean economy the government holds them largely responsible for the country's debt and overcapacity problems. The government wants to restructure the *chaebol* and even to swap assets among them in order to force them to focus on fewer core businesses. If policy makers have their way, the big five *chaebol* – Hyundai, Samsung, Daewoo, LG and SK – will merge their troubled divisions in the semiconductor, petrochemical and other industries suffering from weak prices. As part of the 'Big Deal', the government wants the *chaebol* to swap their key subsidiaries so that each of them emerges stronger in its main field of specialisation. For example the government is pushing Hyundai, LG and Samsung to consider a three-way asset swap: Hyundai would focus on cars, LG on petrochemicals and Samsung on semiconductors. The swaps would also serve to curb overlapping investment and surplus factory capacity. However such deals may not lead to the cutting of excess capacity, debt or employment.

As South Korea recovers, the *chaebol* feel that the pressure of the crisis is easing. An austerity plan has cut imports dramatically, while the low won exchange rate has increased the *chaebol*'s exports. South Korea now has record hard-currency reserves, and interest rates have fallen; consequently the big *chaebol* can eke out enough cash to continue operations without a radical overhaul.

Favourable economic conditions may mean a return to the old game – expanding at any cost. The *chaebol* are jockeying for asset acquisitions to increase their dominance. For example, take the auction of insolvent Kia Motors: Hyundai bought Kia despite its own massive debts and excess car-making capacity. Daewoo and even Samsung participated in the auction – the latter despite its own debt load. Similarly Daewoo has acquired Ssangyong Motors, having been forced by the government to strip down its affiliates to six units and to concentrate on car manufacturing. Daewoo's refusal to repay almost US$60 billion in debt had threatened to derail South Korea's fragile economic recovery. It is still not clear whether the government will be able to implement the announced restructuring plan.

Investors had hoped that the *chaebol* would start peddling assets aggressively. Some deals occurred, such as Samsung's sale of its heavy-machinery division to Volvo and the transfer of all its shares in Hewlett-Packard Korea to its American partner. However such examples remain the exception. Samsung, in particular, appears determined to emerge from South Korea's crisis as a world-class competitor by reducing debt and cutting jobs. But the retention of Samsung Motors is restraining the group's reformation – something that Samsung at last appears to recognise. Most observers think that the Big Five are delaying the inevitable restructuring at the expense of their future wellbeing. Many companies seem convinced that the crisis will eventually blow over and the old practice of emphasising diversification and ever-growing sales over shareholders' returns will reemerge. Some *chaebol* have ignored restructuring altogether. Most have been able to resist change through their sheer size; because of the public perception that the *chaebol* are too big to fail, the latter have been able to raise sufficient money to continue operations as usual. The top *chaebol*'s leverage over

Korea may actually be increasing; but so is the risk they pose to South Korea's economic health, as corporate reform seems vital to the country's long-term development.

CHINESE OVERSEAS NETWORKS

Kinship, Authority and Entrepreneurship

Poor, and usually having borrowed the money to pay for their passage on steamers leaving ports in Southern China, migrant Chinese arrived in Southeast Asia with little more than pillows and sleeping mats (see Haley *et al.*, 1998 for a more complete description). These immigrants faced immense hardship at first, but with thrift and perseverance they worked their way to better lives. Many of the immigrants were from peasant farming stock in southern China, but today they are the pillars of corporate life in their adopted lands. The communist revolution in China triggered another wave of ethnic Chinese diaspora, and many established Chinese capitalists fled to Hong Kong and Taiwan. This group, more inclined towards industry and manufacturing, gradually merged with the existing overseas Chinese network.

Ethnic Chinese have greatly contributed to the development of the private sector in countries such as Indonesia, Thailand and the Philippines. Overseas Chinese businesspersons make up about 10 per cent of the population but control an estimated 80 per cent of all listed companies (Weidenbaum and Hughes, 1996). The overseas Chinese in Southeast Asia number around 50 million and their collective GDP roughly equals that of the 1.2 billion Chinese living in the People's Republic; their per capita income is significantly higher than other groups in Southeast Asia.

Businesses owned by overseas Chinese are family-oriented networks – not a tight group of companies like the *chaebol* or *keiretsu*, but rather loosely organised constellations of partnerships among several families, often with ties to other network groups (Haley and Haley, 1999). Overseas Chinese businesses constitute the nodes of extensive partnership networks under outstanding entrepreneurial ownership. Their low transaction costs are due to the strong ethics and sanctions within their business communities (see Haley, 1999a). Famous entrepreneurs such as Li Kashing in Hong Kong, Robert Kuok in Malaysia and Liem Sioeliong in Indonesia account for a huge proportion of their host countries' industrial output.

In this sense an 'offshore China' exists, with access to vast amounts of capital and managerial expertise. Equally important, overseas Chinese exercise substantial control over access to China, the world's largest potential consumer market and cheapest labour pool. According to Redding (1990), the Chinese family business format has been designed to survive intense volatility – strategic flexibility and speedy response to changing conditions are the major strengths of ethnic-Chinese family businesses. Overseas Chinese businesses are further characterised by kinship and networks of personal contacts, autocratic and centralised leadership and a well-developed sense of entrepreneurship (Haley, 1999b).

The patriarchal founder-owners of overseas Chinese businesses are usually surrounded by an internal network of clan members who occupy all the key positions. Family members or trusted outsiders hold the most important financial and legal posts. Leadership based on kinship and personal contacts seems to be a response to environmental and political uncertainty (Haley and Haley, 1998). In general decision making is top-down and autocratic (Haley *et al.*, 1998). The need for discretion and speed when making important decisions prevents the inclusion of middle and lower managers in decision making. Overseas Chinese businesses are important sources of information about new business ventures, offering risk sharing and providing effective managerial role models for aspiring entrepreneurs (Haley, 1999a).

The Overseas Chinese and Their Core Competencies

In their study of overseas Chinese businesses, Haley *et al.* (1998) found that these businesses practice conglomerate diversification, maintain good relations with the enormous public sectors in which they operate, have strong familial and informal networks and use subjective information as inputs in decision making. The foregoing practices appear to contradict Prahalad and Hamel's (1990) tenets on developing core competencies, but they do not. While the overseas Chinese companies have pursued conglomerate diversification, they have instinctively developed, nurtured and protected their core competencies (see Haley *et al.*, 1998) – their decision-making style, their control over information and their networks.

First, the managers' decision-making style, especially their speed, and their dominant control of information (another core competency) facilitate overseas Chinese efforts to seize business opportunities before competitors even sense that they exist (Haley and Tan, 1996). According to Haley *et al.* (1998) their decision-making style facilitates access to various markets (a requirement for a core competency) with scant data for making analytical decisions. It also allows them to seize opportunities to secure scarce goods and services and transfer them to customers, thereby providing the customers with benefits (another requirement for a core competency). Finally, competitors have difficulty imitating this decision-making style (a third requirement for a core competency) – especially the multinationals, which depend on decision-making techniques that are better suited to industrialised markets; and local businessmen, who lack the overseas Chinese managers' knowledge and hands-on business experience.

Second, according to Haley *et al.* (1998), the overseas Chinese have control over the rich information they obtain through their networks, a rare commodity in non-governmental circles and a core competency. Most notably they control specialised business information, much of which would be considered 'insider information' in the West. They prosper and produce goods in the informational void that they create and perpetuate (Haley and Tan, 1996). Their information arbitrage provides potential benefits to customers, and competitors have difficulty imitating it. The overseas Chinese are generally intensely secretive about over the sources of information that guide their investments.

Finally, according to Haley *et al.* (1998), for the overseas Chinese their networks are a core competency. These networks provide access to various markets, as demonstrated by their ethnic, governmental and familial contacts. Competitors lack and are unable to replicate this web of contacts, and consequently most independent local competitors fail to grow large enough to challenge them in the region.

The broad networks that the overseas Chinese use to promote their connections are referred to in Mandarin as *guanxi* or influential connections. The practice of *guanxi* leads to a high degree of reliance on trust, and this helps to explain why they have tended to keep their individual investments in China small or medium-sized. By doing so they can take advantage of their connections with local officials, who do not have to submit project proposals to Beijing for state approval unless they exceed US$30 million.

The 'complex harmonization of individual technologies and production skills' identified by Prahalad and Hamel (1990) has led to overseas Chinese gaining strategic dominance over the Southeast and East Asian business environments. Neither local competitors nor foreign multinationals can challenge or duplicate their ability to make effective strategic decisions, through their networks, in the informational void they maintain.

Most of the major overseas Chinese businesses in Asia appear to be surviving the economic crisis, although some of their manufacturing enterprises and many of their research units may not survive direct competition with Western firms. This overstretching in areas where there is easy money to be made is symptomatic of many big overseas Chinese business groups.

Taiwanese and Singaporean high-tech firms appear to be exceptions, having developed key strengths in products such as chips and computers (Haley and Low, 1998).

In sum, overseas Chinese businesses are facing increased competition despite their core competencies. For example, under the pressure of recession, political changes and the arrival of new competition, Li Kashing's Cheung Kong Holdings and Hutchison Whampoa are grappling with Western companies in areas as div rse as property, telecoms, ports and electricity.

Efficient capital markets may also eliminate some of the advantages enjoyed by privately financed Chinese family businesses (Haley and Haley, 1999). Publicly held firms that can raise capital through modern investment channels may emerge as more efficient alternatives to network dynasties that utilise enormous private financial resources. Stock and bond offerings are becoming more commonplace as governments continue to lift restrictions on stock exchanges and financial markets, thereby encroaching on overseas Chinese terrain.

CHINESE STATE-OWNED ENTERPRISES

Industrial Restructuring in Post-Deng China

China's reform policy has resulted in an average GDP growth rate of 10 per cent per annum. This impressive growth rate also highlights the economy's historical inefficiency. State-owned enterprises are lagging behind the private sector, which is dominated by joint ventures with foreign companies. China's economic growth is primarily due to foreign investment and China continues to be the developing world's biggest magnet for foreign investors. Although the economy as a whole is growing impressively, the future of the state-owned enterprises appears dark and is even threatened by the overall economic growth. These enterprises, the Chinese economy's workhorses, are still highly inefficient and overmanned.

A possible way out of the dilemma is to restructure the enterprises into network groups, such as those in neighbouring Asian economies. By adopting a strategy of 'grasp the large, release the small' the government hopes to develop sufficient muscle to survive global competition, which will only get tougher when China joins the World Trade Organization. As a consequence, big network groups are currently drawing in unrelated businesses – electronics, automotive, finance, trading and so on.

The government has emphasised that it wants large multinational conglomerates to form China's industrial backbone in the twenty-first century. In 1997 it designated 120 state-owned enterprises for conglomerate status. These enjoy priority when registering on the stock market and obtaining bank loans. They are also permitted to establish finance companies for internal purposes, and trade overseas without going through state trading companies. They even enjoy preferential tax treatment. The top six companies (the software company Beida Fangzheng, the steel producer Baogang, the ship constructor Jiangnan, the pharmaceutical giant Huanbei, the TV manufacturer Changhong and the white goods maker Haier) enjoy even more preferential treatment in other business aspects.

Haier is a good example of a Chinese network group. In the 1980s China had little capacity for manufacturing household refrigerators and the Shandong government selected Haier, at that time a peripheral state-owned enterprise, to fill this market void. A German manufacturer introduced the necessary technology via a licensing agreement and in 1991 Haier acquired two large white-goods firms, followed by further expansion and diversification. Throughout the 1990s Haier ploughed its profits into the takeover of more and more state-owned enterprises – first in Shandong and later in other areas. Since then Haier has acquired 14 firms – besides white goods the firm manufactures pharmaceuticals, television and video sets, and other electric and electronic appliances. It recently announced plans to set up an in-group finance company and is steaming ahead with plans to construct factories in Southeast Asia and Eastern Europe.

China and the Coming Crisis

The Asian economic crisis appears to have affected China less than the neighbouring economies. However it is now falling behind its growth targets, industrial production is slowing down significantly and inventories are up. In 1999 the price index declined continuously, representing a fall into deflation. In response to these problems China has launched a huge programme of public investment in capital projects in order to jump-start the economy. The possibility of a harsh recession or even an economic crash, as experienced by the Southeast Asian countries in 1997, still appears possible. On top of the bandwagon pressures from outside, domestic problems such as the overheated expansion of state-owned enterprises may contribute to a Chinese recession.

Over time the hallmarks of overstretching may also become evident in China – growing indebtedness, a shortage of vital skills and synergies that fail to materialise (Richter, 1999a). Unrelated conglomerate diversification, such as that undertaken by the Korean *chaebol*, the Japanese *keiretsu* and overseas Chinese businesses, figures prominently in China. Due to the fusion between the state and the enterprises, China's future multinationals will probably undertake this form of diversification too. A lack of synergy as a result of activities in different industrial areas constitutes a serious threat to China's effort to create competitive multinational companies.

Yet even as the *chaebol* try spin off and sell assets in order to focus on their core businesses, China is barrelling ahead with plans to bulk up its state-owned enterprises. 'Grasping the large' could turn firms into fairly weak monopolies rather than efficient businesses. The 'bigger is better' mindset ultimately resulted in the *chaebol* being jerked back to earth. Chinese officials, however, insist that the *chaebol* failed because Korea's financial and legal institutions were weak, and that the factors that crippled the *chaebol* – excessive government interference, a penchant for going big and abuse of the banking sector – will not afflict China's state-owned enterprises. Asia has to hope, indeed, that the newly emerging network groups will not fail. If they do the Chinese economy will fail – and if China goes down the impact on the neighbouring Asian countries may prove disastrous.

The Asian economic crisis is unlikely to make Chinese bureaucrats less enamoured of size and scale, but it may result in the modification of the network strategy. This would be a continuation of Deng Xiaoping's cautious approach to economic policy. Deng's heir, Jiang Zemin, has already called for the wholesale restructuring of the state sector – a move as revolutionary as his predecessor's initial reforms.

SOME LESSONS TO LEARN: MANAGING AROUND NEW CORE COMPETENCIES

Untangling Business Portfolios

Western and Asian scholars (for example Fane, 1998; Godement, 1999; Shin and Kwon, 1999; Tezuka, 1997) have recently argued that network groups are generally less capable of adjusting to new economic realities than Western firms. Network groups may sometimes overestimate their strength in the face of adversity because of their past reputation or their implicit mutual insurance schemes within the groups. They may be unfamiliar with severe market competition owing to the presence of in-group customers, or their organisations may have become inflexible simply because of size or age. Therefore network groups may be less capable of entrepreneurial activity than independent firms.

The increasing focus on new core competencies is evidenced by Japanese manufacturers acquiring both expertise in international markets and employees who are familiar with business abroad. Most have their own distribution channels overseas and therefore can sell or buy without relying on the group's trading companies. With regard to the latter, in-group conflict is increasing as – under conditions of crisis and rapid economic restructuring – firms in declining industries are desperately seeking to diversify. At the same time other members are already serving the markets the firms want to enter, creating intragroup competition. The only way out is to sell peripheral businesses.

Many of Asia's big network groups will have difficulty surviving if they do not adapt quickly to the new business climate. Asset sales certainly boost efficiency, but many network groups are choosing to hang on to their inheritance. Some are taking tentative steps by shedding non-core businesses, but many are not. In fact some appear not to realise that the conditions that nurtured these network groups – government patronage, preferred lending, opaque bidding practices – are vanishing in the new area of declining demand, tightened liquidity, weakened governments and unrelenting globalisation. Such network groups may find it increasingly difficult to attract international investors, some of whom now prefer focused companies to diversified ones.

Separating Business and Finance

A lack of transparency combined with the herd mentality of investors and lenders during the bubble euphoria led to high-profile business networks across Asia gaining easy access to cash (Haley, 1997). This in turn perpetuated expansion long after cash-flow deficits should have caused them to put on the brakes. Meanwhile the combination of foreign and domestic investment continued to drive domestic growth throughout the region. A growing proportion of the domestic population found themselves with disposable income and the consumption of imported branded and luxury products escalated, contributing to persistent trade deficits. In the financial sector a pawnbroker mentality prevailed. This translated into a tendency to lend against asset value rather than cash flow. When combined with asset bubbles, this mentality contributed to the rapid expansion of bank assets. Poorly informed investors became a panicking herd, propelled in part by the tendency of several long-serving Asian leaders to blame 'foreign conspiracies' for their own management errors.

Investment capital disappeared with investor confidence. The scarcity of capital has raised its cost across the board in real terms. Asian network groups will have to learn to operate in environments in which capital is limited and pricey; and they will have to convince capital markets that they can use money efficiently. In addition, pressure is rising from multilateral agencies and global markets for greater disclosure of financial data. Asian companies that want to tap international capital markets will have to conform to more stringent reporting requirements.

Asian network groups will also have to redefine the roles of their internal financial institutions, for example that of Sumitomo Bank in the Sumitomo *keiretsu*, Samsung Securities in the Samsung *chaebol*, Bank Dagang Nasional Indonesia in the Gajah Tunggal Group, and SAIC Finance in SAIC. The use of external financing would lower the risk of financing pet projects. A shake-up of the 'national champions' within the league of troubled Asian banks would help as well. The Korean government's promise, for example, to sell the debt-heavy Korea First Bank to American GE Capital and Newbridge Capital indicates that more big banks and insurance firms may end up in foreign hands. Such deals mean that the money-starved banks will obtain billions in fresh capital. Foreign-run banks would also avoid making disastrous loans to Asian network groups, many of which have accumulated debts that are four times greater than their equity.

Supporting Regulatory Changes

In the domain of party politics and the struggle to fund increasingly expensive elections, politicians have sought access to the monopoly rents accruing to the ersatz capitalists by means of black money contributions to election funds. Unfortunately the 'holy grain' became a 'hot potato' as these new blue-chip conglomerates used their political connections to facilitate rapid expansion into other areas. To this end they lobbied to reduce domestic economic competition and gain preferential access to other deals. They then embarked on ambitious investments in underperforming assets as their inexperienced executives used the cash flow from their protected core to expand into new businesses where their organisations lacked the ability to compete.

A core competency of many Asian network groups is their ability to manipulate the bureaucratic process for project approvals. However the reforms demanded by the International Monetary Fund (IMF) and the markets will reduce governments' ability to formulate policies that favour certain companies and network groups. IMF-mandated reforms have already forced Thailand to close down debt-strapped finance companies and Indonesia to end some monopolies. In both countries the IMF has required public bidding for government contracts.

Repositioning the Network Paradigm

Most Asian economies will suffer deficits during the years to come and there is plenty to fix before Asia can emerge from the crisis. The recovery process will take years, maybe even decades, and will proceed in fits and starts. Financial constraints will hinder government help to favoured network groups. Countries are also allowing foreign investment in economic areas that were previously considered sacrosanct or strategic.

The network paradigm is at a critical crossroads in Asia. As Tezuka (1997) states, the networks' success may be the source of the recent economic failure. Drastic changes in internal and global economic conditions may necessitate a far-reaching transformation of interfirm links, largely eroding the traditional Asian network form. Yet many of the benefits of grouping may remain. Information exchange may assume more value as competition becomes global and technology advances more quickly. Sooner or later Asian network groups will have to make a crucial decision about the future shape of their governance structures. New types of network groups will have to lead the region through another transformation.

References

Chen, E. and G. G. Hamilton (1991) 'Introduction: Business Networks and Economic Development', in G. Hamilton (ed.), *Business Networks and Economic Development in East and Southeast Asia* (Hongkong: Centre of Asian Studies, University of Hongkong), pp. 3–10.

Dunning, J. H. (1997) *Alliance Capitalism and Global Business* (London: Routledge).

Fane, G. (1998) 'The Role of Prudential Regulation', in R. H. McLeod and R. Garnaut (eds), *East Asia in Crises. From Being a Miracle to Needing One* (London: Routledge), pp. 287–303.

Gerlach, M. L. (1992) *Alliance Capitalism. The Social Organization of Japanese Business* (Berkeley, CA: University of California Press).

Godement, F. (1999) *The Downsizing of Asia* (London: Routledge).

Haley, G. T. (1997) 'The Values Asia Needs', Editorial and Opinion Section, *Business Times* (Singapore), 24 December, p. 6.

Haley, G. T. and U. C. V. Haley (1998) 'Boxing with Shadows: Competing Effectively with the Overseas Chinese and Overseas Indian Business Networks in the Asian Arena', *Journal of Organizational Change Management*, special issue on 'Strategic Dimensions of Organizational Change and Restructuring in the Asia Pacific: Part I, Strategies for Foreign Investors', vol. 11, no. 4, pp. 301–20.

Haley, G. T. and U. C. V. Haley (1999) 'Weaving Opportunities: Overseas Chinese and Overseas Indian Networks in Southeast Asia', in F. J. Richter (ed.), *Business Networks in Asia. Promises, Doubts, and Perspectives* (Westport, CT: Quorum), pp. 149–70.

Haley, G. T. and C. T. Tan (1996) 'The Black Hole of South-East Asia: Strategic Decision-Making in an Informational Void', *Management Decision*, special issue on 'Strategic Management in the Asia Pacific', vol. 34, no. 9, pp. 37–48.

Haley, G. T., C. T. Tan and U. C. V. Haley (1998) *New Asian Emperors: The Overseas Chinese, Their Strategies and Competitive Advantages* (Oxford and Boston: Butterworth-Heinemann).

Haley, U. C. V. (1999a) *Strategic Management in the Asia Pacific: Harnessing Regional and Organizational Change for Competitive Advantage* (Oxford and Boston: Butterworth-Heinemann).

Haley, U. C. V. (1999b) 'Strategy in the Asia Pacific', in *International Encyclopedia of Business and Management* (London: Thomson Business Press).

Haley, U. C. V. and L. Low (1998) 'Crafted Culture: Governmental Sculpting of Modern Singapore and Effects on Business Environments', *Journal of Organizational Change Management*, special issue on 'Strategic Dimensions of Organizational Change and Restructuring in the Asia Pacific: Part II, Concerns of Local Stakeholders', vol. 11, no. 6, pp. 530–53.

Hall, I. P. (1998) *Cartels of the Mind: Japan's Intellectual Closed Shop* (New York: Norton).

Henderson, C. (1998) *Asia Falling? Making Sense of the Asian Currency Crisis and its Aftermath* (Singapore: McGraw-Hill).

Kang, M. H. (1997) *Chaebol Then and Now* (London: Curzon Press).

Lasserre, P. and H. Schütte (1995) *Strategies for Asia Pacific* (London: Macmillan).

Naisbitt, J. (1997) *Megatrends Asia – The Eight Asian Megatrends that are Changing the World* (London: Nicholas Brealey).

Patten, C. (1998) *East and West. China, Power, and the Future of Asia* (New York: Times Books).

Prahalad, C. K. and G. Hamel (1990) 'The Core Competence of the Corporation', *Harvard Business Review*, May/June, pp. 79–91.

Redding, S. G. (1990) *The Spirit of Chinese Capitalism* (Berlin and New York: Walter de Gruyter).

Richter, F. J. (1999a) 'Industrial Restructuring in post-Deng China: Towards a Network Economy', in F. J. Richter (ed.), *Business Networks in Asia. Promises, Doubts and Perspectives*, (Westport, CT: Quorum, pp. 237–49).

Richter, F. J. (1999b) *Strategic Networks. The Art of Japanese Interfirm Cooperation* (Binghamton, NY: International Business Press).

Richter, F. J. and Y. Teramoto (1996) 'Population Ecology versus Network Dynamics: From Evoution to Co-evolution', in F. J. Richter (ed.), *The Dynamics of Japanese Organizations* (London: Routledge), pp. 151–66.

Richter, F. J. and Y. Wakuta (1993) 'Permeable Networks: A Future Option for the European and Japanese Car Industries', *European Management Journal*, vol. 11, no. 2, pp. 262–7.

Teramoto, Y. (1999) 'Japanese Corporate Groups. From Parenting to Partnering', in F. J. Richter (ed.), *Business Networks in Asia. Promises, Doubts, and Perspectives* (Westport, CT: Quorum), pp. 75–90.

Sako, M. (1992) *Prices, Quality and Trust. Inter-firm Relations in Britain & Japan* (Cambridge: Cambridge University Press).

Scher, M. J. (1997) *Japanese Interfirm Networks and Their Main Banks* (New York: St Martin's Press).

Shin, D. and K.-H. Kwon (1999) 'Demystifying Asian Business Networks: The Hierarchical Core of Korean Chaebols', in F. J. Richter (ed.), *Business Networks in Asia. Promises, Doubts, and Perspectives* (Westport, CT: Quorum), pp. 113–46.

Tezuka, H. (1997) 'Success as the Source of Failure? Competition and Cooperation in the Japanese Economy', *Sloan Management Review*, vol. 38, no. 2, pp. 83–93.

Weidenbaum, M. and S. Hughes (1996) *The Bamboo Network: How Expatriate Chinese Entrepreneurs Are Creating a New Economic Superpower in Asia* (New York: The Free Press).

Yoshihara, K. (1988) *The Rise of Ersatz Capitalism in South-East Asia* (Singapore: Oxford University Press).

Author Index

Subject Index